THE STORY OF
CHORLTON
-CUM-HARDY

THE STORY OF
CHORLTON -CUM-HARDY

ANDREW SIMPSON

The
History
Press

First published 2012

The History Press
The Mill, Brimscombe Port
Stroud, Gloucestershire, GL5 2QG
www.thehistorypress.co.uk

British Library Cataloguing in Publication Data.
A catalogue record for this book is available from the British Library.

ISBN 978 0 7524 8966 7

Typesetting and origination by The History Press
Printed and bound in Great Britain by
Marston Book Services Limited, Didcot

CONTENTS

IMAGE CREDITS

With the exception of the map of Brownhill's Buildings (CPO Order 1972, courtesy of Manchester Libraries, Information and Archives, Manchester City Council), and the detail from the Greenwood map of Chorlton (courtesy of Digital Archives Association, http://www.digitalarchives.co.uk), all the images come from the collections of Oliver Bailey, Angus Bateman, Alan Brown, David Bishop, Rita Bishop, Marjorie Holmes, Karen Lewis, Philip Lloyd, St Clement's parish church, Andrew Simpson, Barri Sparshot, and South Trafford Archaeological Group.

PREFACE

The place, its historians, the historical records, the lost finds and two visitors

Chorlton was not always a suburb of Manchester. In the early 19th century the township was still a small rural community with a system of government stretching back to the Middle Ages, a welfare system derived from Elizabethan Poor Law and an ancient set of rural customs.

There have been plenty of historians who have recorded the town's past. The best known general book is that by John Lloyd, published in 1972. But there have also been countless newspaper articles, two picture books and references to the place in the histories of neighbouring townships. Almost all of these authors draw on twenty-five articles written in the winter and spring of 1885–86 by Thomas Ellwood. These were published in weekly instalments in the *South Manchester Gazette* and reappear as articles in the Wesleyan and parish magazines throughout the late 19th and early 20th centuries. Ellwood in turn drew on an earlier work about the histories of the churches and chapels of south and east Manchester, written thirty years earlier, as well as contemporary documents. But the real strength of his account is that much of it is based on the oral testimonies of some of the oldest inhabitants of the township; people who had been born at the very beginning of Elwood's century and confidently recorded the customs and people of an even earlier time.[1]

Missing from all the histories is a detailed description of the lives of the people of Chorlton in the early and mid-19th century. After all, many of Ellwood's audience would have been familiar with the customs and work practices as well as the township's earlier inhabitants, and so it was not necessary to spell any of it out. But what was once familiar is

---

1 Both drew heavily on the work of the Revd John Booker, who wrote about Chorlton in *A History of the chapels of Didsbury and Chorlton*, Chetham Society, Manchester, 1857.

now remote, as are the people who lived here. Most left few records other than the official ones recording births, marriages and deaths. Their letters, thoughts and personal effects have vanished, and many have lost even the gravestone that recorded their existence.

Likewise there seem to be few detailed studies of any of the townships that surrounded Manchester at that critical moment when the city was fast becoming a major centre for business and industry. So while its commercial dealings, factories, mills, transport network and dwellings are recorded in detail, those places that provided food, labour and in many cases a place of respite have been less well served. The homes of working-class families in Ancoats, Deansgate and across the Irwell in Salford continue to be excavated, recorded and written about, but their rural counterparts are by and large ignored. Of course much rural accommodation was still of wattle and daub construction, which leaves little trace when it is demolished or falls down. But here just as in Manchester speculative builders were putting up blocks of cheap brick housing in the 1830s. These lasted well into the last quarter of the 20th century and have yet to fade from living memory, but no work has explored what they were like and the reasons for their construction. Perhaps we shouldn't be surprised at this, given that no similar academic rescue work is being undertaken on either the few remaining farmhouses or the last homes of the wealthy.[2] This is a real pity because there is so much original source material available. The census returns provide a snapshot of who was here, their work, accommodation and families, every ten years from 1841, and these can be supplemented with street directories, rate books, newspapers and everyday ephemera, like household accounts receipts and bills. And because Chorlton was a rural community it is possible to track land tenure and the type of farming from the tithe map and schedule, which record the amount of land owned and rented and the use it was put to. And that usage is vividly brought to life through contemporary farming textbooks, which laid out everything from how to choose a farm to how best to dig a well and the merits of water meadows. All of this means that we can follow many people around the township, from home to home and workplace to workplace.

The Higginbotham family farmed 36 acres and lived on the Green. They employed Elizabeth Morton, who left their employ in 1849 but was back again by 1851 working again as a servant. She worked alongside carters, cowmen and young farm servants. James Higginbotham buried his first wife and two of his children in the tiny Wesleyan graveyard on the Row. He was active in the local community, as were many of the local farmers.[3]

What local people did, as well as welfare provision and the effects of the great parliamentary elections of 1832 and 1837 through to the '40s and '50s, can be explored – but not all

2 There have been digs at Moston Hall and Northenden Mill, which aimed to introduce the public and schoolchildren especially to archaeology. The dig at Moston focused on the Hall and the Northenden dig on the mill.

3 He was an overseer four times, chairman six times, twice an assessor and once the constable.

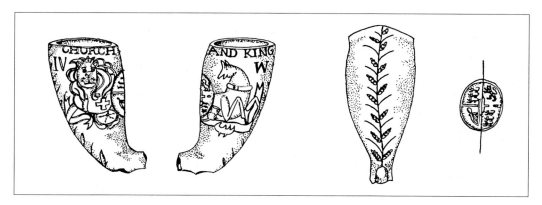

The William IV clay pipe discovered during the excavation of the church site in the 1980s. Fragments of clay pipes crop up across the township, but so far this is the only one with a design that can be dated.

source material has survived. We do not know how the community reacted to the growing social and political unrest during and directly after the long wars with Revolutionary and Napoleonic France. If there were any Chorlton Chartists they have yet to be found. But the township was only 4½ miles from the city and connected by the Duke's Canal[4] as well as roads and by a complex set of trading links. It is highly likely, therefore, that the people would have been aware of what was going on in the wider world and would have formed opinions about the events of the day. In that sense this was not a remote rural community; what went on here reflected the bigger picture. There was an entrepreneurial culture that matched anything the city could offer, along with a growing mobility of labour which is at odds with the idea that few people travelled far. Children were born out of wedlock but do not appear to have attracted moral outrage. Crimes were committed, ranging from murder to robbery as well as drunkenness and vandalism, and they excited equal amounts of interest and condemnation.

Chorlton was typical of the farming communities in the south of Lancashire. As elsewhere there were a large number of fairly small market gardens, serving the needs of the city; and there is evidence that this township was quicker to lose the traditional industry of handloom weaving than some of its neighbours.

Above all this book is about the people who lived here in the first half of the 19th century: their daily lives and the strategies they employed to cope with seasonal unemployment, overcrowding, old age and infant mortality. It is about everything from the landscape and building to whom you had to be polite to.

Some families were in the township before the 18th century and some can be traced across the next century. The Higginbotham family was still on the Green in the 1960s, and

---

4 This is the Duke of Bridgewater's Canal.

descendants of other families like the Nixons, Brownhills and Grestys are still in Chorlton today. It is also still possible to touch their past, for while few of the buildings have survived some documents can be seen and handled. Written in longhand and including signatures of the people we know, they remain a personal link with the first half of the 19th century. Even more revealing perhaps are the few objects that were lost by their owners and rediscovered in the parish churchyard during an archaeological dig in the early 1980s.[5] This was hardly a treasure hoard, being a few coins, part of a clay pipe, a medal commemorating the coronation of Queen Victoria and a few buttons, but it is the stuff of ordinary living.

Some of these objects might have been lost by visitors, for there seem to have been plenty of them. In 1770 a soldier and a few companions walked into Chorlton from Manchester and preached the first Methodist sermon on the Green. A little over fifty years later Richard Buxton came with a group of friends to examine and record the area's botany. He was a remarkable man, whose family had moved from rural Sedgely Park into the overcrowded slums of Ancoats in the 1780s. He was self-taught and lived on the verge of poverty, but he is acclaimed as one of the most important working-class botanists of the 19th century. The plants he identified in Chorlton are only just being rediscovered, and catalogued exactly where he first saw them 180 years ago. Along with Buxton came many others who sought the peace and open countryside as a break from the noise, over-crowding and frenetic energy of Manchester. These were Sunday visitors who walked the 4½ miles, either with their families for a day out or sometimes just to sample the public houses. The writer Edwin Waugh came in the winter of 1857, travelling from the heart of the city on a railway that was just eight years old. It was a journey of contrasts. Leaving 'the huge manufactures, and the miserable chimney tops of Little Ireland, down by the dirty Medlock; we ran over a web of dingy streets, swarming with dingy people ... left the black stagnant canal, coiled in the hollow, stretching its dark length into the distance, like some slimy snake'. And clearing the 'cotton mills, and dye works, and chemical manufactories of Cornbrook',[6] the train entered open countryside before arriving at Stretford station, which had been built in 1849. Standing on the bridge over the railway just outside the station, Waugh had a view of countryside for miles around. The view today is dominated by rows of houses and the Stretford Arndale, but he saw 'this great tract of meadows, gardens and pasture land'. To the south was the village of Stretford, and to the north and east across open land and lost behind trees was Chorlton.

5 The dig was conducted by Dr Angus Bateman during the 1970s and early '80s. The records and finds were deposited with South Trafford Archaeological Group, who kindly gave permission for the report to be used in this book. Descriptions of the dig are also contained in two handwritten accounts by Fife, N., 'Letter to Anthony Walker', February 1984, and 'A time to look back and think', 1981.

6 Waugh, E., *Lancashire Sketches*, Alexander Ireland & Co., 1869, pp.74–5, Google edn, pp.94–5.

one

INTRODUCTION

Summer 1847, the location of the township, the hamlets of Chorlton, Hardy and Martledge, their proximity to Manchester, the people and the rivers and the rival attractions of Stretford

The summer of 1847 promised to be a good one, which was an important consideration for a rural community and a good starting point for our story. After all, ninety-six of our families were engaged in some form of farming, so a good harvest would put food on the table, guarantee work for the many and help the village through the dark cold winter ahead. The harvest was equally important for the sixteen families who made their living as tradesmen and retailers as it was central to their fortunes. Only the gentry might be more relaxed about the weather, but even they would have been aware of the distress and possible social unrest that might follow a bad year in the fields.

Three years earlier there had been a bad summer, which meant a meagre hay crop and even more disastrous harvest. The following year proved little better, and this further aggravated the poor condition of the livestock. And while the cycle of bad summers was broken in 1846, leading to a plentiful harvest, the potato blight that first appeared the year before devastated the crop, and led to the first famine year in Ireland.[7] Lancashire was luckier. It was a very dry and cold winter, and less than an inch of rain fell through January, March, April and July; the summer months proved to be very hot.[8] Wealthy families might well have felt relief. They would have drawn the connection between the bad harvests in France in the last century and the Revolution that toppled a monarchy and unleashed a continental war which lasted twenty-three years. Closer to home, and at the beginning of their own century, there had been food riots in Manchester, and it was only seventeen

---

7 Stratton, J.M., *Agricultural Records AD 220–1977*, John Baker, second edn, 1978, pp.107–8.

8 As it was, the wheat harvest of 1847 had indeed been plentiful if of a poor quality, but the oat crop that was Chorlton's main one was only average, leaving just the barley as a good crop for the year. *Ibid.*, p.108. 48 per cent of the harvest in 1847 was oats, 33 per cent barley and 19 per cent wheat.

Mary Hulme and her father.

years since the rising of the agricultural workers against mechanisation and falling wages that had been fuelled by the poor harvest of 1829 in the south and east of the country. [9]

The township was a small community of just 761 people spread across a number of hamlets. On the northern boundary was Martledge, south of Chorlton Brook was Hardy and at the centre was Chorlton itself. Smaller communities, in some cases just a few houses, were scattered in between. And as if to underline a dependence on the land, each of these small communities was separated by fields and orchards.[10]

Most people lived in Chorlton, which was the area around the Green on the edge of the flood plain. In 1847 it consisted of the church and graveyard, a pond, two pubs, the village school and a collection of cottages and farms. The village green had long since passed into the hands of the Wilton family, who rented it from the Egertons as a garden. It was to remain so until the death of Mary Wilton in 1895, when it was returned as the village green. While it might be more accurate to call this plot Wilton's garden during the 1840s and '50s, it will be easier to refer to it in future as the Green.

---

9 In 1812 a food riot at New Cross in Manchester had only been quelled by the military shooting into the crowd, killing five and wounding many more. The harvests had been poor since 1808 and the price of wheat stood at over £6 per quarter, which was the highest annual average during the Napoleonic Wars. The Swing Riots had been preceded by two successive poor harvests.

10 Rough population percentages based on the 1841 census were Chorlton 50 per cent, Martledge 17 per cent, High Lane 15 per cent, Hardy 10 per cent, Lane End 5 per cent, Dark Lane 3 per cent.

Chorlton at the beginning of the 19th century.

Just to the south-west of the Green was the pinfold, used to hold stray animals. Most villages had one, and this example was sturdily constructed of oak. An animal left to wander could do a lot of damage, and the fine of 1s to release it, paid to the parish constable, matched the seriousness of the offence. The owner was also expected to pay for any damage the animal incurred; and if the animal was not collected within three days it was sold to defray expenses. Anyone attempting to release livestock without paying was liable to a fine or imprisonment. Sometimes an enterprising farmer took a chance and kept the stray. So it was with Mary White, who found a brown pony in September 1850. She farmed 52 acres across the township and lived by the Green not far from the pinfold. Once

The danger of flooding from the Mersey was a regular concern throughout the 19th century. The weir was built to protect the Duke's Canal; here the flood waters have created a lake beyond its wall.

she had ascertained that no one in the township owned the pony she went to the expense of advertising in the *Manchester Guardian* that 'the owner may have it on giving a description and paying expenses. If not owned in fourteen days, it will be sold to pay expenses.'[11]

Running east out of the Green was Chorlton Row, now Beech Road. This road out of the village was dominated at one end by the Wesleyan chapel and at the other by the fine home of James Holt. In between were a beershop, the smithy of William Davies and the homes of Daniel Sharp and Mary Holland, who proudly described themselves as of independent means.[12] Beyond them were the farms of the Bailey and Gratrix families and a few assorted cottages.

To the south of the Row beyond Chorlton Brook was the area known as Hardy. This was a vast expanse of land that stretched out across farmland and meadow to the Mersey. Here the farms were bigger but there were few of them, lonely outposts. Directly south of the brook stood Hardy Farm and beyond were Barlow Farm and Barlow Hall, while away hard by the bend in the river was Red Bank Farm. In all that great expanse of land there were just a few cottages, beyond Hardy Farm and where Hardy Lane became a track on its way to the wooden footbridge across the Mersey. This was the original hamlet of Hardy.

---

11 *Manchester Guardian*, 25 September 1850.

12 Their houses date back to the 19th century. Mary Holland's was later known as Row House but may date back to the beginning of that century. A James and Elizabeth Blomley who lived in Chorlton baptised their son Samuel in 1807 and may have given their name to Blomley's Fishpond, which stretched from Acres Road towards Sutton's Cottage on the Row. Daniel Sharp was in his house which stood beside the Wesleyan chapel from 1841 and his father John Sharp, who is mentioned in various legal documents, may have lived there even earlier.

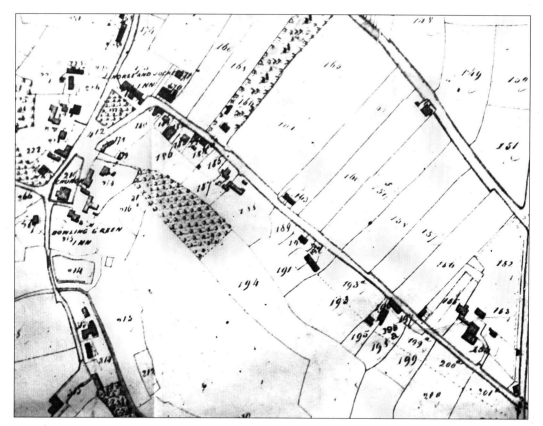

The Village and the Row, now Beech Road, in 1845 – homes, buildings and plots. The numbers denote who owned and rented the land and its use.

The last of these cottages was demolished after the great flood of 1854 had inundated the land to a depth of 3ft. In all directions the patchwork of fields was fed by irrigation ditches and divided by bushes and trees. On warm summer evenings it was an idyllic place, and even in the depths of winter it had a desolate beauty.

To the north of Hardy and Chorlton was Martledge. Less well remembered as a place and now covered by late 19th-century housing, it was for many visitors their first sight of the township. It was the area that today is around the library, stretching back towards Barlow Moor Road and out to Oswald and Longford Roads. In the 1840s there were marl and brick pits here. Marl had been dug for centuries and used on the fields.[13] Later, at the turn of the 20th century, some of this land was bought by the Chorlton Brick Company, and for about forty years there was a brickworks here. Martledge had been commonly known as the Isles. It was an area where lazy streams fed the disused pits, forming ponds and lakes; some of it was wet and soggy ground. Even further north was Dark Lane, a lonely place with just two farms. From here the visitor might walk east, ending at Holt Woods.

---

13 Marl is rich in lime and acts as a good fertiliser. It was dug in Martledge as early as 1598 and possibly much earlier, Booker, John, 'A History of the Ancient Chapels of Didsbury & Chorlton', Chetham Society, 1857, p.248, and Google edn p.277.

The Meadows, when the land was still worked as pasture and meadow land.

In between these three areas were more farms and collections of cottages, sometimes with a pub or beershop. One of these was clustered at Lane End, where today Sandy Lane joins the junction of Barlow Moor Road and High Lane. For a while there was a pub here, as well as the home of William Brownhill the wheelwright, who was also a beerseller and speculative landlord. Away from Lane End running east towards Hough End Hall were more farms and cottages.

In the opposite direction along High Lane was a brick terrace called Grantham's Buildings, now the site of Johns Close. Further down High Lane at the junction with Manchester Road was Pitts Brow, 'one of the most lovely spots in the village'.[14] This house was popularly known as the Glass House and was much admired, which must have gratified William Chesshyre, who lived here with his family. The Glass House stood on slightly higher ground and commanded a grand view south towards the village. It was roughly opposite St Clement's Church on the site of Edge Lane. To the left of the road into the village was an orchard, while away to the right, half hidden by trees, was the small brook that fed Blomley's Fishpond on the Row.

Strictly speaking, these small communities were really part of one of the three larger areas, but they had their own identities and so should be seen as separate.

The township is marked out and divided by its watercourses. Martledge was a place of streams and ponds, but across the area there were other ponds of varying sizes and uses.

14 Ellwood, chapter 4, 1885.

Barlow Woods. There were 10 acres of woodland in the township.

These included the fishpond just beyond the village, rented from the Egerton family by George Whitelegg, tenant farmer and landlord of the Bowling Green Hotel. Along the Row there was Blomley's Fishpond, which stretched up the road and was wide enough to have a bridge across it: it ran from Acres Road as far as Chequers Road. This too has long gone. To the north was Longford Brook, which rises in what is now Whalley Range and winds down and across the township before emptying into the Duke's Canal at Longford Bridge.[15] To the south was Chorlton Brook, which flows into the township at Hough End Hall before skirting the village and running into the Mersey. Anyone tracing its route out of Chorlton would encounter a number of smaller streams that fed into Chorlton Brook. To the north was Dog Kennel Brook, which flowed from Rusholme past Dog House Farm before joining Chorlton Brook at Hough End. From the south, meeting at the same point, was Red Lion or Shooters Brook, which came from Withington; while slightly further east were Platt Brook, sometimes known as the Gore Brook, and the Lay Brook from Lady Barn.[16] In places these smaller streams were buried in culverts, and in the years following the 1840s many were lost, along with the ponds they had fed. One such is the mysterious Rough Leech Gutter, which ran parallel with what is now Sandy Lane before making off across the township. It twisted and turned, running under High Lane and Edge Lane and onto Turn Moss.

15 Longford Brook rises on Withington Road, along Brantingham Road, to Manchester Road, on under Longford Road and then across Longford Park. Ashworth, Geoffrey, *The Lost Rivers of Manchester*, Willow Publishing, 1987, p.50.
16 All appear on the 1845 Ordnance Survey map and are referred to in Ashworth's book, p.48.

One of the footpaths across the Meadows, close by Hardy Farm.

Typical field plants that would have grown on the arable land in Chorlton.

The township was dominated by the Egerton family and the Lloyd estate, who together owned 87 per cent of the land. The remainder was held by twenty-one smaller landowners: some, like the retired James Holt, held enough to have a fine garden estate and farm a few acres running beside the brook, while others, like Alice Bailey, owned just enough to support a row of cottages. During the first four decades of the new century little changed to alter this pattern of land ownership, and on the one occasion when some land became available it was bought to consolidate existing holdings. In 1838 James Jackson was declared bankrupt, and his 'Several Closes and Parcels' amounting to 15 acres were put up for auction. Even then there was an interest in using the land to build houses, and the land was advertised as suitable for 'the erection of respectable villas and [it] possesses advantages for building rarely excelled, there being an excellent supply of sand, brick, clay and pure water on the estate and as there are not any manufactories or works in the neighbourhood, it affords an opportunity for investment seldom met with, at so short a distance from Manchester'.[17] But despite a similar housing development being undertaken by

17 *Manchester Times and Gazette,* 1 September 1838.

The Isles looking from Manchester Road towards Stretford.

Samuel Brooks on the northern edges of the township, James Holt, the new owner, was content to leave the land as it was.[18] The land had been occupied by tenant farmer Thomas Pearson, who may have been there from the early 19th century and was still there in 1835. Ten years later James Holt was farming the land himself. It may be that Thomas chose that moment to retire, or perhaps he lost the tenancy.[19]

It would be easy to think that in that summer of 1847 this was just a remote rural community. And it is true little had changed in hundreds of years. Some of the land had been farmed by the same family for generations, with their land in patches across the township separated by the holdings of other tenant farmers. The regular routine of ploughing and harvesting went on unchanged and each generation continued the cycle of life, marking the major events of baptism, marriage and death in the parish church on the Green and later also in the Wesleyan chapel on Chorlton Row. Their names appear in the records from the 18th century; they often lived close to each other and connected by ties of work and marriage. The great events of state passed them by. No major battle was fought in

---

18 Some of the fields later changed their names but others can be identified. These were Stack Field, Back Barn Field and Middle Field, which lay · between what are now Sandy Lane, the allotments and Chorlton Park.

19 Thomas Pearson described himself as a farmer in 1808 at the baptism of his daughter at the Methodist chapel on the Row and qualified for a vote on parliamentary elections in 1835, but ten years later the tithe shows James Holt farming the land.

their fields,[20] no kings or generals laid waste their land and in the years from 1642 till 1811 the population grew but little. Nor did this appear to change much during the first half of the 19th century. Someone born in the 1780s who had come to maturity as the long wars with Revolutionary France briefly came to an end and was reaching old age in the summer of 1847 would have seen little change. There were a few more houses along the Row, and others dotted about, but these were matched with the steady decline of the little hamlet of Hardy.[21]

Four miles north of the village the city of Manchester had gone from a pleasant Georgian city of 9,000 people to an industrial giant that was home to 90,000, and whose factories and warehouses were seen as new and exciting. Chorlton was never remote from that smoky giant. As an agricultural community it looked to the city as the main market for the food it produced. Some of this travelled down the Duke's Canal from Stretford into the heart of Castlefield, and in return we received night soil, Sunday daytrippers and the wealthy of Manchester, who retired here on the back of money made in commerce and industry. Some of those who laboured in the fields would have tramped in from Hulme just 3 miles away, and may well have passed some of the villagers heading into Manchester to work in the warehouses, offices and calico shops.

Getting into town was relatively easy. For those who could afford it there were the twice-daily packet boats from Stretford along the canal, which transported passengers in comfort and speed. A ticket for the front room cost 6d. and the back room 4d.[22] This was travelling in style. These packet boats were fitted with large cabins, where the passengers could sit 'under cover and see the country' glide by at the rate of 6mph, with two or three horses pulling the packet. If that was not style enough, the lead horse was guided by a horseman in full company livery.[23] It was a pleasant journey, for most of the route was still across open farmland, and it was not till Cornbrook that the landscape became more industrial. The chemical and dye works of Cornbrook gave way to sawmills, a textile factory, a papermill and all manner of wharves and warehouses, before the packet arrived in the heart of Castlefield.

For those preferring the roads there was a regular omnibus service from Stretford, which put down at the Buck and Hawthorn Inn on St Ann's Street hard by the church and square, as well as commercial carriers and even farm wagons. If all else failed people

---

20 During the Civil War parliamentary troops and those of the king came close by, as did a party of the Jacobite army, which camped on 'the slight rise bounded by Whitelow, & Wilbraham Road and High Lane', and a unit of the Scots Greys, who camped in the walled orchard of Hough End Hall on the way to Waterloo. Lloyd, John., *The Township of Chorlton-cum-Hardy*, E.J. Morten, 1972, p.69.

21 The development of the township can be followed in four maps drawn between 1786 and the Ordnance Survey map of 1844. These are Yate's map of 1786, Greenwood's of 1818, Hennet's dated 1830 and the 6in Ordnance Survey map of 1844.

22 This was beyond what most of the township's residents could afford. A domestic servant might earn 2s 9d and a labourer 13s 6d a week.

23 Slugg, T.J., *Reminiscences of Manchester*, J.E. Cornish, 1881, p.223.

walked the 4½ miles, using the country lanes into Hulme and thence into the city. Mary Moore thought nothing of walking back from the markets on a June day in 1838, having missed the farm wagon. Her day had started at 6.30, when she walked the mile from her home on the Green to Dog House Farm, just east of the township, helped to load the wagon and sold the farm produce before making her way back to Chorlton.

The main routes north were from Stretford or out through Martledge and further to the east along Withington Road. The road from Stretford was part of the ancient route from Chester, and passed Stretford before running parallel with the Duke's Canal almost all the way into Manchester. This was easy enough to reach from the village, and travellers had a choice between the old road, which ran out by the parish church before crossing close to Turn Moss and arriving by the canal, or taking High Lane and then Edge Lane. The latter was wider and a fairly straight road, bounded by a few interesting houses. The old road was more remote, twisting and turning as it snaked out of the village along by the Mersey and close by the weir. And for the faint-hearted it involved walking past Sally's Hole, which was reputedly where a woman had drowned.[24]

For those who lived north of the village around Martledge there was the road that ran out by the Royal Oak, continued past Dark Lane and onto Whalley Range before meeting Trafford Lane, which went past Hullard Hall to Old Trafford. And here there was the choice of Chester Road or Stretford Road. Part of this was not much more than an old lane or rough cart road, with deep ditches on either side and overshadowed by trees, mainly favoured by the farmers and those on foot. Nevertheless this was a route that took the Sunday drinker out from the city past the first pubs and beerhouses of the township.

Those prepared to pay could fork off at Trafford Lane and travel along Upper Chorlton Road and Chorlton Road, paying a toll at the turnpike at Moss Lane End. This was still a relatively new road, having been formed by Samuel Brooks back in 1838 to give access to his home of Whalley House.[25]

Mary Moore, mentioned above, would have taken the road that ran all the way from Withington past Hough End Hall and Dog House and into Hulme, before coming into Manchester along Moss Lane.

The canal opened the village to the modern world, but the arrival of the railway in 1849 was to pull Chorlton into a new relationship with the city. The decision to build a railway from Manchester to Altrincham, at the time just a small market town, had been taken in 1844 and construction began the following year. It followed on from the first passenger railway line that had opened between Manchester and Liverpool in 1831, and started a

---

24 There is no reliable source to corroborate the story or to link it to the early 19th century. The pond remained there until the late 1960s when it was filled in, and retained its name until the end.

25 Trafford Lane is now Seymour Grove, and the turnpike at Moss Lane End is now known as Brooks Bar.

The Royal Oak and Renshaw's Buildings both date from before the 1840s but this photograph was taken in the early 20th century.

For those working the meadows south of the village, the parish church dominated the view.

railway craze that in just twenty years created a network of rails across the country. By 1844, in Manchester alone, there were five railway companies connecting the city with Liverpool, Leeds, Birmingham, Sheffield, Bolton, Bury and Ashton-under-Lyne.[26]

Samuel Nixon, who ran The Greyhound by the Mersey, would certainly have seen the building of the railway that passed close to his home, and along with many local people may have been appalled and frightened by the hard-drinking hard-working navvies who built the line with nothing more than shovels, pick-axes, wheelbarrows and muscle power. He may even have known people in the village who were employed to help build the line. Much of the unskilled work was done by local farm labourers. There is no doubt that the sight of these speeding convoys of carriages pulled by an engine belching smoke and steam would have been fascinating. The short walk along the old road that ran out of the village to the Duke's Canal was a perfect spot to observe the trains. For wealthier residents the railway offered an even quicker way into the city. Like the canal it gave the traveller a fine view of the surrounding countryside, but with one difference. From the train window the passenger could gaze down on the roofs and streets as the train made its approach to Oxford Road. For the first time it was possible to see the city in a new way, as a lofty observer detached and isolated from it.

---

26 Liverpool & Manchester Railway, Manchester & Leeds Railway, Manchester, Bolton & Bury Railway, Manchester & Birmingham Railway, and the Sheffield, Ashton-under-Lyne Railway.

The Methodist congregation grew during the first half of the 19th century. They built their first chapel in 1805, a second in 1827 together with a Sunday school. This early 20th-century photograph is of the interior of the second chapel on the Row.

The railway brought other changes. For a while the omnibus service ceased, and the canal began to be eclipsed. By 1850, just one year after the opening of the railway, the Duke's company was longer advertising Stretford as a stop for its packet boats. More ominous was the fall in the quantity of freight, which was now taken by railway and roads. The canal had carried agricultural produce from Altrincham and Stretford into the city and brought nightsoil back. By 1849 this amounted to 873 tons of produce from Stretford, climbing to 1,781 tons in the following year, of which 69 per cent was carried on independent carriers along the waterway. But this would always be expensive, and many farmers used the roads. By 1855 the amount of agricultural produce taken from Stretford into the city by canal had fallen to 239 tons, and while it rose slightly in the following years it was never to rival pre-1850 tonnage.

The farmer William Bailey took his produce by road, returning with loads of dung that according to the receipts from the weighing machines ranged from 22cwt to 34cwt.[27] He also travelled in the opposite direction, south along Barlow Moor Road, to

27 Three of these weighing machine tickets have survived for June 1856 and 1857 and April 1862 in the Bailey collection.

the mill at Northenden, where he paid £4 to have a quantity of his wheat milled in May and July 1858.

Chorlton was a noisy and thriving place – and it would have been the noise of children more than anything that would have been noticeable in 1847. Just under 50 per cent of the population was under the age of fifteen, most being less than ten years old.

In the fields, depending on the time of year, labourers would have been ploughing, seeding, weeding or harvesting. Up by Lane End William Brownhill was carrying out his trade of wheelwright, while at the bottom of the Row William Davies the blacksmith was busy with his mysterious work of heating and hammering. Nor were they alone, for across the township tailors, carpenters, dressmakers and washerwomen as well as domestic servants laboured in some cases into the night. Nor would they have remained in their homes and workshops, for goods had to be delivered, washing returned and cows brought back for milking.

Along with the noise and hurly-burly there would have been the smells, some vaguely familiar and others that would have been less welcome. Even in summer there would have been that powerful smell which comes from wood and coal burning on open fires. Then there were the smells of animals mixing with the less pleasant ones of nightsoil from the privies of Manchester on the farmland, mingling with the smell of cottage privies – some of which were no doubt overflowing.

There was much that we would recognise from our traditional image of an early Victorian village. Many of the cottages were of traditional wattle and daub with thatched roof, and the church, school and pubs were the centre of village life. The system of local government had changed little and was dominated by local farmers. People knew each other and were aware of dark secrets; and some of these secrets were brought out and shared in some of the less pleasant customs, like publicly humiliating wrongdoers and those who had the misfortune to have unfaithful wives or husbands. Less unpleasant and more welcome customs survived into mid-century, although some would soon disappear.

Just as today there were burglaries and darker and more violent crimes. Some, like the murders of Mary Moore in 1838 and Francis Deakin in 1847, are as shocking now as they were then. Others, like desperate acts of infanticide or a thwarted illegal prize fight by the Mersey at Hardy along with poaching, sit in the past.

Other traditional aspects of rural life were missing. There was no squire to dominate the scene and the village pond so loved of country writers was soon to be filled in, while the Green had already been enclosed and turned into a private garden.

As for the people of the township, they were (as now) a mix. Some families like the Pinningtons and Grestys could trace their roots in the community back into the 17th century; others were relative newcomers. James Holt, who like many others will feature in the

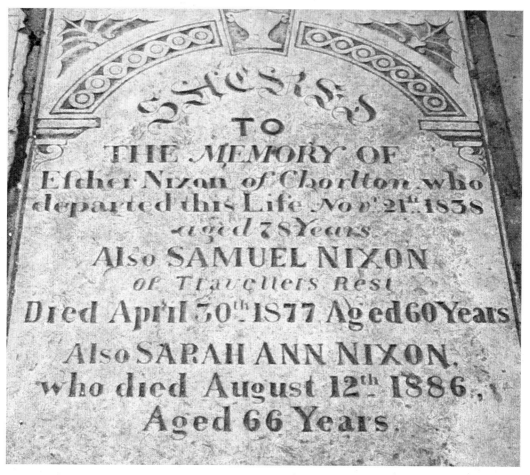

The Nixon family was in Chorlton throughout the 19th century. Samuel Nixon senior ran The Greyhound on the Mersey, his son was the landlord of the Travellers Rest on the Row, and his son ran the stationers and post office. Lionel, the great-grandson of Nixon senior, sold stationery and tobacco on Beech Road at the beginning of the 20th century. Lionel married Hilda Brownhill, whose family had been wheelwrights at Lane End.

story of the township, was a retired businessman from Manchester who retained interests in the city, and combined them with land-ownership here in Chorlton.

There were grand farmers, like Samuel Dean who farmed 290 acres by the Mersey, and lesser farmers, like John Cookson of Dark Farm and James Higginbotham on the Green. Some, like Higginbotham, had moved into the township from his father's farm at Yew Tree in Withington fairly recently. There were market gardeners like William and Alice Bailey, who were to build their business up through the century and were related by birth and marriage to many of the familiar families, like the Cooksons, Taylors, Renshaws and Chesshyres. William Chesshyre (also a market gardener) was himself a newcomer but soon embedded himself in the community, holding the position of parish clerk, and acting as enumerator for the 1841 and 1851 censuses.[28] He played an important part in the life of the township. Lastly there were those families who seem almost to epitomise not only village life in the 1840s but also reflect greater changes that were happening to Chorlton and the country. Samuel Nixon, for instance, was born in 1817 and was landlord of the Traveller's Rest beershop on the Row where it ran in to the Green. Born just two years after the victory at Waterloo, he grew up in a world of horses and oil lamps. His son ran a shop and post office and his granddaughter was a telegraphist.

Nor was this an inbred community. Just over half of the township had been born here, with a few more coming from less than 5 miles away, but the rest were from all over the country.[29] Lancashire might count for most of the 'outsiders' but there were plenty from Yorkshire and Cheshire, as well as some from London, the North-East, the Midlands, Wales, Scotland and Ireland: already by the late 1840s people were becoming increasingly mobile. These outsiders were from all the main occupational groups. Some married into local families and others brought their families with them; and there were plenty who were still single. As late as 1851 there were still only eight who were born in Ireland: two were farmworkers, another two were in domestic service and one was housekeeper to a painter and decorator from County Kerry. Not all of them gave their birthplace in Ireland, but of those that did most were from those areas most ravaged by the famine.[30]

In that summer of 1847 this was a mixed community but one still dominated by farming. And in that respect we were little different from the neighbouring townships of Withington, Didsbury and Stretford. Of these Stretford was the most significant. The Duke's Canal cut across the edge of Stretford village, providing a vital link with the city.[31] Running parallel for much of its route was the main road into Manchester, and many of our people would have taken one of the two to reach it. By the 1840s, Stretford like Chorlton was pouring its agricultural produce into the city. In 1845 over 500 tons of farm produce were coming by road into the city each week from Stretford.[32] These carts were piled high with fruit and vegetables, of which rhubarb was a particularly profitable crop. They left Stretford just after midnight for the markets, and while one family member remained to sell the produce the rest returned with the cart loaded with manure, ready to repeat the operation the following day.[33] 'This prompted one observer to describe the

---

28 As enumerator he was responsible for the collection of data on each household in the township.

29 53 per cent of the township had been born here and another 1 per cent was from less than 5 miles away.

30 These were in the north-west and south-east, where the population fell by over 30 per cent, and the south-west where it dropped by between 20 and 30 per cent during the period 1841–51.

31 It had arrived at Stretford in 1761, and the route into the heart of the city at Castlefield was finished by 1765.

32 Scola, Roger, *Feeding the Victorian City*, Manchester University, 1992, p.105.

33 Leech, Sir Bosdin, *Old Stretford*, privately printed, 1910.

place as 'the garden of Lancashire'.[34] Stretford was also a major centre for the processing of pigs for the Manchester market, as well as the manufacture of black puddings, and had gained the nicknames of Swineopolis and Porkhampton. During the 1830s between 800 and 1,000 pigs were slaughtered each week and sent into the city.[35] Most came from Ireland via Liverpool and were transported into Stretford by barge. On arrival the pigs were kept in cotes kept by the local landlords. The Trafford Arms charged 1*d* per pig a night and had cotes for 400 pigs.[36] Not surprisingly, in 1834 there were thirty-one pork butchers in Stretford compared with one in Chorlton and five in Urmston.[37]

Edwin Waugh, whom we have already met, having left the Manchester train at Stretford, summed up the place well when he wrote: 'Fruit, flowers, green market stuff, black puddings, and swine's flesh in general – these are the pride of the village.'[38] He was full of praise for the black puddings and the local speciality known as the Stretford goose, which was made from pork stuffed with sage and onions. He thought this 'not a bad substitute for that pleasant bird'.[39]

There was also industry of sorts in Stretford – the paper mill at Throstles Nest, built in 1765 on the site of an old corn mill. So the town had much going for it, and in the late 1840s its population was already about six times larger than Chorlton's – which is why the latter may have been a more attractive place to live.[40] Despite being close to Manchester this was still a secluded and attractive rural community with some fine houses, a pleasant parish church and fields to gaze across, as well as pubs to drink in.

34 Scola, *op. cit.*, p.97.

35 Cliff, Karen and Masterton, Vicki, *Stretford: An Illustrated History*, Breedon, 2002, pp.19–22.

36 Brundrett, Charles, *Brundrett Family Chronicle*, The Book Guild, 1984, pp.6–7.

37 Pigot's and Co.'s National Commercial Directory, 1834, p.538, Historical Directories edn p.338.

38 Waugh, *op. cit.*, p.75, Google edn, p.94.

39 Waugh, *op. cit.*, p.75, Google edn, p.94.

40 The township's population was 632 in 1841 and 761 in 1851. That of Stretford had gone from 3,524 to 4,998 during the same decade and even Withington was larger: in 1841 it was 1,277, which rose to 1,492.

FARMING

The farming community, the landlords and their relationship to the tenants, market gardeners,
land and crops, the farming year, and a reminder that this was a rural place

In 1847, 75 per cent of the families in Chorlton derived their living from the land. These were the farmers, market gardeners and agricultural labourers, and they worked land that was concentrated in the hands of the Egerton family and the Lloyd estate, who together owned 87 per cent of the land in the township. What was left was held by just twenty-one people. These smaller landowners were a mixed bunch. Some, like the retired James Holt, held enough to have a fine garden estate and rent out some to locals while others had a plot that accommodated just a cottage.

The Egerton and Lloyd land was rented out to tenant farmers and householders. These tenants undertook agreements or indentures that in some cases stretched over generations. James Renshaw took out such an agreement in 1767 with Samuel Egerton for 4 acres, and the farm buildings and cottage beside the Row.[41] The contract extended for his life and those of his wife and son, and could be binding for fifty years. As it was, the Renshaw/Egerton connection lasted a great deal longer. When James Renshaw's son died the farm passed to his son, and on his death to his niece Alice and her husband William Bailey. The Bailey family continued the tenancy into the early part of the 20th century, which gave a continuity of 146 years.

The rent of £9 10s in 1767 was payable in two equal amounts at Whitsun and Martinmas. Whitsun was always seven weeks or fifty days after Easter Sunday and Martinmas was on 11 November. These were the traditional times of the year to settle debts, and many of the township's tradesmen expected to see their bills paid at this time. The agreement between James Renshaw and Samuel Egerton made it clear that all mineral deposits and timber

---

41 Indenture between James Renshaw and Samuel Egerton, 1 May 1767. Bailey papers.

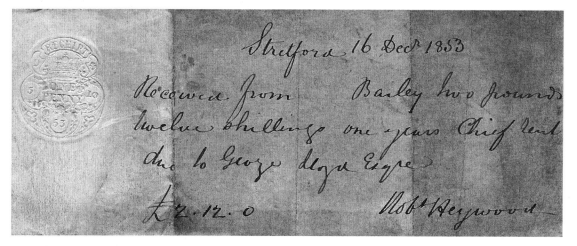

The Renshaw and Bailey family were tenants of the Egertons from 1767 through the entire 19th century and paid rent to both the Egerton and Lloyd estates.

belonged to the Egertons, who as landlords also reserved the right to 'hunt fish fowl hawk shoot and course in upon and through the said Premise or any part thereof and the Game found to take and carry at his and their will and pleasure Exclusive of any such Right Liberty or Privilege to be given granted or allowed to the said James and His Heirs'.[42]

We can follow the fortunes of the farming families over the years. Some prospered and increased their landholdings while others for whatever reason saw their acreage decrease. There were those who rented large estates and those who held onto just a few acres. Some combined their small landholdings with other occupations, like Samuel Nixon who ran The Greyhound,[43] or Alice Baguley who had 3½ acres of land and described herself as a housekeeper. She had been married to Thomas who was a tailor, but by 1851 she managed the land on her own.

Samuel Dean farmed 290 acres at Barlow Farm, which made him the largest farmer in the township. From his farmhouse, his land stretched across the southern end of Hardy down to the Mersey and across towards Withington and back up towards the brook. But most farms were more modest, ranging from the 57 acres of Charles Hayson down to the 11 acres that Charles Renshaw had at Martledge.

Working alongside these farmers were the market gardeners, who made up a bigger proportion of those who rented land. Just fewer than 60 per cent of all landholdings were less than 10 acres, and not all of these would have been viable as a source of income unless the families working them had other sources of income. Martha Deakin took in lodgers, while

---

42 Indenture between James Renshaw and Samuel Egerton, p.1.

43 Today the pub is Jackson's Boat. Nixon's land stretched out along the side of the Mersey, and his son ran the Travellers Rest on the Row.

Farming close to Barlow Hall.

her son William worked as a mechanic and another, Samuel, as an agricultural labourer. This pattern was common across the land to the south-west and north-west of Manchester, with farms varying from upwards of 150 acres and others less than 10 acres. Observers commented on how the farmers in the area were 'liberal in their views and desirous of making any improvements that hold out a reasonable prospect of success'.[44]

Something of the economics of market gardens can be got from the rents charged just across the river at Sale. Here in the summer of 1847 the rent of a good market garden ranged from £3 to £4, with some as high as £5 per acre, while wages about Sale were £1 2d per day for women in the fields and gardens and 2s per day for men, with dinner in summer and without dinner in winter.

The geography of the township determined how it was farmed and indeed what was farmed.[45] By the Mersey and back across the flood plain much of the land was meadow, as befits an area prone to flooding. Almost half of Barlow Farm was either meadow or pasture, while James Higginbotham, who lived on the Green but farmed out towards the river, could count three-quarters of his land as meadow. Meadow was particularly important. It is grassland that is kept damp by the use of ditches (called carriers) that are worked by

44 Wheeler, James, *Manchester: Its Political, Social, & Commercial History, Ancient & Modern*, Whitaker & Co., 1836, p.433, Google edn p.443.
45 There were 490 acres given over to arable, another 680 acres to meadow and pasture and 10 acres to woodland. Contained in this mix were both orchards and market gardens. Tithe schedule 1845.

sluice gates fed from a river. The land is fed with water up to an inch in depth from October to January for about fifteen to twenty days at a time, before the water is run off into the drainage ditches. The land is then left to dry out for five or six days, so the air can get to the grass. The early watering took advantage of the autumnal floods, which brought with them a mix of nutrients and silt that enriched the land. All this requires constant vigilance and Farmer Higginbotham would have expected to visit his fields once every three or four days to see that the water was evenly distributed and that there was no accumulation of weeds. This was not a task that could be entrusted to an unskilled manager, as the weather and time of year dictated the level of water that needed to flow from the irrigation ditches. As the weather got colder it was important to watch for a hard frost: if this was severe enough it could turn the meadow into 'one sheet of ice which will draw the grass into heaps which is very injurious to meadows'.[46] Not that this stopped Alfred Higginbotham annually flooding one of his fields in the early 20th century to provide a skating rink for the village.[47] The rewards for all this care and hard work were many. During the winter the water protected the grass roots from frost, allowing the grass to grow several weeks earlier, while in hot summers it kept the grass lush and provided grazing for the cattle as well as hay.

Much of the meadow land south of the village was drastically altered in the mid-20th century, but hints of it still exist. One irrigation ditch runs south, bordering the cow field close to the brook, while there are those who remember ditches close to Hardy Farm. At least one photograph shows a small footbridge crossing a ditch into Boat Meadow.[48] Ida Bradshaw remembers some of these ditches including the one that ran into Boat Meadow and others up by Hardy Lane Farm. They were roughly knee deep and were crossed by planks.[49]

Beyond the flood plain and stretching north past Martledge and east towards Hough End the land was mainly arable. Today arable weeds can still be found growing in these places.[50] In 1845 the main cereal crop was oats, followed by barley and wheat.

William Whitelegg, who farmed 36 acres at Red Gate Farm, was typical of the mixed farmer. He grew wheat and oats, along with potatoes, swedes, turnips, mangle wurzuls, raspberries and currants.[51] The pattern was repeated across the township, so in February 1849 the much bigger farm of Henry Jackson at Hough End comprised 'about 300 thraves

46 Stephens, Henry, *The Book of Farming*, William Blackwood & Sons, 1852, p.677, Google edn p.696.

47 An event that has yet to pass out of living memory and is attested by a photograph in Lloyd, John, *Looking Back at Chorlton-cum-Hardy*, Willow Publishing, 1985.

48 *Ibid.*

49 'I remember playing beside them when I was young. You had to jump over them but if you went in they were deep enough to cover your knees and you had a devil of a time trying to get out.' Ida Bradshaw, July 2010.

50 Arable weeds like corn poppies and fumitory, which have been discovered growing in an arc from Hough End down to Withington by David Bishop.

51 From an advertisement for the sale of the farm contents of Red Gate Farm, *Manchester Examiner and Times*, 3 November 1855.

The farm at Hardy Lane. This was farmed by the Cook family from before the 1840s until almost the end of the 19th century. In 1841 they farmed 29 acres of arable pasture and meadow land. The farm survived into the middle of the 20th century, was then the site of playing fields and is now cut by the tram line.

of wheat, 600 thraves of oats, 80 thraves of horse beans, 100 tons of hay, 100 loads of potatoes of various sorts, 30 tons of Swede'.[52]

Smaller market gardens were not only a feature of our township but also surrounding areas. Walking along the Row down from Barlow Moor Lane one would have passed plots farmed by Samuel Gratrix, William Bailey, James Higginbotham, John Brundrett and Thomas White. In some cases their holdings alternated with each other, reminding us of the old medieval strip farms. Market gardening may seem a pale imitation of farming, but the land was actually more intensively cultivated. Large numbers of early potatoes, cabbages, peas and other vegetables were grown, and it was possible to draw two or three crops from the land. It was not uncommon for a market gardener to grow 18 or 20 tons of potatoes from just 1 acre.[53]

Potatoes were an important crop and most were destined for Manchester, where by the 1840s the city was consuming 50,000 tons a year.[54] No doubt some of Chorlton's potatoes would have made their way by water from Stretford to be landed in Castlefield; for a brief period in the early 19th century the potato market was moved to be close by. The Oxnoble

52 A thrave equates to two dozen, and was the number grouped together as a bundle when stacked in the fields.

53 Wheeler, *op. cit.*, p.434, Google edn p.444.

54 Scola, *op. cit.*, p.95.

pub on Liverpool Road, which dates from about 1808, is a reminder of the importance of the trade to Castlefield. The oxnoble potato was popular in the late 18th century, but was superseded by other varieties and became the food of city cattle corralled in back yards to provide milk. Potatoes were an ideal crop for the many smaller landholdings or market gardens. On his 12-acre farm at White Hill, William Bennet grew forty-five loads of potatoes in October 1851.[55]

The diversity of produce was important when cash crops followed the seasons and were geared to the needs of nearby Manchester. It was reckoned that farmers who sowed the white Lisbon onions in autumn to send to the Manchester markets in spring could clear their land in time to plant potatoes and other vegetables. Many also had a second crop of onions, which was ready in the summer and might earn £150 per acre. There were also the obvious crops like wheat, apples from the orchard, rhubarb, strawberries and herbs like mint. Cows were also kept, to produce milk for sale.

Across south Lancashire the sale of fruit from orchards and gardens was not only a vital earner for market gardeners but contributed to the income of the larger farms.[56] Mary Moore sold the garden produce of Dog House Farm in the markets of Manchester. Dog House Farm covered over 200 acres around Whalley Range, and was one of the largest farms in the area. She would have made the journey to the city three times a week during the spring and summer. On the June afternoon in 1838 when she was tragically murdered she had successfully sold her entire cart load of gooseberries for 3 guineas. The Baileys who farmed on the Row in the 1840s not only had an orchard but were also growing rhubarb and raspberries.

In all there were twelve orchards in the township listed in the tithe schedule, and some farms had smaller orchards mixed in with their gardens or even their meadows. Francis Deakin, who was murdered in the summer of 1847 leaving a wife and six young children, farmed a market garden of 5 acres, of which 3 were orchard and 2 were meadow. Likewise, Samuel Gratrix's landholding on the Row had over a quarter of his 12 acres given over to an orchard. Its legacy is still there to see in the fruit trees in the gardens along Beaumont Road. Even the Higginbothams who were almost entirely dairy farmers still had 4 acres that were part arable and part orchard.

Some of this fruit travelled on the Duke's Canal from Stretford, where a 40-ton open market boat sailed three times a week to catch the Manchester markets on Tuesday, Thursday and Saturday mornings. This proved so successful that the company had to send the food barge at night and offer farmers seats on the packet boats. It may well be that the

---

55 White Hill Farm was on Barlow Moor Lane close to the present Southern Cemetery.
56 Scola, *op. cit.*, p.121.

The home of the market gardener Samuel Gratrix and his wife Mary. They farmed between 6 and 7 acres of land in the 1840s and '50s, which was one of the larger market gardens and included an orchard.

volume of farm traffic on the old road from the village to the canal was the reason for the raised platform under the viaduct. Anyone caught on the track as a farm wagon passed would have been able to jump into the ditch, but underneath the viaduct there was no such space, and road safety dictated a protected walkway.

The arrival of the train further hastened the decline in water transport, so that by 1860 only 43 tons a year were being shipped along the canal. This fall was reflected in the number of wholesale potato merchants based at the Castlefield wharf. In 1850 almost half these merchants worked from the canal, but twenty years later there was only one operating.[57]

Some farms were almost entirely arable but others were a mix of arable and meadow. Others were entirely meadow, and engaged in dairy farming. Indeed, 100 years after our story the Bailey family still maintained bulls on open land on the north side of the railway line, where the bridge crossed Wilbraham Road, and drove pigs from the railway yard through the streets of Chorlton to their farm at the bottom of Sandy Lane.[58]

Nor were market gardeners any less equipped than their farming neighbours. William Bailey on the Row held 7 acres of land, a mix of arable, meadow and orchard. He possessed

---

57 In 1850, thirteen of the thirty wholesale potato merchants were located at the Duke's Canal at Castlefield, according to the commercial directories, but by 1871 only one of the fifty-seven were trading there. *Ibid.*, p.112.

58 Oliver Bailey, April 2010. There are also a number of photographs dating from 1959 and 1960 in the Manchester Local Image Collection, showing the bulls in the field by Wilbraham Road. The field ran alongside what is now the metro line.

a range of farm machinery, including a horse, three types of cart, a plough, a set of harrows, two saddles and all the horse gear.[59] This may be compared with the contents of William Hayson's farm, a much larger operation of 70 acres employing five labourers. It had:

> a very powerful grey draught mare, rising 8 years old, 17 hands high, in foal; one compact black draught mare, 9 years old, 15½ hands high; one black horse, aged; one year stirk [a heifer or bullock usually between one and two years old], three broad-wheeled carts, with iron arms; shaft and chain cart gears, whitechapel, single iron plough, double wood plough, scarifier, set of iron seen harrowers, summer-work harrow, drill harrow, winnowing machine, patent hay cutter, wheelbarrow, ladders, cart sheet, rakes and pikels, spades and forks, ropes, cow tubs, old iron &c; also about 60 head of poultry.[60]

It was much the same in the Higginbothams' farmyard. Standing in the centre of the yard and looking out towards the Green there was the usual mix of water barrels, odd bits of timber, a drinking trough and farm carts as well as other equipment. To the right was the large barn that faced the parish graveyard, and directly opposite, squeezed into the remaining space, was their home.

There was never an end to the farming year. The late summer may have been full with the cereal harvest, but almost as soon as it was over it was followed by ploughing and sowing for the year ahead. As the cold winter months became a memory, June meant haymaking, and with it the worry of watching the weather and hoping all would be well for the coming harvest. Although the year differed slightly for dairy farmers like James Higginbotham and the arable farmer John Cookson over at Dark Farm, and was different again for the market gardeners like Martha Deakin, whose 3½ acres were given over to vegetables and orchard, there were constants for all of them. The weather might call a halt to many outdoor activities, and in these quiet moments tools were sharpened or repaired, hedges looked to and the manure and marl collected so that it was ready to be spread. For some it was the variety of tasks that appealed. Pulling kale on a December morning with leaves dripping with cold winter water was no fun, but that could be balanced with a harvest break in the late summer sun.

It is easy to forget that so much of this farm work was solitary, accompanied only by the sound of the birds in the sky. Ploughing was one such activity. It was undertaken two or three times a year and was essential for preparing soil for the seeds. On big farms there

---

59 Inventory of William Bailey, February 1887, Oliver Bailey, 2008. The list also included a greenhouse with thirteen lights, a rhubarb house and hay shed measuring 12 by 6yds, a chopping machine and potato scales with weights. One of his carts weighed 15cwt, which may have been average for a small cart.

60 *Manchester Guardian*, 1 April 1865.

One of the farmhouses on the Green. This was on the eastern side close to the churchyard and its barn was near the Bowling Green Hotel. During the middle of the century it was run by the Knight family, who farmed a mix of arable, pasture and meadow land.

might be teams of ploughmen working dozens of horses, but here it was one man with a pair of horses. Alone, working the field, all that could be heard was a sliding sound as the furrow was turned, similar to the noise a spade makes when pushed into the ground.[61] Occasionally the plough might hit a stone and there would be a 'chattering sound'[62] If all went well the farmer might plough an acre in a day, but this could be the equivalent of walking 16 miles. At times it could be dangerous. When a plough hit a stone it might throw the plough handles up into the ploughman's chest, while a tree root could ensnare the plough and waste precious time. All this had to be finished before Christmas, so that the hard frosts of January could help break down the soil.

During the later winter months manure was spread across the fields. This was a slow and back-breaking job, which involved carting manure to the field and spreading it out by hand. The farmers would have obtained marl from the marl pits at Martledge, which for centuries had supplied their needs. There was also nightsoil. The produce of thousands of privies in Manchester, it came to the township along the Duke's Canal and by road. In just one day in the summer of 1836 over 400 loads averaging 2 to 3 tons each passed out of the

---

61 The material for this section has been drawn from a collection of farming memories collected by Margaret Wombwell and covers a number of small farms in north Derbyshire. Wombwell, Margaret, *Milk, Muck and Memories*, Derbyshire County Council, 2007.
62 Howard Davieson quoted, *ibid.*, p.50.

city along the Stretford road and through the toll bar.[63] Farmer Bailey paid 2s for a horse load in March 1857. He may well have spread most of it on the strips he rented opposite his farm on the Row. With the coming of spring it was ploughed into the ground.

Seeds were sown by hand, in autumn for a late summer harvest or in the spring for an early autumn harvest. They were carried in a box on the labourers' chest, hanging from a belt that went over his shoulders. This left both hands free to broadcast the seeds. Following behind was a man with a harrow, which was pulled by a horse and turned the soil over to bury the seeds.

Farmers here grew more oats than other cereals. Oats can grow and ripen in cooler summers and have a greater tolerance of rain, which makes them a suitable crop for the North-West. Martha Deakin and the other market gardeners planted a mix of vegetables – potatoes, mangolds, turnips and kale. Potatoes were particularly tiring to plant: they were dropped into the ground in long rows at intervals of 10 or 12in.

---

63 Wheeler, *op. cit.*, p.435, Google edn p.445.

The farmyard of the Higginbothams, looking east towards the Green. This painting by Marjorie Holms was copied from an old photograph taken in the 1880s.

In 1845 Chorlton grew a mix of oats, barley and wheat. The date of this picture is unknown.

Crops were at the mercy of rats, moles and birds. Birds might be dealt with by killing a few and leaving them on the field, a deterrent that didn't last long. Sparrows were thought to be particularly troublesome, so there was a tradition of presenting dead sparrows to the constable, who paid a bounty from local funds of a halfpenny for each one, or a farthing for an egg. For the young, eager for a little spending money, this was a wonderful incentive, although some enterprising young lads were less than honest when they found a few dead sparrows on a manure heap at Oak House Farm in 1843. The sparrows were given to John Brundrett, who was the constable for the year. There was a hint of irony as it was his farm.[64] But by the time of this great sparrow crime the practice was on the way out. Farmers were realising that the birds performed a valuable service, in eating insects, and Thomas Cookson, a constable and a farmer up by Dark Lane, abolished the custom.

Some farming communities had mole catchers who visited annually. A successful team working in north Derbyshire used poisoned worms, but the more traditional method was traps. This was probably safer as all members of the Derbyshire gang eventually succumbed to their deadly art.

---

64 Ellwood, chapter 8, 1885.

But of all the tasks weeding and singling must surely have been the most disliked. These were chores that were never ending. The latter involved getting down and crawling along the rows, pulling out surplus plants. At best the ground was damp; at worst it was raining. And then there were more weeds to pull. For Martha Deakin, newly widowed and just delivered of her sixth child, much of this work would have been done by her children.

For dairy farmers like James Higginbotham, haymaking was one of the important times of the year. Over 17 of his acres were meadow, which needed cutting during June so that his animals had feed through the dark winter months. This was a labour-intensive task and he may well have called on extra help. John Gresty was a haycutter who lived on the Row, and could have been hired by James as well as helping his neighbour William Bailey. Grass cut in early June took longer to dry because it was still full of sap, but it was reckoned to be better feed than that cut later.

The grass was cut using a scythe which was a long wooden shaft about 5½ft long with two handles and a blade that could be anything up to 2 to 3ft. Holding the top handle in his left hand and the central one in his right, with the blade parallel and close to the ground, the haycutter cut in a long arc from right to left, depositing the cut grass on the left. On bigger farms a team of haycutters appointed a leader, who set the pace and decided when to call rest breaks. Watching the slow and purposeful movement as men advanced with a steady rhythm across the field accompanied by a work chant or song was something to behold. It reminded some of an army of ants and others of the wind gently moving the long grass. The grass was left to dry, then turned during the following day. This too was labour intensive, as the labourers had to turn it by hand with forks. And all the time their fear was rain, which put off the time when the grass could be stacked in cocks. These were small and cone-shaped, sometimes topped with a cap of grass to act as an umbrella. The skill was in knowing when the grass was ready to be gathered and stored: too wet and it would rot; too dry and it would make poor food for the cows. Not that it stopped there: a really dry and hot period might cause the hay to overheat and burst into flames.

Loading and carting was also skilled work. Men pitched the hay onto the cart, while another man stood on top, making sure the corners were solid so it didn't fall off when the cart was on the move. Each forkful was dispatched with a shout, ensuring that the man on top was ready and not too close to the sharp prongs. Accidents happened, of course: men were sometimes caught with the point of the fork, and this could turn into an infected wound. Even the best-stacked hay load might have an accident. Further south in north Derbyshire the farmer John Joseph Briggs abandoned the age old custom of 'harvest home' when the wagon overturned. For as long as people could remember the last wagon from the harvest fields would be decorated and women and children would sit on top singing songs, but on this occasion when the load was lost many sitting on top had been hurt.[65]

Once back at the yard the hay was stacked. This involved laying brushwood and timber on the ground with gaps to let the air circulate and loading the hay onto this platform. The final bales were built into a slope and then thatched.

Most of the farms here were a mix of meadow and arable. James Higginbotham had 7 arable acres along with his 17 acres of meadow, while away to the north in Martledge John Cookson's 59 acres included 26 which were arable. Samuel Dean at Hardy counted a third of his 290-acre farm as arable land. This meant that no sooner had the hay been gathered in than it was time to start the corn harvest. During August John Gresty was working long hours while the sun shone, sometimes even on into the night. Men raked the corn into sheaves or bundles, which were gathered in eights facing north-south, so the sun could get at both sides. It was then moved into barns, and when they were full into corn stacks. These had to be carefully made, ensuring the heads were off the ground. Working from the middle out, the sheaves sloped outwards so the rain ran off. Once the first course was completed the second was made in the same way, but this time working from the outside towards the middle. The stack was then thatched.

Once the corn was in, the task of threshing began. This is really two processes. The first consists of loosening the grain from the stalks or chaff, the second of separating it. Traditionally the loosening was done by beating the corn with a flail on the threshing floor, then throwing it up into the air so that the wind blew the lighter chaff away and the heavier grains fell back down. Threshing was labour intensive, and was an important source of work during October. By the 1790s the first threshing machines were in use, and became a focus for rural protest during the early 19th century.[66]

Meanwhile Martha Deakin and the other market gardeners would be getting in their crops. The back-breaking job of digging up the potatoes would be over by October and this was followed by the collection of mangolds, a winter feed for cattle as well as turnips and other root crops.

By October the apple harvest was in full swing. For weeks the younger children would have been picking up windfalls daily. Most of the apples went to Manchester, but some were retained to be turned into cider.

What united all the farmers and determined their success was the weather. The mid-1840s were not good and the harvests of 1844 and 1845 were poor. Much of 1844 was

---

65 Heath, Philip (ed.), Briggs, John Joseph, *Melbourne 1820–1875*, Melbourne Historical Society, 2005. John Joseph Briggs farmed Elms Farm just south of Derby and kept a diary.

66 The threshing machine was invented by Andrew Meikle in 1788 and production began the following year. The destruction of threshing machines accompanied by rick burning was a feature of the Swing Riots in 1830.

a year of drought and the spring corn germinated late. As a consequence it was not harvested till October, and even November in some places; even then some of it failed to ripen. The winter of 1845 was no better. An arctic spell began in late January and continued till almost the end of March. February was the coldest for fifty years, and there were heavy snowfalls. Much fieldwork would have been difficult, and the poor hay harvest of the previous year coupled with meagre fodder crops meant that the amount and quality of animal feed was much reduced.

The year 1846 proved to be better, but while the wheat crop was good that of barley was below average, bad news for Chorlton given that a third of the cereal crop was barley. Nor were things any more promising for the smaller farmers, who specialised in vegetables and fruit for the Manchester markets. The potato blight that was to bring disaster to Ireland had been reported in Derbyshire and although we were clear some at least of our farmers were concerned.[67] Likewise the hot sunny weather of May and June had brought out vast numbers of insects which had attacked the fruit trees, but as James Higginbotham reported, 'the cold of last week and the rain of this' had killed them off 'and there was still a goodly show of apples left, on the Rose of Sharon branches, which were fresh again, beautiful and healthy and the Newbridge pears clustered upon the trees.'[68]

Farmers, like others in the township, spread their risk when it came to earning money. George Whitelegg ran the Bowling Green Hotel, but also farmed 36 acres in 1845. He was a man inclined to make money, and by 1860 he was into speculative building. In that year he built Stockton Range, fine brick houses catering for the new trade in suburban living that had been made possible by the coming of the railway to Stretford eleven years earlier. These houses still stand. In the same way, but perhaps on a smaller scale, the Bailey family maintained a row of brick cottages at Martledge. These had been built before 1832 by the uncle of Alice Bailey, and were still providing rent in the 1860s.[69] The Baileys also lent money, a practice that was common before the age of accessible banking. In June 1847 they lent William Gresty the sum of £36 with interest.[70] They also borrowed money themselves: in 1838 they borrowed £70 from Thomas Taylor, and in 1851 Alice borrowed £52 from her mother-in-law Margaret Bailey.[71] These were not small amounts, but they were paid back promptly. William Gresty discharged his debt of £36 with its interest of 3s 6d by 5 April 1849, while Alice paid hers back in instalments, with the debt standing at only £2 10s a year later. These appear to have been short-term loans to pay for stock or

67 The *Manchester Examiner*, 19 June 1847, James Higginbotham's potato field stretched along the Rec. beside what is now Cross Road.
68 James Higginbotham's orchard was between the Row and the Green.
69 In 1863 Alice Bailey was rated for four cottages which had rentable values ranging from £5 4s 6d to £4 5s 6d. Chorlton-cum-Hardy Rate Books, Microfilm Rolls 297–9, Archives and Local History Library, Manchester.
70 William Gresty, 5 June 1847, the Bailey Collection.
71 Thomas Taylor, 8 September 1838, Mrs Margaret Bailey, 1 January 1851, the Bailey Collection.

machinery. In the case of Alice she settled £8 14s 2½d soon after taking out the loan, and made a further payment of £50 three weeks after agreeing the loan.

In many rural communities, particularly where the main landowners were absent, farmers like the Baileys and Higginbothams dominated the scene. People might be in their debt, and many relied directly or indirectly on them for a living. Twenty-six of the farmworkers here were employed on six of the local farms and more were taken on at busy times of the year. James Higginbotham's workforce included cowmen, carters and a number of young boys, young enough for the hiring contract to have been agreed between the farmer and the boys' fathers. Farms also generated income for local tradesmen, like William Davies the blacksmith and William Brownhill the wheelwright, as well as the shopkeepers, tailors and shoe makers. As we shall see, these farmers played a prominent part in church affairs and dominated the administration of local government. From their ranks were drawn the local juries that served to make judgements at inquests and sat in the local Vestry to decide the local rate; and they were heavily represented among the few who were entitled to vote.

three

FARM LABOURERS

Jobs, pay, and the hardships and seasonality of work

Working on the land was the main occupation in Chorlton. During the 19th century farmworkers fell into four main groups. There were the farm servants who were hired by the year or even by the quarter. If they were unmarried they usually lived in a farmer's house and received part of their wages in kind – many being paid between 5s and 6s less, to take into account their board and food. It was a system that suited younger workers who were not married and in many cases had only just left home. Although their monetary wages were low they had job security. Although plenty of the labourers were still hired in this way,[72] it was a declining practice; it was becoming more common for labourers to be hired for a year at a time and to live in their own homes. Less attractive was the practice of hiring men weekly or even daily, which meant that there was no job security. Finally there were skilled workers, who contracted for a special job. Traditionally in the north these contracts were advertised in local papers at Martinmas. Popular accounts describe lines of workers on 11 November, often holding or wearing a symbol of their trade and waiting to be selected. When an agreement was reached, both parties signed papers that stated the period of time and the wage to be paid.[73] These were binding contracts backed by legal precedent, as Henry Stephens was careful to spell out in his book about farming, but there were circumstances in which either party could break the bargain.

---

72 In 1881 seven farm servants are listed as living at Barlow Hall Farm and five at Higginbotham's farm on the Green in 1891. Young Thomas Griffin from Ireland was the milk lad and lived in, while the remaining four lived in two rooms over the shippon, which was also the barn or cow house.
73 Webb, Mary, *Precious Bane*, Cape, 1924, gives a vivid if fictional account of a hiring fair.

Across the south of Lancashire and into Cheshire farm servants were hired throughout the year.[74] Our old friend James Higginbotham dismissed more than one of his men for persistent drunkenness or negligence and took on fresh labour when needed. His account book is peppered with references to broken tools, mislaid equipment and absenteeism, all of which led to dismissal.[75] No doubt some workers stayed with their employer for years at a time, but Higginbotham's accounts show a steady turnover. In October 1844 he employed Margaret Turner as a servant on £8 a year, and the following January took on Samuel Mulliner as a carter. He agreed to pay Susannah Clark 3s a week in April the same year, and in spring 1846 he took on young John Royle as a servant boy.[76] Some of these appointments at least were on a monthly basis. Robert Howarth agreed a month's wages or a month's warning in spring 1848, and left on 9 June having turned up drunk and breaking a lamp the day before.

Often, with younger workers, the deal was contracted with a parent. William Carter's mother agreed on his behalf that he should be paid £3 14s a year, while the father of Thomas Whitefield not only agreed that his son should be paid a yearly salary of £4 in January 1847 but received the first quarter's payment of 12s, which was paid to him in April the following year. John Brody's entire yearly wages of £3 10s went to his father.

Farmers had to think of a worker's character and record. This was difficult when farm servants seldom had written references and only named their previous employer. As Stephens pointed out, this was less of a problem if the previous employer was local, but if farm labourers had worked elsewhere it was more difficult. Ten years earlier, in 1839, Robert Mitchell had set up a register in Morayshire 'of the names of farm servants of established character'. For a small fee the worker's name was entered on the list. This proved popular with both employer and employee, so much so that the original list of just 269 names on 31 July 1839 had risen to 1,110 by 1841.[77]

The term labourer is a deceptive one, as it included many different manual and physically exhausting jobs. In the course of the farming year the agricultural labourer had to be proficient at many tasks, including ploughing, harvesting, threshing and haymaking, as well as maintaining hedges, fences and walls. He could be called on to look after the welfare of farm animals, some of which were very valuable. As the 19th century progressed he was expected to use an increasing number of machines.

---

74 Gritt, A.J., 'The Survival of service in English Agricultural Labour Force: lessons from Lancashire c.1650–1851', *Agricultural History Review*, 50, 2002, p.39. This cites evidence that in the late 18th century at Eccleston near St Helens hiring was done throughout the year with a concentration in January, February and March and earlier, in 16th-century Cheshire, hiring was not assisted by hiring fairs.

75 Higginbotham farm accounts. These are fragmentary, only cover the late 1830s and the 1840s, and have only survived in a typed form.

76 There were others, but the accounts do not always include a month.

77 Stephens, *op. cit.*, p.738, Google edn, p.757.

One such man was John Gresty, born in Chorlton in 1817. He grew up against a backdrop of the bitter peace that followed the long wars with France, years in which prices and unemployment rose dramatically – leading to agricultural disturbances and riots in the South and West, industrial agitation, the demand for a minimum wage and an extension of the franchise. The government and the ruling class, fearing social unrest at best and revolution at worst, dispatched the military to the new industrial towns of the North and invoked draconian laws to stifle the protest. John married Mary Helsby in May 1838. She was just seventeen, and by June 1841 they were living in a small wattle and daub cottage rented from the Egertons, on the Row close to the Bailey farm, for which, together with a small plot of land, they paid £5 a year in rent.[78]

John was variously a hay cutter and agricultural labourer, a market gardener and later a coal dealer. As a hay cutter he was expected to work long hours with a scythe, which would probably have been customised to match his height and the length of his arm. Much of the work would have been back-breaking and undertaken in all weathers. At times he must have reflected on his working day compared with that of the cotton spinners 4½ miles away in Manchester, or the even more dangerous work of coalminers. His was, after all, a job with all the pleasures of fresh air and sunlight, not an oppressive, dusty and noisy factory floor or dark tunnels deep underground. He could even grow his own food and had access to much fresh produce. But his labours were long, and mending a fence in a bitter February wind could not have been pleasant.

John Gresty's day began at daylight and lasted as long as there was light. If he was at work at six, his day might have started an hour earlier, as he had to walk to work. In winter he might expect to work from 8am to 4pm and for the rest of the year from 6am to 6pm.[79] Some farmers offered the incentive of a pint of ale for the first man to arrive on the job, as well as giving each man a bottle of beer or cider for the day and providing meals at harvest time. Breakfast was at 9.30am, dinner at noon, afternoon lunch at 4pm and supper at 7pm. This working day was similar to those in the factories, but unlike industrial work the hours varied with the seasons.[80]

Agricultural workers like John could expect variations in their take-home pay depending on the time of year and the weather, and of course their age. Rural unemployment was at its worst in the winter months, with February being particularly bad. There were also differences across the country, with wages in the North being better than the South. Farmers in the growing industrial areas had to compete with wages available in the new factory towns,

---

78 The site of the cottage is either under the present Ivy Court or the electrical substation on Beech Road.
79 'Evidence of Mr Spooner on working hours in the south west', *Reports of the Poor Law Commissioners on the Employment of Women and Children in Agriculture*, HMSO, 1843, p.31, Google edn p.51.
80 'Reports of the Poor Law Commissioners', *op. cit.*, Evidence of Mr Spooner on working hours in the south west, p.31, Google edn, p.51.

and as Manchester was so close by the employers in Chorlton had to be mindful that factory jobs might lure men away. Certain workers like carters and cowmen could expect between 1s and 2s 6d per week more than other labourers. John, as a hay cutter, might receive between 3s 6d and 5s per acre, and perhaps also a quart of ale for each acre mown. Across Lancashire agricultural male wages ran from 11s to 18s, with women earning between 6s 4d and 6s 11d, and children from 2s to over 4s.[81] But these figures varied, depending on the time of year. It is worth noting that women's wages in parts of Lancashire were the highest in the country. Wages at harvest time ranged from 15s a week up to, in some circumstances, 24s, while task work might pay between 14s and 21s, with special work like drainage bringing in 5s for boys and 7s 6d for men. Families might also earn extra at harvest time from gleaning, which was the practice of collecting left-over crops from a farmer's fields; in the 19th century this was a legal right for cottagers. There were also hidden payments, with some farmers providing land and farm produce as well as accommodation. Higginbotham the farmer, for example, was paying 5s down to 1s 6d a week to men employed variously as cowmen, carters and farm servants.[82] Even given the competition from nearby towns, agricultural wages did not compare favourably with the best wages paid in the cotton factories in 1833, where a man in his thirties might earn 22s 8d.[83]

Nevertheless, Alexander Somerville reported in the June of 1847 after his visit to Chorlton, Sale and Northenden, that:

wages are 1s 2d per day for women in the fields and gardens, and 2s per day for men, with dinner in summer and 2s without dinner in winter. Some employers give the dinner all the year over, and in cases it is said to be of the same quality for the men as for the master; they eat together. For mowing, meadow grass 5s and 6s per acre are paid, and 4s and 5s for mowing clover and rye grass. These payments are about double the wages paid for mowing in Wiltshire and Dorsetshire; they are about fifty per cent above the wages paid for the same work in Northumberland and the Lothians. I have mowed grass in East Lothian, which was heavy as any now growing in Cheshire for 3s 6d per statute acre. If a man mows an acre for and a half per day, he will hardly be inclined to dance at night.

Agricultural labourers would have expected to work until old age or disease offered a natural form of retirement. There were not many who celebrated their seventieth birthday and fewer still their eightieth, but of those in Chorlton who had many were still working. Of the fourteen who were between seventy and seventy-nine six still described themselves as at

81 Agricultural Labourers' Earnings, Parliamentary Papers, 1861.
82 Higginbotham's farm accounts, 1845–8.
83 Frow, Edmund and Ruth, *Radical Salford*, Neil Richardson, 1984, p.34.

work, and even more staggeringly two of the four over the age of eighty were still working. It is true that Mary Gratrix and Mary White, both aged eighty, gave their occupation as farmers and employed men to work for them, but of the six who had celebrated their seventieth birthdays and were still working one was a charwoman and two were farm labourers. When Thomas Renshaw was interviewed in 1851 he gave his age as seventy and his occupation as straw joiner (or thatcher). Unlike some of his neighbours, who described themselves as former labourers or infirm, Thomas gave the impression of a man still at work.

Nationally, rural workers might expect to earn their best money and be most comfortably off in the years before they married or just after marriage, and once their children were earning. The years when the children were young and the years after they left were difficult.

Many in the township would have had to turn their hand to a variety of jobs in a year. This may explain why Thomas Renshaw described himself as an agricultural labourer in 1841 and a straw joiner in 1851. The 1841 census had been in June, just as the farming year was taking off again, but the 1851 census happened on 30 March, which was a dead time. Thomas may have moved up the ladder, or perhaps he was engaged on one of those alternative jobs.[84]

For others, especially women, there were opportunities to find field work at the busiest times of the year, like haymaking or the corn harvest. These were labour-intensive jobs that offered casual work to anyone in the township.

Seasonal unemployment was not the only reason why some families struggled to earn enough. In 1847 there were far more people who described themselves as agricultural labourers than were employed by the six farms. Some might have been employed in the large number of market gardens or on farms in neighbouring townships, and others may have worked in Manchester. Perhaps some chose to describe themselves as farmworkers although this was just one of their jobs. A case in point is George Jones, who gave his occupation as weaver and labourer.[85] Many weavers drifted into other occupations throughout the year or left entirely to pursue other jobs before returning later in life to the loom. Weaving had been an important industry across south Lancashire, and as late as the 1850s there were still a few weavers in Burnage and Stretford as well as further south across the Mersey in northern Cheshire.

As we shall see later, some labourers may have relied on the earnings of other family members, whether wife or children. John Gresty was part of this group, and he prospered. In 1841 he described himself as a hay cutter and agricultural labourer; by 1861 he was a market gardener; and twenty years later he was dealing in coal as well as market produce. Two of his daughters were pupil teachers and a third became a schoolmistress.

84 Reay, Barry, *Rural England*, Palgrave Macmillan, 2004.
85 It was at the baptism of his two sons on 27 October 1808 when his occupation was given as labourer when George was baptised and as a weaver when Edward was baptised.

four

ANIMALS OF TOIL
AND ANIMALS FOR THE POT

Horses, pigs, chickens and other useful animals

his was a time dominated by working animals. For centuries the main draught animals had been oxen, and in some parts of the country their use continued until the end of the 19th century and the start of the 20th; but by the 1840s the horse had taken over in most areas.[86]

Horses were a familiar sight in Chorlton. As well as working the fields, they pulled carts and wagons as well as the coaches of the well-to-do. They provided work for the blacksmith and the farrier, and indirectly for the wheelwright. Then there were the men who worked with the horses, of whom the ploughman and the carter earned more than most farmworkers. After all, the carter was assured a regular wage because his horses might be used all year long. James Higginbotham, farmer on the Green, employed a carter and on the 380-acre Dog House Farm just outside the township eight of the men employed were carters. At smaller farms and market gardens the job of caring and working with horses fell to the farmer or his son. The Bailey family on the Row had just one horse, which would have doubled for ploughing and pulling the spring cart.[87] This was the pattern with many market gardens with less than 10 acres of land.

On large farms horses were worked in pairs and there might be two or three teams. The most intensive periods were when wheat or turnips were being sown, mangels were being carted and at harvest time. Many formed close bonds with their horses, a bond that was deepened by the long hours they spent together. This might start as early as five in the morning as the horses were prepared for work, and when the day in the fields was over the

---

86 This was a result of improved breeding and the development of lighter ploughs.

87 The inventory of William Bailey in 1885 recorded one Roan horse worth £14, a Howard plough and a single Howard plough. Just sixty years later the Baileys, now at Park Brow Farm, still had one horse.

horses had to be cleaned of thick mud, then fed, watered and groomed. For this he might be paid just over £1 a week, although James Higginbotham was less generous. During the mid-1840s he was paying his men between 4s 6d and 6s a week. These wages reflected the fact that the men lived in, thus receiving their food and lodging in lieu of part of their payment – but even so they seem rather low.

Horses pulled everything from the light spring cart to the heavier carts used by the carriers and the big four-wheeled wagons. William Bailey's spring cart was a two-wheeled vehicle that was pulled by his single horse. It was an all-purpose vehicle, which might convey his farm produce to market one day and act as a taxi on another and it weighed 15cwt. The more substantial carrier's cart was more likely to be pulled by two horses. These plied the lanes from township to township carrying virtually anything, including people. More often than not the cart was covered, either with a canvas top or a specially constructed cabin. By far and away the largest farm vehicle was the wagon. These usually had four wheels, and were 6ft high and 14ft long. There were different designs and regional variations. James Higginbotham's was made of oak with elm boards; its front wheels were 4ft in diameter and the back ones 5ft. Drawn by two horses in single file when it was laden with the summer hay, it was an impressive sight lumbering away from the meadow.

A carter and his horse worked almost all the year round, and each season brought its own problems. The cold winter months with the ever-present threat of snow and hard frosts might make any journey a trial, but equally long hot summers brought horse flies, which hung around the horse and irritated all in close contact. The better off, of course, could choose when to venture out, and coachmen like George Heath, who lived at Holt Lodge and worked for the Holt family on the Row, might not have had to be out in all weathers. Nor did he have to look after the horses, for the Holts employed a groom.[88] His counterpart Frank Hains might have been kept busier. He worked for William Cunliffe Brooks at Barlow Hall, who regularly travelled into Manchester. There was no groom, so the task of seeing to the horses and maintaining the coach fell to Frank.[89]

I doubt that Cunliffe Brooks would have given a second glance to the animals that were to be found in farmyards and cottage gardens across the township. Chickens were common enough, and many families aspired to keeping a pig. This was bought in the spring from a local farmer – who might wait until the animal was killed and the meat sold before receiving payment in the autumn. This was the only way that some families could afford the animal, which cost between 20s and 25s. These were kept in the back

88 William Needham was nineteen and lived in the family house, unlike George Heath who lived with his family in the lodge house. The Holts employed a number of grooms in the fifty years from the 1840s, but retained the services of George Heath throughout. He was still working for them in 1891 and may have done so till his death in the township in 1896 aged 76.

89 The office of William Cunliffe Brooks Bankers & Co. was at 92 King Street.

garden or yard and could be fed on almost anything. It might provide meat for up to seven months: as well as fresh pork it could provide salted bacon, cured ham, lard, sausages and black pudding.[90] Beyond food, the pig offered its skin for saddles, gloves, bags and footballs, while the bristles could be used for brushes – and an average pig gave a ton of manure a year. Often, though, the pig became a family pet, which made its killing that little bit harder. Slaughtering was usually done in winter, the cooler months being preferred because, in the words of the farming expert Henry Stephens, 'the flesh in the warm months is not sufficiently firm and is then liable to be fly born before it is cured'.[91] The traditional time was around Martinmas in early November, so that cured hams were ready for Christmas. The slaughtering was done by the local butcher, who was often paid in kind. The event was very much a family affair, with everyone pitching in to scrape the hair clean from the body either by immersing it in boiling water or pouring the scalding water over the carcase. Immediately after the pig was killed it was hung and left for the night, before being cut up. It was a time-consuming job to rub salt into the hams, and not a pleasant one either. First the salt had to be crushed from a salt block, and this was then rubbed into the meat.[92] A side was anything up to 4ft in length, and special care had to be taken to rub salt into the bone joints. All of this left the hands red raw. The meat was then soaked in water and dried, before being wrapped in muslin and hung up. Meanwhile some of the pork was cooked in pies and the blood was made into black pudding.

Pigs were part of the local economy, and both farmers and market gardeners found that pig-keeping was a profitable undertaking. The going rate at market in 1844 for a single animal was anything between 24s and 30s.[93] Our old friend Henry Stephens calculated that two brood sows could produce forty pigs between them, and that after retaining six for home use the remaining thirty-four could easily be sold at market. Many of the smaller farmers and market gardeners might well keep at least one sow and use it to supplement their income.[94]

The same was true of poultry, which existed happily enough in a back garden or farmer's yard. A dozen eggs in the summer of 1851 might cost 4d a dozen and rise in price to 8d later in the year. Enterprising farmers and market gardeners might store up summer eggs to sell in the winter: this involved smearing them with butter or lard while still warm and packing them in barrels of salt, oats or melted suet. They were then transported into the city or sold to egg merchants, who visited weekly.

---

90 Porter, Valerie, *Yesterday's Farm*, David & Charles, 2008, p.224.

91 Stephens, Henry, *The Book of the Farm*, vol. 2, 1852, p.697, Google edn p.716.

92 These measured about 9in square and 2ft long.

93 This was for a pig weighing between 56lbs and 70lbs. Stephens, *op. cit.*, p.704, Google edn p.715.

94 There is no doubt that as the population of Manchester increased so did the demand of fresh meat, which was being supplied by local farmers. Scoular, *op. cit.*, chapter 3, pp.40–1.

five

THE WORLD OF WORK

Teachers, tradesmen, domestic servants, women workers, doctors, and working outside Chorlton

There was no squire in Chorlton, and the two most prominent landowners lived elsewhere, which left a bit of a vacuum in the pecking order. There were the well off, who described themselves as gentry, and when that fell out of fashion as independent. They were businessmen, retired businessmen or living off annuities; but while money may mark an individual out it rarely gave a position of authority by itself. The authority figures were the parson and the village teacher.

From the early 19th century until 1851 the schoolteacher was James Renshaw, who ran a day school on the Row. He was much respected by the villagers and was known simply as the village schoolmaster. They consulted him on a range of different subjects, ranging from the law and medicine to science. He was a strict disciplinarian, and was remembered long after he died. Renshaw ran the Methodist day school, which in 1817 was supplemented by the National School. If James Renshaw provided a degree of consistency over the years for the Methodist schoolchildren the same cannot be said for the students of the National School:[95] from 1817 to 1851 there were seven teachers.[96] Renshaw could expect to receive £36 a year, while a male National School teacher was paid £55 19s; his female counterpart just £33 19s.[97] But this was still better than the £25 paid to the schoolmistress

---

95 The first was Edward Wilson, followed by William Bythell (1828–32), Johnson, Richard Higginson (1836), Frederick Hill (1841), Gathercole, James Bugden and Eliza Johnson (1850), John and Ann Ellison (1851), White, Daniel Bostock, James Kay, and John and Elizabeth Ireland (October 1860–January 1885). From Ellwood, chapter 13, 1841, 1851 and 1861 censuses, Pigot's Directories, 1828–29, 1834, 1841, Slater's Directory, 1855.
96 The schoolmaster in 1861 was John Bostock, 1861 census, Enu. 7, p.5.
97 Figures from Census of Great Britain, 1851, *Education in Great Britain*,1854, George Routledge, Table N, Remuneration of Teachers in Public Schools, County of Lancaster, p.100, Google edn p.116.

at the workhouse on Stretford New Road.[98] Moreover, the National School teacher's post came with accommodation. The school house was large and brick built, on two floors with four rooms.[99] James Renshaw, by contrast, lived in a wattle and daub cottage on the Row.

The National School teachers were trained in the National Society's training colleges, of which by 1851 there were five, regularly turning out 270 teachers a year.[100] As the National Society was a Church institution all the teachers were Christians. They were qualified to teach a range of subjects, from the basics of reading, writing and arithmetic to languages, music, drawing and geography.[101] This was complicated by the wide range of age groups that walked through the school doors. Of the seventy-three who were described as scholars by their parents in March 1851, 21 per cent were five or younger, 58 per cent between the ages of six and ten and 21 per cent from eleven to fifteen. The usual way of dealing with this problem was to employ two teachers, or to fall back on monitors and pupil teachers. Eliza Johnson and later Ann Ellison taught the infants, while James Bugden and John Ellison concentrated on the older children. If there were monitors or pupil teachers their names are lost until 1861. Across the country in 1851 there were over 9,000 of them, and their average pay was just £8 a year – or roughly 1s 8d a week.

The blacksmith was at the heart of the rural community, and William Davies supplied the needs of the village, repairing broken tools, forging new ones and shoeing horses, from 1834.[102] He lived with his family at Black's Cottage on land he rented from Lydia Black and John Brundrett.[103] The smithy was well sited on the Row. To the east were the Bailey and Gratrix farms and around the corner on the Green three more. He was at the very centre of the village, surrounded by cottages and the homes of the gentry. When he was hammering and heating at his forge, Davies must have been a centre of attention, with people coming by to collect a repaired tool or bring in a horse that was in need of a new shoe, or just stopping to pass the time of day. There were always requests to personalise a farm tool, such as making a left-handed scythe or widening or narrowing hoe blades that were used to chop out weeds. There would have been an endless procession of labourers who needed tools sharpened, from bill hooks and scythes to axes and all other edged tools. In the process he

---

98 The £25 included board and lodging. Advertisement for the post of schoolmistress, Chorlton Union, April 1848, *Manchester Times and Gazette*, 1 April 1848.

99 The present schoolhouse is much larger and was extended by taking in the old headmaster's office, which had been part of the school. It may incorporate elements of the old schoolhouse.

100 *Education in Great Britain, op. cit.*, p.32, Google edn p.40.

101 The full list taught in National Schools was reading, writing, arithmetic, English grammar, modern languages, ancient languages, mathematics, drawing, music and industrial occupations. The degree to which these were taught varied from subject to subject, and there was a gender split, so while almost all boys and girls were taught the three Rs, few studied modern languages, and while 10 per cent of boys received tuition in mathematics it was just 4 per cent of girls. In contrast 46 per cent of girls were instructed in industrial occupations compared with under 4 per cent of boys.

102 We first come across him in Pigot's and Co.'s National Commercial Directory, 1834, and then in the 1841 and 1851 census returns. Census 1841, Enu. 8, p.4, 1851, Enu. 1, p.6.

103 Tithe Map Schedule, 1845.

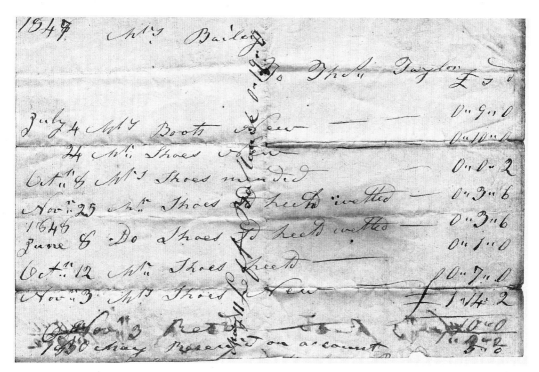

Estimating the cost of living is always difficult, but buying and repairing shoes was essential. The cost of a new pair was 9s, while repairing a pair might cost 3s 6d when a labourer's wage might be 18s to 11s a week.

might replace broken or split staves. He may even have repaired the rake that was broken by the farm boy John Royle who worked for Farmer Higginbotham. On a larger scale, in an age of horse-drawn carts and carriages there would have been a steady demand for him to make good a worn or broken piece of equipment. William Davies was very much part of the community, as was his family: his son Thomas worked for Farmer Higginbotham, who paid him 4s a week in 1846. Thomas was just thirteen years old, but soon went to work for his father. William continued to work the forge through the 1850s until he was succeeded by John Clark, whose family would see out the century working here.

It is easy to romanticise rural life in the middle years of the 19th century, yet the Davies family home seems to have been ideally situated not only for work but also for living. At the back were fields and an orchard. Standing at the smithy's open door William would have looked out on fields stretching north, while directly opposite was Mary Holland's elegant home.[104] This was set in a long garden that went out towards High Lane, to be met by the equally long garden of William Brundrett.

104 This was Rowe House, which later became known as Lilly Cottage. For most of its existence it was a family home but later became the village reading room and ended as an office. It was demolished in the winter of 2007.

William Brownhill, who lived just outside the village at Lane End, was the village's wheelwright. Wheel-making was a skilled trade. William constructed the wheels' hub, spokes and rim, then assembled them into a unit, working from the centre outwards. The hub or nave was made from seasoned elm, the spokes from cleft heart of oak, to give strength, and rim sections from ash, elm or beech. The wheel had to be dished or made slightly concave, so that it resisted the sideways thrust of a load swinging from side to side on an uneven road. Finally lengths of iron called strakes were nailed to the outside of the wheel to hold it together; from the mid-century a solid iron tyre replaced these. This tyre was custom built by the blacksmith, so William Brownhill would have worked closely with William Davies. There was nothing more spectacular than watching as the red-hot tyre was slipped over the 5ft wheel, and just before it seemed the wheel would burst into flames Davies and Brownhill would arrest the impending catastrophe by throwing buckets of water over it. Brownhill's skill rested not only in making products but in buying and laying down the timber to season, which accounted for a considerable amount of his capital. Before making a 12in wheel hub, the cross-cut timbers were bored and seasoned in the bark for up to six years, requiring careful brushing and inspecting for rot. Despite all his skill, knowledge and investment, wagons and carts were not expensive: in 1860 they cost £40 and £20 respectively.

The Brownhills served the community for the whole of the 19th century and some of the next – but they were not alone. In the 1830s John Gratrix and John Mason made and repaired wheels, and later James Griffith worked alongside Brownhill: he started as an apprentice wheelwright in the 1840s. Perhaps in competition was John Gautney at Martledge. Back at Lane End William Brownhill had plenty of work to keep him busy. He ran a beershop and owned and rented out a block of eleven cottages (which bore his name) a little further down the road. Beerselling was not confined to the landlords of public houses, and while there had once been a pub at Lane End it had been closed for rowdiness.

Many wheelwrights also served as carpenters, but in 1841 there were four joiners and a carpenter in the village. While Joseph Renshaw at seventy may have been looking to retire, there were three younger men: Edward Worth, Henry Moulder, who lodged at The Greyhound, and William Pinnington, whose sisters we shall meet later. He was just fifteen and lived on the Green. They repaired houses and farm buildings and undertook what was known as hedge carpentry, which consisted of repairs to field gates, posts and fences. They also provided for other community needs: chairs, tables, even coffins. John Renshaw made a fine coffin for the late James Bythell in 1821. It was lined with flannel and cost £4 9s,

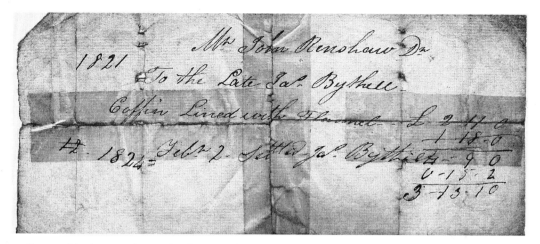

The cost of death was another certainty: it might mean paying for the coffin in instalments.

which was paid in three instalments – the last in 1824.[105] In February 1854 Richard Pearson charged the Bailey family just £2 20s for the coffin he had made.

Nor were these the only craftsmen busy in the village. There were eight shoemakers in 1841. James Higginbotham the farmer paid one of them 2s to mend a pair of shoes, but chose to go into Manchester for a pair of clogs, which cost him 10s. William Bailey spent a total of £1 14s 2d during 1847 on mending shoes and boots, at a cost per repair ranging from 2d to 10s. Tailors and dressmakers worked from home. Theirs was a solitary trade but a busy one. In an age when clothes were still made by hand and made locally there was a steady demand for their work, especially as not all in the township would have had the time or inclination to repair their clothes. Itinerant traders and carriers brought the material into the township and tailors and dressmakers worked to order, in most cases producing simple and utilitarian clothes. In the 1840s there were four of them. The young George Grantham and Thomas Baguley, aged sixty-six, lived on the Row, John Fox at Renshaw's Buildings[106] and John Hale, up by Red Gates Farm.[107] Wealthier members of the community could afford to commission those who worked in town, and were more aware of the latest fashions. In 1841 there were 178 milliners and dressmakers listed in Manchester and 316 tailors.[108] But there has always been a tradition in country areas of supporting local tradesmen, and even if the rich frequented fashionable shops their servants needed uniforms, and these needed repairing.

105 Renshaw, John, 1824, Bailey collection.
106 Renshaw's Buildings were on the site of the Royal Oak pub near the Barlow Moor and Wilbraham Road junction. They were built in the early 1830s and survived until the 1920s.
107 Hale lived in a row of cottages opposite the farm, now the site of the library. They may have survived into the 1940s.
108 Pigot and Slater's Directory of Manchester and Salford, 1841.

The second Methodist chapel on the Row. The photograph dates from 1907.

There was only one dressmaker in Chorlton at any one time. In the 1840s this was Sarah Marshal, who at twenty-five was single and living at home with her parents on the Green. Later in the decade her place was taken by young Harriet Griffiths, also in her twenties and single. The same seems true of painters and decorators: there was only one such in the middle years of the 19th century.

The one trade that was missing in the summer of 1847 was weaving. The high point for weavers had been during the late 18th and early 19th century, when there was a surplus of spun cotton. This was created when spinning moved over to powered machines, but weaving was still dominated by hand-operated looms. George Jones described his occupation as weaver when he baptised his two children at the Methodist chapel on the Row in 1808. He no doubt knew the two weavers who walked over from Stretford and Withington to baptise their children in the same chapel.[109] In all likelihood there were more. Handloom weaving was conducted in a wide arc both north and south of Manchester and in the areas bordering north Cheshire, Derbyshire and the West Riding of Yorkshire. By the mid-18th century cotton had replaced wool as the main textile material, and across the county areas specialised in cambrics, muslins and ginghams. Just over 5 miles to the east, near Gatley, flax had been grown and linen woven from at least the mid-17th century.[110] Exactly what was produced, and how, in Chorlton is unclear. It may be that George and his family undertook each of the processes from carding and spinning to weaving, but it is more likely with the mechanisation of spinning and its concentration in the factories of Manchester that he was only a weaver.

In Stretford in 1826 there were 302 looms providing employment for 780 workers, supporting 151 families,[111] and as late as the 1840s there were still seven, while in Withington there were nineteen cotton weavers, mostly concentrated in Lady Barn and Fallowfield, where they specialised in 'weaving checked handkerchiefs and ginghams.'[112] Further west there were a few handloom weavers recorded in the 1851 census in Flixton and Urmston. Nationally weavers had been the largest single group of industrial workers, and throughout the 1820s, '30s and '40s they came third in the list of occupations, after agricultural labourers and domestic servants. The estimate of the Select Committee of 1834–35 reckoned that 800,000 to 840,000 were wholly dependent on one of the branches of weaving.[113] It was a trade passed down through families, with children beginning to learn at an early age. Samuel Crompton, who invented the spinning mule, remembered starting to spin as soon as he was able and 'at the age of 10 [was] placed for a year to learn to weave'.[114] In most cases weaving was the main economic activity, but in some households it was secondary, undertaken by the wife or adult children. There is also much evidence that many weavers combined working at the loom with other occupations, of which farming was the most common. Some managed a smallholding all the year round, while others concentrated on weaving in the winter and farming in the summer. Likewise, some moved into other trades before returning to weaving later.[115]

---

109 Thomas Jones of Stretford and his wife Mary baptised children in the chapel on the Row between 1809 and 1816, John and Sarah Thorley also of Stretford in 1807 and William and Mary Taylor from Withington in 1820 and 1823. William Taylor was still working aged sixty-five in 1841.

110 Groves, Jill, 'Such a Day as is Seldom Seen, The Memorandum Book of a Cheshire Yeoman, Jon Ryle of High Greaves, Etchells, 1649–1721', *Manchester Region Review*, vol. 4, 1990–1, pp.36–41.

111 Leach, Sir Bosdin, *Old Stretford*, privately printed, 1910, p.23.

112 Williamson, C., *Sketches of Fallowfield*, John Heywood, Manchester, 1888, p.34.

113 Thompson, E.P., *The Making of the English Working Class*, Pelican Books, 1968, p.344.

114 Quoted by Wadsworth, A.P. and De Lacy Mann, Julia, *The Cotton Trade and Industrial Lancashire, 1680–1780*, Manchester University Press, 1931, p.326.

115 During a dispute between the weavers of the parish of Manchester and the Warden and Fellows of the Collegiate Church between 1749 and 1753, one weaver described how he became a tailor after finishing his apprenticeship before returning to the loom later in life, and others either moved from weaving to farming or alternated depending on the season, quoted by Wadsworth and De Lacy Mann, *op. cit.*, p.324.

George Jones, like most weavers, relied on a middleman or 'putter out' who provided the material to be woven on a credit system. When the cloth was finished the weaver delivered it to the middleman, receiving payment and material for the next week's work. These 'putters out' either dealt with the spinners for yarn and the manufacturers for finished cloth, or were agents who worked on commission for a Manchester mercantile house.[116]

The loom was not an expensive item to buy, costing between 6s and 12s in the 1760s – not much considering that a Manchester weaver might earn 3s to 12s a week, depending on the type of cloth that was being woven.[117] Earlier machines worked by a treadle, which the weaver operated, but later models needed the assistance of a boy. In rural areas the loom occupied a room in the cottage. Some weavers started with a single loom, in the course of their working life adding more, before returning to a single machine in their final years. Five or six people had to prepare the yarn for each loom, and the preliminary processes of carding and spinning were usually undertaken by members of the family.[118] In Stretford 321 children under the age of twelve were engaged in one or another of the textile processes, representing 41 per cent of the total workforce.

In urban areas weavers might rent machines in a building that housed a number of looms. Here in Chorlton weavers might have been clustered together as they were in Lady Barn, in a series of cottages.[119] These would have been simple wattle and daub buildings, but it is doubtful that they displayed the characteristic long windows.[120]

It is easy to over-romanticise the life of a weaver. Although he seems to have been well paid, working from home and master of his own time, the reality was different. He was at the end of a long supply and credit line that gave him little control, and he was reliant on others for the supply of his work, the quality of materials provided, and credit and payment. The increase in the number of weavers and manufacturers led to fierce competition. When manufacturers cut the price for which they sold the finished cotton they reduced the money they paid to the weavers. Weavers in north-east Lancashire saw the price paid by manufacturers for a piece of calico fall from 3s 7d in 1818 to 2s 11d in 1824, and a little over 2s 1d a year later.[121] We should also not be blinded into assuming that working from home was liberation from the drudgery of labour. Long hours were worked in the autumn and winter in workshops lit only by candles. There were also problems with poor-quality yarn, which slowed down production and might affect the finished material, thereby low-

116 Turner, William, *Riot, The Story of East Lancashire Loom Breakers in 1826*, Lancashire County Books, 1992, p.5.

117 Dunkerley, Philip, 'The Early Dunkerleys and the Domestic System of Cotton Working', http://dunkerley-tuson.co.uk/jame_tuson_longton.aspx.

118 Turner, op.cit., p.3.

119 Williamson, *op. cit.*, p.34.

120 These, according to some authorities, had originally been designed for weaving wool. Cotton needs a damper environment, and it may be that cellars were preferred as workshops – although it is difficult to believe that any cottages in the township had cellars. Dunkerley, Philip, *op. cit.*

121 Turner, *op. cit.*, p.11.

ering the price paid by the 'putter out'. And ever present was the danger of sickness or injury, which might pitch a family into disaster.

Disaster, indeed, was on the horizon. Manual weaving could not compete with the power loom and although mechanised weaving was only slowly adopted, by the end of the 1820s it was in the ascendancy.[122] While the number of handloom weavers continued to rise in the early 19th century, reaching a peak of 240,000 in 1820, the decline was dramatic, with the loss of 52,000 jobs during the next thirteen years.[123] The collapse in earnings was equally dramatic. In 1790 a Bolton weaver could make £1 10s, and despite short periods of hardship owing to trade fluctuations, earnings remained high. But there was a steady downward trend, which saw wages fall from an average of £1 18s 10d a week for a family of six including three weavers in 1818 to £1 1s in 1823; and a year later it stood at just 19s 1½d.[124] This trend continued into the next decade, and by 1832 according to Dr James Kay, Manchester handloom weavers 'labour fourteen hours and upwards daily, [and] earn only from five to seven or eight shillings per week'.[125] These were mostly skilled workers, and their low wages should be compared with those of factory girls, who could earn between 7s and 9s per week in Manchester and 5s 6d to 6s 6d in the surrounding areas.[126] But even this is to paint a slightly distorted picture, for high earnings were restricted to a minority of weavers: they did not extend to those engaged in fustian weaving or to those who were less well trained and had been attracted to the industry at the end of the 18th century on the promise of easy money.

In the townships around Chorlton the collapse was no less dramatic. There were particularly bad years in 1799, 1807–8, 1811–12 and 1816–21. In Stretford the number of looms fell from 302 in 1826 to just four in 1829, although it is not clear whether this was because of fluctuation in trade, which left the handlooms idle, or an indication of their total abandonment. The distress is all too clear from a song sung at the Theatre Royal in Manchester in the same year:

At Stretford, Prestwich, Eccles too, no weaver could you see sir,
For who would starve at weaving who could find a better trade, sir.[127]

122 The power loom had been designed by Edmund Cartwright in 1784, built in 1785 and refined over the next forty-seven years. By 1850 there were 250,000 in operation.

123 In 1829 there were 225,000 handloom weavers, falling to 213,000 in 1833, and two years later there were 188,000.

124 Turner, op. cit., p.11.

125 Kay, James Phillips, *The Moral and Physical Condition of the Working Classes Employed in the Cotton Manufacturing in Manchester*, James Ridgway, 1832, p.27. Kay was quoting the evidence of Joseph Foster before the Emigration Committee, 1827.

126 Faucher, Leon, *Manchester 1844, Its Present Condition and Future Prospects*, Abel Heywood, 1844, p.61.

127 Crofton, *op. cit.*, p.22.

The same year saw the Revd Dr Elsdale write to the committee that was administering a fund for the relief of distress in Lancashire:

that great want of work prevails among the weavers and consequent distress exists not only among them but all the inferior trades people and workmen with whom they deal. When the Overseer called upon one poor woman she said 'Gentlemen, you have come just at the right time, for I have no work, no money, and no food.' Another with a large family, when a few shillings of relief were sent him, immediately burst into a flood of tears.'[128]

Across the townships to the east and west the industry struggled on into the 1840s and '50s. In Fallowfield there were still fourteen weavers in 1841, but this fell to just one by 1851. Further south and west in that part of Withington running from Hough End Hall down to the village, the number fell from five to one during the same decade.[129] In Stretford this dismal picture was repeated. By 1841 there were just seven weavers, and four at the following census.[130]

Not only were the numbers in decline but it was an ageing workforce. Of the fourteen from Lady Barn and Fallowfield over half were over the age of forty with two in their sixties and a third aged seventy-five. In Stretford it was even more pronounced, with just two of the seven weavers aged thirty and the rest in their sixties and seventies in 1841. While ten years later Margaret Mary Roberts was twenty, the youngest of the remaining three was seventy. Thomas Taylor, who walked across from Withington to the chapel on the Row in the early 1820s was himself an old man of sixty-five in the summer of 1841.

Weavers fought back in the face of such hardships. Against the growing competition from power looms, severe and periodic trade downturns and the loss of jobs and earnings, weavers across Lancashire protested in a variety of ways. A number of weavers' associations and unions from places like Bolton and Manchester attacked the fall in earnings, called for a minimum wage and sent petitions to Parliament. These were met with a mix of indifference and bland platitudes, turning on the economic arguments that there were too many weavers, warehouses were overstocked and that a minimum wage would only serve to protect the handloom weavers. In essence, such actions would interfere with the natural cycle of trade. It was, as ever, a clear statement that an old industry rooted in old practices should not be protected if it could not compete with newer methods of manufacture. The rejection of yet another petition in 1808 led to a strike, with 10,000 to 15,000

128 *Ibid.*, p.22.
129 1841 census, Enu. 4, 1851 census 2a, Withington, Lancashire.
130 These were spread out across Stretford, some on the north-eastern edge by Chester Road and others to the south-west on the way to Urmston.

weavers demonstrating on St George's Fields in Manchester over two successive days.[131] This genuine response to hardship was met with official violence: one man was killed and several were wounded when the military intervened, and a popular manufacturer who supported the minimum wage was imprisoned. This was Joseph Hanson, whose crime was to utter 'malicious and inflammatory words.'[132] More petitions followed, and when these failed the weavers resorted to direct action. These involved demonstrations, arson attacks and frame breaking. Eight men were hanged, seventeen transported and six men and one woman imprisoned during 1812. Most famously, the attempt by 1,000 weavers to march from Manchester to London to highlight their plight was broken up at Stockport.[133]

Many weavers turned to radical politics, and in particular a demand for the reform of the House of Commons. But again the authorities met these expressions of protest with repression. On 16 August 1819 a peaceful demonstration in Manchester in favour of reform was suppressed when the military fired and charged into a crowd of 60,000 people, with the death of fifteen and hundreds of casualties. Many of these were handloom weavers.[134] In the final phase, when the power loom began making major inroads into weaving from the 1820s, the weavers made three consistent proposals: a tax on power looms to equalise conditions of competition, a restriction of hours in power loom factories, and the employment of adult males as opposed to women and children as power loom weavers.

There is no way of knowing how George Jones and his family managed the possible collapse in earnings. As we know, some weavers had other means of income, and in George's case he had a son-in-law who was a farmer. Nor do we know if he was active politically. He is a shadowy figure, turning up twice in the baptismal records of the chapel between 1807 and 1808, and when he remarried on 29 October 1815.[135] George may have been illiterate but many weavers were self-educated, articulate men who were engaged in a rich variety of cultural pursuits, including poetry and the sciences, as well as being politically active in their associations, trade unions and the Chartist movement.[136]

During the 1820s the botanist weaver John Horsefield walked from Prestwich to Manchester and then to Chorlton to 'botanize' with his friend Richard Buxton in the fields along the Mersey. Horsefield was president of the Prestwich Botanical Society for thirty-four years, while Buxton, who was a poor, self-educated Manchester shoemaker, wrote *A Botanical Guide to the Flowering Plants Ferns Mosses & Algae found indigenous with 16 miles*

---

131 St George's Field was an open space between Oldham Road and Rochdale Road.

132 Thompson, *op. cit.*, p.307.

133 This was the March of the Blanketeers in March 1817, so named because each man carried a blanket to sleep in at night.

134 Bush, Michael, *The Casualities of Peterloo*, Carnegie Publishing Ltd, 2005, p.24.

135 'George Jones, widower, and Elizabeth Platt widow, both made their mark', Marriages of St Mary in the city of Manchester 1806–24, Entered by Burton, Lynn Ransom.

136 Thompson, *op. cit.*, pp.324–5.

of Manchester in 1849.[137] Making much the same journey just thirty years later was Edward Waugh, who took the train south in 1857 from Oxford Road in Manchester to Stretford in search of the birthplace of weaver poet John Collier (known as Tim Bobbins), who had been born in Urmston.

Many of the northern local Chartist leaders were weavers. They included William Ashton of Barnsley, a linen-weaver born in 1806 and transported in 1830 for alleged complicity in strike riots, liberated in 1838 and brought back by public subscription – only to be imprisoned again; and Richard Pilling, who began as a handloom weaver before moving to power looms, and was a leader during the Lancashire General Strike of 1842. It is all too easy to underestimate their achievements. Despite long hours, with little or no formal education and in many cases beset by grinding poverty, they mastered complex subjects, spoke with authority and acted in the defence of their community with skill and dignity. In people like Pilling, Horsefield and Buxton we see both what was possible and much that was lost. In later life Buxton reflected that his inability to read 'caused me very much to regret my want of knowledge', and 'with great diligence became master of it,' which resulted in his wonderful catalogue of local plant life.[138]

George Jones was no longer in the township in 1847, and those who carried his surname and may well have been his children had turned to other occupations. He may have taken the advice of a Royal Commission that advised weavers 'to flee from the trade', or he may have seen out his days in what was an increasingly precarious trade, reflecting on the words of a song of the period:

> You gentleman and tradesmen, that ride about at will,
> You pull down our wages, shamefully to tell;
> You go to the markets, and say you cannot sell;
> And when that we do ask you when these bad times will mend,
> You quickly give an answer, 'When the wars are at an end.'[139]

Domestic service was the second largest source of employment in Chorlton. As in the country as a whole it was mainly an occupation for single working-class women. In 1851 there were fifty-three female servants in the township, ranging from governesses to housekeepers, cooks, maids and nurses. It counted for 27 per cent of the labour force, of which 68 per cent

---

137 Buxton, Richard, *A Botanical Guide to the Flowering Plants Ferns Mosses & Algae found indigenous with 16 miles of Manchester*, Abel Heywood, 1849. This remains a remarkable book which is much admired by modern botanists.

138 *Ibid.*, p.iv, Google edn p.11.

139 'The Handloom Weavers' Lament' was collected by John Grimshaw, alias 'Common' of Abbey Hey, and included in a collection of Lancashire songs, Harland, John, *Ballads and Songs of Lancashire*, Whittaker & Co., 1865, p.259, Google edn p.270.

were women; of these 81 per cent were unmarried. By comparison just 22 per cent of single women were engaged as washerwomen and laundresses. But domestic service was not much of an opportunity for local women: only ten of the fifty-three working as servants were born in Chorlton, and just another eleven were from less than 5 miles away. Sarah Bayley was one of these. She worked for the Higginbothams at Yew Tree Farm in Withington during 1841 and later moved to work for Daniel Sharp on the Row.[140] Those households with servants would have heard a mix of accents, including those of Yorkshire and punctuated by voices from Derbyshire and far away Ireland. Part of the reason for this was a concern that locally employed servants might be tempted to divulge family secrets, which could tarnish a household's reputation for generations. It followed that anyone wishing to find employment was often forced to look outside the township. In some cases news of vacancies came from family members who were already employed in a household elsewhere; in other cases local gentry or clergy might hear of vacancies or ask among their friends if anyone needed a servant. There were also hiring fairs and newspaper advertisements. But, as we have seen, the hiring fairs may not have played much of a part in the local economy.

Few servants from the more northerly parts of Lancashire, Yorkshire and especially Ireland could hope to make frequent visits home. Theirs was an isolated existence, reinforced if they were the only servant in a household. This was not a community of large houses, and few employed more than one servant.[141]

For those with pretensions a servant was a necessity, and often the social standing of an individual was judged by their number of staff. In the early decades of the 19th century it was reckoned that the minimum income with which an individual or couple could comfortably afford to employ a servant was £100 a year; but this only allowed for a young maid on less than £10 a year. For couples with children it was deemed that an annual income of £300 was needed to comfortably employ two maids and that a 'gentleman and Lady with children' wanting 'a Cook, Housemaid, and Nursery- Maid or other Female-Servant; with Livery-Servant, as Groom and footman and a Gardener occasionally', would have to be on between £500 and £600.[142] Few in the township could aspire to this, and fewer still were able to match the 'respectable Country Gentleman with a young family whose net income is from £16,000 to £18,000 a Year, and whose expenses do not exceed £7,000' who employed twenty-seven staff.[143]

Only James Holt, the Revd William Birley, Frederick Cope and the banker William Cunliffe Brooks at Barlow Hall had more than one servant. Understandably, given his

---

140 She was just thirteen in June 1841, and ten years later was working for Daniel Sharp who lived on the Row.
141 45 per cent of all households employing servants employed just one, another 27 per cent employed two.
142 Adams, Samuel and Sarah, *The Complete Servant*, Knight & Lacey, 1826, p.5, Google edn p.28.
143 *Ibid.*, p.7, Google edn p.30.

eighty years, James Holt employed a sick nurse along with a housekeeper, two servants and a coachman. The Revd William Birley, who had private means to supplement his annual income of £103, kept up appearances with a governess, nurse, cook, two maids and a footman to minister to his family of seven. The Copes had a large house in Martledge but managed with three staff. Cunliffe Brooks had a household that included a lady's maid, nurse, housemaid, cook, kitchenmaid, butler and coachman, looking after just himself, his wife and daughter. In the rest of the township the servants toiled alone, working mostly in farmers' homes and dividing their time between household and farm duties. These 'maids of all work' were expected to undertake all the domestic chores, as Mrs Beeton testified: 'she has to rise with the lark, for she has to do in her own person all the work which in larger establishments is performed by the cook, kitchen-maid, and housemaid and occasionally the part of a footman's duty, which consists in carrying messages'.[144] A maid of all work was defined as:

A domestic servant, who undertakes the whole duties of a household without assistance; her duties comprising those of cook, housemaid, nursery maid, and various other offices, according to the exigencies of the establishment. The situation is one which is usually regarded as the hardest worked and worst paid of any branch of domestic servitude; it is, therefore, usually filled by inexperienced servants, or females who are so circumstanced that they are only desirous of securing a home, and of earning sufficient to keep themselves decently clad. In many of these situations, a servant may be very comfortably circumstanced, especially if it be a limited family of regular habits, and where there is a disposition to treat the servant with kindness and consideration.[145]

Her day began at six, lighting the fire and preparing breakfast for the family. While they were eating she aired the beds. The rest of the day included preparing and cooking the midday and evening meals, as well as cleaning the house and washing the clothes. It ended at about eleven in the evening, but this was at the discretion of her employer. This was hard work, a real test of physical strength and endurance. For instance, each fireplace in the house might have to be cleaned each morning, with ashes taken out, a new fire laid and then maintained. But for twenty-nine-year-old Sarah Bailey who worked for Daniel Sharp on the Row in May 1851 this might have seemed an improvement on conditions at the Higginbotham farm. She had worked at Yew Tree Farm in Withington for £7 7s in

144 Beeton, Isabella, *The Book of Household Management*, S.O. Beeton, 1863, p.1001, Google edn p.1066.
145 Philip, Robert Kemp, *Dictionary of Daily Wants*, Houlston & Wright, 1863, p.657, Google edn p.668. Originally appearing in parts, it was an alphabetical guide to household management and 'seems likely to prove a useful compilation for families of humbler means', *Literary Gazette & Journal of Belles Lettres, Arts, Sciences*, Saturday 2 January 1858, p.14, Google edn p.21.

1829, her salary rising to £8 the following year.[146] Traditionally a servant was paid at the end of the hiring year, and would expect advances or loans to pay for items she needed during the previous twelve months. So it was with Mary Bailey, who during the course of the year received advances for a pair of stays, four pairs of stockings, a check apron and a pair of clogs, as well as repairs to her shoes, a trip to Manchester and the cost of two journeys home. In all she was advanced £6 7s, leaving her a balance of just £1. This seems much the going rate. Servants' wages at Lamport House in Northampton varied from £8 for a kitchen maid to £9 for an undermaid and dairymaid. A housekeeper might expect £20 to £25 and if as at Lamport she combined cooking with her role as housekeeper this might rise to £40 per annum. Otherwise a cook could be paid £30 to £40 and a coachman £18.[147] This varied with experience, with staff beginning at a lower wage, and there was a rent allowance given to those who lived out.

When the younger James Higginbotham set up as a farmer on the Green in the 1840s he brought with him the young Elizabeth Morton. She was thirteen in 1841 and still living in Withington, but by the following year the Higginbothams had a son and she may well have joined them. She lived at the back of the farmhouse above the kitchen. Her working conditions might have been slightly different from other maids of all work because this farming family was used to sharing the table with farm servants, and she would have been expected to help in the dairy and feeding the livestock. Elizabeth left in April 1849 but was back by the spring of 1851.

Leisure time for such servants was limited, but as mentioned above Mary Bailey travelled to Manchester (for the wakes), and even managed two visits home, including at Christmas 1829. Otherwise her time off would have revolved around walks along the lanes, perhaps in the company of fellow servants and just possibly a male friend. Some employers were very clear about who their servants could spend time with. Later in the century they were entitled to a half-day holiday on Sundays; by 1900 many servants could expect an evening off a week; later still they would expect a week's paid holiday.

Just how many of our young women went out of the township to work as servants is unclear. One who did was Ann Pearson. She was born in 1822 and her parents lived on the Row. By the time she was nineteen she was away from the family home. In March 1851 she was a servant in the house of a grocer in Altrincham; later she was in Manchester.[148]

---

146 Higginbotham farm accounts.

147 Horn, Pamela, *The Rise and Fall of the Victorian Servant*, Alan Sutton Publishing Ltd, Stroud, 1995, pp.211–12. An undermaid was chiefly employed for hard and physically demanding jobs like cleaning and scouring the stoves, grates, coal scuttles, kettles, carpets and floors, making beds, bringing in water and coal, and in the evenings mending and washing linen.

148 She was absent from the family home during the census of June 1841, was recorded in the next census in Altrincham, and in June 1854 according to newspaper reports and evidence at her trial conceived her child in Manchester.

Cleaning another's home was not limited to domestic servants. Mary Hesketh made a living as a charwoman: she was paid by the week and visited daily.[149] This job allowed those who were widowed or single to provide for themselves. For Mary, who was sixty and living alone, charring was an important source of income. Ten years later, in March 1851, none of the charwomen recorded were married: most were single, in their twenties and living at home.

For many married working women the alternative in Chorlton was to wash clothes, either by visiting customers' houses (this was the case in wealthier households) or by taking the clothes away to wash them at home.[150] There were twenty-three washerwomen; most were married, and some of the younger ones worked alongside their mothers. They were by and large concentrated along the Row, up by Lane End and in a cluster by the Royal Oak in Renshaw's Buildings. Before the widespread use of hot water and soap, the traditional way of washing clothes was with cold water and homemade alkalis to dissolve grease: for centuries wood ash was the most common material. The real work came after the clothes had been soaked in the solution of water and wood ash: water was forced through the clothes, by hitting them with a wooden bat. The water was then wrung out, using a wringing post that was set in the ground: the clothes were wrapped around this. In Chorlton there were ready supplies of water, but not particularly close for the washer-women up by Renshaw's Buildings, who relied on nearby wells.

Domestic service brought new people into the township, but they were not the only new arrivals. The community was not as inward looking as one might imagine. It is true that just over half the population had been born in the township and a handful more had come from less than 5 miles away, but the rest, 44 per cent, were from further afield. Skilled trades-men, farmworkers and industrial workers were from Lancashire, Cheshire, Yorkshire, even Shropshire, Staffordshire, Suffolk, Sussex, Wales, Westmorland, Middlesex and Scotland.

All manner of people passed through the village. There were itinerant tradesmen who sold anything from cloth to leather, and would call at each house on the Row. At the first hint of interest they would drop their heavy load and begin pulling out a variety of what-ever they thought would sell to the customer. The same well-worn route was tramped by the tinker, who repaired pans and sharpened knives and scissors on a foot-driven grind-stone. A more regular visitor was the carrier. He had evolved in the age before the railway, and could be relied on to carry almost anything anywhere. Usually he worked a route from the villages and hamlets into town and back, acting as a shopping agent: he took orders from people and bought the goods for them. He dealt in everyday household items, as

---

149 Earlier in the century the going rate was 1s. 11d. per day. Steedman, Carolyn, *Labour's Lost*, Cambridge University Press, 2009, p.305.

150 Thompson, Flora, *Lark Rise to Candleford*, Penguin Classics, 2000, pp.494—5. Miss Lane employed a professional washerwoman for two days every six weeks, arriving at 6 in the morning.

well as luxuries like tea or coffee, even books and newspapers. It was not just one-way traffic: a carrier also took country goods into the town for sale, as well as transporting passengers. The names of the carriers who plied their way around Chorlton are lost, but in 1841 George Royle and John Lowe were listed as carriers working from their home of Green Lane in Flixton, and John Barlow was based in Davyhulme. They offered a service to Manchester every Saturday and might have travelled via Chorlton. It is equally possible that there were local carriers who carried on the trade either full time or as a sideline.

The pull of the city was beginning to exert itself, and the first Chorlton people were working there – only eight of them in 1851, granted, but a start. They were engaged in Manchester's new trades. There were the Bradley brothers, born in Salford and still in their twenties, who were calico engravers employing twenty-four men, Richard Sorton, a warehouseman, and engineers like Edward Bowker, a boiler man, Henry George Morton, a mechanic fitter and tool merchant, and William Deakin, also a mechanic. Finally there were those whose education had secured them clerical posts, like Samuel Walker, a railway clerk, Elisha Brundrett, an office boy, and Thomas Pollitt, a clerk to an accountant. Pollitt later created a stir by taking on the Church authorities over clerical taxes.

SHOPS, PUBS AND BEERHOUSES

A guide to what you could buy and where you could relax with a glass of beer

Before the mid-19th century rural communities had few shops, and those that existed were general stores selling almost everything from clothing to bread to string. The list is almost endless, including cheese, butter, tobacco, snuff, some pieces of meat (usually salt pork), tea, sugar thread, needles and pins, buttons, string, sweetmeats and fruit. At this time farmers tended to be self-sufficient, and the simpler diet of farm labourers was either home grown or bought from local farms. In Chorlton in the first half of the 19th century there were a surprising number of shops, including some that seem to have catered for specialist needs. At various times there was a pork butcher, a druggist, a baker, grocers and even a stationer.

We have seen that there was a blurring of boundaries when it came to making a living: market gardeners ran beershops or took in lodgers, agricultural labourers had different seasonal jobs and still others relied on the wages of children or siblings. So it was with some of the shops, which were not always the only source of family income. Ellen Bythel, whom we shall meet again, was running a shop while her husband William variously described himself as a joiner and a labourer; for a while he ran the shop as well.[151] There was Peter Warburton, a thirty-four-year-old farm labourer in 1851 but a shopkeeper four years later, and Thomas Taylor, who ran the Horse and Jockey but later became the stationer on the Row. Some of the bills and receipts from local businesses that have survived could have been produced locally, and his shop is an obvious source – going some way to explaining why there was a stationer's in a rural community.

---

151 Nor was this confined to the 19th century. As late as the 1970s the landlord of one Chorlton pub continued to work during the day while his wife ran the pub.

The Horse and Jockey. The photograph probably dates from the early 20th century, but the pub would have looked much the same when the inquest into Francis Deakin's murder was held here in 1847, and a year later the prize-fighter Samuel Warburton was arrested while drinking a pint of beer at 7 o'clock one Sunday morning after his contest on the Meadows had been interrupted by PC Wynstanley.

In 1841 there were at least three shopkeepers, maybe more. Up by Lane End was Jeremiah Brundrett who sold groceries. On the Row was Sarah Jackson, a widow who described herself as a shopkeeper, and Lightly Simpson, a chemist and druggist. Sarah Jackson's shop may also have sold beer, as her son Samuel described himself as a beerseller as well as an agricultural labourer.[152] A little earlier Ellen Bythel[153] had sold groceries in a shop behind the National School and was famous for her bread. There were also Thomas Birkett and William Pennington,[154] who ran shops by the Horse and Jockey, and later still Mary Lewis and Mary Wilton who took over Pennington's shop on the Green. Further afield, Ellen Heywood ran a shop from Renshaw's Buildings in Martledge, and Betty Bates would still be remembered forty years on for selling sweets and soft drinks.[155] In the late 1820s and '30s Ann Williamson was a pork butcher, and George Darbyshire was dealing in

---

152 In Pigot's Directory for 1841 the twenty-year-old Samuel is listed as a beerseller, but in the same year in the census as an agricultural labourer. In 1849 he was running a beerhouse on the Green.

153 'An old wood and plaster house behind the National Schools', Ellwood, chapter 24, 1886.

154 Father of Hannah and Susannah, Enu. 8, p.6. Thomas Birkett was a Methodist and in 1851 described himself as a grocer and tea dealer at Brundretts Buildings at Lane End in 1851.

155 Pop's Cottage was mentioned by Ellwood, chapter 4, 1885. The cottage was demolished when the railway came to Chorlton.

provisions, with George Lewis. What complicates the picture is that many of these shops had a short existence, while others might not have bothered with an entry in a trade directory. If a shop was purely an income supplement rather than a full-time career, it might not survive more difficult economic times, or the owner might stop if other opportunities for income came along.

Some of Chorlton's shopkeepers survived well into the 19th century, however. In 1857 Thomas Taylor's stationer's shop became the post office, which his widow continued to run until the beginning of the 1880s.[156] The Whittaker family were running a grocery shop on the Row in 1851, and this came to dominate the village. They prospered, and by the end of the century they had a prime site facing the Green on one side, and the Row on the other.[157] Jeremiah Brundrett, who was selling his cheese and bacon from a shop at Lane End in 1841, became so successful that some referred to the spot as Brundrett's Corner well into the 19th century.

These shops were small and cramped places. Just how small is clear from the two shops that sold beer and stationery on the Row in 1851. The beershop of Samuel Nixon and the stationer of Thomas Taylor were identical in size. The width of each shop was just 11½ft and the original ground floor consisted of two small rooms. The shops on either side of the Horse and Jockey were equally tiny. In 1841 the pub was just the rooms either side of the door; the remaining rooms to the right belonged to other houses. By contrast, Brundrett's grocer's shop was much larger.

In 1847 there were six public houses and a number of beersellers serving an adult population of about 368.[158] There was the Travellers Rest on the Row, the Horse and Jockey and the Bowling Green close to the parish church. Across the Mersey beyond the open land of Hardy there was The Greyhound. To the north of the village there were the Black Horse and the Royal Oak. Added to these there were a number of beerhouses, which owed their existence to the 1830 Beer Act. This was passed in order to try and weaken the gin shops. Gin was a real problem, and was commented upon by many social observers of the period. In Manchester the population doubled and 'the consumption of gin and whiskey has quadrupled ... Drunkenness has infused itself into the bosom of society. Habit has conquered shame, and that which formerly drew a blush from the men, is now regarded as a daily habit by women and children.'[159] The 1830 Beer Act allowed anyone who was a ratepayer and could afford the yearly licence of 2 guineas to brew and sell beer from home. The tax on

---

156 His shop which is now no. 68 and its adjoining property may be two of the oldest buildings. If the Travellers Rest had remained in what is now no. 70 from 1832 when it opened, it means that these two properties are older than anything other than a few farmhouses, 131 Beech Road, Lime Bank and the Horse and Jockey.
157 The family appear in the 1851 census as grocers on Chorlton Row, Enu. 1, p.29, and were still there over a century later.
158 1841 census.
159 Faucher, Leon, *op. cit.*, pp.48–9.

The Bowling Green Hotel with the church to the right. It was built in the late 18th century, and was at first a farmhouse and hostelry; it was the largest of our drinking places boasting a bay window. By the 1840s it was run by George Whitelegg and as well as running the pub farmed 22 acres in 1851.

beer was removed and pubs were allowed to stay open for up to 18 hours a day. The result across the country was an explosion in the number of beershops. In Manchester just ten years after the Beer Act there were 812 beershops compared with 502 pubs; by 1843 there were 920 beershops as opposed to 624 pubs and thirty-one inns and hotels.[160] Ten years later there were 1,572 beershops and 484 pubs. The full enormity of these numbers can be gauged by just four streets in the densely packed warren that ran behind Great Ancoats Street: there were ninety pubs, taverns and beershops here in the years 1841–50.[161]

Beershops often only lasted a short time.[162] Mrs Leach ran a 'superior beershop' on the edge of Martledge.[163] This was a neat detached brick building of two storeys standing in a small garden on the right-hand side of the main road out of the village. It was a double-fronted property with two rooms on either side of the passage from the front door. It may

160 *Ibid.*, p.48.
161 Gun Street and Henry Street ran parallel behind Great Ancoats Street and crossed Blossom Street and Jersey Street. Pigot and Slater's Directory, 1841, Slater's Directory, 1850.
162 1834 Thomas Chorlton, 1841 James White, also Richard Jones and Samuel Jackson, 1847 Mrs Leach, 1851–69 William Brownhill.
163 So described in various newspaper stories in 1847. It was roughly where the modern Wilbraham Road cuts across Manchester Road somewhere near the precinct car-park.

well have been a cut above many beershops, but it was the scene of a violent murder in 1847 – and Mrs Leach was no longer in Chorlton by the time of the 1851 census.[164]

William Brownhill ran his shop alongside his wheelwright business on the corner of Lane End from at least 1851 until the licence was refused in September 1869.[165] Beershops were by their very nature small places, nothing more than a room in a house where the beer was served from jugs or from a wooden barrel resting on a table. It is likely that each of the smaller communities on the edges of Chorlton, Hardy and Martledge had their own beershop. Pubs and beershops were by and large the preserve of men. Women, apart from those who served behind the bar, were rarely seen there. For most men they were a place to relax, often with those they had been working with all day. Conversation might turn to local events, politics or just gossip, and occasionally ended with singing.[166]

The Horse and Jockey was typical. It consisted of two rooms, one either side of the front door, with stone-flagged floors and low beamed ceilings.[167] The furniture was old, battered and solid, stained with years of spilt beer and polished smooth from long use. On a busy winter's night the heat from the fire combined with the smoke of countless clay pipes to create a warm and dense fug, which was powerful enough to survive the cold air entering with another customer. The pub's size, or lack of it, did not prevent it from being used as the venue for the inquest into the murder of Francis Deakin in May 1847. Packed into the place were the twelve members of the jury, the officials, police and witnesses.[168] In some rural communities pubs were the obvious choice for occasions like this: they were larger than the average home, and the only alternative to the village school – which would probably be in use.

Just a year later the same pub was the scene of an early morning arrest, when PC Wynstanley apprehended the young Samuel Warburton for prize-fighting. Warburton had been about 20 minutes into his fight, watched by hundreds of spectators who had gathered in a field up by the Mersey in Hardy, when the law arrived. The crowd and combatants fled the scene, but a little over an hour and half later, at 7am, Warburton was arrested while drinking in the Horse and Jockey.

Away across the Green and half hidden by the church was the other pub at the centre of the village. This was the Bowling Green, a much bigger establishment.[169] It boasted a

164 Francis Deakin was murdered by George Leach on 5 May 1847after a drinking bout that had lasted from 10 in the morning till 4 in the afternoon. *The Times*, 7 May 1847. The inquest was held at the Horse and Jockey on 6 May 1847, the day after the murder.

165 *Manchester Times*, 11 September 1869.

166 See Bonham-Carter, Victor, *The English Village*, Penguin, 1952, p.214 and Thompson, Flora, *op. cit.*, p.64.

167 These are still features of the Horse and Jockey today. Over time it expanded into the shops on either side.

168 All of the jury are or will be familiar. Thomas White was the foreman; there were also Edmund Newton, Thomas Cookson, James Bankcroft; William Gresty, William Brownhill, William Bailey, William Knight, James Higginbotham, William Cheshyre, James Brundrett and Peter Langford. Giving evidence were PC Wynstanley, John Cookson and John Fox.

169 Its first publicans were Edward Mason and his son. The earliest reference for the Masons at the pub was 1814.

bay window, but additions at the side and back gave it a haphazard appearance. Having said that, it was still more impressive than the other pubs. There was no mistaking its name: not only was it painted a little way above the bay window, but there was a large signboard running the length of the building, which had been built as a pub and farmhouse in the 18th century and so might count as the oldest in the township.[170] It had become the chosen venue for sick and burial club meetings, and was no doubt a popular stopping off place en route from the church. Its publican George Whitelegg was a busy man. As well as running the pub he was a market gardener, local builder and played an important part in village life. He was appointed Overseer for the Poor in 1841 and took his turn at chairing meetings of the ratepayers. At one meeting the interests of pub and ratepayers overlapped as the meeting resolved to adjourn to his pub![171] George may have needed many different ways of making money: by 1851 he had four daughters and a son and employed four servants.

In the spring of 1851 the Nixon family ran two of Chorlton's pubs. Old Samuel Nixon, aged sixty, served the intrepid pub goer who ventured out across Hardy and over the Mersey to The Greyhound. He had been there from at least 1834 and not only served beer but also rented 10 acres of land, which he farmed. Despite appearing in the directories as a publican, he chose to describe himself and his son as farmers in the 1841 census. The pub may been granted its first licence in 1801 and had at least four names.[172] One of these, Jackson's Boat, may in part be explained by the pub's site. At some point a farmer called Jackson farmed the land here and kept a boat for ferrying passengers across the river.[173] Although Samuel Wilton built a bridge here in 1816 at a cost of £200, the ferry and the right to transport passengers across the Mersey were still in place in 1832 when the pub and the surrounding land were put up for sale. The advertisement throws some light on the relationship between owner and tenant: the land and pub were owned by James Marsland and tenanted by a George Brownhill, who seems to have benefited from the ferry charges. The new owner was Edmund Howarth, who may well have appointed Samuel Nixon as tenant.[174]

As it was so remote, The Greyhound was perfect for those who came to watch illegal sporting activities, held far away from the prying eyes of the law. On those occasions when the police did arrive, the bridge across the Mersey afforded an escape route into Cheshire, beyond the jurisdiction of the Lancashire constabulary.

---

170 The Horse and Jockey is an older building but only began serving beer at the beginning of the 19th century.

171 It was 19 February 1859. No reason was given in the minutes. Perhaps it was too cold in the school house. Six years earlier, the ratepayers found themselves locked out of the school, but whether the meeting went ahead on the Green or in the pub is not clear.

172 The Old Greyhound in 1821, the Boat House in 1824, the Old Greyhound in 1828, Jackson's Boat in 1832, The Greyhound in 1834.

173 Ellwood, chapter 23, 1886.

174 Howarth lived at Sale Lodge in Cheshire and held a property vote on the strength of owning the pub and land.

Samuel Nixon's son was also a publican: he had the Travellers Rest on the Row. When it first opened in 1832 it went under the name the Robin Hood, but perhaps to distinguish it from a pub with the same name in Stretford it became the Travellers Call; by the 1840s it was the Travellers Rest. It lacked the size of the Bowling Green Hotel or the position of the Horse and Jockey, but it was a natural stopping point for anyone coming down the Row. Grouped around it were a fair few village homes, and as William Davies's smithy was just across the road, it was a convenient port of call for those dropping off tools to be mended or horses to be shoed. It fronted directly onto the road. Inside there was just the one room, lit by a window beside the door.[175] Judging by the size of the room which was just 11½ft wide by 6ft long, this one window was enough. Samuel's customers sat on simple wooden chairs and benches, with just enough room for one table. Samuel and his predecessors described themselves as beersellers, and like other beershops the Travellers Rest might not even have had a bar: it was a simple drinking room. In the remaining three rooms lived Samuel Nixon, his wife, four children and a lodger. This packed arrangement seemed to suit Samuel Jackson, the lodger, who would still be with them in spring 1861.

Away from the village was the Black Horse at Lane End. By all accounts this was a rowdy place; it had a reputation for after-hours drinking on a Sunday under its landlord Thomas Chorlton. It attracted a 'rough and low company'[176] who delighted in watching the nasty contest of badger fighting. The badger was kept in a box which had one opening on the top. Through this a dog was lowered and held by its tail. In the close confinement, driven by fear and aggression, the two animals fought until the dog was pulled out. This was repeated again and again, to see how many times the dog could be withdrawn in a minute while still holding onto the badger. Perhaps because of its clientele and its reputation for after-hours drinking, the Black Horse only lasted from 1832 to 1870.

Up towards Martledge was the Royal Oak, much favoured by farm labourers and by some of the factory workers who walked into the township on Sundays from Manchester. For these visitors the Royal Oak was the first pub they encountered, and after a 4½-mile walk its attractions were obvious. It was a detached, two-storeyed building with a commanding position. To the north was Red Gates Farm, and surrounding the pub were a cluster of cottages. Just next door was the large block known locally as Renshaw's or New Buildings. In all the pub served a little community of about 100 people, its only competition coming from Mrs Leach's beerhouse. On spring days in the late 1840s and early '50s it would have been a busy place, with the first Sunday visitors of the year taking advantage

---

175 The smallness of the room can be gauged from standing in the present shop, which is 70 Beech Road. Nothing now remains of the pub interior. It ceased to be a pub after 1903 and at one stage was a bakery, when it was knocked through with no. 68.

176 Ellwood, chapter 7, 1885.

The Royal Oak was at Martledge. It was much favoured by farm labourers and by those who walked into the township on a Sunday from Manchester. In all it served a little community of about 100 people.

of the improved weather. The locals probably swapped tips on gardening with William Wise, the gardener, while his wife Hannah dispensed beer to her customers. During the rest of the week there would have been a steady trade from farmworkers passing on their way between fields; those who lived in the township and those who were returning from the city might have added to the gathering. One such was Thomas Leigh, who stopped here on his way home from the markets in Manchester. He spent the night drinking with a John Battersby, who then stole 2 sovereigns from Leigh while he slept.[177]

Apart from the Black Horse our pubs were not such terrible places. The Greyhound, Bowling Green and Horse and Jockey all had bowling greens, which in the case of the

---

177 *The Times,* 14 August 1838. Battersby was caught, tried, convicted and sentenced to transportation for twelve years.

Jockey were patronised by gentlemen. The same gentlemen may well have fished in the pond behind the Bowling Green, which was rented out by the landlord.

There was always a blurring at the edges between hotel, pub and beershop. While there was no doubting the place of the Bowling Green in the pecking order, smaller places were more akin to beershop than pubs. Both Samuel Nixon of the Travellers Rest and Thomas White before him, along with Hannah Wise of the Royal Oak and Thomas Chorlton of the Black Horse, were all listed as beersellers rather than licensees of a tavern or pub. And so while the Bowling Green Hotel had an estimated annual rent of £111 and The Greyhound across the Mersey £84, the Horse and Jockey paid just £36.[178] Lower still was Samuel Jackson's business on the Green, which paid £15 a year.

Nor was there any uniform pattern to ownership. The Bowling Green was owned by the Egertons, and was the only pub to be in the hands of a traditional landowner. The rest were either owned by businessmen, who were outsiders, or by local people who were engaged in other activities. The Greyhound, as we know, was sold after the death of James Marsland in 1832 to Edmund Howarth and later passed to Samuel Brooks, none of whom had much connection with the township.[179]

The two most notable local owners were Thomas Taylor and Thomas White. Both were engaged in other business projects and may have become involved almost by default. In the 1840s Thomas Taylor for a time ran the Horse and Jockey as a tenant. He also owned property, which by the 1830s consisted of two houses at the bottom of the Row and four cottages that had once been the Methodist Sunday school. He also ran the stationer's shop and later became the postmaster. In 1832 he or Thomas White applied for a licence to open a beershop in the house beside the stationer's. This was the Travellers Rest, mentioned above, which closed in the early years of the next century. Not all beershops were profitable concerns, but the very fact that the Travellers Rest survived for three-quarters of a century suggests it made money.[180]

Thomas White came from a farming family who lived by the Green. In the early 1830s the family rented 54 acres and during the next decade increased this to 77 acres. His decision to move across the Green into the Row and sell beer could have been for any one of a number of reasons. He was thirty-one, and his father still ran the farm. Thomas had a younger brother, who no doubt helped manage the farm, and there were four servants. Perhaps Thomas wanted a fresh challenge. He and his wife Harriet stayed in the Travellers

---

178 Chorlton-cum-Hardy Rate Books, Manchester Archive Rate Book Microfilm Rolls 297–9

179 Samuel Brooks owned and occupied a house here in the 1840s but did not qualify to vote here.

180 It was still owned by the Taylor family when the shop next door was leased to the son of Samuel Nixon in 1882: indenture agreement between Mrs Jane Taylor (widow of Thomas) and Samuel Edward Nixon, who was the grandson of the second tenant of the Travellers Rest and grandson of the landlord of The Greyhound.

Rest despite the death of his father in 1835 and continued to sell beer into the mid-1840s, when they gave up the tenancy and bought the Horse and Jockey. We can only speculate on whether the sale was funded from the profits of the beershop or from the farm as a way of diversifying their assets. Either way, by 1845 Thomas had returned to farming.[181]

Both Thomas Taylor and Thomas White were typical of the enterprise culture alive in Chorlton. They were a cut above those who ran the beershops. These were small-time family businesses, and in most cases the tenants had little expectation of owning a property. Few seem to have stayed the course, and like some of the shops they may have been a temporary strategy to make ends meet. Samuel Jackson was listed as a beerseller early in 1841, no doubt using his mother's shop, but by June that year he described himself as an agricultural labourer. In March 1849 he was back running a beerhouse on the Green. He may very well have been reacting to the seasonal nature of agricultural work. The beginning of the year through to March was a slack time in the farming community, so Samuel might have had the foresight to make provision for a lack of earnings. A similar case, perhaps, is James White, who was also an agricultural labourer and styled himself as a beerseller in the same year.

Beerselling also offered the opportunity to be independent, whether it was from the vagaries of the farming year or from domestic relationships. Mrs Leach, who ran 'a superior beer shop' at Martledge, was partly driven by the need to earn a living that was not dependent on a husband who drank heavily and absented himself regularly from the family home. This led her to put the beershop in the name of a relation. The business did not survive the dreadful murder of one of her clients by her husband. In 1847 she was open for business, and by the census of 1851 she had vanished. Others lasted longer, gambling that a rural community was remote enough for their infringements of licensing laws to go unnoticed. Ultimately this was proved wrong. William Brownhill had his licence refused after there had been seven convictions in eleven years, and the Black Swan closed its doors because of after-hours drinking.[182] There is no question that such places made money, but even the successful ones were reliant on the earnings of their regulars. Seasonal unemployment must have eaten into their takings. Some landlords, as we have seen, had other jobs, and some, like The Greyhound and the Travellers Rest, took in lodgers.

Chorlton was, of course, not the only place to drink. For those more adventurous spirits, the short walk to Stretford offered a number of drinking opportunities, as did Withington; but most, no doubt, stayed in the township. In the way of things, some would have sat in their chosen pub and reminisced about past landlords. But whichever pub or beer-

---

181 He had retired by 1861 and died in 1872, leaving effects worth under £100. The pub was sold to Joseph Holland in February 1880.
182 *Manchester Guardian*, 11 September 1869.

shop they turned out of in the summer of 1847 all would be clear about who had called time. On the Green there was Joseph Holland at the Jockey, directly opposite was George Whitelegg at the Bowling Green, and around the corner on the Row Samuel Nixon would be watching as his customers disappeared, illuminated only by the moonlight. He may well have been thinking of his father out across the Mersey on the edge of the township. I still wonder how many customers chose The Greyhound, for even on a summer's night the journey home was a long one. And up at Martledge as the Royal Oak closed and Mrs Leach said goodnight to the last to leave, one or two might (if there were still pennies in their pocket to spare) walk up to Lane End on the off chance that the Black Horse or William Brownhill's beershop was still open.

seven

HEALTH

The lack of doctors in 1841, the alternatives including quacks, folklore, chemists and druggists, the workhouse and sick clubs, as well as home treatments and Mrs Beeton. Infant mortality, common childhood illnesses, water and sanitation, the welfare of the elderly and family size

There were no doctors in the township. The nearest was the surgeon George Savage in Stretford and if he were unavailable there was John Hepworth at Crofts Bank on the way to Urmston. Given the distance from Chorlton it is unlikely that either would have been much help in an emergency. This was remedied with the arrival of James Partington, who lived with his family on Nell Lane opposite Hough End Hall.[183] Technically he was in Withington, but for those living on the Row and around the Green he was just a short walk away. Not that this may have been much of a consolation because his fees would have put him beyond the reach of most. The standard charge was 5s, which might represent anything between a quarter and half of a labourer's weekly wage, and this was before the cost of any medicine that might be prescribed. Many expressed the view that this was a crippling cost: as the Revd C. Oxenden said in 1854, 'the doctor's bill is the bill which breaks down the labouring man.'[184]

There were alternatives, however. These ranged from travelling quacks and folk knowledge to the workhouse infirmary and sick clubs. Individually or collectively these coped with a wide range of complaints, illnesses and diseases. Lightly Simpson, the chemist and druggist on the Row, might have been of help, but he too would have been relatively expensive. For most the only solutions were natural remedies and the wisdom of the older generation.

Most illnesses were connected with poor diet, long hours of back-breaking work and the overcrowded and unsanitary conditions that many had to endure. They ranged from

---

183 James Partington was fifty-one in 1847 and lived with his family in Brook Field House, opposite Hough End Hall on Nell Lane; previously he had lived on Oxford Street.
184 Revd C. Oxenden, quoted in Sherren, J., *Evidence on Poor Law Medical Relief Taken before the Select Committee of the House of Commons, on Poor Relief, England*, 1861, p.xvii, Google edn p.26.

rheumatism, influenza, inflammation of the chest, throat and eyes to bowel disorders, heart disease and minor injuries. Set against these were the low-level pain of toothache and skin rashes.[185] There were also those ailments that were more common among infants, children and the old. Finally there were the great killer diseases, which thrived in poor living conditions but made no distinction between rich and poor.

Chorlton was a township where pain was a backdrop to everyday living, and the prospect of wonder cures was an illusion – but there were those who peddled the promise of getting better, as well as those whose advice was based on a degree of medical knowledge. Any illness was unwelcome especially in an age before antibiotics, but if the person falling ill was the main wage earner it could be disastrous. In 1854, 72 per cent of those described as paupers were 'made paupers through sickness',[186] which had repercussions on the whole family. It followed that anything which offered a quick solution would be welcome – but the itinerant quack, dispensing hope with attractively coloured substances and showmanship, was more likely to have entertained than cured.

More useful, and in many cases free, were the vast store of herbs and plants that had been used for centuries. The use of some was revealed by trusted older members of the community, while others were common knowledge. Yet more were listed in self-help books. The wide range of herbal treatments included anemone, which was applied externally as a juice to clean ulceration and infection, burdock, which when crushed and mixed with salt could be used on dog bites, flatulence and tooth pain, and wood betony, good for headaches, belching, cramps, convulsions, bruises and even killing worms.[187] Mugwort induced labour, assisted birth and eased labour pains. Some, like anemone, burdock and mugwort, were commonly available in the township, while many more would have been either grown in gardens or collected from the wild.

Then there were the chemist and druggist shops.[188] Lightly Simpson's was on the Row in the 1840s and he would have dispensed medical advice for nothing and charged only for drugs, which were prescribed by a doctor and he made up. Some druggists had no medical training, and like the quacks they could be dangerous. Official reports and contemporary

---

185 Well into the 20th century it was common for teeth to be extracted at markets and in rural areas by the blacksmith. Many of those seemingly grim-faced working-class women caught in photographs are not smiling because this would reveal their lack of teeth. It was not uncommon for people to have all their healthy teeth removed to prevent problems in the future.

186 Sherren, *op. cit.*, p.xvii, Google edn p.26, evidence of Dr Wallis.

187 Culpeper, Nicholas, *The English Physician*, 1652. Culpeper was a botanist, herbalist, physician and astrologer whose two books, *The English Physician* and *The Complete Herbalist*, are a collection of pharmaceutical and herbal knowledge. *The English Physician* has been almost continuously in print since the mid-17th century. Culpeper was a radical during the English Civil War, translating medical and herbal texts into English from Latin as self-help guides for the use of the poor.

188 Marland, Hilary, *The Medical Activities of Mid-19th century Chemists & Druggists with special reference to Wakefield & Huddersfield*, vol. 3, Medical History Wellcome Trust Centre for the History of Medicine at UCL, October 1987, pp.415–39.

novels reflected on the dangers of these unsound solutions to serious illnesses.[189] For many in Chorlton Simpson might have been the first port of call when illness struck, and his advice probably extended to dentistry and even minor surgery. He may also have sold a wide range of other products, including domestic recipes and veterinary preparations, as well as toilet articles, tobacco, snuff, tea, coffee, herbs and other foodstuffs, and oils, candles and dyes.[190]

There were many branded pills that were advertised in the street and trade directories and were widely available not only in chemists' shops but also stationers, grocers, butchers, hairdressers and publicans.[191] Dr Bardsley's Antibilious Pills for Disorders of the Stomach and Bowels, Giddiness, Sickness and Headache were advertised in *Slater's Directory of Manchester and Salford* in 1850 and were sold by wholesalers across Lancashire. Made by W. Mather, chemist of 105 Chester Road in Hulme, they came in boxes at 7½*d*, 13½*d* and 2*s* 9*d*.[192]

Of all the solutions open to poorer members of the community the most dreaded was the workhouse. Chorlton was part of the Chorlton Union, covering a swathe of land to the south of Manchester.[193] There was no legal obligation to help the sick, but the Poor Law commissioners recognised that 'if a man is able to provide himself and family with food, and lodging, and clothing, whilst in health, but is unable in cases of sickness to provide medical aid, he is entitled to receive medical relief at the charge of the poor rates'.[194] However humanitarian this appeared there were sound economic reasons. If those who sought relief did so because they were ill, the Poor Law commissioners reasoned, it was 'therefore most important to get them cured as speedily as possible', thereby saving them from 'coming on the rates for maintenance'.[195] So the Unions employed qualified medical officers to care for those who applied for help in the infirmary. There were no clear guidelines defining who could qualify: 'in some Unions Medical Relief is withheld except where the families are large and young; in other Unions it is given to all applicants'.[196] It was the job of the relieving officer to assess the needs of the applicants, both those asking for medical help and those requesting general assistance. His assessment was passed to

189 Gaskell, Elizabeth, *Mary Barton*, 1848, Penguin edn, 1970, p.102. John Barton buys an over-the-counter drug to help a friend who has typhus; needless to say the man dies.
190 Marland, *op. cit.*, pp.422–3.
191 *Ibid.*, p.434.
192 Slater's Directory of Manchester and Salford, 1850, p.672, Historical Directories.
193 The Union covered Chorlton-upon-Medlock, Ardwick, Openshaw, Gorton, Levenshulme, Burnage, Hulme, Stretford, Moss Side, Chorlton-cum-Hardy, Withington, Didsbury and Rusholme.
194 Official Circular, May 1845, No. 2, quoted in 'Evidence on Poor Law Medical Relief Taken before the Select Committee of the House of Commons, on Poor Relief, England', 1861, and published by J. Sherren, 1862, p.xvii, Google edn p.26.
195 *Ibid.*, p.xviii, Google edn p.27.
196 *Report of the Poor Law Commissioners*, HMSO, 1840, p.283, Google edn p.298.

the guardians, and if he considered they were eligible for relief he issued an order to the medical officer or doctor who was employed by the Union.

The guardians were always mindful of the need to keep costs down. Before 1842 posts could be put out to competitive tender, which usually resulted in the cheapest and least qualified doctor being appointed. Even so, there were great variations in what was paid to the doctor, so while the average was 2½d per head, Glossop paid just a farthing and Thetford 1s 2¾d.[197] Therefore we shouldn't be surprised that, in the words of the Poor Law commissioners, 'Sufficient care does not appear to be taken in selecting medical men of the highest qualifications for the responsible situation of medical attendant on the poor'.[198] Nor was there any uniformity in how the Unions paid their medical officers. Some paid an annual fixed salary with an allowance for extra medical fees; others omitted to pay anything but a fixed salary; some paid by the case. In our own Union the fee paid was 5s per case, which covered both attendance and medicine.[199] Given that doctors were expected to foot the bill for medicines, there was a suspicion that this method of recompense resulted in some of them prescribing cheaper and inferior medicines.

There were just two medical officers to cover the whole Chorlton Union in its early years. Samuel Nicholson was responsible for the southern half, which included Chorlton-cum-Hardy, Didsbury, Hulme, Moss Side, Rusholme, Stretford and Withington, which amounted to 55,400 people.[200] In summer 1847 those who were sick were admitted to the workhouse infirmary on Stretford New Road, just over 3 miles away. Like every other aspect of the workhouse the infirmary was segregated. On the south side of the building was the Females' Sick Room; separated from it by the dining room and chapel was the Males' Sick Room. Each had its own exercise yard, and each was situated hard by the areas allocated to male and female lunatics. The ten wards were simple places and probably not unlike that of St George the Martyr in Southwark.[201] Each ward in this London infirmary had a fireplace and a lavatory in a recess or lobby, the water closet serving two or three wards. The level of nursing was basic at best, with many nurses drawn from the inmates – who were usually elderly and illiterate. This posed serious problems when administering medicines from labelled bottles. In our infirmary these duties were performed by Jane Grimes, who had celebrated her seventy-fifth birthday by the spring of 1841.

197 *Evidence on Poor Law Medical Relief, op. cit.,* p.xliii, Google edn p.51. The figures remained much the same from 1841 to 1860.
198 *Report of the Poor Law Commissioners, op. cit.,* 1840, p.282, Google edn p.297.
199 Advertisement for the election of three medical officers for Chorlton Union, April 1848, from the *Manchester Times and Gazette,* Saturday 1 April 1848.
200 'The New Poor Law, Report of the Guardians of the Chorlton Union', *Manchester Guardian,* 23 February 1839. Chorlton-cum-Hardy, 700, Didsbury, 1200, Hulme, 20,000, Moss Side, 240, Rusholme, 2,000, Stretford, 30,000, Withington, 1260. By 1848 this had risen to three medical officers, with the south-west district no. 6 comprising the townships of Stretford, Chorlton-cum-Hardy, Flixton and Urmston.
201 St George the Martyr was the subject of a report published in the *Lancet* in 1865 and quoted by Higginbotham, Peter, 'Medical Care in the Workhouse', on his excellent website www.workhouse.org.uk.

With such a grim place to fall back on, many working people chose to rely on the sick and burial clubs. There were a number in Chorlton that flourished over the years. In return for a regular contribution, they provided sick payments when a member fell ill; some also offered the assistance of a club doctor, who was paid between 2s and 3s per member per year. How effective they were is not easy to say. Some members, according to H.W. Rumsey in his evidence to the Select Committee on Medical Poor Relief in 1844, reported that they were 'not generally satisfied with the medical attendant. They like the power of electing him. They expect him to walk in their annual processions, and they thank him for his services at their club feats, but individually they often complain that they are not sufficiently supplied with medicines and attendance.'[202] The records of most societies have not survived, and the medical provision made available in Chorlton is not known. Nor do we know what illnesses the club members succumbed to. The records of other societies suggest that common ailments included rheumatism, influenza, inflammation of the chest, throat and eyes, bowel disorders, heart disease and minor injuries – few of which a club doctor would have been able to cure.[203] The same records show that some members counted their illness in months if not years: this was an added hardship, as benefits were reduced after a fixed term. The rules governing applications were very clear. The sick had to be certified by an official of the club and by a medical person, clergyman or another approved witness.

Only one of the local clubs survived for any length of time, one of them collapsing after the funds were stolen.

For the middle classes in the township, as well as the doctor and the chemist there were self-help manuals, which provided guidance on a range of medical matters. These included *Primitive Physic, An Easy and Natural Method of curing most Diseases* by John Wesley, written in 1785, and *Domestic Medicine* by William Buchan, published in 1798. Both were reprinted well into the 19th century, but for many households it was Mrs Beeton's *Book of Household Management* that was the obvious choice. This devoted three chapters to the care of the sick, along with a short section on Invalid Cookery. There was a guide of what to look for when employing sick nurses, as well as wet and monthly nurses, and clear instructions on how the sick room should be laid out and the level of ventilation.[204] Much was drawn from the experiences of Florence Nightingale, which were quoted at length. But above all it was the descriptions of childhood illnesses, many of which are a distant memory today, which feature in profusion. Diarrhoea, croup, whooping-cough, scarlatina, scarlet fever, measles, chickenpox and cowpox were far more serious in an age before

202 H.W. Rumsey evidence to Select Committee on Medical Poor Relief quoted by Marland, *op. cit.*, p.193.
203 *Ibid.*, p.197.
204 A monthly nurse looked after the mother and baby in the first few weeks.

antibiotics. Measles, 'this much dreaded disease', was treated by first getting the temperature down 'and opening the pores, producing natural perspiration, and unloading the congested state of the lungs [which] in most cases does away entirely with the necessity both for leeches and a blister'.[205] For all the diseases there were homemade treatments. For measles Mrs Beeton recommended aperients powders, consisting of scammony and jalap in various quantities, or a mix of mint water, powdered nitre, antimonial wine, spirits of nitre and syrup of saffron, designed to 'keep up a steady but gentle action on the bowels'.[206] Similar treatments were offered for the other diseases, as were suggestions to deal with bites and stings, broken bones, bruises, lacerations, cuts, burns, scalds and more serious accidents. We should not minimise the effect of minor scrapes and cuts: they easily became infected, even (in the case of dog bites) having fatal results. Arnold Brownhill, grandson of William the wheelwright, died from one such bite in the summer of 1882, after rabies set in.[207]

But there were some diseases that even Mrs Beeton could not be hopeful about. One such was cholera. It is true that 'cleanliness, sobriety, and judicious ventilation' were bound to keep people in a more healthy state, but cholera could not be kept at bay with a clean dish cloth and a sober lifestyle. It attacked rich and poor alike, but its main victims were those who lived in crowded conditions with no access to clean water. Other serious illnesses included typhus, typhoid, tuberculosis, diphtheria, dysentery, scarlet fever and smallpox, all of which thrived in overcrowded conditions. Some were carried by body lice, while typhoid and cholera were transmitted through drinking water that was contaminated with the faeces of an infected person. These diseases were not confined to industrial towns: in the village of Blandford in Dorset 'there were more than forty cases of typhus, and the spread of the disease must be attributed to the people living so densely packed together'.[208] As we shall see, Chorlton's water supplies were at best limited and easily contaminated – but the township seems to have been spared from the ravages of the great killer diseases of cholera and typhus. Asiatic cholera raged through Manchester in the early 1830s and again in 1849, killing 674 people in Manchester during 1831–33 and 828 in 1849.[209] But in Chorlton the death toll was little different from other years. Nor was

205 Beeton, Isabella, *Book of Household Management*, S.O. Beeton, London, 1863, p.1055, Google edn p.1120.

206 Scammony is a bindweed native to the Mediterranean; jalap is a root plant that accelerates defecation; antimonial was a substance that speeded up vomiting.

207 *Liverpool Mercury*, 15 September 1882, Issue 10819: http://newspapers.bl.uk/blcs/.

208 Evidence of Mr Spooner, surgeon of Blandford, *Reports of the Special Assistant Poor Law Commissioners on the employment of women & children in Agriculture*, HMSO, 1843, p.22, Google edn p.42.

209 These outbreaks are well documented by Gaulter, Henry, *Origin and Progress of the Malignant Cholera in Manchester*, Longman, 1833, and Appendix A to *The Report of the General Board of Health on the Epidemic Cholera of 1848 & 1849*, HMSO, 1850. Another 216 died in Salford and thirty-four in Chorlton-upon-Medlock in 1831–33.

there an increase in the number of local deaths during 1847 when there was a typhus outbreak in Manchester.[210]

It was children who were the most vulnerable. The death rate among the very young in Chorlton during the first half of the 19th century was very high. Over 35 per cent of children buried in the parish church in the years between 1807 and 1850 were under the age of one. Child mortality was at its highest among the very young in warm weather, when they were vulnerable to diarrhoeal infections, and again in the late winter and spring from respiratory ailments.[211] So of the twenty-seven children under the age of two who died during this period, eighteen (or 66 per cent) succumbed in the warmer months.

Each death represented a personal tragedy for a family, and a loss to the community. James Higginbotham, the farmer on the Green, buried his first wife and two of his children in the tiny Wesleyan graveyard on the Row in the space of four years.[212] Nor was he alone: most of our families in the decades before 1850 also buried at least one child in either the chapel's grounds or the graveyard of St Clement's by the Green. William Chesshyre was a month old when he was buried in 1831, Mary Bell Whitelegg and John Gresty just three months and William Cardrew Birley, son of the Revd William Birley and his wife Maria, only five months. Some families were unluckier than others: the Hollands lost three of their children between 1840 and 1841;[213] James Gresty buried his two young sons and his wife in just a year.[214] William and Mary Cookson lost their daughter Mary in April 1806: she had survived the uncertainties of infancy to die at fifteen. The death of a child at any age is hard to bear, but perhaps for them the loss of a child so close to adulthood was even greater. The words they inscribed on her gravestone cry out their loss:

Fair and beauteous young and gay
Here she falls to Death a Prey
Bright and glorious good and wise
There she mounts to yonder skies
There to reign in Bliss above
Perfect Peace and perfect Love

210 Throughout the period from 1800 to 1850 the number of burials in the parish church stayed much the same, with only slight variations. On only four occasions did they rise above seven in one year; these were in 1817 and 1836, when there were eight burials, and 1800 and 1838 when there were ten.

211 Reavy, *op. cit.*, p.110.

212 Henry Higginbotham, born 1842, died January 1845, Mary, died in June 1848 aged just five weeks and Margaret mother and wife, died on 17 January 1849 aged thirty-seven.

213 Thomas, 17 December 1840, aged six years and ten months, William, 13 December 1840, seven years and eight months, and Sarah, 16 September 1841, fifteen months, the Holland gravestone, St Clement's.

214 'Mary wife of James died January 6th 1800, aged 37, John their son who departed this life February 8th 1800 aged 5 months. Also Samuel their son who departed this life April 16th 1800 aged 2 years & 11 months.' The Gresty gravestone, St Clement's.

Let not the Tear of Woe
Down thy Cheeck dear Parent Flow
Rather let thy Life's Decline
Praise that Providence divine,
Which from such a World of this
Took thy Child to heavenly Bliss.[215]

Nor should we forget that childbirth was fraught with complications that could carry both mother and infant away. Few in the township suffered this fate, but in the spring of 1778 Mary Lamb and her daughter of just seven days were buried in the same grave, their deaths three days apart.[216]

Personal hygiene was important, but most families in Chorlton had no bathroom and washing was done using a jug of water, each part of the body being washed in turn.

Toothbrushes were not often used; instead, a wet rag that had been dipped in salt or soot was used. The better off in the township may have relied on the advice of Mrs Beeton, who recommended that 'a good wash for the hair' involved pouring boiling water over a pennyworth of borax and a ½ pint of olive-oil, allowing it to cool, then applying it with a flannel. Alternatively, 'Camphor and borax dissolved in boiling water and left to cool make a very good wash for the hair; as also does rosemary-water mixed with a little borax.'[217]

There were plenty of wells, as well as watercourses and countless ponds, but collecting enough water was always a chore. Farmhouses and the larger houses in Chorlton had their own wells, as did some of the cottages, but other families had to share.[218] A family might need several buckets of water a day, which all had to be drawn and carried home.[219] Wells had to be deep. Anything less than 10ft ran the risk of contamination either from surface water entering from above or seeping through the walls, an ever-present problem given the inevitable proximity of privies. This could be eliminated by encasing the first 10ft or so with a stone collar, and also making sure the well stood above the level of the surrounding ground. Henry Stephen, who wrote a farming manual in the 1840s, reckoned that 'the cost of digging a well in clay, eight feet in diameter and sixteen deep and building a ring

215 The Cookson gravestone, St Clement's.

216 Betty Lamb, aged seven days, died on 6 April and her mother Mary Lamb, aged forty-four, on 9 April 1778.

217 Beeton, *op. cit.*, p.981, Google edn p.1064.

218 The Higginbotham family filled theirs in only in the 1960s; the pump at Bailey's old farm on the Row was still standing in the 1970s, as was the well at their farm at the bottom of Sandy Lane. Bigger houses built in the 1860s, like those constructed by George Whitelegg on Edge Lane in 1860, had a well inside the house: their deeds are in possession of Peter Richardson. Wells continue to turn up, like the one found in William Chessyre's new house on Manchester Road.

219 Mrs Williamson, writing in 1883, described how the villagers of Lady Barn regularly had to visit a pond in a nearby hayfield to collect 'buckets of water where with to clean their houses, this being the only supply of any but rain and spring water'. Williamson, W.C., *Sketches of Fallowfield and Surrounding Manors Past and Present*, John Heywood, 1888, p.38.

three feet in diameter with dry rubble masonry is only £5 exclusive of carriage and the cost of pumps'.[220] He was convinced of the usefulness of a soundly built rain water cistern, and many Chorlton homes would have had one, either made from a block of freestone or flags, or from wood. The earliest pumps in the township were made of wood, with the central part a hollowed tree trunk. Lead and cast-iron pumps replaced them later.[221] Shared pumps and wells were focal points, where people met and exchanged gossip. On long hot summer days pumps provided children with a source of entertainment.

Chorlton's wells might have provided a sufficient water supply in the summer of 1847, but there was soon to be a pressing need for alternatives. George Whitelegg built his two fine houses on Edge Lane[222] with a joint well in 1860, but just three years later there was a request to Manchester Corporation to provide piped water, and the following January the Water Works Committee resolved 'to authorise the laying of a service Main in Edge Lane … for the supply of the houses included in the Schedule submitted and situate in Chorlton-cum-Hardy'.[223] The 3in main extended down Edge Lane, along St Clements Road to the Horse and Jockey. Within another twenty years the remaining wells were all but empty and becoming contaminated.

Clean water for drinking and other household needs was a real problem almost everywhere. Despite warnings, many were too shallow and became polluted. It wasn't just in the cities and fast-growing towns that this caused health hazards; waterborne diseases were also evident in the villages and hamlets. As we have seen they were responsible for many child deaths, and were common enough to be remarked on in reports of the period. Sanitation in rural areas was primitive, and simple earth privies were common. They were set away from the houses and required the user to drop earth onto the human waste. Cesspits were an alternative. These were brick or stone lined and were set away from the house. There were also ditches, which over time had become full of all manner of rubbish. One such ran from the Row up to Hardy Lane.[224]

The enterprising George Whitelegg built his new houses with indoor and outside lavatories, which fed into a drain. Further north, where Samuel Brooks began developing Jackson's Moss, he used the brook that ran from Hulme as a sewer for his property.[225] This was culverted, eventually feeding into the Black Brook – which runs south into the township.

---

220 Stephens, *op. cit.*, p.539, Google edn p.558.
221 Williams, Richard, *Village Pumps*, Shire, 2009, and www.villagepumps.org.uk.
222 Stockton Range.
223 Minutes of the Water Works Committee of Manchester Corporation No. 10, 28 January 1864, Archive and Local History Library, M231/1/2/1/10. There were initially only eleven houses along the course of the main, but during the next thirteen years it was frequently extended, until in 1877 a new 12in main was laid from Brooks Bar, along Manchester Road, Wilbraham Road and Edge Lane to Stretford. Ellwood, chapter 22, 1886.
224 The ditch from the Row to High Lane runs under Acres Road. It was flagged and the stones then covered with ash and earth.
225 Samuel Brooks renamed the estate Whalley Range. He lived in Whalley House, which was on what is now Upper Chorlton Road.

eight

MAKING DO ON LESS THAN A POUND A WEEK

Poverty, welfare of the elderly, Poor Law Relief before and after 1834,
the workhouse, sick clubs and charities, emigration

Poverty was never far away in Chorlton, and various strategies were used to supplement family incomes – but there were always unforeseen circumstances, whether unemployment, sickness or death.

When young Francis Deakin died in May 1847 he left a wife and six children. Martha was in her thirty-fourth year; her eldest child was thirteen and the youngest just three weeks old. She was, in the words of the *Manchester Guardian*, 'in a very critical state and her prospects are truly gloomy'. She benefited from a burial payment that usually paid out £10 on the death of the husband.[226] Martha may also have fallen back on charity, poor relief or the help of friends and relatives. Several hundred turned out for the funeral of her husband, and the collection must have been generous; she may even have benefited from the income derived from the sale of the sermon preached on that day by the Revd William Birley. Its title 'The Uncertainty of Life, a reason for Perpetual Watchfulness and Preparation', went on sale soon after the service. However hard their immediate situation, the family survived, and continued to farm the 6 acres that Francis had rented.

Families on the economic margin adopted many different strategies. The garden provided extra food, of course, and others relied on lodgers. Sometimes man and wife were both working, but these were in a minority, as were those families who relied on the wages of unmarried children: just over a quarter of households in Chorlton with one adult at work also had children earning. This was only a temporary solution as children in most cases left home to start their own families. There were also plenty of families in which the children were too young to work.

---

226 This was the Odd Fellows Society, which had a branch in the township. Francis had been a member and the lodge turned out for his funeral. *Manchester Guardian*, 12 May 1847.

One local family, the Suttons, stands for many. They had a teenage boy who like his father was working on the land. In Lancashire boys over the age of ten might expect to earn from 2s to 8s depending on the time of year. This was an important addition to an agricultural family's income, and in the words of one government report was 'so great a relief to the parents as to render it almost hopeless that they can withstand the inducement and retain the child at school'.[227]

Other families, like the Pearsons, illustrate the different fortunes that a family could experience. Richard Pearson was an agricultural labourer who lived on the Row during the 1840s and '50s. Between 1821 and 1831 he and his wife Elizabeth had seven children. Not all survived, but by 1841 at least one daughter was working away, while another two were at home but not working. The eldest daughter might have sent money home, but in June 1841 Richard's earnings could have been the only income. By the spring of 1851 the younger girls were working as domestic servants and living at home, which would have helped. Elizabeth was twenty-one and Mary was nineteen, so we can assume that they had been making a regular contribution to the household income for some time. A near neighbour Mary Turner was receiving £8 a year (3s a week) as a servant from Farmer Higginbotham: this wage took into account her board and food, as she lived in. The Pearson girls were daily staff, so may have earned a little more. Daughters have a habit of marrying and moving away, or at the very least finding employment elsewhere, and there is no record of Mary Pearson in the township after 1851.

If Richarad Pearson earned the average agricultural wage for the north-west he would have been taking home between 11s and 18s in 1841. His rent was 3s a week, and if he was in a sick and burial club his payments would have been approximately 1s 6d.[228] What was left had to be divided between food, lighting, heating and clothes. The cost of these varied regionally, but in 1859 the cost of ten common household items from village shops was 7s 2d.[229] This bought 4lb of bread, 7lb of flour, 1lb of bacon, 1lb of butcher's meat, 1lb of cheese, 1lb of butter, 1oz of tea, 1lb of sugar, 1lb of soap, and 1lb of candles. For those who chose to make their way into town and buy from the markets prices could be slightly lower,[230] but this was not an option for most Chorlton people. Nor was food the only demand on the family budget. The cost of repairing a pair of shoes was put at 2s, while

---

227 *Report to Parliament of 1851 Census of Education of Great Britain*, 1854, George Routledge, p.19, Google edn p.27.

228 Richard Pearson was a Methodist, and if he was in a sick and burial club he no doubt belonged to the Wesleyan Friendly Society. This is the one group for which we have no details of monthly contributions.

229 The estimate was done by collecting 'the shop prices paid by the labouring poor for ten different articles of food' from the counties of Kent, Norfolk and Devon. Purdy, *op. cit.*, p.347.

230 Prices at St John's Market, Liverpool, featured in 'Housewife's Corner', *Liverpool Mercury*, 10 September 1863. A pound of beef was 5½d, a pound of mutton 6½d, a pound of lamb 7d and a pound of fresh pork 6d. A pair of rabbits could be bought for 2s, and a pound of fresh butter for 1s 1d; salted butter was 10d a lb.

a check apron and strings cost 1s 7d and two flannel petticoats were 9s 4½d.[231] By stark contrast a bottle of claret could cost between 35s and 70s and a high-quality Moët 72s.[232]

Given the economic situation for most people, it is surprising that there was support across the classes for the local subscriptions that were an important part of the building programmes in the township. The new church school, built in 1845, and the rectory were partly paid for by public subscription, as were the Methodist chapels and Sunday school. The Methodists were a small group and many were labourers.[233] The building fund for the second chapel came mainly from just eighty subscribers who made subscriptions ranging from 10s up to £50.[234] Perhaps more revealing of the determination of the group comes from the even smaller amounts which were dredged from surplus income and in some cases represented a real sacrifice ranging from 10d to just a few pennies.

Of all the groups who were most likely to encounter hardship it was the elderly. Not that this was an aged community in today's terms: only 7 per cent of the township was over sixty years old.[235] And this small group was diverse. Some were still at work, while others relied on private annuities and one was on parish relief. The elderly could find it hard. Even if they were still working their best years were behind them, and for those still out in the fields or washing other people's clothes their pace of labour and wages reflected their age. In some cases they might move in with their children or be supported by them financially. Such was John Sutton, who aged eighty-four described himself as an infirm labourer, and lived with his son and family on the Row. Overcrowding was eased when grandchildren lived with grandparents. Ann Jordrill, aged eighty-four in 1851, was a widow and receiving parish relief: she was living with her thirteen-year-old granddaughter Ann Kenyon, who was employed as a house servant.[236] Not all the elderly struggled in old age. The farmer Mary White continued to run her 52 acres with the help of her son, and the market gardener Mary Gratrix was assisted by her nephew. Others had independent means: James Holt was a businessman with land in the township; for others it was annuities. Less grand was Sarah Jackson, who had run the grocer's shop on the Row and lived with her son. She rented out part of her house to John Winstanley, the local police constable, and his family. Others spent their retirement as lodgers in another's home. Such was Jane Holland who, aged seventy, unmarried and a former cook, was living with the Higginbothams on the Green.

---

231 Higginbotham's accounts.

232 *Liverpool Mercury*, 14 October 1853.

233 The second chapel cost £690. Later they raised the money to build not only the church on Manchester Road at a cost of £5,600 in 1873, but the Sunday school building in 1885.

234 The Brundrett family alone contributed £154 0s 6d, which came from nineteen members of the family.

235 This was in 1841; ten years later it was 8 per cent.

236 Ann was one of five children, whose parents were John and Ann: they lived at High Lane Cottage.

For those who faced an uncertain future, either because they were widowed or single, and because of frailty and limited funds, as well as those who found themselves unable to earn a wage, there was parish relief. Since Elizabethan times the parish had distributed help to the poor from a fund of money raised from rates, and each parish had an unpaid elected Overseer of the Poor. He was responsible for giving out money or food to those in need, either as indoor or outdoor relief. Indoor relief was given in a workhouse or almshouse and outdoor relief went to the pauper in their own home. Chorlton's parish records do not exist for the early 19th century but those of the neighbouring parish of St Matthew's in Stretford have survived. They show regular payments made by James Mee, the overseer. During 1808–9 he paid out £3 8s for seventeen weeks' relief to John Eccles, with an additional 4s for a pair of clogs, and £7 to Catherine Ashcroft for twenty-eight weeks' relief at 5s a week.[237]

These were hard years. From 1807 onwards until 1813 the harvests were bad in the North and the price of wheat rose steadily until it reached 126s 6d per quarter in 1812.[238] This was the highest it went during the Napoleonic Wars and represented real hardship for the poor.[239] Back in Stretford the money expended on relief in 1811–12 amounted to £1,088, rising to £1,757 the following year: the lowest payments coincided with harvest time when there might be more work available. Harvests after 1815 were generally better and wheat prices fell, but in June and July 1819, forty-three people were still on casual relief.

The system had been undergoing changes since Elizabethan times, partly to restrict relief to local people and partly to change the system of indoor relief, which was more costly. The Settlement Act of 1662 aimed at reducing the relief burden by empowering parishes to restrict the number who could settle in an area. Anyone wanting to settle in a parish had to gain permission in the form of a settlement order. This was granted if the applicant could demonstrate a link with the parish or evidence of financial security. In the century stretching back from 1847 a number of people won the right to live in Chorlton: in 1733 'Ellen Bates wife of William Bates the soldier and Mary her daughter' were granted settlement; during the following ten years 'William, Jane, and Ann, children of George Pennington as well as Mary Statham and Alice Williamson' were allowed to stay.[240] But it could and did work the other way: those who settled without permission could be returned to their original parish. Not long after the Pennington children were granted their settlement order, 'John Edge, his wife Katherine and their sons James and Richard' were removed.[241] During the following seventy-nine years five other families or individuals were

237 'Relief of the Poor, Township of Stretford, St Matthew's', Microfilm MRPR 2042, Local History Library, Manchester.
238 *Ibid.*, Stratton, pp.96–7.
239 A quarter of wheat was 28lb.
240 Lancashire County Records Office, Ellen and Mary Bates, 1733 QSP/1371/4, William, Jane, and Ann, children of George Pennington, QSP/1375/13, Mary Statham, QSP/1534/8, Alice Williamson, QSP/13575/13.
241 John Edge, his wife Katherine and their sons James and Richard, QSP/1554/8.

also issued with removal orders, although two successfully appealed against them. The township also received those who had been sent away by other parishes. On 21 December 1765 'Mary Crowther, single woman' was removed from Stretford to Chorlton, and on 23 February 1809 'Lucy Higham, widow' was also sent from Stretford.[242]

Mary Crowther's is an interesting story. Her parents were Richard and Ellen from Manchester, who in 1732 were granted settlement in Chorlton with their daughters Elizabeth (aged two) and Mary (just six months).[243] When Mary was returned from Stretford she was thirty-three years old and pregnant. Without a settlement certificate, and probably having already requested help with her coming baby, the parish sent her home – not being keen to take on the extra cost of helping a single mother. In such cases fathers often made no contribution. Mary returned to Chorlton, and in the following year buried a son called John. She had three more children out of wedlock: James (born in 1769), Martha (1779) and Thomas (1782). All three were baptised at St Clement's, and the parish might have had to support them. Martha had a short life: she was baptised on 28 March 1779 and was buried on 6 April 1780.[244] Mary lived in one of two wattle and daub cottages on the Row,[245] and died aged ninety in 1837. She is buried in the parish churchyard with her son Thomas, who died the following year. Mary is interesting in another way: she was the last person to be called to do penance in the church some time at the beginning of the 19th century: it is not known why. As was the custom, she was made to walk up and down the aisle of the church with a white sheet over her head.[246]

The whole system of relief had been creaking for half a century, and in order to solve the growing problem of its cost and also to introduce a uniform system the Poor Law Amendment Act was passed in 1834. Parishes were grouped in Poor Law Unions covering a large area. Each Union had a workhouse where relief was distributed. At the centre of the system were two principles: first, making conditions in the workhouse worse than anything the applicant had experienced, thereby acting as a deterrent on seeking relief; second, making it a condition that relief was provided in the workhouse.[247]

The workhouse movement began in the 17th century and spread across the country. Even before the 1834 Act, which turned workhouses into 'harsh prisons', there were moves to make them unpleasant places, and those seeking relief had to do a set amount of

242 Removal Orders, L89/9/10/11 and 22.

243 Lancashire County Records, QSP/1356/7.

244 The baptismal record of St Clement's refers to a Mary Crowder baptising Martha in 1779, but given the vagaries of spelling at the time this may be Mary Crowther.

245 The cottages stood roughly where the Trevor Arms stands today, at the bottom end of Beech Road.

246 Ellwood, chapter 13, 1886.

247 In reality there was still a measure of outdoor relief that might be given to widows with dependent children, the wives of men away in the forces and eventually even to able-bodied men, who were given work to do.

work.[248] Later still there were attempts to allocate relief on a county by county basis, with parishes providing workhouses between them,[249] but the approach remained haphazard and confused. Legislation during the 18th century sought to make the workhouse into a place that cared for the old, sick and infirm, and provided outdoor relief for the able-bodied poor.

Chorlton was part of the Chorlton Union, to the south of Manchester city centre.[250] The combined population of the Union stood at 74,300 in 1834, rising steadily to 76,924 in 1841 and 123,841 by 1851. There were also two almshouses in Chorlton, cottages over-looking a footpath to Hardy Croft.[251] The workhouse was at the junction of Stretford New Road and Leaf Street, and could hold 300.

Much was written on the conditions in the workhouse, and they were hated and feared by those who had to rely on them.[252] Many in the establishment were hostile. These included Thomas Carlyle and Charles Dickens, along with the Tory Richard Oastler, who had long campaigned for factory reform, and the radical William Cobbett. They were joined by *The Times*, which from the late 1830s to the '40s carried letters highlighting some of the worst abuses.[253] Like all campaigning propaganda some of what was written was at best exaggeration and at worst false. The powerful scenes in *Oliver Twist* are a case in point. There was brutality and at times a callous disregard of the inmates, which reaches its high point in Oliver's diet 'of three meals of thin gruel a day, with an onion twice a week on Sundays'.[254] But contemporary accounts and modern research suggest that Dickens's description owed more to his own hatred of the workhouses than reality.[255] However, this should not blind us to what awaited any of those from Chorlton who sought relief in the years after 1834. A precondition of admission was that families were segregated. It mattered little if the couple had been together for almost all their entire adult life or that they entered as a family unit. This policy was particularly hard on elderly married couples – and

---

248 The Work House Test Act, 1723. Between 1723 and 1750, 600 parish workhouses were built.

249 The Relief of the Poor Act or Gilberts Act, 1782.

250 Chorlton-upon-Medlock, Ardwick, Openshaw, Gorton, Levenshulme, Burnage, Hulme, Stretford, Moss Side, Chorlton-cum-Hardy, Withington, Didsbury and Rusholme.

251 Roughly where Albermarle Road runs towards the Green.

252 The second Chartist petition included an attack on the Poor Law system, and during the 1842 General Strike, following Parliament's rejection of that petition, Stockport Workhouse was attacked. This level of fear persisted into the 20th century. As late as the 1960s there were still many older working people who shuddered at the thought of the workhouse despite the fact that they had been abolished in 1930. Many who trace their family history come up against family members who were either born in the workhouse or spent some time there.

253 Many of these were reissued along with other anti-Poor Law material by the radical G.R. Wythen Baxter in his *The Book of the Bastilles*, 1841, John Stephens. It is available as a Google download.

254 Dickens, Charles, *Oliver Twist*, 1837–38, , Penguin edn, pp.12–13.

255 In 1843 Jonathan Pereira examined the workhouse diets along with those of the army, navy and prisons, and concluded that the inmates received 'an adequate supply of wholesome food'. Pereira, Jonathan, *A Treatise on Food and Diet*, J. and H. G. Langley, 1843. This observation is supported by the work of a group of dieticians drawing on contemporary accounts and modern research. Smith, L., Thornton, S.J., Reinarz, J., Williams, A.N., 'Please, sir, I want more', *British Medical Journal*, 17 December 2008, BMJ 2008,337.a2722.

of the seventeen couples in the workhouse in the summer of 1841 most were in their sixties – but it was no less hard on those with young families.

The Stretford Road Workhouse was in the heart of Hulme, just over 3 miles away.[256] For anyone from Chorlton this must have seemed a forbidding place. On all sides there were close-packed terraced houses punctuated by timber yards and cotton mills, a far cry from the fields and woodland of the township. The prevailing sound was of many machines engaged in ceaseless noisy activity, while there was an ever-present pall of smoke from countless domestic chimneys and factories. The isolation from all that was familiar was reinforced by the harshness of the workhouse. For both sick and healthy inmates the regime was bleak and austere. There were twelve exercise yards for the 300 inmates, each dedicated to a particular group.

In 1841 there were sixty-six children in the workhouse. What constituted a child had been set down in 1834: females under sixteen were girls, while males below the age of thirteen were treated as boys; those under seven were regarded as a separate class. Forty-two of the children were on their own,[257] while twenty-four had been admitted with their mothers, who were mostly in their thirties or forties and alone. Most had two or more children. Mothers were supposed to have access to their children and in certain circumstances children under seven could be left with their mother and even share her bed, but this was difficult if they were in different institutions, and the length of contact depended on the guardians. The children's ages ranged from just a few days to fifteen years. Some were there with siblings; some were completely alone. Some were orphans or deserted children, while others were illegitimate; some had been abandoned because of various disabilities.[258] During the period 1831 to 1835, 8,650 children were picked up off Manchester's streets and deemed to have been deserted, while in 1835 in Salford 471 children were recorded as lost: only 138 were found.[259]

The guardians could keep in an orphan under the age of sixteen if they determined that on release the child was in danger. Well might these children have abandoned all hope, for in a real sense they were lost to all but the officials of the institution – and even those

256 It stood on the island formed by Leaf Street, Stretford New Road, Nelson Street and Devonshire Street. It was replaced by the Withington Workhouse built in 1855. In 1858–60 the Manchester & Salford Baths and Laundries Company opened their third public baths on the site. The company had been formed in 1855, and built baths in Salford, Mayfield at Ardwick and Victoria Park. Its assets were bought by Manchester Corporation in 1877. The company added a Turkish bath in 1860, which was the first in a public baths in Manchester. The Leaf Street Baths were demolished in the clearances of the 1970s and today the site is open ground.

257 Some, like young Henry German aged two months, had no known birthplace, and one was simply recorded as 'unknown boy, 18 months old'. Together they made up 34 per cent of all the inmates.

258 Dr James Phillips Kay, Assistant Commissioner, had in 1838 recorded that children in the workhouse included 'orphans, or deserted children, or bastards, or children of idiots, or of cripples, or of felons'. Higginbotham, *op. cit.*

259 Data submitted to the House of Commons in September 1835 by the Manchester and Salford Police, quoted by Wheeler, James, *Manchester Its Political, Social & Commercial History, Ancient & Modern*, Whitaker & Co., 1836, p.197, Google edn p.215.

charged with their welfare might not always have been diligent in promoting their needs. So it was with young Mary 'Penny' in November 1841, who had been abducted from a nurse girl in Hulme, left with another child a few streets away for a penny and ended in the workhouse on Stretford New Road as an orphan, where she languished for eleven months.[260] The admission book showed no record of the baby's entry into the workhouse and the official position was that such events were improbable. This may well have sealed her fate, but for the persistence of her parents combined with the testimony of an inmate, which resulted in the baby's release. It is a bizarre and unusual story, but one that points up more than a hint of what could happen to those with no voice or influence.

Many in the institution were old. After a lifetime of hard work, struggling with low wages punctuated by periods of unemployment and ill health, many were forced into the workhouse as a last resort.[261] So it was for Ellen Warburton who in April 1861 was eighty-five years old and seeking assistance. Her story may be typical. She was born in Chorlton in 1776 and retained her independence well into her sixties, running a home that she shared with her teenage grandson. By 1851 Ellen, aged seventy-five, was living in the home of a married grandson. A decade later the family had moved to Manchester, and Ellen was in the workhouse.

It is only when we peel back the figures and begin to follow the guardians' own policy of segregating the inmates by sex that the full picture emerges. In the summer of 1841 the single largest group was adult women who (as we have seen) often entered the workhouse with children.[262] Many may have been there as a direct result of the emigration of their husbands. In June 1842 the *Morning Chronicle*, reporting on the slump in trade, wrote that 'Chorlton Workhouse is filled with the wives and families of men going or have gone to America in quest of employment ... Emigration is going on extensively.'[263] This was a policy that was actively pursued by the Poor Law commissioners, with parochial aid or assistance from local landlords. The commissioners reported that over 2, 000 people had gone to Canada in 1841, which was an increase on the year before, and that assistance was also being given to move to Australia and New Zealand.[264] There was also a trend for 'men quitting England and procuring a passage to the United States, leaving their families to be forwarded to the country by the parish officers or private individuals'.[265] Not unsurpris-

---

260 The young girl was the daughter of Mr and Mrs Shore, who were shopkeepers on Florence Street in Hulme. She was abducted and then abandoned.

261 In June 1841, 35 per cent of all the inmates were over sixty, 34 per cent under the age of sixteen and just 31 per cent between sixteen and fifty-nine.

262 Once these groups are further broken down by gender, 22 per cent of the inmates were women between the ages of sixteen and fifty-nine, followed by boys and old men on 19 per cent. Men in the sixteen to fifty-nine grouping made up just 9 per cent of the total.

263 *Morning Chronicle*, 11 June 1842.

264 *The Eighth Annual Report of the Poor Law Commissioners*, HMSO, 1842, p.37, Google edn p.58.

265 *ibid.*, p.38, Google edn p.59.

ingly the commissioners expressed 'our strong opinion of the inexpediency of rendering the assistance to the families of persons so circumstanced which is the object of the parties to obtain the desertion of their families'.[266]

Throughout the 19th century it is doubtful that many attached any stigma to applying or receiving parish relief. It was regarded as a matter of course in most parishes, a right for the aged and more generally one of the strategies that might have to be employed by all.[267] Even so, this did not mean that entry into the workhouse was a favoured choice. Conditions could be Spartan at best and usually harsh – but many used it as a short-term solution. Later in the century Flora Thompson wrote of a woman who took herself and her children into the local workhouse for a month when her husband was sentenced to prison for wife beating. Others might be admitted when ill or pregnant or when there was no other source of support. How easy it was for anyone from this group to descend from gainful employment to inmate is evidenced by the case of Elizabeth Pearson. She was born in Chorlton in 1822 and her early years were spent with her parents on the Row. She was a domestic servant, and gave birth in the workhouse as an unmarried mother in 1855.

Those asking for relief expected to be set to work. Well-known images of inmates crushing stones or picking oakum are a vivid reminder of the principle that Poor Law relief came at a price. But some of the Unions explored alternatives, particularly for able-bodied men. In the early days of the new Poor Law, schemes were put in place to encourage the migration of rural workers to the industrial centres of the North, but these foundered during trade recessions. The Chorlton Union had high hopes of its farm on Trafford Moss, which was started in 1840 as an experiment in 'employing the able bodied poor applying for relief in reclaiming and cultivating a portion of waste land, by means of spade and husbandry'.[268] Trafford Moss is about a mile from Stretford and 3 miles from the Chorlton Union workhouse in Hulme. The land belonged to the Trafford family, who gave it to the Union rent free, and given the improvements that were made to the area the Traffords did well. In two years 9½ acres were drained, 'heavily marled and worked by the paupers of the Union', and in the summer of 1842 were 'covered with crops of wheat, potatoes and turnips, which are not to be surpassed on the best managed farms in the best cultivated county in England'.[269] The experiment created much interest, both in the press and with

266 *Ibid.*, p.38, Google edn p.59.
267 Reay, *op. cit.*, p.81. Charles Booth had commented in 1894 on the acceptance of relief by the old, and in his work Seebohm Rowntree had shown the recurrent waves of poverty in a labourer's life.
268 'Employment of the Pauper Population', *Newcastle Courant*, 22 July 1842.
269 *Ibid.*

other Unions.[270] Extravagant claims were made for the improvement in rent that could be obtained for the land and also the value of the produce grown, with the promise that there should be no 'insuperable difficulty in bringing ten acres of land into cultivation every year in every poor law union in the Kingdom by means of pauper labour'.[271] This was perhaps the sticking point, because the paupers themselves were less than happy. Some of them complained to the commissioners of the 6-mile round trip they had to walk, on the inadequate meals they were given or the fact that 'a portion of us are either far advanced in years, crippled, or labouring under some bodily or mental infirmity, and as part of our quota has already been laid up sick in the workhouse'.[272] Supporters argued that as a works scheme it did not set itself up in competition with industry or undercut wages, but its real advantage was that it tested an applicant's determination to work and thereby their eligibility for relief. The *Newcastle Courant* reported that 'hundreds of persons who have applied for relief, stating that they were quite destitute, and who have received orders for employment on their Union farm, have never gone near it, or have left it after earning a single week's wages, thus relieving the Union, and at the same time confessing themselves to be imposters'.[273] As the *Manchester Times and Gazette* pointed out, this was not exactly fair or realistic, given that most of those directed to work on Trafford Moss were not agricultural workers. A pauper had to walk to the farm 'on a cold and wet morning' and was 'engaged on the damp moss till his dinner hour comes; goes into a small wooden shed to eat his morsel of bread and rancid cheese and turns out again to renew his labour on the wet peat earth'.[274]

The scheme folded in 1848. Detractors argued that the sums paid out, ranging from 1s to 1s 4½d, made it unprofitable, although there was disagreement about the number employed and the cost.[275] Defenders continued to praise the scheme, but accepted that it was not a viable solution to large-scale destitution.

There were other alternatives to the workhouse as well. Mutual self-help was important in protecting the working classes against sickness and death, while also ensuring that they could manage on their wages. At one level this involved individuals banding together to buy produce in bulk, which could then be sold cheaply to the participants. Initiatives like this

270 The Preston Union and Sheffield Union were interested and Sheffield set up a farm at Hollow Meadows, 7 miles from Sheffield on the Glossop Road. It was more ambitious in that it covered 50 acres of moorland rented from the Duke of Norfolk at 4s an acre for twenty-one years, *Lloyd's Weekly Newspaper*, 12 August 1849.

271 '... the land a mere bog, not worth a shilling an acre ... is now worth 30s a year ... while the crops are worth £10 an acre.' *Newcastle Courant*, 22 July 1842.

272 'Treatment of Paupers', *Lloyd's Weekly Newspaper*, 22 February 1846.

273 *Newcastle Courant*, 22 July 1842.

274 *Manchester Times and Gazette*, 16 July 1842.

275 The *Preston Guardian* of 15 April 1848 asserted that 553 people had been engaged as labourers during 1847 at a cost of £1,067, while the *Liverpool Mercury* of 18 April 1849 put the figure at 2,569 'men, women and children [who] maintained at an average cost of £5 1s. 3d. per head'.

predated the co-operative experiment of the Rochdale Pioneers in 1844, and can be traced back through Chartist shops to Robert Owen and the Fenwick Weavers Society of 1769.[276]

At the same time trade unions, friendly societies and religious groups offered sick and benefit schemes based on a mutual fund that members contributed to and could draw on in times of need. The distinction between these groups could be vague. When trade unions were made illegal many described themselves as friendly societies. In the same way the early friendly societies acted as trade unions, supporting members who were in conflict with employers. Not unnaturally temperance and religious groups provided similar services.[277] As well as mutual insurance they might offer pensions, savings and loans, and like trade unions offered assistance for members who were travelling to look for work. These mutual self-help organisations were an expression of local community action. They were set up and run by those with little economic power, low status and by and large no political influence.

Here in Chorlton the Methodists set up a sick and burial club in 1836. There was a sliding scale of benefits depending on the amount contributed. A sick member could expect a payment of 6s if he had a balance of £2; this rose to 7s if the balance was £3 and then an extra 1s for every additional pound. There was also a death payment of £8 for the member and £6 for the death of a wife. These payments did not compare favourably with the other sick and burial clubs that operated in the township. The Old Men and Old Women's clubs, which dated back to the beginning of the 19th century, both paid out 8s a week based on a quarterly contribution of 2s 6d. Another two handed out 10s a week, with a death payment of £10 based on payments of 1s 6d and 1s 4d a month. The Methodists included strict rules about poor behaviour and intemperance, which could result in fines or a complete cessation of benefits – particularly if the illness had been brought on by 'intemperance or an irregular course of life',[278] and a member could only receive a death payment for his first wife. The full payments only lasted for the first twenty-six weeks before being halved. The Methodists were not alone in instituting rules that governed the behaviour of members. The Didsbury Female Friendly Society, set up in 1799, had similar strictures 'to suppress and discourage vice, profaneness and immorality and promote virtue, industry, piety, honesty, decency and sobriety, to the Glory of God, her own welfare and the honour of her

276 The Chartists had a co-operative shop in Hulme at 10 Melbourne Street in 1840 selling a 4lb loaf for 7d run by the Hulme & Chorlton Joint Stock Provision Company, *Northern Star*, 7 November 1840. Robert Owen advocated co-operation. The Fenwick Weavers Society had been created in 1761 in the village of Fenwick in East Ayrshire to foster higher standards in weaving but expanded into collective purchasing of bulk food items and books. See *Co-operative News*, 19 December 2008.

277 In Scotland in 1810 the Revd Henry Duncan established a small bank to encourage his congregation to develop thrift, while the Sons of Temperance Friendly Society began in 1860.

278 Ellwood, chapter 17, 1886.

country'.[279] The Methodist club did not meet in a pub like the other clubs. This was not just a moral choice, but may have reflected the fact that two of the clubs expected members to pay 3d a week from the quarterly payment of 2s 6d to the publican as drink money in lieu of rent to the publican. This was a common feature of many of the friendly and mutual clubs and societies, and the enforced contribution made for a lively end to meetings on club night. Annual dinners, which were compulsory and cost 1s, created a bond between members. Thomas Ellwood, writing in 1886, commented that 'on club nights the hotel was a great resort for men of the village, who assembled to sing to, and in other ways amuse the opposite sex', and given that not all who made the contribution were there for its drinking 'it is scarcely a matter of surprise that the members who remained usually went home the worse for liquor'.[280]

There is no doubt that in the absence of a modern welfare service and with only parish relief to fall back on such schemes were attractive. The Chorlton-cum-Hardy Wesleyan Friendly Society lasted for forty-six years while the Old Men and Old Women's clubs both collapsed in the late 1830s after the embezzlement of their funds which left a need for a non-religious sick club. This vacuum was filled by the Conservative Club, which may have been founded in the 1840s and met at the Bowling Green. Members subscribed 1s 6d a month and received 10s per week during illness and £10 on the death of a member. Like the earlier clubs it retained the same drinking customs and annual dinner. A second club was formed in 1843 as the Odd Fellows Lodge, which had been established in Urmston before moving first to the Horse and Jockey in Chorlton and later to the Bowling Green.[281] It was still operating in 1847.

Certain charities were founded in the 18th century to help selected members of the township. For example, when Margaret Usherwood died in 1742 she left money for the instruction and clothing of six poor children, who would receive this help over four years. The trust ensured that their school fees were paid, so the boys were taught to read and write and the girls to read and sew. They were also provided with new clothes every two years.[282] Like many such charities the terms were very precise. The parents of the six 'should or did when living, frequent the Chorlton Chapel, and more particularly bear the surnames of Warburton and Williamson'.[283] If any of the children failed to attend services

279 Million, Ivor, *A History of Didsbury*, J. Morten, 1969, p.101.

280 Ellwood, chapter 25, 1886.

281 It was started by Samuel Cottrell, G. Beswick and John Johnson, and met in the Lord Nelson pub in Urmston. It amalgamated with the Conservative Club in 1862, and by the 1880s was meeting in the Reading Room on Beech Road, by which time it had £700 invested in Salford Corporation and over £200 in the Manchester & Salford Bank. Ellwood, chapter 25, 1886.

282 This included a blue gown, blue cap and a pair of stockings, along with a shirt and pair of shoes.

283 The will of Margaret Usherwood, made on 23 August 1742, proved at Chester on 2 April 1773, from *Further Report of the Commissioners for Inquiring Concerning Charities*, HMSO, 1826, p.190, Google edn p.195.

regularly they no longer received the assistance. Such conditions do not sit easily with most of us today; nor that the clothes provided were a uniform blue and the children were expected to sit in special seats close to the altar. Charity might be pleasing in the eyes of God, but how much better that the community should always see and remember Margaret Usherwood's generosity. Even so, provision of help to the needy in this manner is still help, and it eased the struggle of those in poverty. Such charities were common in the 17th and 18th centuries, and Chorlton shared two others with the neighbouring townships.[284] Such bequests did not always turn out the way the dying intended; in some cases they were so ill defined that they were challenged in law or quietly forgotten by future generations. But the most serious problem was that the money left could not keep up with inflation. Margaret Usherwood recognised that at some point there might be a shortfall, and stipulated that if necessary the trustees 'only nominate so many poor children as might by the yearly interest be clothed and instructed'.[285] And so it was that during the early part of the 19th century this was limited to the provision of clothes for just two children and for a while only the school fees of six. By 1886 the interest was paid directly into the school fund. Nor was it easy to secure trustees. Of the three trustees in 1826, James Gresty was eighty-five and Thomas Taylor had never acted in the trust's management, and was anxious to be discharged. Later in the century there were no trustees.

We should not forget the ad hoc and individual examples of help offered by the better-off to those in need here in Chorlton. No records have survived, but the doing of good works was an expected duty of the well-to-do. Mrs Beeton advised her readers that 'Visiting the houses of the poor is the only practical way really to understand the actual state of each family; there will be opportunities for advising and instructing them, in a pleasant and unobtrusive manner, in cleanliness, industry, cookery, and good management.'[286] How far our families of plenty followed this advice is not known, of course. William and Jane Cunliffe Brooks, who lived at Barlow Hall from 1848, were generous benefactors, and it may well be that they provided for the needy, as might have the daughters of John Holt of Beech House and the equally well-off Morton and Cope families. However, it is most likely that the less well-off and those faced with a temporary crisis did what the poor have always done and sought help from their family and friends. Ann Jordrill was looked after by one of her grandchildren, John Sutton was taken in by his son when he became infirm and Martha Deakin fell back on the sick and burial club when she was widowed.

---

284 These were a fund left by Sir Edward Mosley in 1695 to be distributed 'amongst poor persons not receiving relief' across five townships including Chorlton and a fund left by Dame Ann Bland again for the 'benefit of poor householders within the townships of Withington, Didsbury, Chorlton, Burnage and Heaton Norris, and such person not in the receipt of parish relief on account of sickness, accident, age or having a numerous family'.
285 *Further Report of the Commissioners for Inquiring Concerning Charities*, HMSO, 1830, p.190, Google edn p.195.
286 Beeton, *op. cit.*, p.6, Google edn p.55.

nine

CHILDREN

School, Sunday school, work and play

I n 1847 Chorlton's village school was just two years old. It was the second National School, replacing the first which had been established on the Green in 1817. These were church schools and provided elementary education for the children of the poor. They were the product of the National Society, which had begun in 1811 and aimed to establish a National School in every parish delivering a curriculum based on the teaching of the Church.

The new school had been built with grants from the National Society and the Committee of Council on Education[287] on land given by the local landowner George Lloyd in 1843 'for the purpose of a school for the education of poor children inhabiting the said township of Chorlton-cum-Hardy ... and for the residence of the master of the said school for the time being, such schoolmaster to be a member of the Established Church, and the school to be conducted upon principles consistent with the doctrines of the Established Church'.[288] It was a fine brick building, which could hold 300.

In Chorlton at this time there were 186 children between the ages of four and fifteen: most were at school, a few were educated at home and fifteen were already at work. The youngest of these, aged just ten, was Catherine Kirby, who was born in Ireland and worked as a house servant. The rest were engaged in a range of jobs, from errand boy to farmworker and domestic service. There were slightly more boys than girls and most were born here. There may have been more working, for when William Chesshyre interviewed their parents

---

287 The Committee of the Council on Education was set up in 1839, six years after the first State grants for education had been voted and paid through the National Society, and the British and Foreign School Society. The Committee of the Council on Education gave £150 and the National Society £75.

288 Ellwood, chapter 13, 1886.

in March 1851 some children were described as farmers' sons and daughters. They may have been at school or they may have already begun to work alongside their parents.[289] And, as we shall see, just because parents described their children as scholars was no guarantee they attended school, or even if they did that they were there full time. Many would spend some time working the fields. Seasonal work on the land for children was just part of the rural cycle. One contributor to the Poor Law commissioners on the employment of women and children in agriculture in 1843 said it taught children 'the habit of industry',[290] which fitted in with the belief much held in the countryside that 'the business of a farm labourer cannot be thoroughly acquired if work be not commenced before eleven or twelve'.[291] Despite this, most of Chorlton's children were probably in school for at least some of the time.

In 1851 it was estimated that nationally 61 per cent of all children were in a school.[292] Actual attendances varied enormously. In private schools the number of children attending on any particular day was 91 per cent of the number who should have been there, while in public schools that catered for the labouring classes the number in attendance was 79 per cent.[293] No attendance figures have survived for Chorlton, but attendance figures for south Manchester (which formed the Chorlton Poor Law Union and included our school) are extant. These show that on Friday 29 March 1851 the attendance was 83 per cent.[294] This is not a good attendance figure judged by the expectations of modern schools, but could still be misleading – because March is a quiet time in agricultural areas and if the same count had been done when crops needed picking and the harvest brought in the figure might have been lower.

More boys attended school in south Manchester than girls. While there were 3,286 boys on the books of the thirty-five public schools, only 2,028 girls were registered. In Chorlton it seems there was little difference.

A rigid and austere style of teaching was the order of the day. There was strict discipline and much learning by rote: a passer-by standing on the Green outside the school would have heard repetitive chanting as the children repeated a prepared text row by row. Inside, hanging from the walls, there were embroidered verses extolling the virtues of thrift and hard work. Despite this grim scene there was much that could stimulate eager

---

289 The picture is clouded somewhat by the failure of William Chesshyre to record anything beside the names of fifty-nine children aged between four and fifteen, to describe twenty-five as son or daughter of the householder, another three as with no occupation, and finally two at home.

290 Evidence of Mr Austin on Wiltshire schools, *Reports of the Special Assistant Poor Law Commissioners on the employment of women & children in agriculture*, HMSO, 1843, p.38.

291 *Census of Great Britain on Education*, HMSO, 1851, p.19, Google edn p.27.

292 The exact number of children between three and fifteen was calculated as 4,908,696, and after taking out those estimated as working, educated at home or ill the figure of those in a school was 3,015,405. From the *Census of Great Britain on Education*, 1851 *op. cit.*, p.23, Google edn p.30.

293 *Ibid.*, p.27, Google edn p.35.

294 *Ibid.*, Table L, Numbers of scholars attending compared with number on the books, in registration districts, p.37.

imaginations. There were stirring tales of faraway lands and dramatic episodes from the Old Testament, which had the power to transport the young listeners. Although the curriculum focused primarily on the basics of reading, writing and arithmetic, it also included languages, music, drawing and geography.[295] The degree to which these were taught varied from subject to subject, and there was a gender split: while almost all boys and girls were taught the three Rs, 10 per cent of boys received tuition in mathematics compared with 4 per cent for girls. In contrast 46 per cent of girls were instructed in industrial occupations compared with 3.6 per cent of boys. These opportunities were further defined by the fault line of class: boys and girls from private schools were more likely to study both modern and ancient foreign languages, mathematics and music than their counterparts in the public sector.

It was with some concern that the report to Parliament of the 1851 Census on Education commented:

To find in the schools a large proportion of the children learning the mere rudiments of knowledge, while a small proportion only is engaged upon the higher branches, must be looked upon as an unfavourable sign ... when it is remembered that, of those who appear to have engaged in the more advanced departments of instruction, a majority were probably belonging to the upper and middle classes ... the children of the working classes go to school while very young, and remain but a very scanty period.'[296]

This picture was complicated by the wide differences in ages among those who attended Chorlton's National School. Of those who might have attended in March 1851, under a quarter were five or younger, just over a half between the ages of six and ten and more than a quarter aged eleven to fifteen.[297] The conventional way of dealing with this was to employ monitors or pupil teachers alongside the school teacher. These were abler students who passed on what they had already learned, and learnt how to teach on the job.[298] It was a way of training working-class children for responsible jobs, and a cheap way of extending primary school education: in 1851 a male National School teacher received £1 a week, his female counterpart 6s and a monitor or pupil teacher just 1s. But there were critics who pointed out that the system encouraged larger class sizes, and that monitors were no

---

295 The full list taught in National Schools was reading, writing, arithmetic, English grammar, modern languages, ancient languages, mathematics, drawing, music and industrial occupations.

296 *Census of Great Britain on Education*, 1851, *op. cit.*, p.29, Google edn p.37.

297 21 per cent were five or younger, 52 per cent between the ages of six and ten, 27 per cent aged eleven to fifteen.

298 The system was developed independently by Dr Andrew Bell and Joseph Lancaster. Bell was an Anglican who received support from the Church of England and the National Society, while Lancaster was a Quaker and was funded by the Nonconformist organisation, the British and Foreign Schools Society.

substitute for better trained teachers.[299] The school may also have had a second teacher to teach the infants, but again names have not come down to us until 1850, when Eliza Johnson was employed to teach the infants alongside James Bugden, who taught the older children. The following year John and Ann Ellison were in the school on the Green, and were still there in 1852.[300] Not until 1861 do the names of pupil teachers appear in the records: these are Elizabeth and Martha Gresty, aged sixteen and thirteen, who lived at Martledge with their parents, who made a living as market gardeners.

As ever, concern revolved around standards. The authors of the 1851 Census on Education fell back on the simple test of how many people were able to sign their marriage certificate against those who put a cross or mark. The 'test of marriage marks' was not in itself an over accurate form of assessment, as the report pointed out that 'the art of writing is with great facility forgotten by the poor who find no application for it, while for various causes some who can write nevertheless decline to sign the register'.[301] It showed, however, that the number of people signing with a mark had been progressively dropping from 1839.[302]

Before 1817, when the first National School was built, the Methodist day school was run on the Row by James Renshaw, whose discipline ran from 'strict to severe, especially with scholars not in his favour'.[303] He struck boys on the head with his cane and then applied cobwebs to stop the bleeding, and in the case of William Rhodes he nearly cut off one of the lad's fingers, after throwing a penknife at him when he put his hand on the desk while standing during a lesson. Not that Renshaw always played the dignified pillar of village society. Despite his formidable personality, he could still be bested by his students. In a story still told thirty or so years after his death, James Renshaw was the butt of a schoolboy prank. Each morning one of the schoolboys had the task of collecting the teacher's breakfast from his home and bringing it to the school. His home was a little further up the Row. One morning the conspirators elected Charles Brundrett to bury the spoon and throw the bowl into Blomley's Fishpond opposite the school.[304] While young Charles Brundrett was engaged on this enterprise, one of the class 'split' to Renshaw, who rushed out to prevent the deed happening. Not only did he fail, but on returning he was

---

299 In 1827 David Stow had set up a training school for teachers in Glasgow followed by another in 1836, and both were driven by the idea that teachers at all levels should receive the most effective training.

300 On 18 January they baptised their son Charles John in the parish church.

301 *Census of Great Britain on Education*, 1851, *op. cit.*, p.33, Google edn p.40.

302 In 1839 it was 41.6 per cent, 1840 42 per cent, 1841 40.8 per cent and in 1851 38 per cent. While there was a 4 per cent fall in the numbers of men and women who used their mark, this hid a disparity between the sexes. Men using their mark dropped from 33.7 per cent in 1839 to 30.8 per cent in 1851, while in women it fell from 49.5 per cent to 45.3 per cent. *Census of Great Britain on Education*, 1851, *op. cit.*, p.32, Google edn p.40.

303 Ellwood, chapter 24, 1886.

304 The water ran from where Acres Road joins Beech Road up to just before Wilton Road. Ellwood, chapter 24. Elizabeth Blomley, gentlewoman was living in Chorlton in the mid- to late 1820s.

refused admittance without the promise of a holiday, a tactic repeated by the boys on other occasions and supplemented by hiding their teacher's pipe and tobacco. Charles Brundrett suffered no long-term effects from his prank and grew up to run Oak Farm. Nothing so dramatic would have occurred at the other private school, run by Mary Taylor at Clough Farm at Martledge.[305]

In 1834 Renshaw was listed in a local directory as running a school in Chorlton, and in 1841 described himself as schoolmaster. By 1851, aged seventy-nine, he had retired, and by 1852 he was buried in the grounds of the Wesleyan chapel.[306] Sadly no records of the fees for Renshaw's establishment have survived, but over in Stretford in the early decades of the 19th century Mr Johnson charged '3d. to 8d. per week with 1d. extra for fire money in the winter. The scholars were allowed one quill a week and had to pay ½d. each for any more.'[307] These fees were not cheap, being beyond the means of farm labourers. Schooling provided by James Renshaw and Mr Johnson was limited to the children of farmers and tradesmen. Johnson, like Renshaw, was 'a perfect Squeers, inventing all kinds of queer punishments, and in one case made a lad eat a bad exercise he had written'.[308] Given the harshness of the times, many parents may not have deemed such behaviour as excessive, especially if the child was being well educated.

There was also a Sunday school. The first was set up by the Methodists in August 1805 and was held in the chapel. Later it moved to a building across the road, which had been built from subscriptions the Methodists had raised. When this building was lost the Sunday school returned to the chapel.[309]

Like all new movements the Methodists were proud of their message and were keen to share it with the township. From 1818 the children of the Sunday school set off each Whitsuntide to process around the village. The procession was headed by members of the chapel orchestra who, with a mix of violins, flutes and clarinets, accompanied the children – who visited the homes of Methodist families and sang them hymns. It is still possible to plot the snaking line of musicians and children dressed in white along the Row, where Thomas Baguley lived, to the grocer's shop of Jeremiah Brundrett and the cottage and orchard of George Lunt at Lane End, before heading down High Lane to George Grantham's. The party would have entertained William Griffiths on Lloyd Street before standing on the Green at the homes of Thomas Renshaw and Farmer James Higginbotham, then proceeding past the parish church and following the route of the brook to Oak Farm.

305 Pigot's Directory, 1834, p.68, Historical Directories p.337.
306 Pigot, 1834, p.68, Historical Directories p.337, 1841 census, Enu. 8, p.5, 1851 census, Enu. 1 p.11.
307 Leech, Sir Bosdin, Old Stretford, Manchester City News Co. Ltd, 1910, p.38.
308 Ibid., p.38.
309 Ellwood wrote in 1886 that the Wesleyans failed to convey the building to trustees and that it was sold to Thomas Taylor. He charged them rent until 1827, when they were given notice to leave and the building was converted into cottages. The land was retained by the Lloyd estate.

The parish church followed with a Sunday school some years later. Neither school has left detailed records, but both would have followed a similar routine. This allowed for two sessions, one beginning at about 9 or 9.30am and a second in the afternoon at about 2pm:

> On each occasion school is opened with devotional exercises – such as singing, reading of the Scriptures and prayer. Next, the scholars who have committed tasks to memory repeat them. Then the Bible lesson follows: portions of Scripture having been allotted to particular Sundays, scholars are expected to come prepared, by week-day study of the passage for a catechetical examination by the teacher, who on his part ought to come prepared by similar study, to impart the full meaning of the text, and to enforce its doctrines ... The school concludes as it commenced, with singing and prayer – preceded generally, in the afternoon, by a short address from the minister or some person competent to the task.[310]

As in their day school, boys sat on one side and girls on the other. For some, Sunday schools reinforced or even introduced the skill of reading, for while they 'were a religious institution, for the purpose of inculcating religious truth, and exerting a religious influence',[311] students were expected to be able to read the texts. Those who couldn't read were taught from a box of moveable letters that spelt out a scripture verse, which was explained to them.

Across south Manchester 18,320 children were on the books of fifty-eight Sunday schools, but attendance for Sunday 31 March 1851 was down to 71 per cent, with slightly more girls attending than boys. How Chorlton performed is a little more unclear. The parish church recorded forty students attending in the morning and forty-six in the afternoon. The Wesleyans included their Sunday scholars with the general attendance, but by all accounts the school averaged about eighty pupils.

There is no doubt that adults took activities at Sunday schools seriously. When Jeremiah Brundrett junior was Superintendent of the Wesleyan school, he reminded his students when giving out the hymn one morning, 'Now, lads; if jer can't sing these words and mean 'em, yer must hum th' tune and leave 'em.'[312] That said, the schools could also be places of fun. The Methodists held a Christmas tea party from the mid-1820s. This included raisin wine from Mottershead in Manchester, which was carried in two large stone bottles

---

310 *Census of Great Britain on Education*, 1851, *op. cit.*, p.68, Google edn p.76.

311 *Ibid.*, p.68, Google edn p.76.

312 Mr Lunt, in old age remembering his Sunday school attendance, quoted by Owen, Carter, 'Chorlton-cum-Hardy and its Methodism, A Sunday School Centenary', 18 May 1905, in the collection of The Oxford Centre for Methodism and Church History, Oxford Brookes University.

across the shoulders of Jeremiah Brundrett junior, Joseph Brundrett and others, and currant bread, which was baked in the village and served cut into squares without butter.[313]

Outside school hours there was much to occupy the children's time. The youngest played in cottage gardens and the lanes outside their homes. The older ones were expected to run errands, help around the house and look after their younger brothers and sisters. For those who belonged to farming families there were a whole range of tasks: fields needed constant weeding and root crops lifting, stones picked off the land and birds scared. Animals had to be fed and watered; cows had to be milked. At lunchtimes it might fall to one of the children to take the midday meal to where the work was being done. Dairy farmers like James Higginbotham provided milk for local homes, which his young daughter aged just eight would have to deliver. But all this still left time to wander and explore. There were the woods that still covered 10 acres of the township, including the magical stretch called the Cliffs, which combined water and woodland running alongside Chorlton Brook from the village east towards Oak House and Barlow Moor Lane.[314]

313 Ellwood, chapter 18, 1886.
314 Today these are the gardens of the houses that run along Brookburn Road.

ten

HOUSING

Wattle and daub, sanitation, rents, overcrowding, brick built terraces,
farmers' homes and the houses of the well-off

A walk across Chorlton in the summer of 1847 would have revealed very different forms of housing. There were the modest and in some cases dilapidated homes of the majority, either traditional wattle and daub cottages or newer terraces of brick houses. There were the more robust homes of farming families and finally the much grander homes of the wealthy. There may still have been more than fifty wattle and daub houses at this time. They were constructed from a timber framework with walls made of branches woven together and covered with a mixture of clay, gravel, hay and even horse hair, and topped with a thatched roof.[315] Such houses were easy to build and equally easy to maintain, but there could be disadvantages: the porous nature of walls meant they were damp, and crumbling clay meant endless repairs. This in turn meant that they could be very cold in winter, while the thatched roofs might harbour a multitude of vermin.

Floors made of brick or stone were laid directly on the ground and were almost invariably damp, and in the worst cases ran with moisture.[316] Once the brick was broken the floor became uneven and bare earth was exposed. This was compounded when the cottage floor was below the ground outside or the floor was uneven, which caused drainage problems. Even the proudest wife and mother must have been reconciled to damp and dirt. The only heating was from an open fire. When the coal or wood was damp the smell permeated every room in the house. During the winter months the unheated bedrooms were particularly unpleasant places, and on the coldest nights ice formed on the inside of windows.

---

315 Ellwood, chapter 4, 1885.
316 This practice continued well into the last half of the 19th century in Chorlton, and one house on Copgrove Road built in the early 20th century only replaced its bare brick floor as that century came to an end.

Many rural cottages had just two rooms. This example was on the site of the church on Maitland Avenue and was demolished in the 1930s. As with many cottages of the time the privy was outside, in this case at the rear.

Cottages of this design were often limited to four rooms, and some had only two, with the family living downstairs and sleeping on the upper floor. In some cases access to the bedroom was by ladder rather than stairs, and in many cases bedrooms were left open, giving little in the way of privacy. As for sanitation, this would have been equally primitive. Nationally the rural picture was grim, with privies often draining into open channels that themselves got blocked with refuse, flowing too slowly to allow the waste to disperse.

Samuel and Sarah Sutton brought up their two children in one of two adjoining cottages on the Row. The white walls and wooden beams were partly obscured by ivy and the front door was approached through a small country garden. Behind the house and away from the view of strangers stood the privy and the back garden, where the Suttons grew fruit, vegetables and flowers.[317]

The biggest concentration of such houses was along the Row and around the Green, but in the mid-19th century many were fast disappearing. Some, like those of the Johnsons and the Bythells, were demolished to make way for the National School, while others were replaced by brick terraces. These were built to serve the rising population, which began to increase in the 1820s.[318]

317 Suttons Cottage stood on the corner of Beech Road and Wilton Road, until it was demolished in 1891 soon after Sarah Sutton died.
318 Between 1821 and 1831 the population rose by forty-four, and by thirty-six in the next decade, before leaping up by 129 from 1841–51 and thereafter falling.

There are no examples of these two-roomed farm cottages left in Chorlton. This is the interior of the Maitland Avenue cottage: the downstairs room had a range.

The same room, showing the opposite wall, the entrance to the staircase and the steep angle of the stairs.

The upstairs room, showing the stove. Farm cottages like this one did not often have heating upstairs.

The upstairs room may have served as a bedroom for the entire family. It has been impossible to discover this cottage's residents before 1900, but similar houses were home to large families.

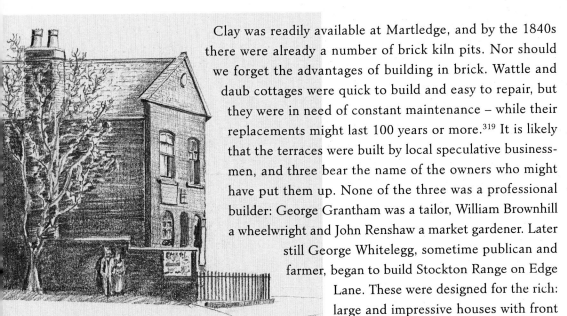

Clay was readily available at Martledge, and by the 1840s there were already a number of brick kiln pits. Nor should we forget the advantages of building in brick. Wattle and daub cottages were quick to build and easy to repair, but they were in need of constant maintenance – while their replacements might last 100 years or more.[319] It is likely that the terraces were built by local speculative businessmen, and three bear the name of the owners who might have put them up. None of the three was a professional builder: George Grantham was a tailor, William Brownhill a wheelwright and John Renshaw a market gardener. Later still George Whitelegg, sometime publican and farmer, began to build Stockton Range on Edge Lane. These were designed for the rich: large and impressive houses with front and back gardens and servants' quarters.

Renshaw's Buildings at Martledge date from the 1830s, and may have been one-up one-down cottages.

By contrast the terraces of Grantham, Brownhill and Renshaw were modest four-roomed properties designed for working families. Grantham's and Renshaw's Buildings had been built by 1832, as both George Grantham and John Renshaw were qualified to vote in parliamentary elections as freeholders of buildings on High Lane 'in the occupation of William Holland and others' and of buildings in Martledge 'in the occupation of James Kenyon and others'.[320]

These men of enterprise and business drawn from different occupations were making their mark in the township and replicating the actions of other small businessmen 4½ miles away in the city. None was exceptionally wealthy, and it is not known if the projects were entirely funded with their own money or whether they collaborated with others. Their ownership was on a modest scale and in most cases was restricted to a single terrace, but there is no doubting their determination. Thomas Taylor was another landlord, and the postmaster from 1857. He charged the Methodists an annual rent for their Sunday school, but eventually in 1827 served notice on them to quit and the building was converted into

319 Three built in the early part of the century survived into the 20th century and photographs of them exist. Renshaw's at Martledge only went in the mid-1920s and the other two lasted till the 1970s, by which time Brownhill's Buildings were long past their best; they were condemned in 1972 and demolished in 1974.

320 'Voting Register Southern Division of the County of Lancaster Salford Hundred', f324.4272 L1 (1832 and f352.04272La1, 1835, Archive and Local History Library.

four cottages.[321] We have no idea how much the Methodists paid, but the cottage rents amounted to £27 a year.[322] He also had the rent from the building next door, which was the Travellers Rest, which amounted to £13. Other landlords were making even more. In 1845 the Renshaw estate picked up £60 in annual rent from ten cottages, about half the number that John Renshaw had owned before his death a year earlier. George Grantham was paid £50, and just a little later William Brownhill received over £61.[323] These were significant sums, and reflect the way in which some of the local businessmen were diversifying. Most of the remaining landlords can be divided between those whose properties came with the land they had bought or inherited and those who had very few houses. The grandest of the first group were the Egerton and Lloyd estates, followed by Lydia Brown, whose property included the smithy on the Row. Properties were often disposed of *en bloc*, and there are plenty of advertisements announcing the sale of a whole row of cottages. On the death of Charles Bracegirdle his five were disposed of in one sale.[324] The latter group were made up of people like William Chessyre who owned just one cottage for which he charged £4 10s, or Alice Moore, who was an agricultural labourer who received rent of £3.

All these cottages were fairly similar, although there were variations in the design, the quality of materials used and the amount of land they were built on. George Grantham's on High Lane had four rooms, were set back with cottage gardens at the front and an orchard to the rear. They were home to, among others, William Ashcroft, a master slater, employing two men, and the widow Elaine Bankes, who lived on an annuity. The front room and front bedroom were 12ft by 12ft and the rear rooms 12ft by 9ft. The staircase was situated in the back room. The floors were stone-flagged and the front room and bedrooms had plastered walls. Some thought and care had gone into the style of the door and window frames. By contrast Brownhill's Buildings were more modest. They were set back at right angles from the road just down from Lane End and consisted of eleven dwellings with no gardens. Less care was lavished on their appearance: while the entrance to each of Grantham's Buildings had a tall brick arch above the door, Brownhill's Buildings were served by a low and mean brick and timber frame. Nor were the windows any more impressive. Not surprisingly these houses were occupied by domestic workers, agricultural

---

321 The Beech Inn on the corner of Beech and Whitelow Roads may be what is left of the four cottages that were once a Sunday school. From maps and the census return it would seem the four ran along Whitelow Road. Until the late 19th century they occupied the same building line as the adjacent buildings of 68 and 70 Beech Road. In the early 20th century the building became a public house, and may have been altered so that it sat back from the building line.

322 Sarah Jackson paid £9 and seemed to have sub-let part of her property to PC Gilpin and his wife, while James White and James Bates along with a fourth tenant paid £6.

323 Renshaw received £4 10s for eight of his cottages, £5 and £5 10s for another two. Grantham charged between £6 and £11 for his six cottages, and in 1865 the eleven tenants of William Brownhill were each paying £6 15s 3d annually.

324 These were sold as a block on his death in 1865, and were homes to Joshua Warburton, Elizabeth Aldcroft, William Lunt, William Barker and Mr Rowland. *Manchester Guardian*, 16 September 1865.

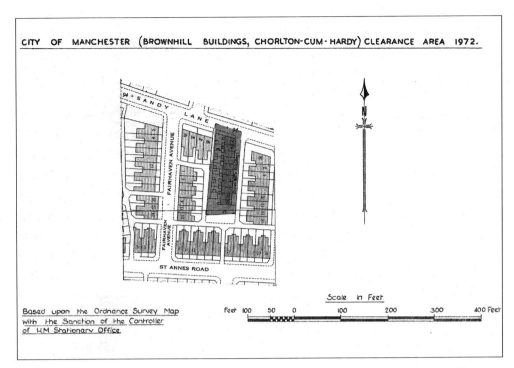

CITY OF MANCHESTER (BROWNHILL BUILDINGS, CHORLTON-CUM-HARDY) CLEARANCE AREA 1972.

Based upon the Ordnance Survey Map with the Sanction of the Controller of H.M. Stationary Office.

Scale in Feet

Brownhill's Buildings were typical of the small brick-built cottages erected by speculative builders during the 1820s and '30s. They were two-up two-down and during the first half of the 19th century were surrounded by fields.

labourers and a shoemaker. John Renshaw seems to have been engaged in something altogether different with his property at Martledge. It too was built at right angles to the road, but its appearance suggests not cottages but a tenement block. This seems to be borne out by the numbers living there during the 1840s and '50s: in 1841 there were fifteen households consisting of fifty-three people, and ten years later there were ten families of forty-five people. Maps show the property as six units of four rooms each, which suggests that some rooms were being sub-let – or perhaps Renshaw's Buildings were in fact one-up one-down dwellings, which were common enough in Manchester. Renshaw's portfolio seems to have been the most extensive. His will, dated 1844, shows that he left eleven cottages to members of his family, along with Renshaw's Buildings.

Cottage rents varied. In 1848 John Hooley was paying James Holt an annual rent of £10, while Richard Pearson paid £8 for his cottage and George Heath (who was a coachman) paid £5. These work out at weekly rents of 3s 8d down to 1s 9d, which might be a substantial part of a family's weekly income – given that the average rural wage in the North West was between 11s and 18s. Rural overcrowding was every bit as bad as its urban equivalent. Surveys by the Board of Agriculture in the early 19th century revealed the degree of overcrowding across England and Wales.

The Poor Law commissioners in 1843 reported that in parts of the South West the level of overcrowding was so severe that some families were forced into agreements with neighbours, whereby the daughters of one family slept with the daughters of another and in return the boys from both families were accommodated in the other house. But this was rare: as the report said, it was more common for 'three or four persons to sleep in the same bed ... the only attempt that is or can be made to separate the beds, with occupants of different sexes, and necessarily placed close together from the smallness of the rooms, is an old shawl or some article of dress suspended as a curtain between them'.[325] This practice might well have happened in Chorlton. One of the surviving farm cottages has a large upstairs room directly off the open staircase, which suggests a curtain might have been used. It was also a common practice in rural areas to send children to live with relatives. During the 1840s Thomas and Susannah Renshaw shared their home on the Green with their two grandchildren; by 1851 eleven families were doing the same. But the data can be a little misleading, for while some of the grandchildren were young others were much older, and in one case may have been working for the family. Likewise there were other households where grandchildren were living with their grandparents because of a widowed or unmarried parent.[326]

In 1841 just under a third of the households on the Row had six or more people living in each house, an arrangement which did not alter much during the rest of the half-century.[327] If the total population of the township is compared with the available housing stock, it amounted to 632 people and 128 houses in 1841, while ten years later it was 761 people and 146 houses.[328]

The homes of our farmers were more comfortable than those of their labourers. Henry Dean farmed 3 acres just outside the village on the lane that ran up to High Lane.[329] He lived in a sturdy brick-built house dating from the 18th century which he shared with his wife and four adult children. It had six rooms and its open staircase led into the main upstairs room. Given that he had two sons and two daughters, the curtain option may well have been employed.

The Bankcrofts of Park Brow Farm could boast an even larger farmhouse, as befitting tenant farmers of 60 acres. Their house had eight rooms. A visitor entered from the south through the garden. Off the hall to the left and right were the main living rooms, with the

---

325 Evidence of Mr Austen, *Report of Special Assistant Poor Law Commissioners on the Employment of Women and Children in Agriculture*, HMSO, 1843, p.19, Google edn p.39.

326 In 1851 there were 115 households, eleven of these had grandchildren, and of these five were under the age of seventeen, two where one of the parents was widowed and two who admitted the parent was unmarried. In all eighteen grandchildren lived with their grandparents.

327 The figure fell from over a third to a quarter by 151, but the figure for homes with five people had risen from 8 to 26 per cent.

328 *Annual Report of Registrar General*, 1851, Population tables, Vol. 11, p.40, www.histpop.org.

329 The house is still there on St Clements Road.

Higginbotham's farmhouse on the Green was the family home from the 1840s. It dates back to the 18th century and was one of the larger farmhouses in the village.

kitchen, pantry and scullery to the rear, and here too were the stairs that led to the upper floor. This was spacious accommodation for a family of six. There were three farmworkers, but it is likely that they slept elsewhere: it was still common for employees to share rooms above the cow shed or barn.[330] James Higginbotham may well have lodged his workers in the farm shippon; certainly later in the century his son did. The Higginbotham farmhouse was large, containing ten rooms. There were five rooms on the ground floor. The hall led past the two front rooms to the staircase up to the bedrooms, while another staircase at the back of the house gave access to a servant's room. On the north side was an outhouse with a cellar and barrel-vaulted ceiling. The ground floors were stone flagged and in the kitchen and pantry were stone benches, which were ideal for keeping food cold. There were small gardens at the back and front, and the family well was in the back garden.

More modest was the home of William and Alice Bailey on the Row. It consisted of four rooms, two up and two down, and was attached to the hay barn. The entire Bailey household possessions amounted to a value of £44 8s. In the kitchen there was the usual mix of cooking pots, saucepans and a frying pan, along with jugs, basins, pots, mugs and a coffee pot. But the prize possession was the Dutch oven, which was a cast-iron cooking pot with a tight lid that was used for slow cooking and could be suspended over an open fire.[331] From the parlour one looked out on the Row and the fields beyond. In this room

---

330 Oliver Bailey, December 2009.

331 Inventory of William Bailey, 1887. We have to be a little careful because some of these may not have been in use during the 1840s. The Bailey collection.

there were a round table, a horsehair sofa and easy chairs. The family kept some of their more precious possessions upstairs. In one bedroom was the four-poster bed, a secretaire (an enclosed writing desk) and their silver, which included a silver cream jug, two silver salt cellars and two silver spoons, coffee and tea pots, four tablespoons and seventeen silver teaspoons. The other bedroom was a little less grand; it contained an iron bedstead.

Any visitor to the township in the 1840s could be excused for ignoring the wattle and daub cottages; nor would the brick rows cause much stir – as similar ones could be seen all over Manchester. Even the farmhouses set among their farm buildings were unlikely to have provoked much interest. What would excite an observer's curiosity were the homes of the wealthy, and while these were nothing in comparison to the ancient piles of Hough End and Barlow Hall, these homes were the grandest in the township.

One of the grandest was Beech Cottage, owned by James Holt. He had made his money from making engraving blocks for calico printing, and the family continued in business well into the century. They had an extensive property portfolio in Manchester, which at one point included most of the houses on the southern side of St John's Street along with more humble dwellings in the neighbouring streets and two public houses. Here in Chorlton he owned 17 acres, making him one of the largest landowners after the Egertons and the Lloyds. His land stretched from Barlow Moor Lane along the Brook

Barlow Hall was the grand house in the township. During the 19th century it was the home of the radical Thomas Walker, the Whig businessman Shakespeare Phillips and from 1848 William Cunliffe Brooks and his family.

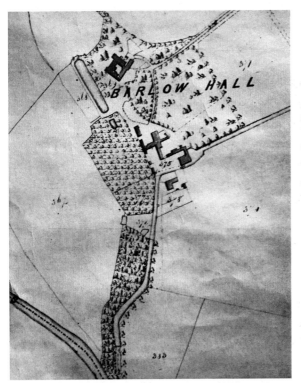

Barlow Hall, 1845. The Hall is to the north and Barlow Hall Farm, home to the Dean family, is to the south. In 1845 Samuel Dean rented 290 acres from the Egerton estate.

towards Hough End. For our inquisitive stranger the real attraction would have been Beech Cottage and the gardens surrounding it. Not that the term cottage does justice to the Holts' home. It was a huge building with an impressive frontage of tall windows and high chimneys, set in its own grounds of an acre and surrounded by high walls. The estate stretched from the corner of the Row along Barlow Moor Lane to Lane End and then down High Lane, before cutting across the fields back to the Row. Tall lines of trees skirted the gardens and hid the family from uninvited gaze.

Equally grand was Oak Bank, situated on the edge of Martledge. This too was set back from the main road and hidden in an extensive garden and orchard, surrounded by meadow and arable land. Once the home of William Morton, by 1847 it was owned by the wine merchant Frederick Cope, who lived there from 1850 to 1855. It consisted of 'three entertaining rooms, six bedrooms, excellent kitchen, scullery, cellars, &c. The outbuildings consist of two coach houses, stabling for four horses, gardener's room, wash house, laundry, &c. There are good gardens well stocked with fruit trees and about three acres.'[332] It had a gross rentable value of £120, rising later to £130, which set it apart as the most expensive domestic property in the township.[333]

Equally desirable was the house that was advertised for sale in the summer of 1836:

A Commodious and tasteful country residence with an adjoining cottage (fitted for a gardener or other outdoor servant), stable, coach house, garden with fountain, greenhouse, tulip beds and other appurtenances, situated in Chorlton-cum-Hardy, and containing in the whole 1400 superficial square yards of land. The situation is airy and healthful, the soil good with fishing streams in the immediate neighbourhood. The house (containing in addition to the usual apartments, a recently erected picture gallery), and the grounds in

---

332 'Valuable Property in Chorlton', *Manchester Guardian*, 28 June 1845.
333 'Chorlton-cum-Hardy Rate Books, 1844–76', Microfilm Rolls 297–9, Local History Library, Manchester.

excellent condition, and the latter elegantly laid out, and abundantly supplied with water at all seasons of the year, and, being within four miles from Manchester Exchange, would constitute an eligible family residence for a gentleman engaged in business.[334]

More accessible were the homes of Daniel Sharp and Mary Holland. These were on the Row, only a short walk from Beech Cottage. Daniel Sharp also described himself as a gentleman of independent means, and his house reflected that wealth. It was a tall two-storeyed building set back from the road and protected by a brick wall. It had ten rooms as well as cellars. Visitors had to climb a series of stone steps before reaching the elegant front door, beyond which was the hall leading to the main living rooms and the staircase. From any of his front windows Daniel could look out on open fields with an uninterrupted view to High Lane, while at the rear of his garden were meadows and an orchard.

Strictly speaking, Lime Bank and Charles Morton do not qualify to be included with the homes of the wealthy. Morton's home was far less grand than the others – but he was a prominent member of the community who played an important part in Chorlton's admin-istration, and he could boast at least one servant. In many ways Lime Bank was better situated than the other houses. Set a little way down from Barlow Moor Lane, it stood in open countryside with views of the tree-lined Chorlton Brook to the south and the Row almost directly opposite. The lane to Lime Bank from Barlow Moor Lane petered out just beyond the house, although a field track carried on to Hough End Hall. Even though it was some way from the Row, it was clearly visible to those heading out of the village and on dark mornings the lamps of Lime Bank would have been a focal point.

There were also two fine Tudor buildings that had once belonged to our traditional landed families. Hough End Hall, just outside the township in Withington, had been home to the Mosleys, while Barlow Hall on the southern edge of Chorlton had been owned by the Barlow family. Both in their different ways fit into the conventional picture we have of old landed families. The Mosleys had moved into commerce in the late 16th century, sided with the Royalist cause in the Civil War and suffered from spendthrift gambling members in the 18th, finally selling the Hall to the Egertons in about 1751. The Barlow family had settled in the area by the 14th century.[335] They appear to have lived a quiet existence until, like many, they were caught up in the conflicts over religion in the 16th century. They adhered to the old faith and were persecuted during the reign of the first Elizabeth.[336]

---

334 *Manchester Guardian*, 19 July 1836.

335 The earliest dated document mentioning them is 1390, but undated sources put them here much earlier.

336 Anthony Barlow died in August 1584, having been imprisoned following raids on fifty wealthy Catholic houses looking for priests. While in prison he and others 'had suffered great hardships for their faith'. Booker, Revd John, *A History of the Chapels of Didsbury and Chorlton*, Chetham Society, 1857, p.253, Google edn p.282. Later still another Edward Barlow who was a Catholic priest was executed at Lancaster in 1641 for disobey-ing the proclamation ordering all priests to leave the country.

Hough End Hall from the rear. In the 1840s the Hall was converted into a farmhouse, but it remained an impressive building

The family continued to live at the Hall until the last died in 1773, and the estate was sold to the Egertons twelve years later.

Hough End Hall was built at the end of the 16th century. By 1847 it was a farmhouse, and was the home of Henry Jackson who farmed 220 acres beyond the eastern boundary of the township. This made it one of the largest farms in the area, and Jackson employed thirteen labourers, nine of whom lived in the Hall. It was an impressive sight, leading one observer to write that its 'ivy-covered walls, its clustered chimneys and its gabled roof, present a picturesque and pleasing appearance'.[337] Neither the ivy nor its functional purpose as a farm obscure its classic Elizabethan design. It was built of brick with three storeys; the centre was flanked by a bay at each end and a small advance bay in the centre that gave it the characteristic E shape.[338] The large communal areas were later partitioned into smaller rooms and the census of 1911 describes Hough End Hall as having eleven rooms.[339] It was best reached along the tree-lined lane from Barlow Moor Lane. There was a clear view of it from some distance away, but only in the last few yards was its full majesty revealed. A low stone wall either side of the gate gave way to a large open area beyond which, partly

337 *Ibid.*, p.167, Google edn p.190.
338 The most detailed description of the Hall can be found in the *Victoria County History, A History of the County of Lancaster, Volume 4, Townships; Withington*, 1911, pp.288–93 and available online at www.british-history.ac.uk.
339 A ground-floor plan exists from 1938.

hidden by hedges and trees, stood the main building. Someone, perhaps even Henry Jackson himself, had grown the hedge into an arch above the gate.

Barlow Hall was even older. While there may have been a building on the site dating from the Middle Ages, the present half-timbered structure dates probably from the reign of Henry VIII. Little of the original structure was visible by the 1840s. Most of the timber work had been covered in plaster or hidden under ivy. The old great hall, which occupied most of the building and was open to the roof, had been divided to create two storeys, with the lower floor given over to three entertaining rooms.[340] During the latter part of the 18th century and into the next it had been home of the radical Thomas Walker, later to the leading Whig businessman Shakespeare Phillips and in June 1848 to William Cunliffe Brooks.[341] According to various observers Cunliffe Brooks was keen not only to preserve the building but also to share his love of the Hall. This interest never appeared to have left him, and led Mrs C. Williamson to write in her *Recollections of Fallowfield* that his 'love for old things is so great that every relic is sacred to him, and even mindful alterations are made in such close imitation of old, they look the real thing'.[342] This was a passion that was to lead him to display a piece of the original timber which had been exposed after a fire in 1879, and our own Chorlton historian may well have been speaking from first-hand experience when he advised that 'Mrs Brooks's morning room is worthy of a visit, with its quaint old china, and the vestibule containing some fine old Furniture and an engraving of Wellington with his autograph'.[343]

340 Booker, *op. cit.*, p.292, Google edn p.321.
341 William Cunliffe Brooks died in 1900. Chorlton Golf Club, which had been founded in 1902, leased the Hall and grounds from the Egertons in October 1905 and bought both in March 1959.
342 Williamson, Mrs C., *op. cit.*, p.33.
343 Ellwood, chapter 2, 1885.

HOUSEWORK

Sarah Sutton, on the Row, Margaret Higginbotham on the Green,
and Jane Elizabeth Cunliffe Brooks of Barlow Hall

Sarah Sutton, who lived in a wattle and daub cottage on the Row, had a hard life. Unlike the wives of the well-to-do or even some of the farming families she had no servants to help her. In the spring of 1851 she had two children under the age of eight, was married to a labourer and had the added responsibility of an infirm father-in-law. Tracking her working day is a good way of understanding the daily routines of running a house. As we have already seen, keeping a wattle and daub cottage clean was no easy task. Plaster walls tended to crumble, the thatched roof could be home to vermin, and the stone or brick floors were damp and had to be swept three or four times a day using damp tea leaves spread on the floor to attract the dirt.

Sarah's day began at 6am in the summer and not much later in the winter months. Most tasks had to be undertaken during the day, as the light available from candles and lamps was so limited. One of the first chores was the collection of water. This might come from a well or the pump in the Bailey farmyard opposite. She may also have used the fishpond on the Row, which was next to her cottage. In having a supply so close Sarah was lucky; for other people on the Row the regular daily journey back with a bucket of water would be time consuming and tiring.[344]

Water was needed for cooking, drinking and washing, and there would be a number of journeys to collect it. The next task of the day would have been laying and lighting the fire. This may have used wood or possibly coal. But traditional wattle and daub fireplaces were large and not suited for burning coal, which needs a smaller fireplace and an efficient flue

---

344 Mrs Williamson, writing in 1883, described how the villagers of Lady Barn forty years earlier regularly had to visit a pond in a nearby hay field to collect 'buckets of water where with to clean their houses, this being the only supply of any but rain and spring water'. Williamson, Mrs C., *op. cit.*, p.38.

to draw the flame. The compromise was to reduce the size of the fireplace, to allow the use of coal now readily available from the Duke's Canal. The move from wood to coal may have been under way during the 1850s and while no one was selling the fuel in the township in 1851 there were a number of coal dealers recorded a decade later.

Once the fire had been made and breakfast served, there were beds to be aired, plates washed and the floor swept. Rugs and mats were taken out and banged against the wall, and even before the floor was swept and scrubbed in damp weather the stone flags had to be scrapped with a an old knife blade to loosen the trodden-in mud. But this simple task could only be done after Samuel had gone off to work and her son John (who was seven) to school. This left baby Ann, who was just a year old and therefore requiring frequent attention. It is likely that Sarah could have relied on one of her neighbours to help mind her child. The midday meal needed to be prepared, and if her husband was working too far away his meal would either have been got ready before he left or taken out to him, which might have fallen to her son John.

Most rural families like the Suttons had a diet heavily based on vegetables. Some of these were available from the cottage garden, including the all-important cabbages and potatoes as well as onions, carrots, parsnips and broad beans. They were lucky enough to have an orchard behind their home and there may have been opportunities to collect windfalls. As in many cottage gardens there were also currant and gooseberry bushes, raspberry canes and rhubarb.

Sarah would also have grown some flowers. One that has survived and still grows on the site of her cottage is greater celandine.[345] It has beautiful yellow flowers and, like many that Sarah and others grew, had medical properties: although it is toxic, in the right doses it has therapeutic uses. She may well have used it as a mild sedative to treat asthma, bronchitis and whooping cough as well as other complaints, including warts. In the back garden there may have been an area reserved for keeping chickens, and a pig.

But despite these vegetables and animals, much research has shown that at best the garden could only supplement food that had to be bought.[346] Even so, there were wild fruits and plants that could be gathered for nothing. Wine might be made from a variety of flowers and fruit, and for those who knew where to look there were plants that enhanced cooked dishes.[347] These free sources of food were important, as village shops were marginally more expensive than their urban counterparts.

---

345 It still grows on the site at the corner of Wilton and Beech Roads, and may be one of the last survivors of the cottage gardens.
346 Reay quotes the work of Rowntree and Kendal, who estimated that home-grown food amounted to just one twelfth of food consumed, p.77.
347 The local botanist David Bishop came across a woman collecting the plant sweet cicely (myrrhis odorata), which she used as a flavouring ingredient for stewed fruit. The crushed leaves smell strongly of aniseed. During the Second World War when sugar was rationed local people used it as a sweetener.

Judging from popular recipe books, which aimed to waste little and use up leftovers, there were many meals available to Sarah that were simple and cheap.[348] The *Family Save-All* recipe book provided numerous ways of using up leftover meat and cheap cuts, like the 'capital dish of Rice, with extract of Bones' or the 'Frugal, Agreeable and Nutrive Meal for Eight Persons, that will neither Lighten the Purse, nor Lie heavy on the Stomach'; this included scotch barley and a leg of beef. It is doubtful if Sarah regularly put meat on the table or had access to such books, but the recipes themselves would have been common knowledge. No doubt she would have made a variation of 'Cheap and savoury Herb Pudding made with spinach, beets, parsley and leek'. This involved taking a handful of the ingredients and washing, scalding and chopping them finely, then mixing them with onions, sage, a quart of groats and a pound of lard and boiling them in a bag. She may also have pickled her own fruit and vegetables as well as making jam.

Washing and ironing the family clothes was a hard and time-consuming job. Gradually the centuries-old use of cold water was being superseded by the use of hot water: more people used coal instead of wood to heat the home which meant less wood ash was available for cleaning. Instead the wash had to be done using soap, which needs hot water to work properly. This involved heating vast amounts of water and collecting more from the well for rinsing, as well as frequent journeys to fetch coal so the fire could be fed. While using hot water was preferable to cold, there was extra work and cost. Books of Victorian household management[349] are very clear about the long and elaborate process, which began with sorting the clothes, repairing them and treating stains before putting everything in to soak. This was best done on Saturday night, allowing a full day before the Monday wash. On that appointed day, perhaps before dawn, Sarah was up to make the fire, before wringing out the clothes that had been soaking all Sunday, grating the amount of soap she needed from the block and adding hot water to the tub, not forgetting to empty the dirty water from the soaking tub, collecting fresh for later and refilling the copper to ensure a steady supply of hot water. The cleanest clothes were put in the hot water and moved about using a dolly, a long pole shaped like a cone or a three-legged stool. The washboard replaced this later. The first batch was then rinsed before being wrung out and hung up to dry. The process was repeated, all the time making sure there was a steady supply of clean and hot water, and coal. There were still those who hung out clothes to dry on hedges as well as the line. Later in the week clothes were ironed. Some in the township might have held to the old custom of the great wash which involved hoarding everything for weeks before embarking on a huge washing exer-

348 *The Family Save-All*, W. Kent & Co., second edn, 1861.
349 Mrs Beeton, *op. cit.*

cise. But this practice depended on a family having lots of spare clothes and bed linen, thereby making a visible statement of the household's wealth.

Difficult as washday was, the volume of washing was nowhere near as high as today. Underwear was certainly washed frequently, but thick top clothes tended to have to last, with dirty spots being sponged off. One sheet from each bed was washed weekly with the last week's top sheet becoming the next week's bottom sheet. The blankets were washed once a year, in good drying weather during the summer.

By 1851 there was a dressmaker in Chorlton, but it is unlikely that the wife of a farm labourer would have paid to have someone make her clothes.

Farmers' wives like Margaret Higginbotham may appear to have had it slightly easier; after all, she employed a servant. But Margaret would not only have been expected to run her home but also to do her share of work on the farm. On smaller farms this could mount up.[350] The Higginbothams had a dairy herd and some of the milking, and certainly butter- and cheese-making would have fallen to Margaret. In *The Book of the Farm* Henry Stephens was at great pains to describe how to lay out the milk-house and cheese-room next to the farm kitchen.[351] These rooms had to be cool and roomy and facing north, or failing that east, to get the sun early in the morning. The Higginbothams' farmhouse had a pantry and an outhouse, facing east, part of which was below ground and therefore perfect for storing milk and making cheese and butter. Most of the butter and cheese was destined for the family, and once the calves had been weaned by the end of June there was more milk available. Margaret could sell fresh butter and cheese at the market or salt it for other families or for dealers.

The Higginbothams were married sometime after June 1841 and moved to the Green later in the year.[352] During the next seven years Margaret gave birth to four children while running the home and helping with the farm, and had to cope with the loss of two of them. Henry, her first born, died in 1845, Mary, her third, in 1848 – aged just five weeks. Margaret herself died in January 1849 at the age of thirty-seven. All three were buried in the Wesleyan chapel on the Row. James was only thirty-six when Margaret died. It was not uncommon for the bereaved to remarry, which James did in 1851 or 1852. Elizabeth Cook was from a family that farmed up by Hardy. Their first child was Sarah, born in the

---

350 Part of the farm accounts has survived. In 1829 Mary Bayley was paid £7 7s, which was increased to £7 10s the following year. In 1851 James Higginbotham was employing Elizabeth Morton. The servants' quarters were above the kitchen at the back of the house, and a separate staircase led from the ground floor to the bedroom. However, these accounts start in 1817 and concentrate on the years 1829–48: as James and Margaret Higginbotham are unlikely to have taken up residence at the farm on the Green until 1841, they must refer to Yew Tree Farm in Withington. Sarah Bayley was working at Yew Tree Farm in 1841: she may have been the sister of Mary Bayley who featured in the accounts for 1829–30. Elizabeth Morton, aged just thirteen, was working as a servant at the farm, and ten years later was at the Chorlton farm on the Green.

351 Stephens, Henry, *The Book of the Farm*, p.268, Google edn p.288.

352 In June 1841 James was still living in Withington at Yew Tree Farm, but his first son was born between October and December 1841 in Chorlton.

spring or early summer of 1852. Elizabeth had another three children, and outlived her husband by thirty years.[353]

Jane Elizabeth Brooks at Barlow Hall could afford to cultivate a more leisurely lifestyle, the sort of life described by Mrs Beeton in her *Guide to Household Management*,[354] which put much emphasis on how to behave in public and participate in charitable activities, but above all how to manage the home. And in this role a woman who employed servants had to be like a 'commander of an army or the leader of an enterprise'.[355] Mrs Beeton was insistent that after breakfast the housewife should inspect her servants' work and discuss the order of the day. Relationships between servant and mistress were to be, in the words of one manual, 'firm, without being severe, and kind, without being familiar'.[356] Once the inspection was complete, she might spend time with her children before the midday meal.

One of the real tests of the servant/mistress relationship was the large social gathering, anything from breakfast for guests to an evening meal for twelve or a picnic for forty. On all of these Mrs Beeton was a sound guide, and her advice on the choice of food, seating arrangements and general conduct is a world away from that of Sarah Sutton or Margaret Higginbotham. Breakfast might be a buffet of cold and hot dishes, attractively arranged with fruits that were in season. The choice of dishes suggested is staggering, including collard and potted cold meats, fish, game and pies, along with steaks, kidneys, sausages, bacon, poached, scrambled and boiled eggs. Dinner likewise involved a selection of fish and meat dishes, and invariably ran to three courses. But the great social divide between the Suttons, Higginbothams and Jane Elizabeth at Barlow Hall was most pronounced when it came to the set evening meal for six to twenty or more people. Mrs Beeton suggested five courses, with varying numbers of dishes for each course. For September there were four different menus. One of these consisted of mock turtle soup, salmon and lobster sauce, fried whitings and stewed eels, followed by veal cutlets, scalloped oysters, curried fowl and grilled mushrooms, then haunch of mutton, boiled calf's head *á la Béchamel*, braised ham and roast fowls *aux cressons*, and a third course of cabinet pudding, iced pudding, compôte of plums, damson tart, cream, fruit jelly, prawns and lobster salad, and finally dessert and ices.

Along with these big events was the round of visiting or receiving visitors, which involved a strict protocol: a card was left if the person one was visiting was out, and one only visited if invited. One handbook on how young ladies should conduct themselves

353 He died aged sixty-three in 1876, leaving £600. Elizabeth ran the farm until her death in 1904, which was no mean feat given that in 1881 it consisted of 62 acres and employed five men.

354 Beeton Isabella, *op. cit.*, first published in twenty-four monthly parts between 1859 and 1861 before being published in a bound edition in 1861.

355 *Ibid.*, chapter 1, p.1, Google edn p.50.

356 Adams, *op. cit.*, p.10, Google edn p.33.

read: 'Do not visit a friend in the country, or another town, unless you have what is called a standing invitation', for it may be that the invitation was 'designed only to make a show of politeness'.[357] Before arriving at the house, the guest was supposed to inform her host 'of the exact day and hour when she may expect you'.

Social engagements would only have been part of Jane Elizabeth's activities. Mrs Beeton also stressed the importance of charitable work: 'Visiting the houses of the poor is the only practical way really to understand the actual state of each family; and although there may be difficulties in following out this plan in the metropolis and other large cities, yet in country towns and rural districts these objections do not obtain. Great advantages may result from visits paid to the poor; for there being, unfortunately, much ignorance, generally, amongst them with respect to all household knowledge, there will be opportunities for advising and instructing them, in a pleasant and unobtrusive manner, in cleanliness, industry, cookery, and good management.'[358] The Brooks were known for their generosity, and Jane Elizabeth probably visited the homes of deserving cases. There were also activities that combined good works and social gatherings. Of these the church bazaar committee is a good example. This was formed to raise money for the new parish church and culminated with a bazaar held at the Royal Exchange during Easter 1862. It included the wives and daughters of gentry, farmer's wives and married women from the larger houses.[359] But this was one charitable task that Jane Elizabeth did not participate in. William Cunliffe Brooks was against the building of the new church on Edge Lane, and continued to support the old one on the Green.

Such might be the lives of three representative women of the township.

357 Leslie, Miss, *The Behaviour Book*, Willis P. Hazzard, 1839, p.10, Google edn p.19.

358 Beeton, *op. cit.*, p.6, Google edn p.55.

359 They were Mrs Edward Booth, The Rectory, the Misses Holt, Beech House, the Misses Morton, Lime Bank, the Misses Dean, Barlow Farm, Mrs Whitelegg, the Green, Mrs J.B. Wilkinson, Brook Cottage, Mrs Tunder, The Grange, Mrs Law, The Lodge, Urmston, Mrs Aders, Bella Villas, Whalley Range, Mrs Burghardt, Whalley Range, Mrs Findeisen, Holly Bank, Mrs Meredith White, Thorn Cottage, Pennington, Brookfield House, Mrs Droughton Lowe, Longford Terrace, Longford, Mrs Dewhurst, Myrtle Lodge, Longford.

twelve

MORALITY

Mary Crowther, the township code including riding the stang and other public humiliations, and attitudes to illegitimacy

Small communities are not always good at keeping secrets. After all, there are very few places where people can go without being seen, and once seen their business usually becomes common property. There were times when the bounds of decency or lawful behaviour were crossed and as Chorlton was still very lightly policed it fell to the community to maintain order, and to remind those who strayed from commonly accepted values and morals that they would be punished. So it was with Mary Crowther, who was made to do penance in the church at the end of the 19th century. It is unclear what she did, but during the closing decades of the 18th century she had given birth to three illegitimate children.

More raucous was the custom of riding the stang, or rough music as it was also known.[360] This practice dated back to the Middle Ages and was common across Europe. 'If a man was known to beat his wife, or if he allowed himself to be henpecked; if he was unfaithful to her, or she to him, the offending party, if living in the village, was serenaded with a concert of music, consisting of cow's horns, frying-pans, warming-pans, tea-kettles, &c., in fact, any implement with which a loud, harsh, and discordant sound could be produced. This hubbub was generally repeated several times, and seldom failed to make a due impression on the culprit.'[361] In Larkhill much the same happened to an adulterous couple. Effigies of the two were made and carried on poles by torchlight to their house, to the accompaniment of the banging of pots, pans and coal-shovels, the screeching of tin

---

360 Thompson, E.P., *Customs in Common*, Penguin, 1993. The practice of public humiliation can be traced back across medieval Europe, and was still in use in both rural and urban areas in the 19th century. In the 20th century it has been evident in the treatment of strike breakers, in the denouncing of disruptive children to their parents' workmates in Soviet factories and during the Cultural Revolution in China in the 1960s.
361 Ellwood, chapter 8, 1885.

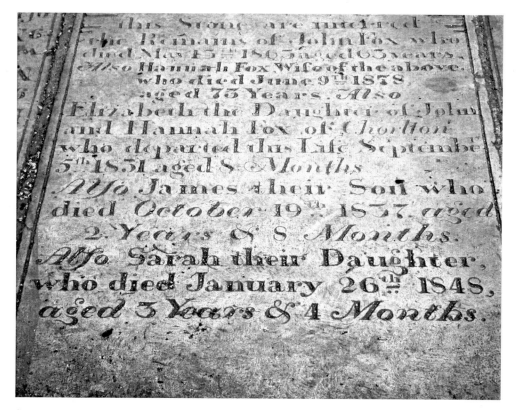

Children were the largest single group in Chorlton, and child mortality was high. The Fox children were buried close to the western corner of the church.

whistles and mouth-organs and cat-calls, hoots and jeers.[362] Nor was this the only form of humiliation. A brush tied to a cottage chimney was a statement to the entire village that the occupier had been deserted and that half a bed was to let.

Public humiliation can also serve to engender sympathy for the victims, and riding the stang was never as popular in the township as some members of the noisy and jeering crowd might have thought. It never extended to those mothers who gave birth to children out of wedlock. Although there was a certain stigma that hung around unmarried mothers and their children, 'this was certainly not as pronounced as one might infer from the declamations of Victorian middle class moralists ...'.[363] These attitudes were reflected in Richard Redgrave's painting *Outcast*. Painted in 1851, it turns on the drama of a young mother turned out of her home by her stern father, while around the room family members swoon or cry and her mother stoically comforts her son, with an expression that

362 Thompson, Flora, *op. cit.*, p.140.
363 Reay, *op. cit.*, p.212.

seems to mingle sadness and bewilderment. Such might have been the stir created in the village when Susannah Pinnington (or Pennington) announced she was about to have a child out of wedlock in the early months of 1837.[364] The child's father was James White, a farm labourer living on Lloyd Street[365] just off the Row. He was aged twenty-two when it was alleged he fathered Thomas Pinnington, and by 1841 he was married with two children. His eldest was just a year younger than Thomas. There is little evidence of his desire to support Thomas. The boy was baptised on 3 March 1837, and James's name does not appear in the record. Two months later the parish served a 'Notice of Intention to apply for an order against James White for maintenance of his bastard son by Susannah Pennington May 9th 1837'.[366] This was an attempt by the parish to recoup the cost of maintaining Thomas.

Susannah was not alone in her plight. In the seventeen years before the birth of her son Thomas, there were seventeen other women who stood in the parish church and baptised their children without a husband, and in the following five years another five.[367] In most years back into the 18th century as many as three women a year baptised a child with no father present.

That women had children outside marriage is no surprise; what is perhaps surprising is that this may not have been met with the degree of shame that we assume was the case. In one Norfolk village the local vicar was moved to write that 'I find cleanliness on the increase in the parish but no diminution of illegitimacy. The girls see nothing sinful in it and their mothers apparently connive in it.'[368] Many of those giving evidence to Poor Law commissioners in the South West in 1843 were in no doubt that overcrowding was a prime reason for illegitimacy.[369] This belief was confirmed by evidence from the North East: 'when we find that a whole family – father and mother, and children of both sexes and all ages live together, and have to sleep together in one and the same room, any degree of indelicacy and unchastity ceases to surprise, and the only wonder is that the woman should behave as well as she does'.[370] How far overcrowding played a part in Chorlton is difficult to assess. Certainly it existed, but it would be a giant leap to suggest that this was the sole cause for illegitimacy. Some of the mothers were working away from

---

364 Susannah was the sister of Hannah and perhaps the daughter of William, who ran a shop on the Green next to the Horse and Jockey.

365 Lloyd Street is Whitelow Road today.

366 Lancashire County Records Item QSP/3066/34, 9 May 1837, Bastardy.

367 They included Elizabeth Warburton on 17 November 1839, Harriet Axon in January 1840, Elizabeth Turner in September 1840, Jane Kenyon in June 1841 and Mary Griffiths two days before Christmas 1842.

368 Revd B.J. Armstrong, vicar of East Dereham, Norfolk, from Herbert, B.J., *A Norfolk Diary 1850-1888*, c.1949, quoted by Russell, G.E and K.F., *The English Countryside*, Bloomsbury, 1953, p.172.

369 What exercised the report more than anything was how far the practice of men and women being together in the fields created opportunities for sexual relationships. Apart from haymaking time it was argued that overcrowding was more to blame for illegitimacy.

370 Doyle, Sir F., evidence to *Reports of the Special Assistant Poor Law Commissioners*, p.299, Google edn p.319.

Chorlton when they gave birth and only returned afterwards.[371] Some lived with parents until they eventually married the father or found someone else. Betty Turner, who was twenty-five in 1841, lived with her parents John and Mary and her son James, who was nine months old.[372]

In the three small villages of Boughton, Dunkirk and Hernhill in Kent, 50 per cent of brides in the 19th century 'were either pregnant when they stood in front of the altar, or had actually given birth before their marriage'.[373] Flora Thompson, describing her own village in the 1870s and '80s, recorded that illegitimate births passed without much comment, 'for these would be the children of couples who had married after the birth of their first child, a common happening at that time and little thought of'.[374] According to the commissioners themselves, 'We used to be told that clergymen in many county parishes hardly ever marry a couple of the labouring classes, of whom the woman was not far advanced in pregnancy.'[375] Only occasionally did Flora Thompson's villagers become upset at blatant illegitimacy, as when a young unmarried woman settled in the hamlet with four children, but even she became accepted once she had proved herself to be a clean, hard-working mother. Most in Larkhill reserved their indignation for adultery.

Of the sixty-seven illegitimate births during the seventy-two years from 1770 to 1842, some were a second or a third child. Some family names reappear, suggesting that some mothers may have been related, and in one case might even have been mother and daughter. In some years there were no illegitimate births, and in others there were more than six.

Before 1820 the baptismal records are silent about the status of women who baptised their children in the absence of a father. The description 'single woman' only appears from 1820, along with the occupational details of the husband and place of residence; before that date there is only a mother's name. Of course it may be that some of these women were married but for whatever reason their husbands were not present. Mary Renshaw, for instance, baptised two children between 1778 and 1783: her husband was present for the first ceremony but not the second. However, she is the exception.

In 1834 the way in which the parish dispensed help to women with illegitimate children changed for the worse. Before this date there was a greater recognition of the father's responsibility, and women could turn to the law for help.[376] Some of these records have

371 Mary Crowther had been living in Stretford in the 1760s before being removed to the township because she was pregnant; Mary Griffiths was also in Stretford but returned in 1842; Ann Pearson conceived and gave birth in Manchester.

372 Betty had been baptised in June 1816.

373 Reay, Barry, *Microhistories: Demography, Society and Culture in Rural England, 1800-1930*, Cambridge University Press, 1996, p.180.

374 Thompson, Flora, *op. cit.*, p.138.

375 Head, Sir Edmund, *Report of the Law of Bastardy*, HMSO, 1840, p.15, Google edn p.17. *Sixth Annual Report of the Poor Law Commissioners*, p.155, Google edn p.168.

376 In 1664 Ralph Bibby of Levenshulme and Francis Goulden of Chorlton-cum-Hardy appeared before the Quarter Sessions for Bastardy and in 1724–25 so did John Gibbons, a farmer, and Elizabeth Rowebotham. Lancashire Country Records, QSP/264/3 and QSP/1233334/17.

survived from Stretford, including the Orders for Maintenance of Bastard Children, 1702–1811 and bastardy bonds from 1715 to 1794, which identify the adult male who would support the child, as well as other miscellaneous Orders Relating to Bastardy for the period 1716–56.[377] They reveal a straightforward system designed to identify the father and bring him to court. This might begin with an examination of the mother by a magistrate, or if she was already in labour by a midwife: these examinations were common in the early 18th century. Having achieved the information, a bastardy warrant was issued, ordering a constable to bring the father before the magistrate. If the case was successfully made then a bastardy order was issued, which identified the man and stipulated the amount he was to pay. The documents were pre-printed with spaces for the magistrates to write the names of the mother and father and the amount that had to be paid. Some of those for Stretford for the years 1702–1811 reveal the estimated costs that the father was expected to pay.[378] Often the sum was decided on a yearly basis, to be paid quarterly. This variable amount may have been based on circumstances. The figure of 26s for the year payable until the child was fourteen appears in some of the documents, but others set an initial payment to cover the birth ranging from £2 down to 10s, specifying that further payments should be made weekly: these varied from 30d to 7d. In some cases the mother was expected to contribute, and this could be 18d.[379] Attempting to make sense of these awards is difficult, but some idea of their monetary worth can be gauged by making a comparison with wage rates and some examples of the cost of living. Just twenty years later in 1830 Mary Bailey and Higginbotham the farmer[380] agreed an annual salary of £7 10s, from which she bought a pair of stays for 10s 6d and a new cap for 1s 8d, and repaired her shoes for 2s 8d. The cost of renting a cottage on the Row varied from 10d to 5s a week.[381] The day rate for women workers in the South West was between 7d and 10d.[382] Against this backdrop, magistrates often determined that the cost of maintaining an illegitimate child was 7d a day. But the system was flawed, and there were many in the early 19th century who said so. Moralists argued that payments to a single mother only encouraged illegitimacy, and pointed to those who had more than one child.

No records have survived to indicate whether Susannah Pennington went into the workhouse. By 1841 she and her son Thomas shared a house on the Green with her sister Hannah and brother William, and sometime around 1843 she married Daniel Chester.

377 Bastardy Bonds 1715–94, Manchester Archives, Manchester Libraries, L89/9/14.

378 Orders for Maintenance of Bastard Children, 1702–1811, St Matthew Overseers of the Poor, Manchester Archives L89/9/14.

379 Bastardy documents from 1807.

380 Higginbotham's farm accounts, op. cit.

381 Properties were assessed annually to determine the individual poor rate and this was based on the rateable value of the property. Chorlton-cum-Hardy Rate Books, Manchester Archive Rate Book, Microfilm Rolls 297–9.

382 Reports of the Special Assistant Poor Law Commissioners on the Employment of Women & Children in Agriculture, p.7, Google edn p.27.

They stayed in Chorlton, first off High Lane, later on the Green and finally in 1871 in Church Road. They had six children, and Thomas was still with them in 1861. He went to live in Hulme in 1871, where he was married with a family and employed as a packer.[383]

Susannah was not alone in finding a husband after giving birth outside marriage. Charlotte Kenyon baptised her daughter Harriet in 1823 when she was just eighteen, and her son George in May 1828, before marrying James Walley. He was twenty-two years older than her, and it may be that George was his son.[384] He was no longer around by 1851, and Charlotte had married again.

For some unmarried women the future as a single parent proved too daunting a prospect. A few abandoned their infants, and in the summer of 1841 in the Stretford New Road workhouse there were two such.[385] There were others who in their desperation turned to a darker remedy. Newspapers of the period reported cases of infanticide, in often lurid detail, focusing on the mother's shame and guilt and graphically describing how the child died. Readers were left in no doubt that in some towns this was a crime on the increase. As we shall see later there were two known infanticides in Chorlton, both of which created a stir. But this crime was difficult to prove, and the courts as well as the public were often sympathetic to the accused mother.

And so we return to Mary Crowther, who did penance in the parish church in the closing years of the 18th century. She continued to live in the village just where the Row runs into the Green. Here in one of those wattle and daub cottages she lived out her life, unmarried, with one of her sons.

383 1871 census, Enu. 67, p.35, Hulme. Ten years later he was a widower and living in Stretford, working as a carter, 1881 census, Enu. 9, p.17.

384 George took the surname Walley, while his elder sister remained Kenyon.

385 Henry German had been born in April 1841 and was to die later in the summer and Robert Sherwood was born in February 1841. There are no records of their mothers' deaths around that period, so they may well have been abandoned.

thirteen

RELIGION

The parish church of St Clement's, its charities and landholdings, the Methodist chapel and
the Methodist congregation, the sick and burial society, religious attendance

I n 1847 the church on the Green was just forty-seven years old, having replaced a
far more ancient church that had been built in about 1512. There is no doubt that
this earlier place of worship fitted much better the idea of a village church. It was
half timbered, with walls of wattle and daub and large irregular-spaced windows.[386]
By comparison the new church was less than attractive, built of red brick with a tower at
the west end and a rounded apse to the east. To the casual observer it resembled a rec-
tangular box, not improved by the addition of aisles on the north and south side in 1837,
which added to the impression of a building too short in length and over-tall in height.
But this description does not do it justice. There was a sense of permanence and purpose
about the place. Parishioners approached the church from the north through the graveyard, and at this point the building dominated the view. The sheer height of the building
combined with the tall windows and soaring tower were as forceful a reminder of the
power of religion as any great cathedral.

The small doorway at the western end beside the tower admitted the worshipper into a
tall expanse of light. On each side were three high circular-headed windows complemented
by another four at the west end.[387] But it was the east wall that truly opened the church
up. Reaching almost to the domed roof was a central window flanked by two others, serving to focus the eye on the altar, which stood directly in front of this blaze of light.[388] The

---

386 Remnants of the brick foundations were found in the archaeological dig in the 1980s.

387 Mr Cunliffe Brooks paid for the side windows to be altered to give them a 'more ecclesiastical character' Ellwood, chapter 9, 1886.

388 A new window was donated by Cunliffe Brooks. Delicate twisted patterns in the glass rose and met four spectacular images of winged animals
topped by Our Lord seated on a throne. And above the window the domed apse was decorated by a silver star which burst out across the blue
painted ceiling. The ceiling was remembered by Majorie Holmes who recalled the church in the 1930s and last visited it just before its demolition in
1949; but as the church went through at least one redecoration it is not certain that the star on a blue background was there in 1847.

font by the north-west door might remind parishioners of their own baptism, and was made of marble, resting on a stem with claws. There was nothing very elegant about the pulpit, but from here William Birley, the minister, gazed down at the worshippers, seated either on older oak pews or newer ones made of deal. They in turn could, when the sermon dragged, stare at the painted and varnished walls, or more likely ponder on those buried at their feet, for here were the great and good of the township: people like Margaret Usherwood who in life gave a silver tankard to the church and in death left £160 to help bring up the children of local families; or Daniel and Mary Lamb, who were buried with six of their children. In all there were nine gravestones inside the church, five of these in the nave and another four at the south-west end. Some interred here had reached a ripe old age,

The silver tankard donated by Margaret Usherwood and Jane Gee in 1734.

but many died young. Thoughts of mortality would be lifted by the sound of the organ, newly installed five years before for the sum of £100, raised by subscription. The church also boasted two Arnott stoves, which, as the advertisement proudly claimed, were cheap and efficient because by their 'circular and oblong bronzed corrugated body, the heating surface becomes multiplied nearly three times and by means of the self regulating valve the admission of air to the fire is so regulated that it only needs replenishing with fuel once every 12 to 18 hours'. How many parishioners enjoyed this long-lasting and cheap warmth is impossible to say. The church could seat 420,[389] with those who could afford to paying for the privilege of listening to the minister. In midsummer 1853 William Bailey, farmer on the Row paid 10s 6d for a year's pew rent and another 1s 6d towards the organist's salary. Those who couldn't afford the pew rent sat in one of the 300 free seats. In worship as in the rest of life your wealth or lack of it was paraded for all to see. William Chesshyre, the clerk, was responsible for collecting these pew rents, and in 1847 he was judged of good

389 Census of Religious Worship, 1851.

character by Archdeacon Rushton who visited the church.[390] The visit proved quite a success, with the archdeacon reporting favourably on the state of the church and graveyard. The headstones were well kept and regular and the grass was mown.

This was not a wealthy church, despite some donations made during the 18th century and a grant from Queen Anne's Bounty, which supplemented the income of poor clergy.[391] With this money the church had bought a farm, Wall Bank Hill in Bramhall, worth £60 a year and another at Heyhead in Northern Etchells worth £32.[392] The 13-acre farm at Bramhall was bought in 1728 and sold to the local railway company in the summer of 1847 for £4,000.[393] The farm in Northern Etchells was bought in 1773 and covered 17 acres.[394] Finally there was an acre of land at Hazel Grove.[395]

Of all the incumbents it was the Revd William Birley who seemed to make things happen. During his sixteen years in the township he was successful in building the new village school and the rectory from subscriptions. The school was a fine-looking building, and served the community for over thirty years. As for the rectory, opinions differed. It was a large brick-built house on three floors with an impressive stone porch. The ground floor had tall windows which looked out on a garden that was screened from casual observers by a row of trees. The rooms had lofty ceilings and were always gloomy and a touch too cold.[396] The place had an air of solidity and a degree of splendid isolation that marked Mr Birley out as someone apart from most of his flock. Indeed the rectory stood beyond the village, so that anyone wishing to call first had to take the road north from the Green, past the Horse and Jockey and out to Pitts Brow.[397] But in his defence Mr Birley had brought his home closer to the heart of Chorlton. Before this rectory was built he lived on Upper Chorlton Road at the corner with Wood Road, and before that at Irwell View, Old Trafford.

William Birley was an interesting character. He was born in 1813, and his first living was at Singleton near Poulton-le-Fylde, a small township of just 501 people in 1840. The following year, while living at Singleton Lodge, he described himself of independent means. What is striking is that in 1859 he exchanged the rural isolation of Chorlton for St Stephen's in Salford. This was a plain brick building dating from 1794, comfortably

390 It formed the basis of his report, Archdeacon Rushton's Visitation Returns, Reference Number MSF 942.72 R121/Vol 39, Manchester Archives.

391 Queen Anne's Bounty had been established to supplement the income of the poorest clergy. The fund was derived from a tax on the income of all the clergy. Originally this had been paid to the Pope, but after the break with Rome went to the Crown instead. In time it was also used to provide and repair the parsonages of poorer clergy.

392 Booker, Revd John, *History of the Ancient Chapels of Didsbury and Chorlton*, Chetham Society, 1857, p.301, Google edn p.330.

393 This was the Manchester and Birmingham and North Staffordshire Railway, and formed the line that ran from Manchester through Bramhall to Macclesfield.

394 This was only sold in 1921, and the land is now part of the runway and car-park of Manchester Airport.

395 The Hazel Grove plot was sold in 1921 to Bucklow Rural District Council.

396 This at least is how they appeared in the mid-20th century, by which time the building was suffering from damp and wood rot.

397 Today this journey would be along St Clements Road to the crossroads where High Lane joins Edge Lane.

The old school was the second on the Green. The first was built in 1817, and was replaced by this building in 1845. The Vestry or ratepayers' meetings were held here. Over the centre doorway was the inscription 'St Clements's Sunday and Day Schools, erected by private subscription A.D. 1817; rebuilt A.D. 1845.'

fitted and containing three galleries and an organ.[398] It may well have been a much larger living, but it was in the heart of Salford surrounded by rows of terraced housing, which hid smaller houses and dark courts as well as a gasworks and timber yards.[399]

Not all in Chorlton worshipped at the parish church. Since the beginning of the 19th century there had been a small but growing Methodist congregation; in 1847 the Methodist chapel had been standing for just twenty years, its predecessor, dating from 1805, having become too small. Not that the very first Methodists needed a chapel, for in those early days they worshipped in each others' houses or (in the summer months) on the Green, or in the barns of Thomas Moores and John Holland. Both chapels were simple buildings made of brick. The first was a Spartan place where the congregation stood in two segregated blocks. As if to emphasise the seriousness of worship, latecomers were accommodated on a pew beside the door called the 'sinners' form'. The chapel was not heated. By contrast the second building was bigger, heated by a stove and lit by oil lamps as well as candles. Even so, it was more austere than the parish church. It had no spire and the

398 Duffield, H.G., *The Strangers Guide to Manchester*, 1850, reprinted by Neil Richardson, 1984, p.29.

399 The church was demolished in 1962 and the site is now a small park between Trinity Way and St Stephens Street.

The old parish church from the north. Approaching from this direction would take worshippers past the graves of previous generations.

The interior of the parish church looking east. There are those who can still remember how the light shone through the great east window to illuminate the whole church.

building resembled a brick, 36ft by 80ft; but it was a practical building and as such had a certain simple beauty. A small graveyard occupied the space between the Row and the chapel. In 1847 there had been forty-eight burials since the first chapel opened in 1805. The names of the interred encompass the early Methodist families: the Lunts, Brundretts, Mortons, Granthams and Renshaws, along with the Higginbothams and Moores. It is a short step from this place of rest to the small porch and into the chapel. There were rows of box pews, the first three of which accommodated the orchestra. Running along three sides was a gallery, which when the chapel was built was the only seated area. Twenty years after its opening there were 280 seats, of which 100 were free, and there was free space or standing room for seventy more. Tall arched windows ran the length of the west side. Two windows on either side of the entrance and another two above provided a blaze of natural light. To the left of the entrance was the vestry, which was also used as the Sunday school.

The popular story goes that Methodism came to Chorlton in 1770 when a soldier and a few of his companions arrived in the township and began preaching. The message took hold: by 1800 a Methodist society had been formed and Wesleyan ministers were visiting each Sunday. But perhaps because there were only five society members, there was just one preacher who attended the afternoon service at 3pm. James Baguley, who lived behind the Green, is credited as being the first Methodist in the village, but the group expanded

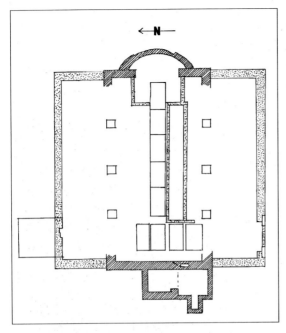

The plan of the parish church. In the centre were the graves of the wealthy and respected.

to include John Johnson, whose cottage on the Green was used for services – as were the homes of Thomas Baguley on the Row and James Baguley, who lived on what is now St Clements Road. Many of these Methodists were still young when they became active in the movement. The most prominent were in their early thirties and forties when the first chapel was built, and may have been even younger when they first embraced the Methodist message. James Renshaw, the schoolteacher, would have been in his twenties, for example. This was a new and dynamic movement. When our first Methodists were gathering in 1800, it was just sixty-two years since the Wesley brothers had returned from America and begun to preach.

It says much for the confidence and commitment of the Methodists in the township that the two chapels and a Sunday school were funded through local subscriptions.[400] The building fund for the second chapel came mainly from just eighty subscribers, who made subscriptions ranging from 10s up to £50.[401] Even smaller amounts were dredged from surplus income, in some cases representing a real sacrifice. £4 15s was subscribed this way. The total from Chorlton was £275 12s 6d.[402] As well as money came contributions of land and labour. Jeremiah Brundrett the elder gave the land for the first chapel, and gave more for the second. His son, Jeremiah the younger, matched his father's £50 donation and gave his labour freely, assisting in the digging of the foundations, and slaking the lime and carrying water from Blomley's Fishpond on the other side of the Row. In the summer months before and after work he put in many hours, starting at dawn and finishing at dusk. This belief in their message and the importance of a permanent place of worship led the Methodists to commit to a loan to bridge the difference between the £404 they

---

400 The second chapel cost £690. Later they raised the money to build not only the church on Manchester Road at a cost of £5,600 in 1873, but also the Sunday school building in 1885.

401 The Brundrett family alone contributed £154 0s 6d, which came from nineteen members of the family.

402 Further sums came from outside the township: £30 from Manchester, £17 17s from Withington, £14 17s 6d from Sale and £6 8s 1d from Altrincham, with a further £66 4s 6d raised in collections.

had collected and the £689 needed to build the new chapel. Three loans were taken out for a total of £350 at 4½ per cent interest from three Methodists.[403]

Methodism appealed across the social classes, but perhaps because this was a rural community the congregation tended towards farmers, labourers and tradesmen. If there were any gentry at worship in the chapel they have yet to be revealed: those rubbing shoulders with the farmer John Brundrett were labourers, weavers and tailors. One of these was William Rhodes, a gardener who lived on High Lane, whose father had been active in the first chapel. William was a preacher and visitor to the sick, services which he continued to perform for forty more years.[404] Also among the flock were George Grantham, who made his living as a tailor, Jeremiah Brundrett, shopkeeper, and James Baguley, farm labourer.

William Rhodes was a gardener. He lived on High Lane and was a preacher and visitor to the sick, services that he continued to perform for 40 years.

In total the names of seventy-two Methodist families who were active in the years up to 1851 are known. Not all of these have revealed their occupations, but seventeen were farmers and market gardeners, nine were in trade and retail, forty-four were labourers, while Betty Moores was a charwoman and one was a servant.[405] There were also a policeman, a coachman and a sailor. Few of the farmers worked large amounts of land; most were market gardeners making a living from less than 5 acres. But even given this middling to low economic status, Chorlton Methodists represented a large number of those entitled to vote in the reformed Parliament. Of the twenty-one electors in 1832 eight were Methodists, six were freeholders and two were tenant farmers.[406] Some owned modest amounts of land.

This was a close-knit community. William Rhodes married the daughter of George Grantham, who in turn was connected to the Holland and Pinnington families, and the

403 John Holland loaned £100, Jeremiah Brundrett the younger £185 and James Renshaw £80.
404 William was born in 1816.
405 Beech Road Baptismal Records 1807–47 from the Register of Baptisms, in the Wesleyan Chapel Radnor Street Circuit 1830–7, microfilm MFPR2120, Local History Library Manchester City Council Libraries, Beech Road Baptismal Records 1807–50, own MSS volume.
406 The six freeholders were William Brundrett, Jeremiah Brundrett, John Brundrett, George Grantham, William Morton and William Griffiths. The tenant farmers were William Gresty on 12 acres and John Holland on 20 acres.

Cookson, Chesshyre, Taylor and Kenyon families were also connected by marriage. Many were close neighbours in a stretch along High Lane across to Lane End and beyond. There were also ties of business. Thomas Birkett, who described himself as a tea dealer and grocer, may well have been in partnership with Jeremiah Brundrett. Both operated from the same place in the 1840s and '50s, and when Thomas left the area the shop was again taken over by the Brundrett family.[407]

The Methodists initially excited both opposition and derision, but in Chorlton no evidence has come to light of a deep division between those of the parish church and those of the chapel. William Chesshyre, who attended the Wesleyan chapel and baptised some of his children there, became a respected parish clerk for many decades, and some Methodists attended services in both places of worship; some were baptised and buried in the parish church. Even the rivalry that centred on the annual walks of the two Sunday schools was more to do with putting on a good show than anything else.

There is no doubt that Chorlton was a God-fearing community. The parish church was well maintained, and the subject of such loyalty that the issue of building a new parish church split the Anglican community and caused division that long outlasted the 19th century. The smaller Methodist congregation dug deep to build their chapels. In total the parish church and the Wesleyan chapel had 770 seats, for a population that still only stood at 761. However, across Lancashire attendance in Anglican churches never rivalled that in other parts of England. In 1851 attendance in the county on Sunday 30 March 1851 at all churches was 44 per cent.[408] For the Anglican community this was just 18 per cent and for the Methodists 9 per cent.[409] The figures present some problems, because they do not distinguish between those who attended parish churches in the morning and a Methodist or non-denominational chapel in the evening. Nor were attendances much better when the census recorded what happened in the Chorlton Poor Law Union, which included Ardwick, Burnage, Chorlton-upon-Medlock, Chorlton with Hardy, Didsbury, Gorton, Hulme, Levenshulme, Moss Side, Rushulme, Stretford and Withington, which had a combined population of 123,841. Across this area attendance was 12.7 per cent for the Church of England and 18.2 per cent for other Protestant churches, which included the Wesleyans.[410] But again the picture is muddied. For while Chorlton and the neighbouring areas of Withington, Didsbury and Rusholme were still sparsely populated and

---

407 Jeremiah was at Lane End, describing himself as a cheese factor in 1841; Thomas is there from 1850–51; and by 1861 the Brundretts are back in occupation.

408 The 1851 Census of Religion was a separate census carried out at the same time as the main census. It assumed that everyone was Christian, and tried to discover which group was most numerous in each district by counting how many people attended each church on the census Sunday. It was published in 1854, Command Number 1690, and is available in Google Books.

409 The 1851 Census of Religion.

410 *Ibid.*, p.ccxc.

rural, Chorlton-upon-Medlock was a densely packed industrial community where church attendance was low.[411] In nearby Cheshire the figures were slightly higher.[412] Set against these figures Chorlton's were better. On that March Sunday of 1851 there were 140 attendances at the parish church and 290 at the Methodist chapel on the Row.[413] During the first fifty-one years of the 19th century 852 baptisms were recorded in the parish church, roughly sixteen a year, and there were over 1,000 burial services carried out in the same period.[414] The Wesleyans baptised 200 in their chapel and buried fifty-three in the slightly shorter period of 1807–50.[415] Not all of these would have been regular attendees, and some were not resident in Chorlton, but even allowing for some inaccuracies the picture is still one of a community that saw religion as part of its way of life.

---

411 Total attendance for all churches in the Chorlton Poor Law Union was 31.9 per cent, compared with 33.2 per cent for Manchester and 31.9 per cent for Salford.

412 In Cheshire they were 52 per cent in total: 24 per cent Anglican, 17 per cent Methodist.

413 Individual census returns from the 1851 Census of Worship. But beware statistics: the Wesleyans included Sunday school attendance in their overall total, while St Clement's returns were expressed separately. When these were included the parish could boast 196, which amounted to 26 per cent of the population.

414 Compiled from parish lists for St Clement's, which differ from other lists in being slightly higher than the parish certificates, and also included some who were non-residents.

415 Beech Road Baptismal Records 1807–47 from the Register of Baptisms in the Wesleyan Chapel Radnor Street Circuit 1830–7, microfilm MFPR2120, Local History Library Manchester City Council Libraries, Beech Road Baptismal Records 1807–50, own MSS, vol. 42.

fourteen

ENTERTAINMENT, CUSTOMS, SPORTS

General customs, Easter celebrations, the Wakes, sports

During the long hot summer of 1847 many in Chorlton would have been thinking of the harvest to come. Harvest celebrations began with the harvest home, where the last wagon loaded with the harvest was decorated and escorted back to the farm, accompanied by workers and their wives and children.[416] Later there was a special harvest supper, where the farmer rewarded his workers with food, alcohol and music. Later still there was a religious thanksgiving. Such celebrations served to underline the rural aspect of much that passed for customs and entertainment in the first half of the 19th century. Many of them were long established and were mirrored across the country, some even surviving as pale imitations in towns. They incorporated elements of popular history and frivolity, and there was an ever-present eye to making money. Processions of locals dressed in outlandish clothing and carrying all manner of props visited the homes of the gentry and farmers, putting on a show and expecting rewards in return. These rewards often eked out a household budget.

In Chorlton some of the most important celebrations were played out during Easter week. By far the most spectacular was the custom of pace egging, where a group of the younger villagers dressed up and acted out the story of St George triumphing over his enemies. Dressed:

with cardboard, tinsel, ribbon, calico, &c., of various colours, and presenting a very gaudy appearance, [they] would set off on the dawn of Good Friday for a tour of the village and the surrounding district, calling at the farmsteads, various residences, and public-houses,

---

416 In some places the leading reaper took the part of the Lord of the Harvest, dressing up and asking for money from onlookers.

the occupants of which, expecting the call, were quite prepared to receive them. The company comprised 'Open the Door', 'Saint George', 'Bold Slasher', 'Black Morocco King', 'Doctor', 'Doubt', and 'The Devil', and each carried a sword, with the exception of the doctor, who carried a large stick and bottle. One of the number was dressed as a lady, whose duty it was to carry the basket for the receipt of eggs and other gifts.[417]

This play (or a similar one) was acted out across the country. In most plays St George vanquished his opponent, who was then revived by the doctor – representing the Easter message of death and rebirth. Part of the fun was the interaction between crowd and players. Chorlton's 'lady', in some places known as Tosspot, held a long straw tail full of sharp pins in one hand. This she swung at anyone who tried to grab her basket, while at the same time encouraging onlookers to make a contribution. Only when the basket was full did the play begin, and after the valiant fight and some knock-about humour and ribald exchanges with the audience, the play ended with the Pace Egging Song:

Here's one or two Jolly Boys, all of one mind
We've come a Pace-Egging, and hope you'll prove kind
We hope you'll prove kind with your eggs and strong beer
And we'll come no more nigh you until next year.

For some of the actors it would have been the beer that was the main attraction, particularly when the performances were outside one of the local pubs. Here there was an audience whose generosity was fuelled by beer, and a landlord who reaped the benefit as the crowd celebrated with a drink. As the players moved off to the next venue they would inevitably be followed by a procession of children, who added to the noise and fun of the event.

The young of the township were not alone in dressing up and parading:

The middle-aged men of the village also formed themselves into companies, generally about half-a-dozen, placing a white shirt over their ordinary dress, tied at the bottom, and stuffing it with hay or straw, with masks over their faces to disguise themselves. They promenaded the village with the skull of a horse's head fixed on the top of a short pole, carried by a person concealed under a horsecloth, who worked the jaws of the horse's mouth with a small lever. One of the party was dressed as a lady, to carry the gifts received.[418]

417 Ellwood, chapter 8, 1885.
418 Ellwood, chapter 8, 1885.

In keeping with the Easter fun there was also the tradition of lifting or heaving. 'On Easter Monday the men lifted the women, and on Easter Tuesday the women lifted the men. The process was performed by two lusty men or women joining hands across each other's wrists, then, making the person to be "heaved" sit down on their arms, they lifted the individual aloft two or three times, often carrying the victim several yards along the road.'[419] Like our other Easter customs it was practised across Lancashire and Yorkshire, and may have originally echoed the Easter message of resurrection.

Less strenuous but no less popular was 'the custom of singing May songs. These started about the middle of April, and continued until the end of the month. The two songs called "Old May Song" and "New May Song" were sung at the gentlemen's residences and farmhouses in the neighbourhood by some half-dozen men, accompanied with violin, flute or clarinet.'[420] They were sung across Chorlton into Stretford and beyond. In Stretford the singers paraded at night. Standing underneath the window of a sleeping family, they named each member of the family. As the sleepy occupants came to the window they were saluted with a shout of 'Merry May' by the men below.[421]

Some of the festivities in Chorlton centred on the church, such as the wakes. These were once popular all over England, and were linked to celebrating the day of the saint to whom the parish church was dedicated. In Chorlton's case this was the third Sunday in July.[422] The custom whereby villagers brought fresh rushes to spread on the church floor after the old ones had been swept out gave the day its other name of rush bearing.[423] It is likely that Chorlton celebrated the day in the same manner as in Fallowfield. There a procession followed the rush cart, a farmer's flat cart decorated with garlands, branches of oaks, ribbons and flags, drawn by twenty or thirty young men harnessed in pairs and covered in garlands and ribbons. They were accompanied by men carrying banners, as well as pipers, drummers and bellringers.[424] As with all festivities, the villagers dressed up, left their doors open and entertained relatives and friends. In the morning many attended the church service and the rest of the day was spent in eating, drinking and enjoyment – which lingered on through the rest of the week.

Many rural customs celebrated the strength of animals – or indeed the strength of villagers. In bull-baiting a bull was pitted against a dog in a ring hemmed in by spectators. Chorlton's bull ring was in the centre of the village green. The bull was fastened to a chain,

419 Ibid.
420 Ibid.
421 Waugh, Edwin, op. cit., p.78, Google edn p.97.
422 St Clements' Day is 23 November, so the festival of wakes on the third Sunday in July may be connected to the church's dedication in about 1512 or possibly to when the new church was built in 1780.
423 Both hard and soft rushes were common in the flood plain, and both flower in the summer months. Soft rushes flower between July and August and hard rushes between June and August.
424 Williamson, Mrs C., op. cit., pp.99–100.

about 20yds long, which allowed him enough space to fight. The dog tried to seize the bull by its nose, but if the bull was well practised he endeavoured to get the dog on his horns and throw him high into the air; the fall would break the dog's neck or back. To avoid this, the villagers were ready to catch the dog, to break the force of his fall. Eyewitnesses often recalled seeing dead dogs left in ditches and hedgerows. If the bull was slow, the dog could hold on until the bull stood still, which was termed 'pinning the bull'. Only one dog was allowed in the ring at a time. These contests of strength were usually staged during the village wakes, and also at Easter and Whit Week. Naturally the main sponsors were the landlords of the Bowling Green and the Horse and Jockey, who had the most to gain from a gang of excited spectators outside their pubs. Not that they were alone in profiteering from the event. The owner of the dog that successfully pinned the bull was awarded a prize, and no doubt some went away the richer having betted on the winner. In the 1840s there were those who could still remember the notable contests and spoke of the victorious bulls, like Young Fury, son of Old Fury, who was regularly baited, and the bull men like Edward Simmer, commonly known as Ned, who afterwards was converted to a religious life and finally became a Methodist preacher. At the inquest of Francis Deakin in 1847 John Cookson boasted that he 'had been bull ward in the bull ring, and once kept one of the gamest bulls in the country'. However, the sport's popularity was on the wane, and for some years it all but died out before being revived by a butcher called James Moores, from Deansgate in Manchester. This revival was not welcomed by everyone: as James Moores and his bulls travelled south from the city he brought hundreds 'of men of the very lowest character to witness the proceedings'. [425] The sport suffered another blow when Samuel Wilton enclosed the village green, turning it into his garden. Perhaps it continued in the pinfold or moved to a remoter corner of the township: John Cookson lived up at Dark Lane, far enough from the village to cause less stir – and there was the added advantage that it was on one of the roads to Manchester. which might have allowed the 'Manchester trade' to come and watch. Either way the last bull bait in Chorlton took place at the wakes in 1835.[426]

Cockfighting suffered the same fate. It had been practised by a large oak tree at Lane End, the spot still known as Cock Clod well into the 1880s. But badger and dogfighting could still be found if you knew where to look: in the case of badger baiting this was at the Black Horse at Lane End.

These sports attracted people from outside Chorlton, as did foot racing, wrestling and prize-fighting. The least violent of these was foot racing, which was a test of endurance. The contestants agreed a distance to be run and wagered on who would win. Early in the 19th

425 Ellwood, chapter 7, 1885.
426 The 1835 Cruelty to Animals Act prohibited bear-baiting and cockfighting and extended earlier legislation to protect bulls, dogs, bears and sheep from 'cruel and improper treatment'.

century these races covered large distances and involved staggering amounts of money. The same was true of wrestling. In September 1834 a travelling team advertised a show on the bowling green of the Northumberland Arms on Stretford Road. There were prizes and a charge for admission. This was close enough to the village to draw interest, but there must also have been local contests. Prize-fighting was a more brutal but lucrative sport that in most cases was more a test of endurance than skill. Two powerful men often in the prime of life exchanged body blows and insults, along with kicks and headbutts, which while illegal were often ignored by the referee. They fought with bare knuckles, and contests went to many rounds with little in the way of rules.[427] During the 1830s William Thompson, better known as Bendigo, fought contests that lasted from twenty-two to ninety-two rounds. Each round lasted for no set time, ending when a fighter was knocked down or thrown to the ground. Once on the floor he had 30 seconds to come up to the 'scratch', which was a marker set in the centre of the ring. Once engaged in the bout neither combatant could take a break, and if pain or exhaustion forced one of them to a standstill they could be disqualified. Prize money varied. Bendigo fought for a purse of £25 in 1835, but later in the decade this rose to over £200. Big-name fights could draw crowds of between 10,000 and 15,000, and emotions ran high. There was often that potent mix of alcohol and partisanship, fuelled by heavy betting, which could turn into mob violence. The fact that fighting for money was illegal meant that these events took place away from the village, close by the Mersey. The land here was open and could accommodate the hundreds who came to watch and wager on the outcome – and if the police arrived the crowd could escape across the Mersey into Cheshire. So it was in the summer of 1848 when Samuel Warburton was 20 minutes into a fight, watched by 200 to 300 spectators. The police were alerted by Samuel Dean of Barlow Farm, alarmed at such a large gathering at 5.30 on a Sunday morning.[428] The crowd and the boxers duly escaped but a little after 7am Samuel was arrested in the Horse and Jockey. PC Winstanley, who had led his force of seven police officers to the fight, had 'changed my Clothes and pursued the Parties and the Prisoner I apprehended in a Public House, the Horse and Jockey in Chorlton-cum-Hardy about 7 o'clock yesterday morning. I told him that he was charged with being one of the Combatants and he said that he was not. There were bruises upon his face and lips and blood flowing from some of them.'[429] The following day Samuel went before the magistrate at the New Bailey Court House in Salford and was found guilty on the evidence of Wynstanley, Samuel Dean and

---

427 The first real rules were drawn up by Jack Broughton (c.1703–89) in 1743, and were the only written rules for over a century until superseded by the Marquess of Queensberry rules in the 1860s. Broughton was variously a waterman and prize-fighter, and ran his own boxing amphitheatre. Later still he ran a boxing academy and even served as a Yeoman of the Guard.
428 Lancashire Quarter Sessions, 17 July 1848, Lancashire County Records Office.
429 Lancashire Quarter Sessions 1848, 17 July 1848, Lancashire County Records Office.

John Davies. But despite being found guilty Samuel was discharged on sureties.[430] He was just eighteen, and he may have been bankrolled by his sponsor.

During the evening after that dramatic arrest at the Horse and Jockey there may have been some who wanted to talk about another local prize-fighter. This was Ned Painter, who was born in 1784 in Stretford and became famous before retiring to run a pub in Norwich. His father John was a butcher who moved to Chorlton and lived at the top of the Row, where later John Holt built his home. In his heyday Painter fought some of the best. In 1818 he went thirty-one rounds with Tom Spring. During the first round Painter was hit on the side of the throat and went down, hitting his head and shoulder on a stake that held the ring together. Despite this he fought another thirty rounds before succumbing, and in the forty-two-round re-match it was Painter who seriously damaged his opponent by opening a gash over his eye.

Not all entertainment was violent or cruel. Since the 1820s there had been a brass band in Chorlton. It had twenty-four members, including William Chesshyre, William Moore, William Gresty, George Lunt and John and James Axon. It folded, but started up again in 1850, with the addition of Daniel Thomas, James Gresty and William Renshaw.[431] These were not wealthy men, so funding was a challenge. In the case of James Axon this meant making his own drum, which proved too large to get through the door of his cottage! More than once the band resorted to raising subscriptions from the township, and after its second formation they raised £28.[432]

Festivals and sporting events may have been the high points of village entertainment, but everyday activities should not be ignored. Some, like the pub, went on all the year round, and were almost exclusively male orientated. Others were confined to lighter evenings and better weather: a summer evening walk with the family or a foraging trip for wild fruit. Cottage gardens had to be tended, with time spent cultivating flowers and vegetables, and keeping an eye on chickens and perhaps the family pig. No doubt some people were engaged upon reading and writing, while others administered sick and burial clubs or attended Vestry meetings.

Manchester was just 4½ miles away, which opened a cornucopia of opportunities. Mary Bayley, who worked for the Higginbothams, recorded her visit to Manchester in June 1830 to watch the wakes. The city offered markets, theatres, churches and an opportunity to be part of a big bustling place. There were also zoological and botanical gardens. To the east of Manchester, just 2 miles away, was Belle Vue. This opened in June 1836 with an Italian garden, lakes, mazes and a hothouse, as well as an aviary. Three years later it added elephants, lions and other exotic African animals, and in 1847 a racecourse was opened. Its owner John Jennison

430 Lancashire Quarter Sessions 1848, 17 July 1848, Lancashire County Records Office.

431 Ellwood, chapter 25, 1886.

432 Later still they were able to call on the generosity of Samuel Mendel, who until his trading business with the Far East collapsed was a very wealthy benefactor.

advertised in the summer of 1850 that the attractions included a 'Museum of Curiosities, with stuffed animals as well as two very fine specimens of the Lion and lioness, a new monkey hall, a gymnasium, a variety of other African animals'. There were also an 'extensive sheet of water, an Elizabethan maze, spacious dancing platforms, and a powerful brass band'. Mindful of the weather, 'accommodation is provided in the gardens for the shelter of thousands'.[433]

Closer to home were the Botanical Gardens on Chester Road and the Pomona Gardens at Cornbrook in Hulme.[434] The Botanical Gardens was a more gentle place, with what one observer described as 'fine specimens of trees and shrubs in the extensive arboretum and plant houses and conservatories ... holding beautiful specimens of plants collected from around the world'.[435] Pomona Gardens was, in contrast, another of those boisterous gardens of fun. It boasted a similar mix of attractions to Belle Vue, including 'the magic bridge, Gymnasium, flying swings, bowling green, rifle shooting, romantic walks and a promenade for both adults and juveniles as well as boat trips on the Irwell'.[436] In the summer of 1850 it pulled out the stops with its 'Splendid representation of the ERUPTION OF MOUNT VESUVIUS, as it occurred in 1849, the most terrific on record'. Here was the 'magnificent Bay of Naples, painted and erected by the celebrated artist Mr A.F. Tait, and extends the whole length of the lake covering upwards of 20,000 yards of canvas and is one of the Largest ever Erected in England'. These places truly played to the Victorian desire for self-improvement with a dash of raucous fun. When in 1857 Manchester staged an art exhibition at the Botanical Gardens it was a great success, attracting large numbers of people – not all of whom were from the more privileged sections of society. Special excursion trains catering for working people were organised, with some travelling from the North East of England. The gardens were not cheap, however. Belle Vue originally charged a subscription ticket of 10s for a family and 5s for an individual, while Pomona Gardens demanded 1s for adults and 6d for children in the summer of 1850. These prices were beyond the reach of labouring families. Sound commercial sense won out in the end, and at Belle Vue subscription tickets were abandoned in favour of a general admission price of 4d, which rose to 6d in 1851.

Just how many chose to leave Chorlton and enjoy these attractions is impossible to say, but there were probably few who sought to travel this far. The daily round kept most labourers close to home, and what little time was left over was spent in cottage or garden.

---

433 Slater's Manchester and Salford Directory, 1850, p.7

434 The Manchester Botanical Gardens on Chester Road occupied the area around White City, while the Pomona Gardens was situated where the Cornbrook joins the Irwell. Cornbrook Road is still visible for a short distance, sandwiched between the Irwell and the Bridgewater Canal; it runs from Chester Road alongside the Bridgewater Way and joins Pomona Strand. The rather forlorn Pomona Palace public house sits on the corner of Cornbrook and Chester Road.

435 Manchester Botanical Gardens, Old Trafford, http://manchesterhistory.net/manchester/gone/botanicgardens.html.

436 Slater's Manchester and Salford Directory, 1850, p.51.

fifteen

CRIME

Murders, robberies and poaching, drunken behaviour and infanticide

pring 1847 brought tragedy to two families in Chorlton, and reminded people of other darker events nearly a decade earlier. In May 1847 young Francis Deakin was murdered in a beershop in Martledge, bringing back memories of the awful murder of Mary Moore nine years earlier. This was not the peaceful rural outpost that some believed. During the years that separated these two murders there were plenty of examples of lesser crimes.

The death of Francis Deakin was particularly shocking. He was killed in a brawl over the wife of a neighbour. Francis was a market gardener, who rented 6 acres from the Egertons. By all accounts he was hard working and loved Martha, his wife. She had given birth to their sixth child just three weeks earlier and was still confined to bed. It was a Tuesday, and Francis had been drinking in his neighbour's beershop, just behind his own home. As beershops went it was a cut above most of them. A neat detached brick build-ing of two storeys, it stood in a small garden on the right-hand side of the main road out of the village. Unusually for such houses it was double-fronted, with two rooms either side of the passage from the front door. It was run by Mrs Leach, who had not had an easy life. George, her husband, was a mechanic who worked for the Manchester & Leeds Railway Company. He was well paid, but as he was the first to admit much of it 'going on the spree'. On one occasion he disappeared to France, and it was while he was away that his wife opened the beershop with the help of friends. Mrs Leach was a prudent and industrious woman. Fearing that if her husband returned he might sell the furni-ture and her possessions, she had the beershop put in the name of one of her relatives, Charlotte Hayson, who lived with her son and family at Hobson Farm. Sure enough, George returned when he heard about his wife's comfortable position. He got his old job

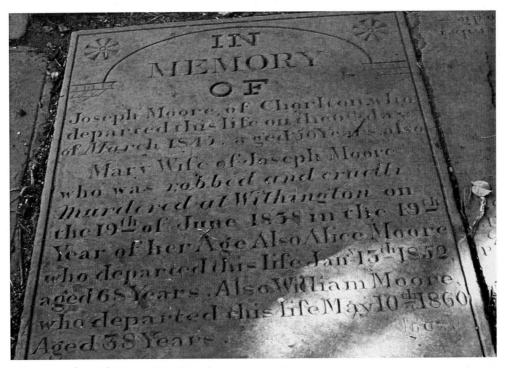

Mary Moore was a well-known and popular member of the village community who worked at Dog House Farm just outside the township. She was murdered in June 1838 on her way back from the Manchester markets.

back, but even though he moved back in with his wife he was still prone to wandering off for a week, or even a fortnight.

On the day in question Francis and George had been drinking from about 10am. Early on they were joined by John Cookson, who like Francis was a gardener. John and Francis had known each other for about sixteen years, and John was local, living on Dark Lane. At 4pm, after they had drunk about six quarts of beer and some rum that John had brought with him, there was a row between George and his wife. Perhaps the drink inflamed things: George had been drinking the day before and into the night – and when he had suffered a head injury some years earlier his surgeon had warned him that drink might make him liable to 'extraordinary excitement'. In the course of the quarrel George became very abusive. He called his wife 'Mr Satan's whore' and Francis remonstrated with him, saying 'do not call her that bad name; I don't think she is deserving of it, for I never saw anything but a decent prudent woman'. At this point George Leach ran into the kitchen, picked out a long, sharp carving knife and went into the passage. Francis followed, and George turned on him. He said, 'I'll have no man interfering with me and my wife,' and then stabbed Francis. Immediately he seemed mortified by what he had done. He let the knife be taken from him, and waited with John Cookson and John Fox, the tailor who lived just across the way at Renshaw's Cottages. Fox had been passing, and it was he who sent for the constable. George continued to mutter that Francis was not dead, which turned into a desperate ' I hope he is not dead,' and finally 'I would give anything if I could restore him.' Together PC Winstanley and John Fox accompanied Leach to the Stretford lockup.

The inquest was held the following Thursday at the Horse and Jockey. The jury consisted of Thomas White, the foreman, Edmund Newton, Thomas Cookson, James Bankcroft, William Gresty, William Brownhill, William Bailey, William Knight, James Higginbotham, William Chesshyre, James Brundrett and Peter Langford. After the witnesses had all given their evidence the jury was left alone for a few minutes, before returning a verdict of wilful murder.[437] At George's trial in Liverpool a full four months later the jury returned a verdict of 'not guilty of murder but guilty of aggravated manslaughter' after a 2-hour deliberation. The defence made much of the fact that 'the prisoner had been irritated by the conduct of the deceased; that there had been drunken quarrels between them; and that it was under the influence of these feelings the blow had been inflicted'.[438] George escaped the hangman, and instead was transported for life.[439]

The township turned out for Francis's funeral. Several hundred of his neighbours, including members of his sick and burial club, were in attendance. The Revd William Birley gave a 'very impressive funeral service' and later his sermon was advertised for sale, the proceeds of which may have gone to the widow. Mrs Leach left the village, and the Deakin family survived the awful murder. Martha took over the market garden, helped by her children, and for a while took in lodgers.[440]

The tragedy reveals much about the social attitudes of the period. George had given up alcohol and so, when he went back to drinking, the surgeon Francis Brook Wragg, a member of a temperance society and 'an enemy to drink', went to the beershop 'in order to reclaim the prisoner'. Drunk as George was, it was Francis who revealed the conventional prejudice to the temperance movement, by saying with a 'sneer that [Wragg] should have half a gallon of Buttermilk and that ale was the stuff'. In contrast George was conciliatory and keen that Francis should not insult Wragg, because 'he is able to answer you any question you may ask him'.

Petty burglary and robbery plagued the community from time to time. How much is difficult to say, but some notable incidents were recorded and there must have been more. In March 1837 the home of William Chesshyre at Pitts Brow on Edge Lane was broken into and robbed. It may be because he was the parish clerk, responsible for stor-

437 *Manchester Times and Gazette*, 7 May 1847.
438 *Manchester Guardian*, 18 August 1847.
439 *Daily News*, 19 August 1847.
440 William, b. 1834, Samuel, b. 1835, Francis, b. 1840, Thomas, b. 1843, Hannah, b. 1845, Ellen, b. 1847, 1851 census Enu. 1, p.2.

Little of the silver plate has survived. Some was stolen in March 1837, but this piece, donated by Lady Ann Bland in 1733, is still in the possession of the church.

ing the church plate and vestments, that his house was burgled. In the early hours the minister's hood, the church communion linen, some silver spoons and a new copper kettle were all stolen. Handbills were issued the following day offering a reward, and a few hours later two policemen in Manchester picked up the two robbers, John Crossly and John Birmingham. They were arrested on Peter Street with the kettle still in their possession.[441] It is interesting to note the speed and ease with which the village publicised the crime.

Organised gangs also seem to have been active. In the winter of 1840 one gang worked its way down from Stretford, breaking into the big houses along the road to Chorlton. They met their match with old Mr Hacking, the ropemaker on Chorlton Lane. When they woke him up in the dead of night he shouted for help, and they ran away having got nothing. Contemporary accounts record how they used chisels to force their way in, and pushed little bits of flagstone into the gap to act as wedges. The same gang was active a few nights later, when it broke into another house to steal a quantity of bacon and other provisions, before taking the garden tools from the school at the Deaf and Dumb Asylum at Old Trafford.[442] Later in the week another gang was apprehended after attempting a serious robbery on a house in Chorlton, and another two crimes were committed just outside the township by 'an expert prowling thief'.[443]

Not all the criminals were anonymous. In the winter of 1837 Thomas Leigh had two sovereigns stolen from him by John Battersby. Thomas had come back from selling hay in Manchester. It was a cold November night and, happy with the £5 he had made, Thomas stopped for a drink at one of the local pubs. He began drinking with John Battersby and Richard Marsland. By the end of the night Leigh had had a lot to drink and accepted Battersby's offer of a bed for the night. The next morning when he awoke two sovereigns were missing, and to cut a long story short Battersby was found guilty and transported for twelve years.[444]

441 *Manchester Times and Gazette*, 14 March 1837. The two policemen were PCs Armitage and Howarth. The robbery took place on Tuesday 10 March. The two were committed for trial but there is no record of what happened to them. Given that other criminals were transported for similar crimes it is probable that this was their fate.

442 *Morning Chronicle*, 17 December 1840.

443 *Manchester Guardian*, 29 October 1855.

444 *The Times*, 14 August 1838.

The most frequent rural crime was poaching or stealing from fields. For some this was an acceptable practice.[445] Sometimes it took the form of stealing game or produce from a local landowner, with the justification that the landlord had much and the labourers had little. These crimes were usually committed by people who lived in the same neighbourhood, but Chorlton's close proximity to Hulme and Manchester meant that some crimes were committed by urban visitors. For example, in October 1855 an organised gang from Hulme descended on the farm of William Knight and stole eight loads of potatoes, only to return the following Sunday in an attempt to take another two and a half loads.[446] The names, addresses and occupations of the thieves all survive.

Just outside the township in the preceding decades there were cases of poaching, fraud and robbery. Peter Gleave was fined £5 after being caught setting snares in the grounds of the Trafford family.[447] James Hall stole money from the farmer who employed him,[448] and three men were apprehended for repeatedly passing fake banknotes.[449]

Alcohol-related crimes posed a real problem, and much of this it seems was caused by Sunday visitors who made their way from Hulme and Manchester to drink in the township. It is the sheer numbers of these visitors that is surprising: there appear to have been organised outings, and filled with beer they resembled a mob. Eye-witnesses on one occasion talked of a group of six men playing pitch and toss in the road, vandalising the property of locals and turning to intimidation when they were asked to stop. Thomas Johnson, who lived close by, was beaten up, and perhaps only saved from worse treatment by the intervention of another group. To make matters worse the same gang, reinforced by another twenty men, reappeared the following week to attack property and threaten the inhabitants, before fleeing when the police and a group of locals arrived.[450]

The level of drunkenness in Manchester was regularly commented on by writers in the 1840s,[451] and there is no reason to believe the same was not true in rural communities. There were five pubs in Chorlton and varying numbers of beershops, all of which stayed open all day and late into the night. During 1846 and 1848 the farmer Higginbotham recorded many instances where his carters were too drunk to carry on working. Between 6 April and 27 April George Badcock was drunk on six occasions: once he had been drinking all afternoon and another time all day. His replacement was Thomas Davies who fared

445 Reay, *op. cit.*, pp.76–7.
446 *Manchester Guardian*, 29 October 1855. William Knight's farm was just north of the Royal Oak pub.
447 *Manchester Times*, 14 November 1828.
448 *Manchester Times*, 24 January 1829.
449 *Manchester Times and Gazette*, 8 August 1829.
450 *Manchester Guardian*, 29 October 1855. The beerhouse was the Royal Oak, which was the first on the route from Hulme and Manchester. The cottages can be traced to a collection of cottages beyond William Knight's farm.
451 Engels and others described the level of drunkenness among sections of the working classes in Manchester.

little better. Having been sent to town to collect dung, he spent the day drinking and left the cart in Manchester. This decision might with hindsight have been wise, for only a few years earlier, and on the road that Davies would have used, a carter was killed in an accident caused by the drunkenness of another driver.[452]

There were problems with pubs and beerhouses in Chorlton. The licence of the Black Horse at Lane End was finally withdrawn for breaking the drinking laws, as was William Brownhill's. Nor should we forget the part played by alcohol in the death of Francis Deakin. Just over the township's border another drunken group of men threw stones and potatoes at one of the packet boats passing through Stretford on a Sunday evening in 1832, seriously injuring a young child.[453]

There were even darker moments – when the township was stirred by stories of infanticide. This crime regularly filled the newspapers, which reported events with a mix of moral outrage and lurid detail. The accounts invariably followed a set pattern, which stressed the mother's feelings of shame and guilt at giving birth to an illegitimate child along with her often helpless situation. There might be a passing reference to the feckless father, as in the case of Rachel Atkinson aged nineteen – who had 'been seduced and abandoned by her seducer' in Manchester in February 1837. More often it was the nature of the crime and the way the child died that excited the interest of the journalist. Here were laid out 'the particulars ... of a child barbarously murdered and secreted in the Old Park Wood, and on Saturday last another case of child murder of a more revolting character [where] in a brown paper bag was found to contain the trunk of the body of a new born child, the head, legs and arms having been cut away'. Few recognised the part played by 'poverty and deplorable ignorance', but portrayed infanticide as a crime on the increase. *The Times* was in no doubt that this was attributable to the practice of burial clubs, who paid anything up to £5 on the death of a child to working-class families, despite the fact that the cost of a burial might only be 20 to 30s, 'so that the surplus is a direct premium on the death of a child'. It should be no surprise that *The Times* confidently claimed that 'cases are frequent in which children are insured in several clubs, one is mentioned in which the father of a child ten months old, insured in three clubs, received twenty pounds; in another case a man had made payments in nineteen different burial clubs'. The same accusation was laid before the Parliamentary Committee on Friendly Societies in 1854 by a procession of respected worthies, who lined up to confirm the link between child deaths and burial clubs. These included Mr Justice Wightman, the governors of Chester Castle and Kirkdale Gaol, and a solicitor from Stockport, all of whom brought lists of poisoned children whose parents

452 *Manchester Times and Gazette*, 21 September 1833.
453 *Ibid.*, 29 September 1832.

had benefited from club payouts. Not to be outdone, the chaplain of Preston Gaol, who freely admitted that he had no knowledge of 'murders to obtain burial money', confidently, asserted that 'temptations to neglect children were induced by burial societies'. He could advance only one example, but proffered the fact that 'the percentage of deaths under five years of age was ten per cent for the wealthy and middle classes and 60 per cent amongst the poorer and working classes. In one burial club it was 62 per cent and in another 64 per cent.' Given the conditions of the time, there would have been many who drew the conclusion that such figures owed much more to low wages, poor sanitation and diet than benefit fraud. It was left to those who worked for or represented the societies to correct some of the misleading assertions about the cheapness of child burials, contradicting the charges that parents in receipt of burial payments had been found guilty of murder and reaffirming that there 'was a strong disposition among the working population to bury members of their family … in what was called a respectful manner'.

Such weighty debates about the cause of the crime probably did not feature in the township when the bodies of two infants were discovered in autumn 1849 and summer 1855. These deaths appeared gruesome and their mothers were judged guilty, but infanticide was difficult to prove; the courts as well as the public were often sympathetic to the accused. An infant might die of any one of a number of natural causes, and even when the evidence seemed clear cut the verdict was often reduced to concealment of the death. Therefore we will never be sure how many cases of infanticide occurred in the township. However, the circumstances of the two infant deaths in 1849 and 1855 appear to have been fairly clear. Both Mary Ann Page and Ann Pearson were single women whose babies had died mysteriously. The child of Mary Ann was discovered hidden in her bedroom, while Ann Pearson's was left in a ditch. Neither publicly said who the fathers were, and both appeared to have good reason for losing their child.

Mary Ann Page arrived in Chorlton in early August and took lodgings with a Mrs Phillips, who lived in Brownhill's Buildings on Sandy Lane.[454] She was described as a servant who was 'out of place', and may well have come from Manchester: there was a Mary Page living in Deansgate in Manchester in 1841. She was twenty years old and lived with her mother, father and sister. Chorlton would have been a sound choice for someone from the city who was expecting an illegitimate child. It was relatively easy to get to, but sufficiently far enough away to escape from family and friends. Mary Ann took up lodgings on 6 August and by the beginning of September was feeling and looking unwell. She asked Mrs Phillips to go into town to purchase some herbal tea from someone at Bank Top. This

---

454 Hannah Phillips 1818–81, Brownhills Buildings, 1851 census, Enu. 8, p.15, no. 51, died 29 October 1881 aged sixty-five, St Clement's burial records.

was on London Road very close to the railway station, and during most of the 19th century there was a market on the site.[455] It was clear to her landlady that Mary was pregnant and she was asked to leave immediately, but after much pleading she was allowed one last night. That night would have tested the strongest heart and soul. She was alone: isolated from her family, abandoned by her unborn child's father, in a house full of strangers. During that last day and night she slipped into labour. There was no one to comfort her or to dissuade her from her intended course of action. Twice during the night she was seen standing in the yard for some considerable time, and at half past five she arose and left the house again. Returning from the yard, she asked for a pair of scissors. Mrs Phillips told the court that Mary had explained she wanted them 'to cut a knot in my stays'. Not that Mrs Phillips was convinced: she decided to search the room and, perhaps for moral support, asked her neighbour Mrs Silgram to help.[456] Mary Ann must have feared the worst, for she denied 'that she had been delivered', but the body of her newly born baby was found in a large box, with puncture marks to the temple and cheek. The inquest found her guilty of wilful murder and she was sent to Kirkdale Gaol for trial at the assizes. In such an unforgiving age it is easy to assume that Mary would have been given a capital sentence, but the jury found her not guilty of murder and she was sentenced to two months' hard labour.[457] At the same assizes in Liverpool two brothers were sentenced to six months' hard labour for manslaughter, while at York another was given twenty years' transportation for the same crime, and a young mother and her father were acquitted for concealing the birth of a child.[458] A number of newspapers carried the story, but only a few conveyed the anguish that Mary Ann must have gone through.[459]

It is likely that some people in Chorlton would have felt sympathy for a young woman who chose to give birth alone in a strange place. How the same people felt about the discovery of Ann Pearson's son in a ditch just six years later would have been coloured by the knowledge that Ann was a local girl. She had been born in the township and her parents still lived on the Row. They were poor but 'respectable' and had attended the Methodist chapel. Ann's fate was to be abandoned by her child's father and left to have her baby in the workhouse. She was a domestic servant who had been working away from home since at least her nineteenth birthday. In the spring of 1851 she was in the house of a grocer in Altrincham, but had been living in Manchester when the child was conceived. Her story, which unfolded at the inquest in the Horse and Jockey, was no less tragic than that of

---

455 Between 1804 and 1824 the site was occupied by Bank Top Market and from 1824 to 1878 by London Royal Market. Mary's knowledge of the herbal tea dealer perhaps indicates that she came from Manchester.

456 Hannah Silgram lived on the Row, 1841 census, Enu. 8, p.5.

457 Lancashire Criminal Registers, 1849, p.163.

458 *Northern Star and National Trades Journal*, Leeds, 22 December 1849.

459 *Ibid.*, *Freeman's Journal and Daily Advertizer*, Dublin, 12 September 1849, *Hull Packet and East Riding Times*, Hull, 14 September 1849.

Mary Ann and must have struck a chord with many. She 'had fathered the child in the Court House on Brown Street' and moved into a house on Silver Street in early January.[460] Many might have speculated about where she had been during the missing months, and Ann remained silent. Nor did she reveal any details of the father at the inquest. Silver Street was a good choice in that it was close to the workhouse, and the woman she shared a room with showed no moral outrage at a single unmarried mother, and agreed to nurse the child once it was born. On 8 February Ann was admitted to the workhouse, gave birth within its forbidding walls on the 27th and left three weeks later, returning briefly for five days before going back on the 29th to Silver Street. Her companion, the widow Jenny Burrows was in no doubt that all was well because on the following day Ann explained she was returning to the workhouse 'until she got the first weekly payment and then would return and agree the terms for nursing' the child. But Ann came home to Chorlton, arriving at her parents' house at about 11pm on 31 March. She told her mother that 'the child was dead and buried' and remained in the family home until she was arrested on 12 April. The baby boy had been found in a ditch close to the main road into the township from Hulme, and in all probability had been smothered to death at about the time she returned. As no one had seen Ann's baby in the family home, the inquest drew the conclusion that she might have disposed of the child on her way into Chorlton. During the inquest she uttered no evidence in her defence, and when asked if she had any response to make to the charge, replied 'I don't wish to say anything.' It is therefore all the more remarkable that in August at her trial she was found not guilty.

Mary Ann and Ann's fate at the hand of the courts was not unusual, but popular feeling in the village may have run the other way. In the case of Ann Pearson, there had been no attempt by her friends or family to engage professional help on her behalf and she seems to have left the township.

---

460 *Manchester Guardian*, 18 April 1855. The Manchester Borough Court House was on Brown Street close to where it joined Market Street, according to Slater's Directory of Manchester and Salford for 1850; the Court House was 5 Brown Street. Brown Street joined at 64 Market Street.

sixteen

THE MURDER OF MARY MOORE

Her character, her employment, the murder, the inquest and subsequent trial

I n some ways, far more disturbing than the murder of newborn children was the murder of Mary Moore, 'who was robbed and cruely murdered at Withington'.[461]. Her death was a gruesome crime for which no one was prosecuted, and which sheds much light on life in Chorlton and in the wider world.

June 1838 was an eventful month. In London preparations were well advanced for the coronation of the new queen, the People's Charter had been written, and in Manchester there was industrial unrest – with further signs that the economic depression was showing no sign of abating.[462] For local people the month was to be remembered for a brutal murder.

Mary was forty-nine years old and married to Joseph Moore; they lived on the Green. She was employed by the Chorlton family of Dog House Farm to sell vegetables and fruit at Smithfield Market. This had opened in 1822, and according to one writer 'it would be difficult to point out anything in the three kingdoms of nature – animal, vegetable, or mineral – that cannot be procured here'.[463] There are no pictures of the market at this time, but maps show that it covered a large area in the island formed by Shudehill, Swan Street and Oak Street.

Her employers had to trust her: on any one day Mary might take a considerable amount of money. Not surprisingly, therefore, she was described as a 'remarkably steady woman

---

461 From her gravestone in the parish churchyard.

462 Queen Victoria was crowned in London on 28 June. In Manchester there were plans for firework displays at Ardwick and Salford. The People's Charter had been published in May, calling for an extension of suffrage to all men over the age of twenty-one. The *Manchester Courier* for 23 June carried a story attacking the attempts by the stone mason's union to maintain a closed shop. There had been a trade crisis in 1836–37 and again in 1839–42.

463 Duffield, *op. cit.*, 1850, p.17.

not at all addicted to liquor'.[464] During the spring and summer months she took the journey to market three times a week. On 19 June Mary left home at 6.30am carrying a basket and umbrella. Her route to the farm is unknown, but more than likely she walked from the Green up the Row before reaching Lane End and walking down Moss Lane to Dog House.[465] At that time in the morning the lanes would have been busy with other farm-workers, and in each of the farms along the way there would have been the purposeful stir of people about their business. Retracing her journey today along modern roads takes about 30 minutes, so Mary might have reached the home of her employer not much after seven o'clock.

The produce would already have been loaded, and Mary and Thomas Hooley, who drove the farm cart; would have aimed to be at Smithfield as early as possible. Their journey would have taken them through what is now Whalley Range and Hulme before they joined Chester Road into the heart of the city. It would have been a pleasant enough ride through open fields; only when they were closer to Manchester would they have encountered the grim rows of cottages, factories and industrial waterways. The last part of the journey through crowded streets would have been much slower. As well as the normal traffic there must have been many other farm wagons from the Chorlton, Withington and Stretford areas, known for their apples and other fruits.[466] People like the Woods of Didsbury, who ran a pub, a mixed farm and a shop, regularly sold their fruit in Manchester and Stockport during the first quarter of the 19th century.

Smithfield would have been teeming with the noise of wagons, the smells of cheese and dried fish and the ebb and flow of people who bought everything from food to china, from glass to clothes. The sheer volume of activity in the market and the surrounding streets must have been overpowering. After all, here was one of the major centres of Manchester that had increased its population by 34.000 in one decade, and which was becoming famous across the world as a new type of city. It was, in the words of Asa Briggs, 'the shock city of the Industrial Revolution'. Here were the rows of workers' homes surrounding the dark and noisy cotton factories and engineering works, in turn dominated by the lavish show-warehouses designed to market the finished textiles. And above all there were the new and exciting forms of transport, from the network of canals, linking the North with the Midlands and beyond, to the first passenger railway, which was only eight years old.

It being June, much of Mary's load would have been gooseberries, which are in season by the middle of the month. Across Lancashire there were gooseberry societies locked in

---

464 *Manchester Courier*, 23 June 1838.
465 This is the most logical route based on the 1844 Ordnance Survey map. Chorlton Row is now Beech Road.
466 Maps of Chorlton in the first half of the 19th century show how many orchards there were in the township. Farms advertised fruit 'for sale locally and which is a clear sign that the sale of fruit provided at least some part of the income of many farmers'. Scola, *op. cit.*, p.121.

competition: the fruit was favoured by handloom weavers and cotton spinners as produce to grow in their cottage gardens.[467] Mary may have sold the fruit from a stall on the street directly to passersby, or possibly conducted business with one of the many middlemen who were beginning to act as intermediaries between the grower and customer.

The day was successful. Mary told a friend that she had a 'good market', selling her 'gooseberries at 3d. per quart', and she may have made over £3 – a substantial amount. By eleven o'clock she had loaded the empty baskets onto the cart, having arranged to meet Thomas at Brook Street. But for some reason she failed to keep the appointment, and after waiting for a while Thomas made his way back arriving at the farm at about 2pm. Mary, having missed Thomas, walked back from Manchester. On the way she met Mr Mee, a local farmer. The two had known each other for about twenty years, and as they walked they talked about food prices and Mary's successful day. A little before 2pm they parted company, Mary was only about 10 minutes from the farm. Mr Mee looked back, but a bend in the lane hid her from view.[468] She didn't arrive at the farm, and neither did she go home.

The following day a search was mounted. John Brundrett, her brother-in-law, and William Leigh, who worked for the Chorltons, searched for her in 'the pits, lanes, fields and culverts' of the neighbourhood. Just after 8pm, not much more than 100yds from Moss Lane and the entrance to Dog House Farm, they found her body along a field lane, in a water-filled ditch. She was lying on her face 'with her head towards one bank, and her feet to the opposite bank. Her head appeared to be much cut on one side and her bonnet and cap awry.' Mary had died from two blows to her head, which had been delivered by a blunt instrument with such force that her skull had been driven into her brain. Death had been instantaneous. Her market money was missing, but her personal cash, amounting to 'two half crowns, and four shillings and also two half pennies', was still in her purse. Her basket and an umbrella were also missing.

The awfulness of Mary's death was reinforced by the place in which she was found. The path through the field led neither to her home nor to Mrs Chorlton's. Mary had probably been taken to this remote and empty spot against her will. Worse still, her lifeless body might have been dragged to the spot and thrown into the ditch. Later in the day a large stick, which might have been the murder weapon, was discovered at the corner of Three Lanes.[469]

---

467 Buxton, *op. cit.*, p.35. There is a reference to the competition among handloom weavers to grow the biggest gooseberries.

468 The Mee family had the nearby farm of Hobson Hall, which they were still farming in 1911; it was at the junction of Manchester Road and Wilbraham Road. Later it became known as Briton's Farm.

469 The corner of Three Lanes has long disappeared, but using the Ordnance Survey maps for 1844 and 1888 and a modern street plan it is possible to track the scene to the island between Wilbraham, Withington, Kingsbrook and Saint Austell Roads.

With no forensic science or CCTV evidence available to them, the authorities relied on eye-witness accounts and supposition. Very soon after the murder it was reported that during Tuesday there had been four men just 10yds from the gate into the field where Mary was found. 'Some strange men having been in the morning and afternoon of Tuesday in the lane, playing at pitch and toss, it was suspected that they were the murderers and the police instantly commenced an active search for them.'[470] The police were helped by descriptions of two of the men, although these were limited to their height, the colour of their jackets and the fact that one of the four was left-handed. Three other witnesses saw the men during the day, and it became apparent that they had been looking for work at some of the nearby farms. The breakthrough came the following day, when an informant was able to identify four men who fitted the description of the gamblers and provided an address for one of them at Riga Street in Hulme. In an effort to draw the men out, the police asked one of the witnesses who had been asked for work on Tuesday to visit Riga Street and offer the men work. Much to the police's disappointment the men were not there, but it transpired they were working on a tunnel in Water Street linking the River Irwell to the Rochdale Canal. Fearing that an attempted arrest in the tunnel would fail, the police contrived to leave a message for the men to go to the Commercial Inn on Liverpool Road. Only one of the four accepted the offer. This was Joseph Wilson, and on his arrival at the pub he was arrested. Two more were arrested later: Thomas Wilson and Charles Leach. All three fitted the description of the men at the corner of Three Lanes. While they admitted they had been there, they said they had returned home by midday. The fourth man was John Wilson, who was working at a main sewer in Moss Lane, but he absconded before the police could arrest him.

At this point in the story the press reports began to make wild assumptions. Two baskets and an umbrella were found at Riga Street, but they had not been identified as belonging to Mary. Likewise, 'In the trousers of one of the men was … discovered a piece of ribbon, which there is some probability, was part of the poor creature's cap.' The press was also quick to draw conclusions from the crime scene: 'The field where their victim was found was a very secluded spot. The grass was much trodden down near the pit as if the murderers had endeavoured to throw her in there and near the place where the body lay, it was in a similar condition, as if persons had been rolling there regularly in a deadly struggle. The deceased had some grass similar to that which grew by the side of the pit clutched in her hand.'[471]

The inquest was held at the Red Lion in Withington and dragged on for three weeks. Witness after witness was called and slowly, despite the earlier belief that the arrested men

---

470 *Manchester Courier,* 23 June 1838.
471 *Ibid.*

were guilty, the evidence began to fall their way. All four had been seen in Manchester in and around Quay Street and St John's Church on the afternoon of the murder. One witness remembered the day vividly: 'it was the day a boy was drowned and the flood in the tunnel prevented them from working'.[472]

Even before these events, suspicion had begun to fall on William Hodge. He was twenty-five years old, lived in Hulme and was an ex-marine. On the day of the murder he had been seen trying to hide a parcel in a hedge on Jackson's Lane in Hulme, and on the following morning had attempted to go back to retrieve it. It was Hodge's bad luck that the witness confided in a James Swettenham, who went to look in the hedge himself and found two parcels, each containing thirty silver shillings. When Hodge was arrested and searched by the police, they 'found in his pocket a piece of blue paper that exactly corresponded with the paper in which the money had been wrapped, and with some scraps that were left in the basket of the deceased'.[473]

Until a month earlier Hodge had worked for the Chorlton family, and it was the testimony of one of his workmates, Charles Kenyon, that proved crucial:

I live at Chorlton and am a gardener for Mrs Chorlton. It might be between a week and a fortnight before (I can't say to a day or two) he left, and left about a month before the murder, that the prisoner Hodge, who worked along with us – there were five of us regularly working at that time – said to me – 'Charles this garden of yours maces (makes) a deal of money in summer time.' – 'Yes,' says I, 'it does.' Then Hodge said 'Which way does Mary Moore come home from market?' I told him she chiefly came down the lane. He then asked, 'Does she come late or soon.' I said, 'She's never late. What makes thee to ask that?' He said 'It's much no one nips her.' He asked me at first if she came through the fields or the lane; and I said 'Chiefly by the lane.' The only lane she could come was by Moss Lane.'[474]

This was one of the only moments when William Hodge spoke, and he angrily interjected: 'What's the good of saying that? Because I know what time she came home generally. Thou'rt telling a lie.' This outburst did little to convince either the coroner or the jury. As the coroner later reminded the court, William Hodge had been seen in the lane and in the field where the body was later found, only hours before he was spotted 'secreting something' in the hedge in Hulme. It took the jury just 15 minutes to decide that William Hodge was 'the very man that has committed this murder and by the bludgeon that

472 Ibid., 7 July 1838.
473 Ibid.
474 Ibid.

has been shown here', and they were in agreement that the other four prisoners 'to be innocent men'. In releasing the four, the coroner expressed sympathy with their plight and hoped they would be compensated for the loss of time, but reflected that their detention had been necessary 'for the ends of justice'. And with that the four had their 'handcuffs unlocked, and they were liberated. They were immediately joined by the wife of Joseph Wilson, whose delight and thankfulness at the result appeared too deep for utterance.'[475]

No such bright comments were vouchsafed for William Hodge who, having been found guilty 'of this wilful murder', was to 'be taken to Kirkdale ... to be tried for the offence at the next assizes at Liverpool'. In chilling words that must have echoed around the hushed room, the coroner concluded 'that you stand in a very perilous situation; for to say the least of it, the circumstances against you are exceedingly suspicious and I think it is your duty to prepare for the best defence you can possibly make at your trial'. William was then allowed a few minutes to speak to his father, who had been determined to see his son before the journey to Liverpool, and while William maintained that he was as 'innocent as the child unborn', he hoped his brothers would not fall 'into bad conduct as he had done'. Meanwhile the four innocent men 'were the happiest of groups ... once more enjoying the open air in liberty with their characters freed from stain or disgrace. Joseph Wilson and his wife were together, the others at a little distance.' In the aftermath of their acquittal collections were made for them at the door of the Red Lion.

William Hodge was conveyed by open coach from Withington to Manchester. 'A great crowd, considering the population of the place, assembled at Withington to see the prisoner as he was brought from the Red Lion and placed in the coach. All the way to Manchester the road was thronged; in many places many hundreds of persons assembled and Oxford Road had the appearance of a fair, such was the anxiety manifested to learn the result of the inquest.'[476]

Mary was well known in the village, and the distress at her death must have lingered on for many years. She was buried in the parish church, and seven years later her husband Joseph was reunited with her.

William Hodge stood trial in Liverpool the following August, but during the course of the 9 hours it was not proved that the money found in the hedge belonged to Mary Moore. The judge concluded that while it was possible that Hodge had placed the money there, 'he might have obtained the money in any other way as by committing murder' and that 'more than one person had been concerned in the murder'.[477] Given that summing up, the jury acquitted Hodge.

475 *Ibid.*
476 *Ibid.*
477 *Manchester Times and Gazette*, 18 August 1838.

William Hodge was an interesting figure. During the course of the inquest something of his earlier life came out. He was born in Chorlton-upon-Medlock sometime in October 1811 or 1812. His mother had died when he was fourteen and he lived with his father, five brothers and sister in the same house in Moss Side for most of his adult life.[478] He worked at a number of casual and unskilled jobs before, aged seventeen, having 'got some drink' in the Red Lion in Deansgate, he enlisted. Within a week he was sent to London and there transferred to the marine artillery. During the 1830s Britain supported the liberal government of Spain against a conservative uprising. The war proved popular with certain sections of the British and French public, and a foreign legion was formed to fight in Spain. Little is known of the British Auxiliary Legion: it consisted of 9,600 men who were volunteers from line regiments, and some may have been deserters from Ireland.[479] According to William, 'Our duty was to remove the British legion from one coast to another according to orders ... and there we fought for the Queen.' This included the capture of a Spanish town and the reorganisation of its defences. Much of his service was seen on the warships *Phoenix* and *Salamander*, which were used to transport the British Legion and give close support. As in other civil wars, the brutality shown by each side was vicious, and prisoners of war were executed. William served abroad for about seventeen months, returning to Plymouth in October 1837 while the *Salamander* was refitted.[480] Here he was involved in the theft of sugar, rum and other articles from the ship's stores. Although he denied the offence, he was discharged from the navy in November that year.

By the beginning of December William had returned to Manchester, staying at first with his father and then at lodgings on Oxford Street. During this time he had a number of casual and unskilled jobs which took him to Leicester and Altrincham before he was taken on as a gardener at Dog House Farm. He lasted just two months, and at the time of the murder had been unemployed for a month: 'I have had no constant work since. I have had to borrow money from my brother and any other person I could.'[481] None of the records explain why he failed to stay in employment. There will be those who judge him as a drifter who was unable to hold down a job in adult life, or just a petty criminal who was caught for a less than petty crime. Others might advance the death of his mother and the growing economic downturn as factors in his descent into casual work and crime. However, the evidence at the trial was not enough to convict him.

---

478 George Hodge was the father; the children were Alfred (b. 1800), James (b. 1803), George (b. 1817), John (b. 1820), Mary (b. 1822), Thomas (b. 1824).

479 National Archives The British Auxiliary Legion and the Carlist War 1835–38: http://yourarchives.nationalarchives.gov.uk. There are no references to individual British soldiers taking part in the Carlist War. This may be because the British Auxiliary Legion was in the pay of the Queen of France.

480 HMS *Phoenix* and *Salamander* were steam paddleships launched in 1832. *Phoenix* had six guns and Salamander had four. In 1836 *Phoenix* was commanded by Lord John Hay, who had lost an arm in 1807.

481 *Manchester Courier*, 7 July 1838.

Dog House Farm survived longer than most, only being demolished in 1960. The last tenant was Norah Templar, who moved there with her family in 1912 and left forty-six years later in 1958. She remembered the farmhouse as a 'historic 300-year-old twelve-roomed cottage ... Most rooms faced south or west. A large barn and coach house sheltered it from the north and east winds. In the cobbled yard was a pump and trough close to the kitchen.'[482] It does not stretch the imagination to place Mary in that cobbled yard, by the trough or standing in the cottage kitchen discussing the day at Smithfield. There is one other way in which Mary and Nora are linked. Nora was a keen historian of Chorlton and wrote many articles, including accounts of the farms and farmers. Her writing not only drew on the articles produced by Thomas Ellwood, but was steeped in her own knowledge acquired over a lifetime in the township.[483]

---

482 *Chorlton and Stretford Journal*, 1977.
483 Norah was born in 1910 and lived into the 21st century. In her years at Dog House Farm she saw 'the landing of the first small aeroplane in the fields ... the first aerodrome built by the Government at Hough End, a barrage balloon and hospital trains at Alexandra Park station' – *Chorlton and Stretford Journal*.

seventeen

RADICAL POLITICS

The years of unrest, Thomas Walker, a local radical

The decades since the victory at Waterloo[484] had been stormy ones, with the threat of social unrest and even revolution never far from the surface. The bitter peace that followed the end of the long wars with Revolutionary France had been set against a backdrop of high prices and economic depression. The political turmoil that followed the French Revolution had not gone away. In the south and east agricultural labourers had risen in the Swing Riots against falling wages and the advance in mechanisation, while in the new towns of the North and Midlands industrial workers had been engaged in an equal struggle to defend living standards. Sitting alongside this struggle and arising from it were the demands for the extension of the franchise to all males over the age of eighteen.

Chorlton was rural, and events in agricultural regions to the south and east would not have escaped the attention of labourers there. Some would have shared the bitter disappointment that followed the rejection by Parliament of the second great Chartist petition in May 1842. This had been signed by over 3 million, and its rejection by 287 votes to 47 was followed by a wave of strikes starting in the Midland coalfields and spreading to Scotland and the great textile areas of Lancashire and Yorkshire, involving up to half a million workers. During August workers across the North West went on strike. Ashton, Stalybridge and Oldham struck on the 8th, followed by Manchester and Stockport on the 10th and Preston by the 12th. The smoke from hundreds of factory chimneys cleared and machines were silenced as groups of strikers marched from town to town spreading

---

484 In 1815 a combined British and Prussian army had finally defeated Napoleon and ended the Revolutionary Wars that had started in 1792 and taken the ideas of 'Liberty, equality and fraternity' across Europe, often on the point of a French bayonet.

the strike and reinforcing the anger at Parliament's arrogance. Even before the factories had fallen silent there were riots in Manchester, which led to the reading of the Riot Act. Nor was Manchester alone in this: in Oldham, Rochdale, Stockport, Preston, Bacup and Burslem the authorities confronted the strikers with the threat of extreme force.[485]

The events of 1842 echoed earlier Chartist action, which had led Chorlton's James Holt when still a Manchester magistrate in 1839 to sign a proclamation 'to prevent, put down, and suppress such meetings and proceedings' which were unlawful and endangered 'the public peace'.[486] Those in the township with longer memories might have recalled the events of Peterloo when a peaceful demonstration at St Peters' Field in August 1819 calling for the vote had been broken up by the military, leading to the deaths of fifteen people and the wounding of many hundreds.[487] It is inconceivable that Chorlton escaped this political and economic ferment; after all, it had been an almost permanent feature of people's lives for over sixty years. Carriers brought newspapers into the village, and itinerant tradesmen reported events that were unfolding just 4½ miles away. Those field workers who tramped in from their homes in Hulme and Chorlton-upon-Medlock were coming from places where Chartists held meetings, and even ran their own cooperative shops.[488] Many residents would have been in almost daily contact with the city as well. All those who sold farm produce in Smithfield would have passed close by New Cross at the junction of Great Ancoats Street, Oldham Road and Swan Street. This had been an assembly point for protest for generations, having seen food riots at the start of the 19th century, greeted strikers coming into the city and on the night of Peterloo been the scene of a second outburst of military violence, when, fearing another gathering of protesters, a combined force of soldiers and police fired on the crowd, killing one man and injuring many more. George Leach, later transported for the murder of Francis Deakin, had been involved in industrial action as a railwayman in 1847 and stood trial for conspiracy. No doubt he discussed his 'picquetting' and the wider issues with others in the township.

The demands for change and greater freedom, and the opposition they engendered, were not confined to the city. In 1793 in the neighbouring village of Didsbury an effigy of Thomas Paine had been burned on the Green by members of the Huntsman social club. Thomas Paine had supported both the American and French Revolutions and written a series of books and pamphlets that proposed a written constitution with a national assembly similar to that of America, the elimination of aristocratic titles and a wide-ranging set

485 Jenkins, Mick, *The General Strike of 1842*, Lawrence & Wishart, 1980.

486 Part of the public notice issued by the magistrates on 9 May 1839, *The Times*, 9 May 1839.

487 Bush, Michael, *The Casualties of Peterloo*, Carnegie Publishing Ltd, 2005, p.3.

488 These were run by the Hulme and Chorlton Joint Stock Provision Company. There were two shops, one at 26 Clarendon Street, Chorlton-upon-Medlock and the other at 10 Melbourne Street, Bradshaw Street, Hulme. They were operating in 1840. *Northern Star*, 7 November 1840.

of social policies benefiting the poor and under-privileged. This made him unpopular with the establishment, and like other radicals he faced persecution for his ideas.

Even closer to home was the radical businessman Thomas Walker, who lived at Barlow Hall. He was indicted for treason and had his warehouse and home in Manchester attacked by a 'Church and King' mob. The son of a Bristol merchant, Walker had led the successful opposition by Manchester manufacturers to the Fustian Tax in 1784[489] and had been appointed as borough reeve for the city in 1790. This was an important and prestigious post and reflected his standing in the community. Just how important can be gauged from his own description of the office: 'The town of Manchester has neither mayor, nor bailiffs, nor any officers of a body corporate. The regulation of the police is in three officers, viz a Boroughreeve or Head-Borough, and two constables. These officers are annually elected in October by a jury of the Leet summoned by the Lord of the Manor. The Borough reeve is considered the principal officer, presides at public meetings, is applied to upon all public business, has the distribution of certain charities ...'[490] His wealth allowed him to live in Manchester during the winter at 7 South Parade, which faced St Mary's Church, and spend the summer in Chorlton. From 1785 the family lived at Barlow Hall but later moved to Longford Hall. Their ties with the township remained close and some of the family, including Thomas, were buried in the parish churchyard. So while his business and political interests lay in the city he regarded Barlow Hall as home, for as he said, 'I have a very great stake in it, my wife and six children.'[491] It is true that his life was played out a full sixty years before most of the events described in this book, but the ideas he advocated were still resounding in the city and no doubt in the village in the 1840s.

Thomas Walker was at the centre of radical political thought and argued for civil liberty, constitutional reform and the abolition of the slave trade. He corresponded regularly with all the leading radicals, including Thomas Paine, Joseph Priestley, and the abolitionist Thomas Clarkson, as well as Samuel Coleridge and even the conservative Edmund Burke. The Whig politician Charles Fox wrote seeking advice on the opinions of the northern manufacturers. He exchanged letters with John Cartwright about the evils of slavery while they simultaneously dealt with matters of business. In one letter John Cartwright condemned 'that Christian wickedness, whereby an hundred thousand Africans are annually murdered', and in another asked Thomas to help his brother Edward by procuring 'me a list of Wool Spinners and other manufacturers to whom our papers might be sent with

---

489 This was a tax of 1 *d* per yard imposed on all bleached cotton manufactures, if under the value of 3 *s* per yard and 2 *d* if exceeding that value and was on top of an existing duty of 3 *d* per yard. Fustian was worn by the working classes in the 18th and 19th centuries and such a tax would have pushed up the price of fustian clothes.

490 Walker, Thomas, *A Review of some of the events of the last five years*, 1794, p.23, Google edn p.194.

491 *Ibid.*, p.46, Google edn p.216.

effect'.[492] As chairman of the Manchester Anti-Slavery Committee along with Thomas Cooper and others, Walker saw the opportunities for building on the growing opposition in Manchester to the slave trade. He turned the visit of Thomas Clarkson in 1787 into a major propaganda event by persuading Clarkson to preach at the city's Collegiate Church. It was a great success, as Clarkson remarked: 'when I went into the church it was so full that I could scarcely get to my place; for notice had been publically given. I was surprised, also, to find a great crowd of black people standing in the pulpit.'[493] The success of that Sunday sermon was followed up by a petition to Parliament which the committee had already planned. In all over 11,000 people called for an end to the African trade. This amounted to a fifth of the city's population, reflecting working-class opposition to the slave trade and the practical campaigning skills of Walker and the others. The same keen sense of injustice led Walker to argue for the abolition of the laws discriminating against Catholics, non-conformists and those of the Jewish faith.[494] These were the Test and Corporation Acts, introduced in the 17th century, which prevented any one who was not part of the established Church from holding public office.

But above all it was the French Revolution that engaged much of Walker's time and commitment. Like other radicals he welcomed the events in France, which gave hope to all 'friends of civil and religious liberty'.[495] In 1790 he formed the Constitutional Society, which argued for a more democratic Parliament, resolving that 'in every civil Community, the legitimate authority of the Governors can only be derived from the consent of the Governed'.[496] This, as he pointed out, was hardly the case when 254 members of the House of Commons were elected by less than 6,000 people. In part the Constitutional Society was established to argue the case for progressive politics, but it was also in direct response to the revival of the Church and King groups. These dated back to the previous century and had re-emerged to oppose the moves to repeal the Test and Corporation Acts. The Test and Corporation Acts were, according to the Manchester Church and King Club, 'the great bulwarks of our constitution in church and state and therefore ought never to be repealed'.[497] Church and King mobs targeted anyone who supported parliamentary reform, and singled out for special attention the non-conformists who dissented from worshipping with the Church of England and were also often supporters of reform. The clash of ideas was reflected in the actions of the rival clubs. When a group

492 Correspondence of Thomas Walker, quoted from 'Culture Minister defers export of anti slavery campaigner's letters', Department of Culture, Media and Sports, 25 February 2010.
493 Clarkson, Thomas, *History of the Rise, Progress, and Accomplishments of the Slave Trade*, John Parker, new edn, 1839, p.244, Google edn p.263.
494 Axon, William, *Annals of Manchester*, John Heywood, 1885, p.119.
495 *Ibid.*, p.45.
496 Resolution 1, Manchester Constitutional Society, Manchester, October 1790, Walker, *op. cit.*, p.17, Google edn p.188.
497 Principles of the Church and King Club, Manchester, 23 June 1792. Walker, *op. cit.*, p.19, Google edn p.190.

of Manchester clergy formed a Church and King dining club, Thomas Walker responded with a Bastille dinner, which was held at the Bridgewater Arms with tickets at 3s 6d to 'celebrate as a subject of exultation, the overthrow of despotism and the establishment of civil and religious liberty in France'.[498] Earlier, when the attempt to repeal the Test and Corporation Acts failed, the Church and King Club paraded in uniforms and issued medals commemorating the defeat.

There was a bitter exchange of ideas between those representing the establishment and those advocating change. The two Manchester newspapers were on the side of the *status quo*, and so it followed that in March 1792 Thomas Walker and Thomas Cooper began publishing a radical alternative called the *Manchester Herald*. Its purpose was 'The great cause of liberty [which] demands the steady support of the brave, the just, and the philanthropic – for should oppression triumph, the vengeance of power will know no bounds; racks and tortures, Bastilles and Inquisitions, will be the punishment of those who have dared to avow themselves the Friend of Liberty'.[499]

These were tense times and the radicals came under increasing attack. In June 1792 drunken gangs formed in St Ann's Square and attacked a dissenting chapel. This was followed in September by a concerted attempt to bar the Constitutional Society from meeting in 186 of the city's inns and alehouses, which forced them to meet at Thomas Walker's home at South Parade.

The establishment newspapers now carried attacks on the radicals as 'insidious vipers who would poison the minds of the people, level all distinctions and all property and make one general wreck of the happiness of the empire'.[500] At the same time public meetings hostile to them were staged in Salford as well as Manchester. On 7 December 1792, just across the river in Salford, a large crowd called for the suppression of 'all seditious meetings and to discountenance and prevent the propagation of all seditious and treasonable publications',[501] going on to request that Joseph Harrop, the borough reeve of Salford, set up a committee to coordinate these activities. This was the same Joseph Harrop who owned one of the Manchester newspapers, and who only days earlier had described the radicals in the most inflammatory way.

Events moved towards a violent conclusion. On 11 December another anti-radical meeting was held, this time in Manchester. As the meeting broke up there were already fears and rumours that with the coming of night there would be riots. And so it was.

---

498 Manchester Constitutional Society Annual Dinner, 15 June 1791, Walker, *op. cit.*, p.22, Google edn p.193.

499 *Manchester Herald*, 28 April 1792.

500 *Manchester Mercury and General Advertiser*, 4 December 1792, Walker, *op. cit.*, p.45, Google edn p.216.

501 The meeting was held at the Court House, Salford, and called on Joseph Harrop to set up a committee to coordinate activities. Walker, *op. cit.*, p.50, Google edn p.221.

Emboldened by drink and fired on by agitators, groups hostile to the radicals began to gather around the city. Walker was in no doubt that this was pre-planned: 'Parties were collected in different public houses, and from thence paraded in the streets with a fiddler before them, and carrying a board on which was painted with CHURCH and KING in large letters'. There was little attempt by the city authorities to stop these events. One magistrate was overheard to say that if called upon to stop the growing menace 'I would not act against them'. One special constable said: 'I'll give you a guinea for every one of the Jacobins' [radicals] houses you pull down.'[502] However, given that these accounts come from Walker, it is possible that they are at best exaggerated and at worst highly distorted. In the course of the next few hours, though, a Church and King mob attacked the offices of the *Manchester Herald* in Market Place, and the following day attacked Thomas Walker's warehouse and home. On four separate occasions a mob gathered outside South Parade, broke his house windows and attempted to force their way in. Supported by friends, Walker was forced to fire into the air to disperse the crowds. The magistrates did nothing, and while a 'regiment of dragoons was in town, booted and under arms'[503] and ready to disperse the rioters, no order was given. As if to add insult to injury, the main concern of the magistrates when they finally met Walker was that he should not fire at the crowd again if the mob returned! These attacks were matched by similar ones in Birmingham and Nottingham. Nor were these ordinary riots, inflamed by drink; they were carefully orchestrated attacks. When the mood of the mob subsided, it was 'repeatedly reanimated by persons of respectable appearance who went among them whenever they seemed to drop, applauded and cheered them, sometimes with whispers, sometimes with "Church and King for ever lads, down with the Rump".'[504] Other eye-witness accounts reported that the crowd were determined to get inside Walker's house, ignoring his warnings that he would shoot, and 'fell upon his house with increased fury'. When neighbours attempted to intercede, pointing to his record in getting the fustian tax abolished, which showed him as 'a good friend to the town and trade of Manchester', they were shouted down. This blatant act of intimidation and official negligence was followed by Walker's indictment with others for treason. The government set out to show that Thomas Walker and others had tried to 'unlawfully and seditiously conspire combine and confederate with each other and also divers disaffected and ill disposed subjects of our said Lord and King, to overthrow the constitution and government of this kingdom as by law established and assist the French then and

502 *Ibid.*, p.56, Google edn p.227.
503 *Ibid.*, p.64, Google edn p.235.
504 *Ibid.*, p.59, Google edn p.230.

there being enemies to and in open war with our said King ...'[505] This was held in April 1794 at Lancaster, and it was by no means certain that the accused would be able to prove their innocence. The key witness was Thomas Dunn, an Irish weaver, who by his own admission had been caught circulating a seditious newspaper. The core of his evidence was that he had heard Walker and the others discussing treason. But the case turned on the evidence of a defence witness who testified that Dunn had confessed both to lying and taking a bribe in order to implicate Walker and the others. The case collapsed and all were set free, while Dunn got two years in Lancaster Gaol.

The case had taken it out of Walker, and he took a back seat after 1794; however, he did record the events that led up to the trial and added a clear warning about how the public can be manipulated, often because 'they have been in the habit of believing that men who are often more ignorant than themselves, have the exclusive monopoly of political knowledge ... Public Ignorance is the sole cause of Political Evil, and the greatest Bane of Human Happiness.'[506]

Walker died on 2 February 1817 and was buried in the parish churchyard. There is some evidence that he and his family had suffered because of the persecution he underwent.

The radical ideas promoted by Thomas Walker continued to form part of the great political debate about the nature and future of the country. Whether or not the *Manchester Herald* or later the Chartist *Northern Star* were widely read in Chorlton is impossible to say, but the ideas and events they reported would have been discussed.

505 Gurney, Joseph, *The Whole Proceedings on the Trial of an Indictment against Thomas Walker*, T. Boden, Manchester, 1794, p.x, Google edn p.15.
506 Walker, *op. cit.*, p.127, Google edn p.298.

eighteen

PARLIAMENTARY POLITICS

Parliamentary elections, local voters and the issues that engaged them,
voting records of leading residents

I t is against the backdrop of more than half a century of unrest that we should
discuss the politics of the township. In the strictest sense, and using parliamentary elections as a measure of political entitlement, few were active: in 1835 only
thirty-one men in the township were entitled to vote.[507] These were a mixed bunch
of freeholders and tenant farmers. In an age when voting was still conducted in the open
there was always the possibility of intimidation. A tenant cast his vote under the watchful
eye of his landlord, and the tradesman shared his political choice with all his customers –
so he might well feel obliged to follow the political line of his landlord or chief customer,
especially as the record of his vote was recorded in the poll books, some of which still exist.

There were other avenues of political expression. Some ratepayers participated in the
ratepayer or Vestry meetings, which were responsible for the administration of the township, depending on the value of the land they owned or the property they occupied; some
even had more than one vote. Methodists ran their sick and burial club, while members
of the parish church had a say in the selection of their churchwardens, while all male
ratepayers might be called on to take part in a jury. But these were no substitute for a
parliamentary vote.

It may well be that when the Great Reform Bill finally passed into law there were those
in the village who echoed the words of Wordsworth on the French Revolution: 'Bliss was
it in that dawn to be alive.' The Act was for some the opening instalment on a wave of
change that would modernise the country, sweep away aristocratic influence and permit

---

507 This was just 16 per cent of all men over the age of twenty-one, and 9 per cent of the entire adult population. This was still better than the
national average, which in 1833 stood at just 7 per cent. Cook, Chris, *Britain in the Nineteenth Century 1815–1914*, Routledge, 2005, p.68.

many more who made the wealth of the country to share in its direction. But again there were others who saw in its passage the very death knell of their world. What it did was to abolish some of the more indefensible ways of electing MPs, widen the electorate to some of the middle class and give the great northern manufacturing towns representation in Parliament. But it also deprived some working people of the vote, ignored women and did not banish bribery or intimidation. Treating electors was common, shady practices were embraced, and violence and alcohol went hand in hand.

After 1832 Chorlton-cum-Hardy was part of the parliamentary seat of South Lancashire. It covered most of what we now know as Greater Manchester, had an electorate of over 10,000 and returned two MPs. Of our thirty-one electors, one did not even live here. This was George Lloyd, the second largest landowner. He lived in Yorkshire but by his landholding had a vote in the township. The others will be familiar. There were three members of the Brundrett family, who were prominent Methodists. They were entitled to vote because they were freeholders, a qualification they shared with Jonathan Brown, Jonathan Hall and William Morton of Oak Bank. Other freeholders included George Grantham, the owner of Grantham's Buildings, John Renshaw, farmer and owner of Renshaw's Buildings and other cottages, William Griffiths and four more. The remaining voters were all farmers or market gardeners who qualified because they occupied land. Among their ranks were John Cookson of Dark Lane, James Dean of Barlow Farm, William Whitelegg from Red Gates Farm, and Samuel Nixon, who was both a smallholder and landlord of The Greyhound. What is all the more remarkable is that a quarter of the group were Methodists. There are no reliable figures for the size of the Wesleyan congregation in 1835, but eighty people subscribed to the building fund for the new chapel which was completed in 1827, and the building had a capacity of 274. Even more remarkable was the absence from the list of James Holt of Beech Cottage on the Row and Shakespeare Phillips of Barlow Hall. Both may have lived in the township but they were registered in the city.

Over the next twenty years the number of electors changed little. In 1831 there were twenty-one; four years later this rose to thirty-one, only to fall in 1854 to twenty-seven.

The 1832 general election saw the Whigs swept to power, and the Tories who had opposed reform won just a quarter of the national vote. There had been two years of a Whig government, which had paved the way for a uniform system of local government, created a new system of administering benefits to the poor, unemployed and old, abolished slavery in the Empire and made some inroads into factory reform. But after two years there were divisions in its ranks and some who were unhappy with its record. The radicals were disappointed that the Reform Act had not gone further, and was now seen as a curb to further parliamentary change. The urban working class were again organising themselves industrially, and through the Chartist movement they were demanding a vote in elections. In rural areas poverty led to widespread riots at the beginning of the 1830s and the Whig government made martyrs of six Dorchester farm labourers who protested at falling wages.[508] And while certain sections of the population thought the government had been too hard on the Tolpuddle Martyrs, there were others who felt the Whigs had not gone far enough in quelling rural disturbances. However, both the urban working classes and rural farm labourers were hostile to the 1834 Poor Law, which had created the Poor Law bastilles and stigmatised any who needed parish relief. Against this background there was a Tory revival, which saw the party gain ten seats in by-elections in 1832 and 1833.[509]

In 1834 the general election was called, and from the outset the Tories were determined to win. Their leader Robert Peel had issued a clear statement of policy that appeared to promise both change and stability. It was contained in an address to his own electors in Tamworth, but its real intention was to signal to the country that the Tory party could deliver reform where it was most needed but would also conserve the best of the old. The Reform Act was a reality that he would not overturn and in the same spirit of improvement there was to be 'a careful review of institutions, civil and ecclesiastical, undertaken in a friendly temper combining, with the firm maintenance of established rights, the correction of proved abuses and the redress of real grievances'.[510] But there was to be no further extension of the vote: 'the reform bill was a final and irrevocable settlement of a great constitutional question', and the Tories were opposed 'to a perpetual vortex of agitation'. This statement was cleverly designed to appropriate the high ground of moral change while reassuring traditional certainties. For all those middle-class electors who demanded a share in the political nation but trembled at the idea of the vote in the hands of the working man, Tamworth was a sensible compromise. It would split them from the radical movement, which at its edges flirted with Republicanism but still allowed religious dissenters the hope that their grievances could be addressed. Dissenters and Catholics were still barred from entering universities and lay professions. They could not marry in their own places of worship and had to rely on Anglican churches for registering births and deaths. During the election campaign in South Lancashire this was to become an issue that the political parties argued about. In Chorlton this issue was of real importance, given that eight of the electors were Methodists who still felt the hand of exclusion.

South Lancashire had been won by the Whigs in 1832. Lord Molyneux had gained 56 per cent of the vote with a majority of 2,493, and George Wood his fellow Whig 55

---

508 The six known for ever as the Tolpuddle Martyrs formed a trade union to campaign against a reduction in their wages. Wages for farmworkers had been 9s in 1830 and were then steadily reduced to 8s, then 7s and by 1834 were down to just 6s. Support for the union grew, and the authorities acted by arresting the men in March 1834 under an obscure law banning secret oaths. All six were found guilty and transported. The subsequent public outcry and campaign led to the government remitting their sentence in 1836.

509 Bloy, Dr Marjorie, www.historyhome.co.uk.

510 This letter to Peel's electors was delivered on 18 December 1834 in the run up to the election, and became known as the Tamworth Manifesto.

per cent and a majority of 1,759. The Tories managed just 30 per cent. And so the Whigs entered the election supremely confident, and appeared to maintain this until the end of the campaign. The *Liverpool Mercury*[511] asserted that the canvas returns were so favourable that 'Molyneux and Mr G.W. Wood must succeed. The majority in their favour is so large that several hundred votes might be struck off without changing the result.' It was this over-confidence that might have been their downfall. Molyneux himself signalled his concern even before the election was called that the Whigs must 'make some extensive exertions'.[512] The Tories realised how much work needed to be done: they were 'moving heaven and earth to carry their point'[513] and 'were clever, active and resolute opponents admirably organised early in the field and fighting for political existence'.[514] The extent to which this was the case will be revealed later.

The Whig candidates represented different strands of their party. Molyneux was an aristocrat with extensive estates in the county. He was from an old Catholic family that had lived at Croxteth Hall outside Liverpool from the 16th century. They had fought for the king in the Civil War and were bound up with the politics and government of the area. George Wood had been born in Yorkshire, made his money from manufacture in Manchester and was an active dissenter. Both had been engaged in extending the religious rights of non-Anglicans. Molyneux introduced a Bill to allow Catholics to be married by their own priests, and Wood moved the second reading of the Bill to admit dissenters into universities.[515] Wood represented the commercial interests, a fact he never tired of telling the electorate. However, neither could be said to be a radical. Molyneux welcomed the legislation improving factory conditions, but also put on record his concern for how factory owners were portrayed as 'child murderers'.[516] He was 'one who had a large stake in the agricultural prosperity of the country ... [and] the tried friend of commerce and manufactures'.[517] Likewise Wood, in the words of one his supporters, would 'be a constant and zealous though not a rash reformer of abuses.'[518]

Ranged against the Whigs were Lord Francis Egerton and Richard Bootle Wilbraham. Both men came from wealthy families with estates in the county. Egerton's uncle was the Duke of Bridgewater, the same duke who in the 1760s had built the canal into Manchester. Lord Egerton and Wilbraham made great play of the fact that they supported

511 *Liverpool Mercury*, 16 January 1835.
512 *Morning Chronicle*, London, 1 December 1834.
513 *Liverpool Mercury*, 26 December 1834.
514 *Liverpool Mercury*, 16 January 1835.
515 Hansard, Molyneux, HC Deb., 10 June 1833, vol. 18, c553, Hansard, Wood HC, 20 June 1834.
516 Hansard, HC Deb., 25 March 1833, vol. 16, cc1001—3.
517 Mr Blundell of Crosby proposing Molyneux, *Preston Chronicle*, 24 January 1835.
518 Edward Jeremiah Lloyd of Oldfield Hall, Preston Chronicle, 24 January 1835

the Tamworth Manifesto. Egerton argued, like Peel, that there should be no 'further sudden change in the constitution of Parliament, [but] this did not imply any opposition to the march of improvement'. Indeed he would be pleased 'if the accelerated march of our progress can be maintained within safe limits'.[519] It was all about conserving the best of the old and introducing the best of the new. This produced one of the fault-lines of the election. The Tories wanted to 'maintain inviolate the connection between Church & State', while Molyneux and Wood believed 'that the people might enjoy the first fruits of that great act of justice and constitutional right' and that they the 'Whigs were the advocates of change', change that would put 'the great body of the English people on equal footing with respect to civil rights'.[520] Nowhere was this more so than in the right of dissenters to be admitted to the universities and lay professions. Such a policy would be popular in towns like Manchester where dissent had a strong following. It might well also have been popular with those of Chorlton's electors who were themselves dissenters. For many Tories this was tantamount to an attack on the Established Church – but even here the fault-line was not so clear nor the differences between the two parties so wide. True, Egerton and Wilbraham were opposed to admitting dissenters to universities, but Egerton conceded the unfairness of blocking their entry into the professions, and when the Whigs came up with a compromise on entry to the universities he voted for it.[521]

To the casual non-partisan voter the differences may not have seemed so clear cut. When Molyneux made the claim that he spoke for both landed and commercial interests, he merely echoed Egerton, who spoke of a 'community of interests' and pointed to his huge estates and his connection with the Bridgewater family. This, however, ignores the great constitutional battles that had occurred just four years before and culminated in the Reform Act. Egerton had voted against, while Molyneux and Wood had been in favour. And despite his apparent moderation there is no getting away from Wood's record on reform, which he proudly presented to the electorate: 'It was my first duty to watch over the commercial welfare of [my constituents] ... and obtain redress for their general or individual grievances and protection for their industry and prosperity.' He also spoke of his efforts to free up trade with China, to break the commercial monopoly of the India Company, improve trade with France and engage in promoting the tea trade and 'the Municipal Corporations, the Education of the People ... And I have had the nobler gratification of contributing my votes to the extinction of Slavery throughout the British dominions'.[522]

519 Speech made at the Liverpool Exchange, 24 December 1834, *Morning Chronicle*, 27 December 1834.
520 Lord Molyneux, *Preston Chronicle*, 24 January 1835.
521 This involved the establishment of London University, which was open to all.
522 Election address, *Liverpool Mercury*, 12 December 1834.

However good the candidate and however noble the policies, it is the election swing that counts. Of course a well-heeled party machine helps, and this the Tories had. On the day of the nomination of candidates both sides mustered their supporters. Despite the bitterly cold day and snow there was a carnival atmosphere: Whig supporters were decked out in their colours of pink and green, but the Tories stole the day. Their people, and many of them were fashionable ladies dressed in white and blue, the Tory colours, occupied the booths opposite the hustings.[523] The Whig press had anticipated that the Tories would 'make a great muster' and were resigned to hoping that the Whigs would do so too.[524] As it was, only about 1,300 people turned up, and of these perhaps only half were registered voters. It was a rowdy and at times light-hearted affair, with shouts of approval, heckling and an enormous amount of laughter. The newspaper reports do not say how far the heckling went, but at an earlier meeting in Rochdale one side had employed a band of drummers to drown out the speeches of the opponent, while at another meeting fights had broken out.[525] The efficiency of the Tory machine and the predictions of the Whig press were all too clear when the vote was taken: the Tories had a clear majority.

The Tory machine ran equally smoothly at the nomination meeting in Manchester, when they 'engaged all the cabs and hackney coaches they could meet with for the purpose of conveying voters to the respective polling booths'.[526] Even before the poll the Tories appear to have seen the importance of registering their supporters to vote and excluding their opponents. The Whigs were well aware that 'numerous inaccuracies have been discovered in the Register, arising apparently from electors having changed their residences since they qualified',[527] but it is unclear how they tacked the problem, other than issuing an apology to any of their side who was not canvassed. Likewise, how the Tories tackled registration is unknown, but organise them they did.

The Tory machine had already been in evidence in the 1832 general election. Facing an uphill electoral battle against the Whigs, they tried to maximise their vote in Manchester by concentrating on one of their two candidates. This was known as plumping, and allowed a voter to cast his two votes for just one candidate. In that election the two Tories got 221 and 257 plumper votes, compared with the Whig candidate who got just 28.[528] This did not help the Tories in the end, as the swing was against them. James Holt of Beech Cottage exercised his plumper vote, voting twice for the Tory candidate in the

523 *Preston Chronicle*, 24 January 1835.
524 *Leeds Mercury* quoting the *Liverpool Mercury*, 17 January 1835.
525 'Disgraceful Outrage at Rochdale', *Manchester Times and Gazette*, 3 January 1835.
526 *Manchester Times and Gazette*, 24 January 1835.
527 Committee for conducting the election of Mr George Wood, *Manchester Times and Gazette*, 27 December 1834.
528 *The Electors Guide 1832*, 'being a list of how electors in Manchester voted at the first election held on the on the 12th, 13th & 14th of 1832', BR 352042 M45, Archives and Local History Library, Manchester.

1832 election. Shakespeare Phillips, who resided at Barlow Hall, cast his votes for the reforming candidates.

As with all elections at this time, the question of corruption, vast expenditure and spin was not far away. During the 1834–35 election campaign, according to some newspaper reports, the Tories had presented Egerton as a reformer in order to win votes from the Whigs and even suggested that Molyneux had withdrawn as a candidate. The same papers complained bitterly at the amount the Tories spent; but it was voter intimidation that most upset the Whigs. Although the Tories claimed the Whigs owed a 'very great proportion of their votes to the direct interference of the [Whig] Earls of Derby, Sefton and Sheffield', and '200 votes were given to Lord Molyenux and Mr Wood at Ormskirk because Lord Derby had expressed his sincere good wishes in their favour',[529] this pales in comparison with the actions of the Tory landowners to their tenants. According to the *Manchester Times and Gazette*,[530] Thomas Joseph Trafford[531] of Trafford Park instructed his tenants to vote for Egerton and Wilbraham, while Lord Wilton instructed his tenants to vote for Egerton and use their second vote for the candidate of their choice. Lord Wilton was in fact Thomas Egerton, 2nd Earl of Wilton, and so loyal a Tory that in January 1835 he was appointed Lord Steward of the Household in the short Tory administration of Sir Robert Peel. In Stretford all but one of Trafford's tenants voted the Tory party line. The level of potential intimidation was all too clear from the one tenant who refused to follow the line. He expected 'in the spirit of the olden times, to hear of Tory vengeance'.

According to a London newspaper, quoting the *Manchester Guardian*:

Mr Egerton of Tatton, we understand personally headed up his tenants, and waited on the booth whilst they voted. The stewards of Lord Wilton of the High Sheriff, and of some gentlemen took a similar course. This was in Manchester. At Newton and Wigan the thing was even grosser. At the former place, the Tory gentry of the vicinity stood in the booths all day; and the voters, many of them, were brought up with as little appearance of will on their parts as cattle going to a slaughter-house. They brought them up like pigs were the expression to us of a gentleman who watched the proceedings with disgust and indignation. At Wigan the thing was perhaps even more systematic and methodical. The agents of the Tory landowners stood with books or papers in their hands, containing lists of the tenants, and marked off each man's name in succession as he voted. To call such persons thus brought to

529 *Hull Packet*, 30 January 1835.
530 *Manchester Times and Gazette*, 3 January 1835.
531 Thomas Joseph Trafford (1778–1852) owned Trafford Hall and land in Trafford and Stretford.

the stalls independent voters would be an abuse of language, of which, whether friend or an opponent profit by it, we will never be guilty.[532]

Not unsurprisingly the Tory vote in these areas was decisive, and the *Leeds Mercury* was only one of the Whig papers to present an analysis highlighting the connection between the high Tory votes and prominent Tory landowners: 'Other townships in the agricultural parts of the division, exhibited we believe, still more striking proofs of the sort of influence which had been exercised by the owners of the soil; and the majority of the Conservative candidates was in great part made up of votes of this description.'[533]

Area	Landowner	Votes for Wood	Votes for Egerton	Total number of votes	per cent share for Wood	per cent share for Egerton
Radcliffe	Lord Wilton	9	55	64	14	86
Farnworth	Lord F. Egerton	13	33	46	28	72
Prestwich	J.T. Trafford	6	28	34	18	83
Barton	J.T. Trafford	57	149	206	28	72
Stretford	J.T. Trafford	4	42	46	9	91
Withington	W.Egerton	5	10	15	33	67
Didsbury	W.Egerton	9	20	29	31	69
Chorlton-cum-Hardy	W.Egerton	7	19	26	27	73
Worsley	Lord F. Egerton	12	52	64	19	81
Totals		122	408	530	23	77

How far this level of intimidation worked in Chorlton is impossible to say. Of the sixteen tenant farmers entitled to vote, twelve worked land that belonged to the Egerton family.[534]

---

532 *Morning Chronicle*, London, 27 January 1835.

533 *Leeds Mercury*, 31 January 1835.

534 These were James Dean of Barlow Hall Farm (150 acres), John White, on the Green (53 acres), William Knight, on the Green (46 acres), William Whitelegg of Redgates Farm (42 acres), John Jackson of Brook Farm (42 acres), William Jackson at Hardy Farm (33 acres), John Cookson at Dark Lane (36 acres), Thomas Cookson (29 acres), William Williamson at Sand Bank (27 acres), Thomas Hayson of Hobson Hall Farm (24 acres), Edward Mason at Chapel End (23 acres) and William Gresty on the Green (11 acres). Using the 1845 Tithe map it is possible to track eight of the twelve tenant farmers who appear on the voting register in 1835 on land belonging to the Egertons. The remaining four do not appear on the tithe schedule, but the land they farmed also shows up as Egerton land.

These men had a real stake in the township, and their prosperity depended on their relationship with their landlord. Two were on the committee of the Manchester Agricultural Society, whose president was Wilbraham Egerton and vice-president George Egerton MP.[535] The remaining fifteen voters were a mixed bunch, who qualified by virtue of being either a landowner or freeholder. In some cases their wealth put them beyond intimidation. The most notable was George Lloyd who had bought into the township near the end of the 18th century and was the second largest landowner. William Morton, who lived at Oak Bank, may well have been one of the wealthiest men in Chorlton:[536] he worked for the very respectable banking firm of Jones Lloyd in Manchester and earned £20,000 a year.[537] But there were those who, while strictly speaking not beholden to the Egertons, might have had to think carefully about coming out against the interests of the largest landowner. These included Jeremiah Brundrett who ran the grocer's shop at Lane End, who would have done business with many of the Egerton tenants. Then there was James Renshaw who owned Renshaw's Buildings and another eleven cottages, but was also a tenant farmer of the Egertons. His family had farmed Egerton land since 1767 and were to continue to do so throughout the century. Here might be bonds of loyalty as well as financial ties.

Intimidation could also take a more subtle twist. Just knowing the voting intentions of the influential might colour how people voted. For example, Thomas Taylor and his son owned freehold houses, but they also had dealings with George Lloyd and had bought houses from him at the bottom of the Row.

This still left a few who could exercise their independent will, men like James Jackson and Edmund Howarth who owned land and held the freeholds of pubs in the township, which on the surface at least left them free of vested interests. Distance might also have had a part to play: not all the voters lived locally. In 1835 three lived outside the township: George Lloyd lived near York, while James Jackson resided at Jackson Lane in Hulme and Edmund Howarth at Sale Lodge in Cheshire.

But however we try to examine the role of intimidation, it is still true that Egerton took nineteen votes compared to Wood's seven. This is not conclusive proof that intimidation played a part in the Tory majority. Chorlton was a rural area and may have been naturally conservative.

The 1835 general election proved a political sensation. The Whigs made much of Tory intimidation and the large amounts of money that had been spent, but in part it may have been their supreme overconfidence that was their downfall. They entered the election as the favoured ones, ignored the lesson of party organisation and, in the words of one jour-

535 James Dean and William Whitelegg, *Manchester Times and Gazette*, 27 September 1834.
536 Close to the modern junction of Wilbraham and Barlow Moor Roads.
537 Grindon, Leo H., *Manchester, Banks and Bankers*, Simpkin Marshall & Co., 1877, p.179.

nalist, were 'too supine and left the field to the plodding Tories. This and the neglect of registration have occasioned our defeat.'[538] Of course there was also the political swing. Even in some of the urban centres like Liverpool the Tory share of the vote was 49 per cent, while in Manchester it was a creditable 42 per cent. Nationally they did as well, with the Tories gaining ninety-eight seats and the Whigs losing fifty-six. The measure of their success can be gauged by the change in the share of the popular vote: in 1832 the Tories achieved just 26 per cent compared with 67 per cent for the Whigs. Two years later this was transformed, with the Tories winning 40 per cent. South Lancashire continued to return Tories for another decade, but in 1846 at a by-election one of the two seats went Liberal. The following year the Liberals took both seats. The 1847 general election was fought during the summer against a backdrop of famine in Ireland and a divided Tory party.[539]

We can only guess at how the electors of Chorlton voted in any of these elections. Some of the tenant farmers may have felt the need to follow the Egerton line, while those who feared for the future of agriculture may have stuck with the Tories who opposed the repeal of the laws protecting the price of home-grown corn. Equally, though, they could have decided that free trade – a key Liberal policy – had merit, particularly as the great manufacturers and businessmen 4½ miles to the north believed it would benefit Manchester and indirectly the neighbouring townships.

The demand for parliamentary reform produced a great fault-line in British politics and indeed in the establishment, and it is not surprising that both sides were represented in Chorlton.

---

538 *Leeds Mercury,* 24 January 1834.
539 The election ran from 29 July to 26 August. The Tories remained divided over the issue of free trade, which had split the party in 1841 when Peel had repealed the Corn Laws.

nineteen

OTHER FORMS OF DEMOCRACY

The Vestry, local protest, the politics and opinions of working people,
the sick and burial clubs and jury service

While it is true that very few in Chorlton could participate in parliamentary elections, there were opportunities to engage in the local democracy of the village and surrounding area. At the Vestry or ratepayers' meetings it was possible to have a say in setting the local rates, and indirectly in assessing new properties for their rateable value, as well as administrating the provision of poor relief and maintenance of the local highways. There were several meetings during the year but the most important was always in March, at which various officers were nominated for the next twelve months. Of these the surveyors of highways and the overseers were the most important. The surveyors were responsible for seeing that the highways in the township were kept in good repair, and they determined and collected a highway rate. The two overseers had more onerous duties: they were responsible for collecting the poor rate, which was used for the relief of the poor, as well as the county and police rate, and passing these to the various spending authorities. They were also expected to prepare and publicise the list of those entitled to vote and sit on juries, and all these tasks were carried out without pay. At the same meeting two ratepayers were nominated and appointed as assessors of property, with the task of setting a value for all new property.

Less popular was the post of constable, also selected at that meeting. All able-bodied men between the ages of twenty-five and fifty-five who were ratepayers were liable to serve. The main responsibility was to patrol the village and keep order, which extended to supervising events like the annual 5 November celebrations, for which the constable was expected to provide a supply of fuel. There were also other duties, which earlier in the century included summoning and supervising the militia. All this took a working man

HIGHWAY ASSESSMENT, FROM MARCH 25, 185*0*, TO MARCH 25, 185 *1*

Progressive No.

When laid	Occupant's Name.	Property liable.	Annual Value. £ s. d.	Rate. d.	Amount. £ s. d.
1850	Mrs Bailey				
Septem 4	Barrett	Cottage	4 3 9 4		1 4½
	COMPOSITION............				4½
		1 Quarter of			

N.B.—WE, the Surveyors of the Township of Chorlton-cum-Hardy, have, with the concurrence of a Town's Meeting, made a Rate of *4* Pence in the Pound, upon the annual value of all rateable Property throughout the said Township, for the Repairs of Highways.

Settled

Thos White   Thomas White ⎫ SURVEYORS
                Thomas Hanson ⎭ OF THE HIGHWAYS.

The highway rate was one of the payments made by Alice Bailey for the upkeep of the roads.

away from his means of earning a livelihood, and was not free from danger. In the previous decades Chorlton had seen burglary, robbery, infanticide and murder along with illegal prize-fighting and poaching. Therefore some who were appointed chose to pay a substitute.

The procedure for electing the nominated overseers was something of a halfway house between the public parliamentary ballot and a secret ballot. Each ratepayer received by hand a voting paper with the names of the nominees. He wrote his name against his preferred candidate and signed the paper. Two days after the voting papers were issued they were collected, and the count took place.[540] Thus democracy was carried out in private, but the results were open for all to see – not least because the voting record was retained for two years.

During the 1840s a more businesslike approach was adopted. In June 1848 Edward Smith was appointed assistant overseer as a salaried official. He was paid '£12 a year for collecting the poor rate of Chorlton-cum-Hardy and of writing out the July list and all other meetings'.[541]

Those who regularly attended in the 1840s were a cross-section of the community.[542] At the March 1840 meeting, prominent in moving or supporting resolutions were

---

540 Voting papers were issued on 5 April and collected on the 7th. Lumley, G.W., The *Poor Law Election Manual*, third edn, Shaw and Sons, 1867, pp.5–6, Google edn pp.18–19. The same procedure was adopted when Chorlton voted for incorporation into the city of Manchester in 1904.

541 Minutes of the Overseers for Chorlton-cum-Hardy, June 1848, M10/8/8/30 Manchester Archives.

542 James Alderley, Thomas Baguely, Jonathan Brown, John Brundrett, William Chesshyre, John Cook, John Cookson, Thomas Cookson, Samuel Dean, Thomas Eason, William Gresty, Peter Langford, William Marshale, John Renshaw, Thomas Taylor, George Whitelegg, William Whitelegg, Thomas White.

Samuel Dean, John Cookson, William Whitelegg, Edward Newton, Thomas White, George Whitelegg, Peter Langford, Edmund Newton, John Brundrett, John Cook and Thomas Taylor. Many were local farmers, and the degree to which these men dominated local politics is all too clear from the fact that six of those listed (54 per cent) were farmers or market gardeners. The same was true in other rural communities. They were the main employers for regular and casual labour, and the blacksmith and wheelwright depended on their trade, as did shopkeepers, shoemakers and even washerwomen and dressmakers. Their success as farmers might well determine how good a year the township had. This commanding position was reflected in their hold on the Vestry. Between 1840 and 1858, 58 per cent of the overseers, surveyors of highways, assessors and even constables were farmers or market gardeners. Farmers may have predominated, but perhaps only because few others were interested. One who took an active part and was not a farmer was Charles Morton. From 1848 until his death in 1858 he was variously an assessor and chairman.

The better off were conspicuous by their absence: neither James Holt nor Daniel Sharp took an active part in Vestry politics. And as with committees throughout history the activists were a minority. The list of the movers and shakers at the March 1840 meeting was by and large still the same as the one that was recorded seven years later. Whether it was because of vaulting ambition or a sense of duty some of the Vestry officers reappear year after year. They may have moved from chairman to overseer to assessor to supervisor of highways, but in the absence of new people they merely rotated the jobs. James Higginbotham, farmer, held twelve posts between 1840 and 1858, while Thomas White held nine and Thomas Hayson and Thomas Holland six each. In total thirteen of the thirty-one officers held more than one post, while sixteen held more than two officerships.

Nothing of the politics of Chorlton has come through from the Vestry meetings. There is no evidence, for instance, that members were organised along party lines, but it would be naïve to think that the members had no political preferences and that these did not come into play during debates and votes. Unfortunately minutes only record decisions and nothing of the discussions.

In February 1849 the Vestry agreed unanimously 'that this Township do not take any part of the movement at present being made for a reduction in the County Rates'.[543] This was a county-wide movement prompted in part by the rising expenditure on prisons, which led the guardians of the Poor Law Unions in January 1849 to push for a parliamentary Bill to set up a county financial board with a majority drawn from the Poor Law Unions.[544]

---

543 Minutes of the Overseers for Chorlton-cum-Hardy, 14 February 1849.
544 DeLacy, Margaret, *Prison Reform in Lancashire 1700–1850*, Manchester University Press, 1968, p.165.

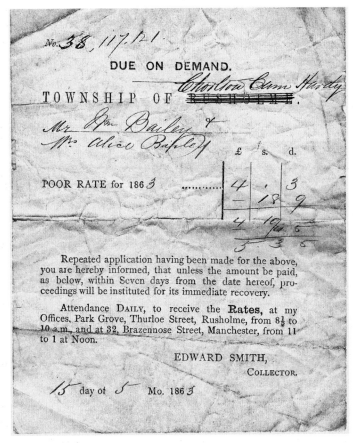

The following is a reproduction of a rate demand notice:

DUE ON DEMAND.

TOWNSHIP OF ~~RUSHOLME~~ *Chorlton Cum Hardy*.

Mr *Wm Bailey* &
Mrs *Alice Bailey*

	£	s.	d.
POOR RATE for 186*3*	4		3
		18	9
	4	19	6
	5	3	5

Repeated application having been made for the above, you are hereby informed, that unless the amount be paid, as below, within Seven days from the date hereof, proceedings will be instituted for its immediate recovery.

Attendance DAILY, to receive the **Rates**, at my Offices, Park Grove, Thurloe Street, Rusholme, from 8½ to 10 a.m., and at 32, Brazennose Street, Manchester, from 11 to 1 at Noon.

EDWARD SMITH,
COLLECTOR.

15 day of *5* Mo. 186*3*

The rate was set by a meeting of the Vestry or ratepayers every year in the old school house on the Green.

Much of the blame for this rise had been heaped on the guardians who were responsible for collecting the county money along with the poor rate. The fact that the expenditure had been authorised by JPs was lost, and instead critics pointed to the salaries of prison staff in Lancashire, which were the highest in England with the exception of York Castle and the London prisons of Newgate and Coldbathfields.[545] In an effort to contain the JPs, the Bill gave the guardians two thirds of the seats compared to just a third for the JPs. We will never know with what passion Thomas White, the forty-nine-year-old farmer, argued his case, or the logic he deployed in proposing the motion against the reduction in the county rate. Did he sympathise with the JPs, believing that more prisons were the answer to the rising crime rate, or was he just opposed on principle to the hard-faced guardians, who had a reputation of being penny-pinching heartless autocrats?

---

545 *Ibid.*, p.166.

Likewise, the decision not to appoint a village constable is unexplained. When this was first agreed in 1850, James Higginbotham argued that because the services of the constable had not been called on during the previous year 'there should be no Constable returned for appointment this year'.[546] When the decision was repeated in 1853 it was, as James White said, because 'the Township is sufficiently protected by the County Constabulary that there be no special constables returned'.[547] Nevertheless one wonders if there were any dissenting voices, as the previous decades were marked by all manner of crimes and disturbances – as we have seen.

Recreating the outrage and determination of the Vestry members to recover missing funds is a little easier if only because the record trail is more extensive. This occupied ratepayers during the whole of 1848 and was no doubt as exciting and important as the events that were preoccupying mainland Europe. The summer that year was a fine one, and newspapers were predicting another good harvest. For Charles Morton the short walk on the early evening of Tuesday 20 June from his home at Lime Bank to Chorlton Green would have been pleasant enough, down the Row from his home to the Green, and to the school where he was to chair a meeting of the Vestry. Charles would have had lots to think about. This was the year when revolutions were shaking the ruling classes in a way that had not happened since 1789. The fall of the monarchy in France and the proclamation of a second republic were matched across Europe by uprisings and demands for change.[548] In England the government and establishment were bracing themselves for the delivery of the third and largest Chartist petition, demanding the vote for working men. All across the North the army was deployed to face unrest at best and revolution at worst. In Chorlton the talking point was missing money. On 8 June, just twelve days earlier, the ratepayers had demanded the repayment of just over £85, money collected by the previous two overseers: Charles Wood and William Whitelegg.[549] This money had been collected in the township to be passed to the Poor Law Union, to help the poor and needy across south Manchester. The issue at the 20 June meeting was how the money could be recovered. As well as Charles, there would have been the usual mix of people in attendance: those with a strong point of view, others with a sense of civic duty and perhaps others with little else to do. The first decision of the night was to pay Edward Smith '£12 a year for collecting poor rate of Chorlton-cum-Hardy and of writing out the July list and all other meetings', a role he continued to perform until

---

546 Minutes of the Overseers Meetings, Chorlton-cum-Hardy, 26 February 1850.

547 Minutes of the Overseers Meetings, Chorlton-cum-Hardy, 13 February 1853.

548 In January there had been risings in Milan that spread across Italy; in February the French monarchy fell; and by March the German states and the Austro-Hungarian Empire were engulfed.

549 Charles Wood lived at Hardy House Farm and farmed 60 acres off Barlow Moor Road opposite Chorlton Park; William Whitelegg lived at Red Gates Farm and farmed 68 acres in Martledge near Chorlton Library.

well into the 1850s. But this was just a preliminary for a discussion about what had happened to the £85 and when the overseers were going to make it available. Although it was reported that £20 had already been recovered, the debate may have centred on the scandal of public money going missing. Samuel Dean, who farmed 300 acres at Barlow Hall Farm, moved the resolution 'that the overseers John Cook & Thomas Hayson[550] should visit the magistrates to take their opinion respecting the steps to be taken to recover the balance of £65 1s. 2½d. to the Township by the late overseers Mr Charles Wood and Mr William Whitelegg'.[551] This was seconded by Thomas Hayson and carried. In the absence of a detailed record of the meeting it is impossible to know whether this resolution arose during the meeting or was a premeditated and calculated act on the part of Samuel Dean, Thomas Hayson and others.

In July the previous two overseers were issued with a warrant for the recovery of the money. On 13 December, at the regular meeting to fix a new poor rate, Thomas White moved and Samuel Dean seconded 'a motion that there be no Poor Rate made in the Township until the Arrears due from the retiring Overseers in March 1848 are paid and that the present Overseer be requested to wait upon Mr Charles North Auditor for the District and intimate to him the decision of this meeting and request him to take steps for their immediate recovery which was, carried unanimously'.[552] It is impossible not to think that Thomas White and Samuel Dean were acting on a carefully worked-out plan, and if confirmation of this was needed the second resolution provides it. Moved by William Gresty and seconded by Thomas White,[553] it called for 'the Arrears of Poor Rates which from the Rate Book at March 25 1848 appear to be due from the cottages be excused'. This too was 'carried unanimously'.[554]

Eventually it was decided to ask the ratepayers to give a voluntary contribution to make up the deficit. In the meantime it was judged that Charles Wood was responsible for the loss. A 'warrant of distress was issued against him and his effects were sold; but all the money was taken to pay the expenses and the township had not got a farthing'.[555] He had 'managed the overseer's affairs and was a defaulter in that amount'. William Whitelegg 'had had nothing to do in the management of the affair', and in the opinion of their counsel he was not responsible for the conduct of his colleague 'and asked the overseers why they did not get a warrant of committal against Mr Wood'. This allowed William to remain

---

550 John Cook lived at Hardy Farm and farmed 29 acres at Hardy Lane. Thomas Hayson lived at Hobson Hall and farmed 37 acres at Whalley Range.

551 Minutes of the Poor Law Meeting, 8 June 1848.

552 Minutes of the Poor Law Meeting, 20 June 1848.

553 William Gresty was a market gardener living on Moss Lane, now Sandy Lane. Thomas White was also a market gardener living on Chorlton Row, now Beech Road.

554 Moved by William Gresty and seconded by Thomas White.

555 *Manchester Guardian*, 24 February 1849. The rate levied was 4*d* in the pound, which should have raised £29 – of which £25 had been collected.

active in Vestry duties, but he was never an overseer again. Charles Wood prospered in the forthcoming years, but seems to have had nothing more to do with local government.

Across Europe different fates awaited the revolutionaries. In England the genuine hopes and aspirations of a generation of reformers collapsed when many of the signatures to the great petition were shown to be forgeries. Chartist agitation continued during the summer of 1848, but was broken by systematic police attacks on its meetings and the arrest of most of its active members.[556]

It is unlikely that these great events went unnoticed in Chorlton. In the tap rooms and the fields, not to mention workshops and servants' quarters, the great issues of the day would have been discussed and opinions given. Later in the century socialist meetings were held on the Green and progressive politicians were elected in Chorlton.[557] The absence of any records of political thought or activity in the 1840s does not mean it did not exist. In places where historical records have survived the opinions and actions of working people are evident. Not all were violent, or as organised as in the South and East during the Swing Riots, but there was widespread opposition to the establishment. In some cases this took the form of threats and vandalism against farmers or the theft of their property. The farmer James Higginbotham recorded a series of broken farm tools during the 1840s, along with absenteeism because of drunkenness; he may not just have been the victim of lazy and clumsy workers. Likewise, poaching was sometimes as much about taking from those who had plenty as it was about putting food on the table.

We know from other parts of England that the division between rural and urban worker was no gaping chasm. Chartist campaigners argued their case in villages, and farm labourers were active on the side of industrial workers. Even the issue of whether to abolish the laws that protected home-grown corn by keeping cheap foreign corn out of Britain was not a clear-cut division between town and country. The Anti-Corn Law League, which campaigned for the abolition of those laws, was successful in getting its messages across in some rural areas.

One such was Alexander Somerville, who had been persuaded by Richard Cobden to join the Anti-Corn Law League in August 1842 and travelled through the countryside arguing the case for free trade and an end to the Corn Laws. In the June of 1847 he was here in Chorlton and recorded his conversations with local farmers James Higginbotham, Thomas Holland and Lydia Brown. He even came across a potato which went by the name 'Radical' because it had been introduced by Joseph Johnson who had been active in radical politics. Johnson was on the platform in St Peter's Field during the Peterloo Massacre and

556 Morton, A.L., *A People's History of England*, Lawrence & Wishart, 1974, p.439.
557 As well as many political meetings, Harry Kemp, the chemist, stood and was elected as a Progress candidate in the first municipal elections after Chorlton was incorporated into the city of Manchester.

was arrested for 'assembling with unlawful banners at an unlawful meeting for the purpose of inciting discontent.' He was found guilty, imprisoned, and on his release in 1821 settled in Northenden. Alexander Somerville, while in the army, had been flogged for his support of the Reform Bill in the May of 1832; he was quoted by Frederick Engels in *The Condition of the Working Classes* and his accounts of his travels through rural England were published in three volumes under the title *Whistler at the Plough* between 1852–53.

We cannot assume that Chorlton was an island entire to itself. A case in point was the opposition to the church rate, which since 1839 had been determined locally at a meeting of the parish. This tax covered the expenses of church services, fabric repairs to the church and the salaries of church officials.[558] Nationally nonconformists objected to supporting the Established Church, as did the Catholic population of Ireland. The newspapers were full of stories of the opposition to the rate and advertisements stressed that properties were 'exempt from tithes and church rates'. Candidates at parliamentary elections voiced their determination to abolish them and there were calls in Parliament to set up a select committee to examine the case for their abolition. At their convention in April 1851 the Chartists included the abolition of church rates and tithes in their Programme.[559]

In Chorlton as elsewhere the opposition had mixed motives. For some it was an issue of principle, while for others it was the cost of the church rate, which had risen during the last decade. Before 1839 it had been set by a parish meeting in Manchester and collected locally in each township by the churchwardens, who in turn paid it to the Manchester churchwardens on the last Sunday of each month. In the case of non-payment the offender's name was passed on and proceedings were taken against him. It is not difficult to see why some in Chorlton were unhappy. Before 1839 the rate levied at the Manchester parish meeting was generally 1½*d* in the pound upon the annual value of all property throughout the parish,[560] but in the late 1840s the local rate was set at 2*d* in the pound. This was not a big difference, but enough for people who could see no justification for paying a church rate in the first place.

And so to the meeting on Tuesday 30 July 1850 where the church rate was challenged. This was publicised with a notice on the church door that announced 'the purpose of laying a church rate for the coming year in Chorlton-cum-Hardy'.[561] The vicar, the Revd William Birley, chaired the meeting and, anticipating a small attendance, decided the meeting was to be held in the vestry. Of course those of a conspiratorial frame of mind may well have concluded that this was to limit the attendance. As it was, the twenty-seven

558 The Manchester Rectory Division Act, 1839.

559 'The Chartist Programme, II The Church', *The Times*, 23 April 1851.

560 Ellwood, chapter 13, 1886.

561 Defeated attempt to set a church rate, *Manchester Times*, 26 April 1851.

people who crowded into the room judged that it was too small, and moved that the meeting be held in the church; but the vicar refused – and not for the first time in the evening ran roughshod over the wishes of those gathered there.

The authorities set out the arguments for maintaining a 2*d* rate. There were problems with the roof estimated at £9[562] and the 'salary for sweeping and cleaning the church, lighting fires & £6, apparitor's salary washing surplices, tolling the bell, coals, soap, candles, bread and wine for the communion and repairing a small hole in a pew floor – these were put down at £11'.[563] On top of this there were the 'impossible to foresee' issues, which were judged as costing £2, and the need to hand a balance over to the successors.

Mr Birley clearly misjudged the meeting's mood. When the opposition opened by questioning the legality of the church rate to pay for anything more than repairs and communion expenses it was brushed aside, as was the question whether a public collection in the church could be used to pay for the 'necessary purposes'. Birley hastily tried to push the meeting towards accepting a church rate of 2*d*, but was met with an amendment: 'the levying of compulsory church rates is contrary to the spirit of genuine Christianity, subversive to the true intentions of the church, and an unwarranted violation of the rights of conscience; and therefore, moves that no compulsory church rate be levied for the present year'.[564] It was an attempt to take the moral high ground and challenge the Church on its own terms, but it fell at the first post as Birley refused to put it to the meeting. The opposition then moved a second amendment to reduce the rate to ½*d* in the pound, which was again disallowed. If Birley felt confident that this stonewalling would win the day he was to be disappointed, for when the vote was taken to levy the full rate of 2*d*. it was defeated by fifteen votes to seven. Not deterred, the vicar refused to accept the vote, falling back on the empty excuse 'that he was bound to administer the law as he found it and was sorry to see so much objection to a church rate which had hitherto been laid and collected quietly'.[565]

But this was not the end. Like many before and after, some of the opposition refused to pay what was to them an unfair tax. One of these was Thomas Pollitt, who was duly summoned to the court at the New Bailey in April 1851 for non-payment – for him the rate was increasing from 10¾*d* to 1*s* 2½*d*.[566] He was a clerk in an insurance firm and lived with his wife and daughter at Grantham Row. During the court hearing it became clear that not only was there some confusion about who was entitled to vote but also that the very basis of the rate calculations was incorrect. The Church authorities claimed that they had lost

---

562 These roof problems were to continue into the 20th century, and may have been created when the aisles were built on.
563 *Manchester Times*, 23 April 1851.
564 *Ibid.*
565 *Ibid.*
566 The rateable value of Thomas Pollitt's home was £7 8*s* 8*d*.

by just one vote, and that some of those who had voted against the rate were not actually ratepayers and so were not entitled to vote.[567] To any impartial observer this last admission suggested that the Church authorities had been lax in their handling of the meeting and underlined a more serious flaw, that the church had not undertaken an assessment of the rateable value of the property in the township, instead relying on the figures from the Poor Law rate assessment. It was this technicality that resulted in the case against Thomas Pollitt being dismissed. There were those who now argued that 'every penny the church-wardens have collected for church rates in the past year, and no doubt on previous years had been illegally obtained from the rate payers'.[568] There were also suggestions that the money should therefore be returned to the ratepayers. As it was, the church rate became an optional payment in Chorlton, and was finally abolished in 1868.[569]

There were other opportunities for the township's working people to express their views. Although there were trade union branches, co-operative ventures and mechanics' institutes in towns, cities and some rural communities, there is no evidence that any of these existed in Chorlton; however, there were sick and burial clubs, mentioned earlier. There was also the Odd Fellows Lodge, formed in Urmston in 1843 before moving first to the Horse and Jockey and later to the Bowling Green. It was still operating in 1847, when its members attended the funeral of Francis Deakin.[570] The longest surviving club was the Chorlton-cum-Hardy Wesleyan Friendly Society, which lasted for forty-six years. What all these groups had in common was that they were run by local people who were charged with the responsibility of administering records, collecting subscriptions and deciding how to allocate resources. Some societies even voted on the appointment of a club doctor.

Throughout the 19th century and into the 20th working men and women gained confidence and skills from being part of these and other organisations, including trade unions, churches and Sunday schools. One such was William Rhodes, who was born in 1816 and gave his occupation as gardener. He was a stalwart Methodist and much admired as a powerful communicator, a skill he learned from preaching in the chapel.[571]

There was one last opportunity for members of the community to have a say and that was jury service. It is easy to overlook this civic duty, and yet it reaches right to the heart of a community, in its way defining the role of the citizen. Those twelve men who assembled

---

567 Emanuel Turner, one of the churchwardens present, claimed that voting was fourteen against and thirteen for.

568 Report of the Chorlton-cum-Hardy Church Rate, *Manchester Times*, 26 April 1851.

569 The Compulsory Church Rate Abolition Act 1868, Chapter 109 31 and 32 Vict.

570 It was started by Samuel Cottrell, G. Beswick and John Johnson, and met in the Lord Nelson pub in Urmston. It amalgamated with the Conservative Club in 1862, and by the 1880s was meeting in the Reading Room on Beech Road, by which time it had £700 invested in Salford Corporation and over £200 in the Manchester & Salford Bank. Ellwood, chapter 25, 1886.

571 Thomas Ellwood, himself a Methodist, in his history of Chorlton-cum-Hardy said of William Rhodes: 'for more than 50 years ... [he] ... has been for that time a regular attendant at the preaching'. Chapter 17, 1886.

in the Horse and Jockey to investigate the deaths of two infants and the murder of Francis Deakin were in a real way seeking to maintain the peace and security of the township.[572] In the case of two of the inquests they were sitting in judgement on people they had known. Not that everyone could participate: as with the Vestry meetings there was a property qualification to be a juror. Of the twelve jurymen who assembled in 1847 to hear the facts about the death of Francis Deakin, all either rented land or were property owners.[573] Five were farmers, farming between 29 and 60 acres, one was a tradesmen and property owner and another was of independent means.[574] Likewise, when Frederick Cope and William Heywood were summoned in May 1852 to serve on the grand jury it was on the basis that they were men of property. Grand juries existed to determine if there was enough evidence for a trial. They could have up to twenty-three members, met in secret and heard the prosecution case without the defendant being present. They reached their decisions by a majority if all members could not agree.[575] Whether either man thought their time on the grand jury was worth the journey from Chorlton to the New Bailey prison is not known. The chairman said in his opening remarks that the 'charge to the grand jury contained nothing of any great public interest. The calendar contained the names of 51 prisoners charged with felony, and 5 with misdemeanour'; but he warned that the 'number would probably be somewhat increased before the end of the session'.[576] Some of these would no doubt have been women, but in May 1852 one would have looked in vain for the name of a woman juror, or for that matter a woman member of the Vestry meeting; and certainly no women would have cast a vote in a parliamentary election.

572 The inquests were into the death of Francis Deakin in 1847, and the discoveries of the infant child of Mary Ann Page in 1849 and the infant of Ann Pearson in 1855.

573 They were Thomas White, foreman, Edmund Newton, Thomas Cookson, James Bankcroft, William Gresty, William Brownhill, William Bailey, William Knight, James Higginbotham, William Cheshyre, James Brundrett and Peter Langford. *Manchester Times and Gazette*, 7 May 1847.

574 Edward Newton, independent, and James Brownhill, wheelwright and landlord of Brownhills Buildings. The farmers were James Bancroft (60 acres), Thomas White (52 acres), William Knight (43 acres), James Higginbotham (37 acres) and Thomas Cookson (29 acres). The remaining five were market gardeners: William Chesshyre (6½ acres), William Bailey (4½ acres) and Peter Langford and William Gresty (1 acre).

575 Hostettler, John, *A History of Criminal Justice in England & Wales*, Waterside Press, 2009, p.142.

576 *Manchester Times*, 26 May 1852.

twenty

COMINGS AND GOINGS

Arriving from the city, field workers, carriers and itinerant tradesmen, the Sunday trade,
Richard Buxton's walks and wealthy families

The roads south out of Manchester took the traveller along busy and noisy thoroughfares, past great warehouses and factories and mean workers' dwellings, then past the fine mansions of the well-to-do before reaching fields and farms. Withington, Didsbury and Northenden all had something to commend them, but Chorlton had all that a casual visitor could desire. Some who visited we have already met: the field workers, the carriers with their carts, and the itinerant travellers with all manner of cheap, cheerful and necessary items. The lanes, shops and pubs resounded with the accents of domestic servants and farmworkers who had been born elsewhere. The Sunday trade from Manchester that was particularly evident in the summer months was a welcome diversion for some and a disquieting intrusion for others. Families brought their children for a day out away from the noise and grime of the city, and others came to visit relatives.

But of all those who tramped to Chorlton it is Richard Buxton who deserves special mention. He was a remarkable man. Although he was self-taught and laboured on the margin of poverty all his life, he was a respected botanist, whose book is still consulted more than 160 years after it was published. In the summer of 1826 he set out from Hunts Bank with some companions to walk to Chorlton.[577] It had been 'one of the hottest and driest summers that I can remember, and there had been no rain in the neighbourhood for two or three months; but on the day appointed for our meeting, very heavy rain came on about five in the morning'. With great honesty he continued: 'I should not have thought of stirring

---

577 It was probably June. He was with James Percival, a Prestwich gardener, Thomas Heywood of Cheetham Hill and John Shaw, an Eccles gardener. Hunts Bank is the area in front of Victoria station.

out of doors; but, having made the appointment, I thought it just possible that my friends might come, and I would not on any account disappoint them. We all went in the rain, through Manchester to Chorlton-cum-Hardy. After staying at the last named place sometime the weather changed and a fine day ensued.'[578] Perhaps it was on this journey that he discovered the autumn crocus where Chorlton Brook runs into the Mersey.[579] Here there was a small bridge over the stream, put up by Charles Walker and later washed away.[580] Buxton's route from the city might well have drawn him to this spot, for having walked south out of Manchester along Chester Road his entry into the township would have led him to Turn Moss. Having crossed the brook at this point, with

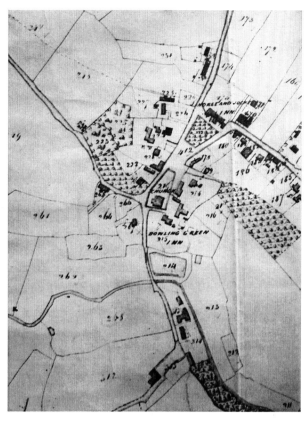

A walk through the village using the tithe map.

the sun beating down on their backs, the botanising companions would have followed the Mersey, crossing at Jackson's Boat (where they found more specimens), before by degree moving on to Baguley Moor and Hale Moss, 'and after having botanized there ... returned to Manchester at dusk, all pleased with our day's excursion'.[581] Sadly Buxton gave no more details of the journey home, but whichever route they took the contrast between the rural lanes and their destination couldn't have been greater. Buxton lived in Ancoats, in a densely packed area of factories and working-class dwellings.

This contrast between city and country is probably what brought the wealthy of Manchester to Chorlton. Unlike Richard Buxton these were people of substance. Many

578 Buxton, *op. cit.*, p.vii and viii.

579 Over 180 years later local botanist David Bishop rediscovered the plants growing where Buxton had first come across them.

580 It was built by Charles Wood and was known as the Mosley Bridge. Charles Wood was the son of Thomas Walker, the radical, and lived at Longford Hall; the bridge connected his land on either side of the brook. Tithe Schedule 1845. In the 1830s it was destroyed by a flood, and a new one was built where the brook joins the Mersey. Ellwood, chapter 1, 1885.

581 These included green winged orchids, meadow saxifrage, adders tongue fern and wild daffodil. Of these only green winged orchids seem to be extinct.

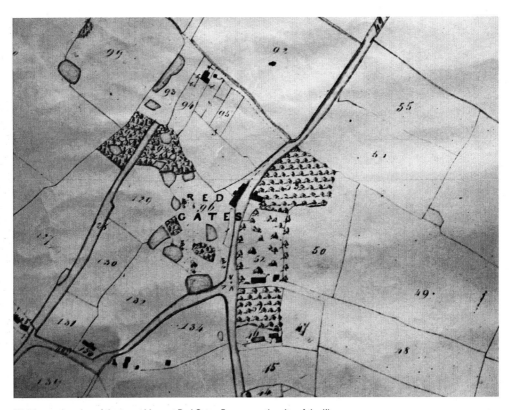

Walking to the edge of the township past Red Gates Farm, now the site of the library.

had made their money in the city and either preferred to commute from the township or had decided to retire there. Throughout the early 19th century house advertisements for Chorlton stressed the pleasant air and open fields, while the opportunity to build fine houses was also emphasised when plots of land were put up for auction. Frederick Cope moved to Chorlton from Oxford Street in 1845. He described himself as a spirit and wine merchant and was in partnership with his brother: they had a number of premises across the city including 12 Exchange Street, opposite the Exchange and close to St Anne's Square and St Anne's Church.[582] The family bought Oak Bank,[583] which consisted of 'three entertaining rooms, six bedrooms, excellent kitchen, scullery, cellars, &c. The outbuildings consist of two coach houses, stabling for four horses, gardener's room, wash house, laundry, &c. There are good gardens well stocked with fruit trees and about three acres.'[584] As well as the house and gardens there was a stretch of land running along

582 These included 12 Exchange Street opposite the Exchange and close to St Anne's Square, and St Anne's Church, 126 Deansgate, 78 Bridge ·
Street, and 16 St Mary's Gate, Slater's Directory of Manchester and Salford, 1850, p.79, Historical Directories edn p.498.
583 Oak Bank stood in a parcel of land bounded by Wilbraham Road, Barlow Road, Sandy Lane and Corkland Road.
584 'Valuable Property in Chorlton-cum-Hardy', Manchester Guardian, 28 June 1845.

Barlow Moor Lane to Lane End, which was a mix of woodland and meadow land; this was rented. Later still Frederick bought the farm tenanted by Thomas Cookson at Dark Lane, Martledge. The estimated rental value of Oak Bank was £130, and with its rateable value of £120 it was the highest rated domestic property in the township. The farm at Dark Lane also commanded an estimated rental value of £130.

Like other wealthy families that moved into the township, the Copes played little part in the politics of the community. Although Frederick was active in the 1830s, calling for an improvement into the policing of Manchester, and tried to secure a property vote in 1841, while twice serving on the grand jury, his name does not appear in any Chorlton records – nor were any of his family buried there. The family remained rooted in the city, their business continuing

Walking across the township from the east to the west along the old road to Stretford, from the parish church, out to Turn Moss, along the banks of the Mersey, taking in a weir, paupers' graves and two bridges.

to expand. In 1857 the partnership acquired the Exchange Tavern on St Mary's Gate, and also may have owned the court that bore their name just off St Mary's Gate; which was given over to businesses.[585] In 1853 Frederick's daughter was married not in Chorlton parish church but in Manchester Cathedral.[586]

James Holt was also a man of substance. He made his money from making engraving blocks for calico printing and lived at the impressive 11 St John Street.[587] This was the only double-fronted house on the street and it reflected his wealth: there were four fine rooms on the ground floor and an elegant staircase leading to two more floors, and there was a series of bow windows behind the staircase. Holt's politics also reflected his wealth. In the 1832 general election he cast his two votes for the Tory candidate against the Whigs.[588]

585 In 1850 it was occupied by Gladstone, Bond & Co. who were foreign produce brokers, and later a leather factor and share brokers. Slater's Directories of Manchester and Salford, 1850 and 1863.

586 On the 29th at the cathedral by the Revd F. Cope, BA. Curate of Birch, Josiah Hunt, Esq. of the city of Westminster, to Barbara Anne, daughter of Frederick Cope, Esq. of Chorlton-cum-Hardy, Manchester Times, 2 July 1853.

587 By the early 20th century the family owned half of the southern side of St John Street and many properties in the neighbouring Artillery and Camp Streets, along with two public houses. When James's grandson died in 1906 he left £41,912, which amounts to over £3m in today's value.

588 The Electors Guide 1832, BR 352042 M45, Archives and Local History Library, Manchester.

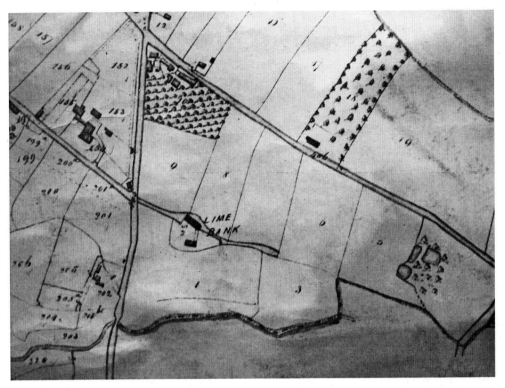

Travelling south through the township to Hardy and the Mersey, starting at Lane End, past Lime Bank and across Chorlton Brook.

Seven years later, against the backdrop of worsening class antagonisms, he was one of the fifteen magistrates of Manchester who met on 4 May 'to consider the measures necessary to be adopted for preserving the peace within the borough'.[589] This was in response to the arrest of Chartists who had allegedly been drilling with weapons. The magistrates resolved 'to prevent, put down, and suppress such meetings and proceedings', which were unlawful and endangered 'the public peace'.[590]

But James Holt had already taken up residence in the township by 1834, and four years later bought 15 acres of land at public auction from the bankrupt James Jackson.[591] This purchase, along with his existing estate, made him the third largest landholder after the Egertons and Lloyds in 1851.[592] The family home and estate dominated the land beyond the village, where the Row ran into Barlow Moor Lane. The Holts' house was set

589 *The Times*, from the *Manchester Guardian*, 9 May 1839.

590 Part of the public notice issued by the magistrates on 9 May 1839, *The Times*.

591 The land was at Round Thorn, which is the area north of Chorlton Brook roughly covering the stretch from the allotments and part of Chorlton Park down to Nell Lane.

592 The size of his land was recorded in the 1845 tithe schedule; the rateable value comes from the 1847 rate book.

South from Hardy Lane, and to Jackson's Bridge. The photograph dates from the early 20th century, but apart from the bridge (which was rebuilt in 1881) the scene would have been much the same half a century before. The first bridge was built in 1816, but the rights to charge for rowing people across the river were still held by the landlord of The Greyhound in 1832.

in a large walled garden laid out with ornamental gardens, and an orchard. The upstairs windows commanded fine views south to the Brook and the Mersey beyond. Holt's 17 acres of land, along with the house and gardens, amounted to a rateable value of £130. He also rented out land to two tenant farmers, which had a combined rateable value of £40. His own land was a mix of meadow and arable and was mainly located along Chorlton Brook.[593] By contrast, his immediate neighbours on the Row lived in homes that were valued at under £10.

There is little evidence that Holt played an active part in Chorlton's affairs. His name does not appear in the minutes of the Poor Law meetings, and in all likelihood he was buried in St John's in Manchester. In his turn James's son was to retire to the township after his father's death, and also seems to have made little impact on the community. However, James's grandchildren, Sarah and Hannah, were active on the bazaar committee, which raised funds for the building of the new church in the early 1860s; Hannah was

593 In what is now Chorlton Park between Barlow Moor Lane and Sandy Lane. The size of his land was recorded in the 1845 tithe schedule; the rateable value comes from the 1845 rate book.

Hough End Hall was best approached along Nell Lane, which gave this fine view of the building. Now the scene is obscured by an office block.

still helping thirty years later.[594] Their brother John was remembered by his sister Martha with the donation of an altar cross to the church after his death.[595]

Not everyone remained in Chorlton for life, although a fair few returned to baptise their children and in some cases to be buried in the parish churchyard. The reasons why they left are varied.

James and Barbara Renshaw moved to Hulme from Chorlton. James was born in 1813 and had settled in Hulme by 1841. To the north of Caton Street, where they lived in Hulme, there were glassworks and cotton factories. Just one street away was the workhouse, a brooding reminder of where those who had bad luck might end up. The area, which formed an island of 174 houses, was home to 834 people.[596] James was a gardener, which seems an odd occupation for an area so heavily built up, but there were plenty of houses with large gardens along Oxford Street.[597] As pleasant as these may have been, there were no gardens

594 'The Christmas Fair', parish magazine, Christmas 1896.

595 'Brass Altar Cross emblazoned with stones 2ft 8in high, presented to St Clement's in memory of John Holt of Beech House by Isaac and Martha [Holt], Hordern, October 1906.' The terrier of St Clement's. John died in August 1906 and was buried beside his sister Hannah, who had died in 1901, in Southern Cemetery.

596 The area comprised part or all of Clarendon Street, Kingston Street, Eagle Street, Phoenix Street, Medlock Street, Stretford Road, Caton Street, Devonshire Street, Elvington Street and Duke Street.

597 This part of Oxford Street is now Oxford Road. Here there were large houses with extensive grounds, for example Oxford House, between what is now Grafton and Nelson Street; while opposite there was the even more impressive Chorlton House.

Cow Lane, typical of the little lanes the casual traveller would encounter while exploring watercourses, ponds and various forgotten roads and footpaths.

near Caton Street. The open plots of land south of the workhouse were no substitute for fields, and in any case these would soon be covered with more houses.

The Renshaws' house was built before 1844, and so did not need to adhere to the byelaw that insisted all homes should be provided with running water and a lavatory either in the house or the yard: the nearest pumps were about 100yds away. The two-up two-down house was shared with another family.[598] It was here that the Renshaws' first son was born in 1841; he died just two years later. But this was not Ancoats or Little Ireland, which had been festering slums for generations. Hulme had been built later and the houses were generally of a better quality. The family's neighbours had a mix of manual, skilled and even clerical occupations.[599] In 1841 the open countryside was still within easy walking distance. Edwin, the family's surviving son, became a solicitor's clerk, and their daughter moved from dressmaking to retail while her husband became a school attendance officer. They were not the only ones to leave. The Revd William Birley swapped his church for

---

598 By common consent this part of Hulme was inadequate, and later in the century it was the focus for a series of reports highlighting poor housing conditions. Nearby streets were demolished in the first slum clearance in 1930.

599 They included an agricultural labourer, warehouseman, cotton duffer, coachman, cotton spinner, labourer, piercer, foundry labourer, joiner, mechanic, weaver, fustian cutter, plaster, brewer, plasterer, pocket book man, engineer, silk throaster, book keeper, shopkeeper, publican, salesman, hairdresser, agent and draper manager.

the church of St Stephen's, Salford.[600] In 1859 Birley left Chorlton, where he had been for seventeen years, exchanging the small rural living for one in the heart of Salford. The contrast between Salford and Chorlton could hardly have been starker. Perhaps it was the wish to bring a message of religious hope to an inner-city parish that motivated Birley. After all, his income at St Stephen's was £145 a year, just £42 more than at St Clement's.[601] Birley chose to live some distance from his parishioners in Leaf Square, a pleasant and elegant spot.

Some families remained in Chorlton for generations. John Clarke was just thirty when he set up home at the smithy on the Row, taking over from William Davies who had worked the anvil since 1834. Clarke was born in Cheshire, and I doubt that as he paid his £55 to Elizabeth Lowe for the business's goodwill, pigsty and wooden shed he thought that his family would still be hammering and heating metal in the village until the mid-20th century. The same was true of William Bailey, who had been born in the north of the county and married into the Renshaw family in the 1840s, and who had run a farm on the Row since 1767. His descendants would still be milking cows and rearing pigs in the township in the 1960s.

John Clarke was the blacksmith on the Row from 1860 and his family continued to work metal well into the 20th century. The document detailed his purchase of the goodwill, fixtures, and forge as well as the pigsty for £50 in 1860. Before him William Davis had run the smithy from 1834. Marjorie Holms remembers watching 'old Mr Clarke hammering and heating at his forge' in the early 1930s.

---

600 In 1861 they were at 28 Queen Street, a long and narrow thoroughfare with a machine factory and spindle works at one end and an ironworks at the other. Behind the block they lived in were a series of hidden courts accessible only by narrow alleys from Queen Street.

601 Lewis, Samuel, *A Topographical Dictionary of England*, vols 1 and 3, S. Lewis & Co., 1840.

twenty-one

WALKING THROUGH CHORLTON

Into the village and onto the Green and out to Stretford along the Lanes from Lane End

The Row

Beech Road is a fine place to start a series of gentle walks around the township. In 1847 it was known as Chorlton Row or the Row, and what is now Barlow Moor Road still went by its old name of Barlow Moor Lane. Standing at the point where the two meet and looking down the Row, the traveller of 1847 would recognise today the twists and turns the road makes on its way to the Green.

In 1847 the Row was dominated by three fine homes of the wealthy, two farms, a fair number of cottages and the smithy, along with the Wesleyan chapel, two shops, a beerhouse and a fishpond. The finest of these fine homes was that of James Holt, which changed its name from Beech Cottage to Beech House. It stood in its own walled grounds at the top of the Row and what is now the bus terminus, Malton Road and the parade of shops stretching all the way to High Lane stood in the eastern part of the gardens. This was a very big house, standing taller than any nearby.

A little further down the Row at the western edge of the Holt estate was one of the brick-built rows of cottages which were replacing old wattle and daub homes. It stood at right angles to the road and was roughly opposite Reeves Road.

This is a good point to stop and take in the views. With our back to Beech Cottage and looking south, we would have had an uninterrupted view across the fields to Chorlton Brook. From any one of their grand windows the Holts would have been able to see much further. On a clear day beyond the Brook and across more fields was Hardy Lane, and obscured by the trees of Barlow Wood was the Mersey. Looking west down the Row towards the Green there was a good view of the first of the farms. This was occupied by

Samuel Gratrix and later became known as Bowling Green Farm. Set back from the Row, it occupied what is now the corner of Beech Road and Beaumont Road and its farmland stretched towards the Brook.

Walking just a little further past Gratrix's home would bring us to the Baileys' farm, where a block of sheltered flats stands today facing the recreational ground. Strictly speaking both these farmers were market gardeners, and neither rented more than 7 acres. But they were also dairy farmers, and the Baileys owned property.

The recreational ground, or Beech Road Park, was part of a series of fields running down from Cross Road as far as Acres Road and back to High Lane. Most of the land was owned by the Egerton or Lloyd estates and were farmed by a number of farmers. In an echo of the old medieval system where no one farmer had all his land in one place, these strips of land were held by William Bailey, James Higginbotham, George Whitelegg, John Brundrett, Thomas Holland, Thomas White and Mary White. In the case of the Baileys, their holdings alternated with those of the other tenants.

At the western edge of the Rec., bordered by Wilton Road, is a good place to stop and take stock again. This was the site of Sutton's Cottage, which was a wattle and daub house, where the Sutton family lived for much of the 19th century. The cottage conformed to that traditional view of a country home: a thatched roof, supported by oak beams, walls made of branches covered with a mix of mud, hay, horsehair and, in some cases, animal blood and manure. It was set back from the road with a garden at front and back. The building may have dated back to the 18th century, and was demolished in 1891.

At this point the Row became more crowded. Looking across the road and down the south side, which today is dominated by rows of shops and the old police station, our 19th-century traveller would have seen more cottages. Sticking to the north side, just beyond Sutton's cottages was Blomley's Fishpond, which stretched way down to Acres Road and was crossed by a wooden footbridge. The pond was fed from a little watercourse that ran from High Lane. Little better than a ditch, it had become polluted and was covered with flags, which in turn were covered with a mix of earth and cinders. This became the footpath called the Acres.

Just past Acres Road was an attractive Georgian house, directly facing the pond. Sadly it was demolished in 2007, and has been replaced by shops, houses and flats. This may well have belonged the Blomleys, who were living on the Row in the early 19th century. Samuel and Elizabeth Blomley baptised their son Samuel in the parish church in 1807 and were listed as living in Chorlton during the 1820s and '30s, but do not appear in the census of 1841.

Directly opposite was William Davies's smithy. It might seem odd to the modern visitor that anyone with money should choose to live beside a smithy, but that is what Daniel

Sharp, who described himself as of independent means and a gentleman, chose to do. His house, which has stood beside the smithy for perhaps 180 years, is another fine example of an early 19th-century townhouse, set in a walled garden. Even in the early 21st century, after years of neglect, an unsympathetic extension and two serious fires, which destroyed half the roof, it remains an elegant building. If Daniel Sharp was not bothered about living next to a smithy, he may not have been over-troubled by the Wesleyan chapel that stood on the other side of his home. The first chapel was built in 1805 and was replaced with a larger building in 1827. This is the one that we see today, shorn of its upper storey. For years it was a furniture warehouse, and has undergone another change of use. It is still possible to view the gravestones of some of the Methodists who were interred in its little graveyard.

We are now almost at the end of the walk along the Row. Back in 1847 beyond the chapel were more wattle and daub cottages, including the home of James Renshaw, the schoolteacher, and Ellen Warburton. Earlier in the century one of the cottages had been home to Mary Crowther, the last woman to do penance in the parish church. Today this site is occupied by the Trevor Arms and a row of shops, the last of which for most of the 19th and 20th centuries belonged to the Whittaker family, who sold groceries.

Directly opposite on the north side of the Row and facing the Green were the stationer's shop run by Thomas Taylor, which later became the post office, and Samuel Nixon's beerhouse, the Travellers Rest. Today they are still shops, having undergone major internal renovation as well as having the height of their roofs increased. They still have a single front window and open directly onto the street; the original floor plan is fairly clear. In the case of no. 70, which was the Travellers Rest, the two rooms were very small, measuring just 11½ft wide by 6ft long.

On the corner of the Row and what is now Whitelow Road stands the Beech Inn, which has been a pub for over 100 years. There has been a house on this site since the early 19th century. This may have been the school and Sunday school that the Methodists built by public subscription. For reasons that are unclear it reverted to the Lloyd estate and was bought by Thomas Taylor, who later converted into dwelling places. In 1847 this corner of the Row was occupied by a block of houses that may have been the result of Thomas Taylor's conversion, which consisted of four properties, one of which faced the Row with the remaining three bordering Whitelow Road. Forty years later one of the middle units was altered, its front outer wall being set further back from the road. Later still the four properties were either rebuilt or converted into one building. This involved taking the rest of the front wall back so that it was in line with the middle unit, and creating the open area that is still a feature of the corner. It may well be that this happened when the Beech opened in the early 20th century.

Chorlton Green

From the Row, the most obvious walk is around Chorlton Green. It takes very little imagination to place this in a rural setting. Stand on the Green and all the features of a country village are there. At one end are the lych-gate and graveyard, opposite is a half-timbered pub and on the remaining two sides are the old school and two farmhouses. However, the timbers on the Horse and Jockey are no more than 100 years old, and one of the farmhouses was an office for most of the last half-century. Even the lych-gate only dates from 1887. None of this hides the fact that for perhaps 1,000 years this was a village green.

In 1847 the Green was the private garden of the Wilton family. It was enclosed in the early 19th century and remained a secret place behind tall hedges until 1895, when with the death of Miss Wilton the land reverted to the Egerton estate, which promptly reinstated it as the village green.

The Wiltons lived in one of the houses in what is now the Horse and Jockey. Originally the pub was much smaller, consisting of perhaps four rooms, two up and two down on either side of the front door. The rest of the building consisted of a number of other houses, including two shops. During the 20th century the pub expanded to take over the rest of the block, although there was still a separate dwelling as late as 1949 on the west side of the entrance. Photographs from the 1930s show it as having its own front door and picket fence, but not the imitation oak beams that were already a feature of the rest of the front of the building. In the same year the pub and the picket fence featured in a short film, *Bella's Birthday*.[602] During the 20th century this block underwent some profound changes. To the east of the pub entrance there used to be an outhouse that jutted out towards the road. The remaining part of the block, where it joins the shop on the corner, was a three-storey structure, which only lost its top floor sometime after the 1920s.

The forecourt of the Horse and Jockey affords the best views across the Green. Back in 1847 the tall hedges of the Wilton garden on the Green would have obscured much of what can be seen today, but some of the village buildings were as they are now. To the west, where today a group of late 19th-century houses sits beside a modern development, were two farms. For part of the 20th century one of the farmhouses was the offices of a garage, but today it is a home again.

Higginbotham's farmhouse at the end of the Green is a wonderful survival of an 18th-century building. It stands behind its own high hedges at the corner of the Green by the

---

602 *Bella's Birthday* is a short film made of outtakes from *School for Randal*, and was made by Film Studios Manchester Ltd. The film company operated from 1948 to 1953 from the converted Wesleyan chapel in Rusholme on the corner of Dickenson Road and Oxford Road. The clip is available online from Mancunian Film Archives.

graveyard. Some of the surrounding buildings were once farm buildings, and the barn just to the south of the farmhouse was where the first Methodists held some of their services before the chapel on the Row was built. The late Anthony Walker, whose family's building yard was situated in this complex, remembered coming across a stone inscription recording the Wesleyan services. Alas it has not survived.

From here, it is just a short step into the graveyard. Before the lych-gate was constructed in 1887 there was a plain brick entrance, with iron gates flanked by stone square pillars. The graveyard was full of headstones, some lying flat on the ground and others standing erect, with several more impressive monuments. Here were interred hundreds from Chorlton, as well as others who had moved away but wanted to be buried with their family. The earliest burials were closest to the church, with the great and good being buried inside the building. Some of the original gravestones survived the landscaping of the churchyard in the early 1980s, but most no longer rest where they were originally placed. Many more were broken up and taken away. The path from the entrance meanders towards the church, which was a tall building with a side aisle and a steeple at the west end. The church was closed in 1940 because of frost damage and was finally demolished in 1949. The layout has been preserved, along with the headstones that rested inside. Standing on the red and black tiles it is possible to get a sense of the size of the church. The six stone blocks supported cast-iron pillars that held up the roof, and the rust marks from the pillars are still visible.

Just beyond the south wall of the churchyard is the Bowling Green Hotel, built in 1908 to replace a much older building. This earlier pub was situated a little to the east of the present one, occupying the area roughly bordering the bowling green. It boasted a bay window, and with additions at the side and back had a haphazard appearance, as if it had yet to be finished off.

Then as now it was possible to walk back to the Green along the east side of the churchyard. Today this amounts to an often overgrown path running parallel with the edge of the Finney Drive estate. This mix of houses and flats was built in the early 1960s on the site of a third farm. It was the barn of this farm that ran along the full length of the track – which in 1847 was a much wider road, as befitted the main thoroughfare from the village past the farmhouse down to the Bowling Green Hotel. It was no doubt this route that was regularly taken by a group of gentleman who rented the rights to fish on the village pond, which was just beyond the old pub. As the pond also bordered Brookburn Road, its fish may have been a target for poachers and children. Like Blomley's pond on the Row it was filled in, and part of the pavilion and some garages stand on the site.

The third farm stood at the corner of Crossland Road and the Green. It was a good example of a local farmhouse and judging by the windows and chimney pots consisted of six rooms. There are still a few who remember it, and from the late 19th century it was known variously as Laburnum Cottage, Ivy Green Farm and more recently Greenwood's Farm. Like other farms in semi-urban surroundings the outer buildings were converted into other uses. Marjorie Holmes remembers that her father, who was a carpenter, had his workshop and store on site, while there were also a garage and smithy.

Standing at this corner today a traveller from 1847 would no doubt be impressed by the new school and schoolhouse that were built in 1876, replacing the school of 1845. The earlier school was a fine building but had become too small. Here the ratepayers met to conduct the Vestry meetings, and the National Penny Bank opened a branch in about 1887. It was open to adults and children, and once a depositor's account had reached £1 it was transferred to the Manchester & Salford Savings Bank.[603] This perhaps reflects the difference between the old rural part of the township and the new area, which was developed during the last quarter of the 19th century at Martledge. Around the Green there were still many farm labourers, while away towards the junction of Barlow Moor and Wilbraham Roads were new inhabitants, many of whom worked in the city. The Green had a penny savings bank, while the new Chorlton had commercial banks.

We are now back by Wilton's garden. Beyond the school looking north there was only open land up to the cottages at the end of the Row.

High Lane from Lane End to Stretford

Like many of the walks around the township, the route from Lane End along High Lane to Stretford was a pleasant stroll with few houses and plenty of trees and fields. From Lane End west to Stretford, it was the northern wall of the Holt estate that was first visible: the wall was high and mature trees further obscured the view, but it was still possible to glimpse tall chimneys. The same corner is taken up today by shops and a large detached house, once the home of Dawson the estate agent and property developer.

Today it is almost impossible to get a sense of the geography. The lie of the land and the watercourses have been hidden by the buildings. It is perhaps difficult to realise that walking away from Lane End the land begins to rise. The houses that run west towards Brundett Road and beyond sit on what was known as Scotch Hill.

Directly opposite was Mrs Dunster's cottage, the garden of which jutted out into the road. This was on the south side, roughly where the old church hall stands before Wilton Road. We know little about Mrs Dunster except that she rented her home from John

---

603 Advertisement for the Chorlton-cum-Hardy Savings Bank, St Clements's parish magazine, 1896, p.4.

Brundrett. She appears in neither the 1841 or the 1851 census, but she was there in 1847. Standing in her front garden, Mrs Dunster would have seen only fields in all directions. Her nearest neighbours were the Suttons on the Row, and brick cottages further down High Lane on the other side of the road. These were Grantham's Buildings, now St John's Close. These cottages were well placed. To their rear was an orchard, while across High Lane just to the west was the garden of William Brundrett; the rest was fields. Grantham's Buildings survived into the last quarter of the 20th century, being pulled down in the 1970s. For years the site remained an overgrown waste and a short-cut from High Lane into the roads behind. It is worth reflecting that the present development of St John's Close has packed more houses onto the same piece of land. Some of the last tenants still speak fondly of Grantham's Buildings, despite the fact that they lacked electricity in the 1950s and had no bathrooms. In the 1970s John and Carol Hayes brought up a large family in one of them, and remember that bath night consisted of filling the tin tub in the kitchen. The children and then the parents took it in turn to bathe.

From here down towards the St Clement's Road and Manchester Road junction the houses are a mix of impressive piles and smaller villas. These were built after the 1860s as family homes; some were converted into multi-occupancy properties in the 1960s and '70s. Often inhabited by a transitory population and neglected by their landlords, they have now begun to be converted into family homes again. The cold and uninviting bedsits sharing a down-at-heel bathroom are now bedrooms, dining rooms and studies. Some are too big for modern families and are being transformed into desirable flats.

It is worth stopping at the junction with Acres Road. This is much narrower than any of the other roads running into High Lane, and in the 1840s was little more than a track. The eastern side of this road, now occupied by small brick terraces, was meadows, while the western side from the school down to Hardy Avenue and to what is now Beech Road was the garden of Mary Holland, extending along High Lane to the boundary of the school.

Two churches follow in quick succession. St John's dates from the 20th century, while St Clement's was built in the 1860s to replace the old parish church. However, some continued to worship at the original church in the heart of the village, and the two coexisted until the old church was closed in 1940.

This is another convenient point to stop. Here High Lane becomes Edge Lane and crosses two other old roads that would have been familiar to our traveller in 1847. To the south is St Clements Road, which runs back into the village, and heading off north is Manchester Road. Just before the junction the old Rough Leech Gutter crosses High Lane by way of a culvert before snaking off down Acres Road to join Blomley's Fishpond, although it may also divide at this point, with part of it running onto Turn Moss and flowing into a pond. This watercourse may well be responsible for the 'Edge Lane Lake', which often forms across the road at its junction with St Clements and Manchester Roads. Although long forgotten, it was a prominent feature in 1847, running from what is now St Werburghs Road, just north of Park Brow Farm, at the bottom of the modern Sandy Lane.[604] It then headed south-west to this junction, and it is possible that it lies for part of its route under Corkland Road before skirting Oak Bank House and Clough Farm, on either side of Barlow Moor Road, then roughly following Wilbraham Road before turning again to meet High Lane.

Many thought this corner of Edge Lane and Manchester Road was one of the most beautiful parts of Chorlton. The stretch of land opposite the modern St Clement's was known as Pits Brow. Here lived William Chesshyre, market gardener, clerk to the parish church and census enumerator for 1841 and 1851. Two cottages here variously went under the name of Pits Brow Cottages or the Glass Houses. Set back from the road, they commanded a fine view south to the village and Green and were surrounded by gardens and orchards. This idyllic spot caught the attention of the farmer, innkeeper and property developer George Whitelegg, and in 1860 he built Stockton Range on the site of the Glass Houses. This was Lloyd land, and before Stockton Range was built George Lloyd built a new house for the Chesshyres on Manchester Road, all but facing their old home. The building still exists, and sits in a garden protected by tall stone walls and iron railings. Stockton Range (actually two houses) also remains. In its way this building also marks a transition point in the history of the township. When these two houses were built the provision of water was still a problem: most houses either had access to a well or pump, or relied on the brooks and ponds. Stockton Range had its own well, which was inside the house – but within four years Manchester Corporation had built a water main to supply Chorlton. This ran along Edge Lane and down St Clements onto the Green.

This idyllic setting may have been the reason why this was the site of the parsonage, in 1847 home to the Revd William Birley and his family. It was a large and impressive building but one not easily seen from the road: the long garden and screen of trees isolated it from all but the persistent of observers. Had we ventured into the garden we would have been met by a brick building on three floors. The ground floor had tall windows looking out east across the garden, with smaller windows above. The front door was entered through a tall stone porch. It was still very new, having only been erected in 1847 by subscriptions collected through the exertions of the Revd William Bailey, who until then had been living on Upper Chorlton Road at the corner with Wood Road. No doubt Bailey was pleased with it, but it was by all accounts a gloomy, damp and cold place, which finally fell victim to wet rot, as well as its huge size in the middle of the 20th century. It lasted only

---

604 This was Moss Lane, running from Lane End down to Park Brow Farm.

a century and when it was replaced by something smaller the incumbent was not sorry to see it go.[605] The cellar of the old rectory is still visible in the garden, and has often been mistaken for a sunken garden.

The road continued past fields and orchards before reaching the edge of the township at Turn Moss Road. It would have been just a short walk to the farm, but for those of a nervous disposition not a journey to be taken after dark: here, where today the Stretford sign welcomes you to Trafford and on the site of a modern townhouse, stood what was reckoned to be a haunted barn. Not I suppose that this ever bothered the rational-minded Thomas Walker, who was both a radical politician and successful businessman and who lived in Longford Hall opposite the barn until his death in 1817. The Walkers continued to live in the Hall until it was sold to the Rylands, who tore it down and replaced it with the present building.

From here it is a short walk to the Duke's Canal and Stretford. Our journey today passes a collection of mixed housing, some quite pleasant and some very ordinary – but 160 years ago the route would have been dominated by just four houses, of which only one was visible from the road. Ahead was the canal. By 1847 it had been here for over eighty years, and there would be no one left who could remember the mixture of fear and excitement that came with its construction. The canal builders were a rough and ready bunch, skilled at their work but prone to heavy drinking and hard living. Local communities were not always happy to have the navvies in their midst, despite the opportunity to make money from them. The canal was the highway to the city, and the swiftest and most comfortable way of commuting into Manchester. From our vantage point on the bridge the sheer scale of the operation would be clear to see. Independent carriers as well as the Bridgewater Company plied the route, and depending on the time of day it might be possible to catch sight of a packet boat arriving or departing from the Watch House, a little further east – close to where the canal went over the old road by Cut Hole Aqueduct.

Within two years of our walk to Stretford in 1847 the railway had arrived, and the bridge over the line afforded a wonderful view not only of Stretford but the surrounding countryside. Waugh, who stood on this spot in the winter of 1857, was moved by the 'great tract of meadows, gardens and pasture land'.[606]

Beyond where we stand on the bridge over the canal is Stretford, and we have two choices for the return journey. We could take the Stretford Road to Trafford Bar, and travel down Seymour Grove to the junction with Upper Chorlton Road and Manchester Road, thence south through Martledge. Alternatively, after following the towpath of the canal

---

605 Ida Bradshaw remembering the rectory, May 2010.
606 Waugh, *op. cit.*, pp.74–5, Google edn pp.94–5.

to the Watch House we could go under the canal and take the old road past the weir and Mersey, skirting Turn Moss to arrive back at the village. Travelling along Stretford Road follows the route into Manchester taken by the stagecoach and the carriers, but the road is busy and the scenery dull. The old road takes us along a peaceful track bordered by trees and the promise of wildlife.

twenty-two

WALKING IN THE NORTH OF THE TOWNSHIP THROUGH MARTLEDGE

Past the houses of the rich, cottages, a pub and a few farms

Barlow Moor Lane, Barlow Moor Road, north to Martledge

Barlow Moor Lane is a long road. Standing at the point where the Row joins Barlow Moor Lane we have a choice: turn north and journey to Martledge and then out of the township by various routes to Hulme and Manchester, or south to Hardy Lane and to the Mersey, Withington and Didsbury.

Martledge is much overlooked in most histories of the township, so north it is. We start with the Holt estate again. Leaving the Row and heading north up Barlow Moor Lane, we follow the east wall of the Holts all the way to Lane End. Everything on this side of the road dates from after 1908, when the last of the Chorlton Holts died and the estate was sold off. Directly opposite where Sandy Lane begins today was the grocer's shop of Jeremiah Brundrett. This was a large house, at one time named Lilly Cottage. The Brundretts were there long enough for the spot to become known as Brundretts Corner. Facing the shop, roughly on the site of the church, was the home of Caleb and Ann Jordrill. Here was one of the last wattle and daub cottages.

Continuing north along the lane, our journey passes open fields until we reach the edge of Martledge. To the left was Clough Farm and to the right Oak Bank House. The farm stood roughly between Groby Road and Silverwood Avenue. In the summer of 1847 it was occupied by Margaret Taylor, and it would have been her farmland we would have seen as we walked up Barlow Moor Lane towards her home. All the land that today runs from Silverwood Avenue back towards High Lane and Lane End was rented by her from the Egerton estate. There were 10 acres in all, a mix of arable, meadow and clover. It included

Jeremiah Brundrett, landowner and leading Methodist.

part of Scotch Hill.[607] From these fields Margaret could have gazed across at Oak Bank, once home of William Morton and later the Cope family. Oak Bank was a substantial building standing in its own grounds close to the modern junction of Barlow Moor and Wilbraham Roads. Nothing now exists of the house, but the path leading to it has become Needham Avenue. The house was situated in a garden that covered the area running on either side of Needham Avenue as far as Barlow Moor Lane in one direction and Corkland Road in the other. The estate also included a large meadow and a small wood, stretching from Needham along Barlow Moor Lane to Lane End. William Morton was there from 1821, and on his death his will stipulated that the house and land had to be sold within five years.[608] When this happened is not known, but in 1845 a Miss Crofton was there, paying rent to Mr Morton's executors.[609] By 1847 the house and land were in the possession of Frederick Cope, who rented both to John Hilton. This was a short-term arrangement, and by 1850 the Cope family were living at Oak Bank.

William Morton described himself as a member of the gentry.[610] Frederick Cope was a wine merchant who ten years earlier had been living with his wife and children on Oxford Street, close to where the university now stands. Elizabeth had died by 1851.

Leaving the Taylors and Copes, our 19th-century route would have taken us over Rough Leech Gutter, which cuts across this part of the township, along the line of Corkland Road, before swinging round just above Oak Bank and heading off towards High Lane. Its name seems rather unglamorous and also very unfair. Far from being a gutter, this was a watercourse on a par with Chorlton Brook, and more impressive than Longford Brook to the north. At this point the modern traveller crosses the junction of Barlow Moor and Wilbraham Roads. Officially this is known as Chorlton Cross, a name bestowed by the city planners and not one that is widely used. Place-names tend to grow out of people's experiences and survive long after the reason for them has been forgotten. So it is with this junction: for perhaps three generations it was known as Kemp's Corner, taking its name from Kemp's the chemist. Harry Kemp was a Liberal politician, and his chemist's shop

---

607 Scotch Hill runs back from High Lane towards Brundrett Road and extends down to Whitelow Road.

608 It was made on 19 August 1836 and was proved in London on 13 July 1839, just two months after his death in 2 May 1839.

609 Rate Book for Chorlton-cum-Hardy, 1844–76, Microfilm 297.

610 Pigot's and Co.'s National Commercial Directory, of 1828–9, p.282 and Pigot's and Co.'s National Commercial Directory, 1834, p.334.

stood from the beginning of the 20th century on the corner of Barlow Moor Road where it joins Wilbraham Road. The clock above the chemist made it a local landmark, and as such it was a recognised meeting point. Today the same spot is referred to as the Four Banks, which given the fact that there is one on each corner makes sense – and is a version of its earlier name, Bank Square.

Had we rested at this point in 1847, with the Rough Leech Gutter at our back, we would have had uninterrupted views of open fields to east and west. Ahead there was a sprawl of properties, including farmhouses, cottages and a pub, and ending at Red Gates Farm where the library now stands. Dominating this stretch was the tall block of Renshaw's Buildings. This was demolished in the 1920s to make way for the Royal Oak, which still stands on the site. The cottages' path is still on the eastern side of the pub, and it retains the stone pavement and road sets. Beyond Renshaw's, on what is now a double-fronted set of shops, stood the old Royal Oak. This was a detached, two-storeyed building with a commanding position. Not only was it on the route to and from the city but it was the only pub hereabouts, in all serving a community of about 100 people. Its only competition came from Mrs Leach's beerhouse. In those spring days of the late 1840s and early '50s it would have been a busy place.

As in so much of the township, the natural geography of the land has been obscured. Watercourses have been culverted, ponds drained and slight rises hidden by buildings. This is particularly true as we move further north – and the first clue to all this is the road itself, twisting and turning, following ancient field boundaries and natural obstacles. Manchester Road snakes its way from the village to Martledge, where the shopping precinct stands – and for a short distance ceases to exist. The break was occasioned by the creation of the precinct car-park. Sections of the Manchester Road appear to have had different names. From Edge Lane to what is now Wilbraham Road was known as Chapel Lane, terminating at Ash Tree, so called because of the tree that grew there in the road. The lane which then crossed what is now Wilbraham Road before disappearing into the car-park and reappearing at Nicolas Road was known as Chorlton Lane. This was the site of the finger-posts, and for a while the area was also known as

James Bracegirdle, another prominent Methodist and property owner. In 1845 he owned cottages by Oswald Field. In that year his tenant Joshua Warburton paid 6s a week. Oswald Field was roughly at the end of Fielden Avenue.

Martledge Green. It is perhaps worth noting that what we now know as Wilbraham Road did not exist until the 1860s.

Had we not turned east at Ash Tree, we could have continued north towards Oswald Field. This is the start of Oswald Road today, and in 1847 it would have taken us past Martha Helsby's garden on our right and through the 4 acres she rented from the Lloyd estate, before the track came out beside the Longford Brook. Just beyond the car-park are the school and houses bordering the long roads of Longford, Nicholas, Newport and Oswald. Here is the site of Isles, where little streams fed ponds that had once been marl pits. Marl was used to enrich the soil, and has been dug here from the 16th century if not before. Later still the clay was used for bricks, and a little further west of Oswald Road were the brick kiln pits, which had already been excavated and filled with water by 1847. Even later this was where a company made bricks for the villas and terraces of the township. Today St John's School stands on part of the old brickfields, while the occasional brick still turns up on or near the football pitch.

This has taken us away from our walk north. Manchester Road, while it continues to twist and turn, never deviates from its northerly direction. With the marl pits to our west now buried under the old cinema and snooker hall, the road opens out to the modern library on the site of Red Gates Farm. This was tenanted by William Whitelegg, and his land ran out to the west. Directly opposite and behind Red Gates were orchards, which gave out onto fields. This was a lonely and open road, not much more than a rough cart track, with deep ditches at each side and overshadowed by trees, mainly favoured by farmers and those on foot. The only house between Red Gates and the border with Whalley Range was here on the corner with Dark Lane. Today, just over the railway bridge where Clarendon Road West joins Manchester Road, was Dark Lane. It stretched east towards Manley Park. On that corner of Manchester Road and Dark Lane was the home of Thomas Cookson. His nearest neighbour was John Cookson, who lived close to the Independent College.

Dark Lane takes us out of our way again: our route must continue north. Where today Manchester Road joins Seymour Grove and Chorlton Road you had a choice – a choice that depended on your pocket. For those who could afford it there was Chorlton Road. This was just nine or so years old in 1847, cut by Samuel Brooks to link his new housing development of Whalley Range south to Chorlton and north to Manchester; but it was a toll road and it cost to use it. The alternative route was to take what is now Seymour Grove to Trafford Bar and the Chester and Stretford roads, which then as now ended at Manchester.

twenty-three

WALKING ACROSS THE TOWNSHIP FROM EAST TO WEST

West on the old road past the river, the weir and terminating at the Duke's Canal

A large part of the old road west from Chorlton and across Turn Moss to Stretford is through open land. To be more accurate, this is no more the old road than any that take us out of the township, but unlike the others it is less used today, half hidden behind trees and bushes, and has a sense of being very ancient. Before starting out it is worth mentioning that there is another stretch that runs from the village past the Bowling Green Hotel, through Chorltonville and out towards High Lane. Strictly speaking only part of this was a road: just beyond Brookburn School it became a track that ran to Hardy Lane Farm, with another track splitting off and heading towards the Mersey at Jackson's Bridge. It is still possible to follow both. The route directly east from the school runs along Brookburn Road before cutting through what is now Chorltonville. The popularly known 'stumps' that connects South Meade to Hurstville Road may be all that is left of the original footpath, which once took the traveller to Hardy Lane.[611] More promising is the other footpath, which still traces its old route along Brookburn Road, past the entrance to the football ground and south across the modern Meadows. But both of these were really just access points for the fields on either side; this west section of the old road ended with the last cottages at Brook Farm.

So west it is by way of the village, Turn Moss to the Duke's Canal and Stretford. It is little more than a narrow paved track, but for centuries it was one of the main routes to Manchester. Along this road went the farmers with their wagons heading for the Bridgewater Canal, villagers wanting to join Chester Road and cowmen driving their cows

---

611 The 'stumps' is just a little far north to be on the line of the old footpath, and it may be that this route was created when Hurstville Road was cut from Hardy Lane, acting as a convenient route out of Chorltonville at this point.

Brook Farm, close to the present school on Brookburn Road. From here in 1845 Lydia Brown farmed 73 acres of arable and meadow land rented from the Lloyd estate. She also owned land herself, renting out the site of the smithy to William Davies on the Row.

back from the Meadows to the farms around the Green.[612] This was called Back Lane and ran past the parish church, across the Meadows and ended just beyond the canal. Over the years parts of the road have changed their name, and there are now houses along some of its course. Our route would have taken us from the Green past open land all the way to Stretford. Today that means picking it up at Ivygreen Road opposite the graveyard hard by the Bowling Green Hotel . But nothing is simple, and Ivygreen Road splits while still retaining one name for both sections. We need to take the turning that leads to Hawthorn Lane, then through the barrier and under the trees to really start our walk.

In some ways little appears to have changed in the last 160 years. Just as then hawthorn, oak, hazel and ash trees line the road, and the banks made from countless years of leaf deposits trapped under the hedgerows are still there. The hazel trees show evidence that they were once coppiced, but probably not for half a century or more.[613] We cannot pass Sally's Hole without pausing and taking in the scene. Today it is easy to miss, having been filled in at the end of the 1960s, but there is still a depression surrounded by trees at the start of the lane. Arrive at a certain time of day, perhaps in the late afternoon in February with the light fading fast, and it becomes quite eerie. The popular myth is that a girl named

612 The sight of Mr Higginbotham bringing his cows home for milking has yet to pass from living memory.
613 Coppicing is the practice of harvesting wood by taking shoots from the tree base (also known as a stool). These shoots are cut at regular intervals, usually between eight and thirty years, depending on the product required and the species of tree.

Sally drowned here. The trees crowd in and the stillness is overpowering – but knowledge of the area is a strong weapon in banishing anxiety. Until quite recently the pond was in open land, with no trees overwhelming it, and it was just one of a number of similar ponds across Turn Moss fed by small streams running from the old Rough Leech Gutter and the Longford Brook.

The road twists and turns, following the old field divisions and avoiding natural obstacles, before running up beside the river bank. This is our first warning of the power of the Mersey: here there is no gentle river bank sloping down to the water's edge, but instead a towering bank, added to over the centuries as the main defence against a powerful threat. Generations of farmers have laboured to construct this wall to repel the Mersey's flood waters. Chorlton and the surrounding farms were all built beyond the flood plain, but this was not always sufficient protection. The Mersey has on countless occasions risen and breached these towering banks, sometimes even sweeping away the defences themselves. This was why a weir was built at a bend in the river, just beyond the point where the brook joins the Mersey – to divert flood water from the Mersey down channels out to Stretford and the Kicketty Brook.[614] Not that it always worked: soon after it was built flood water swept it away, and during the 19th century neither the weir nor the heightened river banks prevented the Mersey bursting out across the plain.[615] In July 1828 flood water transported hay ricks from the farm behind Barlow Hall down to Stretford, only later to bring them back, while later floods were even more destructive.[616] It was, wrote Thomas Ellwood, 'no uncommon thing to see the great level of green fields completely covered with water presenting the appearance of a large lake, several miles in circuit'.[617] On a cold, bleak and rain-swept morning it is possible to sense the importance of the weir. Stretching out from the wall is a deep and placid pool of water, but how different it must have been on a stormy night, when the swollen river burst over the weir. These historic floods were quite sudden. One such event left a farmer just enough time to release his horses from the cart and let them stampede to higher ground, while on another occasion a man was forced to take refuge in a birch tree all night. Although these floods were destructive, they also deposited silt onto the land, and it was common practice to 'open the sluices or floodgates

614 After a heavy flood in August 1799 broke the banks where Chorlton Brook joined the Mersey, there were fears that the Bridgewater Aqueduct across the flood plain could be damaged by flooding, so it was decided to build an overflow channel improving the course of Kicketty Brook and also build the stone weir. Lloyd, John M., *The Township of Chorlton-cum-Hardy*, p.71.

615 This happened in 1840, and in the following year it was rebuilt by the engineer William Cubitt. After litigation the cost of repair was borne by the Bridgewater Trust (£1,500), the Turnpike Commissioners (£500), Thomas Jos de Trafford (£1,000) and Wilbraham Egerton (£1,000). The cost of maintenance was agreed between the Bridgewater Trustees (half), Thomas Jos de Trafford (quarter) and Wilbraham Egerton (quarter). Lloyd, *op. cit.*, p.71.

616 Ellwood, chapter 1, 1885. Ellwood describes serious floods a few years later that destroyed a bridge across Chorlton Brook and six major floods between December 1880 and October 1881. The last time the weir took an overflow of flood water was 1915.

617 *Ibid.*

in order to get the advantage of such sewage upon the land as the river affords, thus saving the trouble and expense of carting "management" there'.[618]

In the midst of life there is death, and anyone who walked the old road after 1885 might well have stopped to gaze at the gravestones of Stretford Cemetery. Well away from the other burials is a line of headstones, in neat rows of five and running parallel for perhaps ten rows. Each contains upwards of six burials; only names and a date record these lives. It is likely that they are paupers' graves.

Beyond the cemetery are the canal and railway line. Many of those making their way along the old road in the late 18th century and mid-19th century would have marvelled at both.

The Bridgewater Canal was built in 1765 to ship coal from the mines of Worsley to the homes and factories of Manchester. So successful was the venture that the price of coal dropped, and the Duke was assured a handsome return on his investment. The canal also carried farm produce into the city, much of which would have been food and must have come from Chorlton. The road gradually became busier as more heavy traffic made its way from the township. This might explain the raised pavement under the canal bridge: out on the open road a traveller could jump into a nearby field if a cart approached, but under the canal this was not possible, so a raised pavement offered protection.

What the canal was to the late 18th century the railway was to the 19th. As Ruskin said, they were 'a device for making the world smaller'. Not that most of the people travelling by road would have been able to afford the railway. Train fares did come down later, but in the early years of the Manchester South Junction & Altrincham Railway the people of Chorlton and Stretford might have wondered at its brash speed and magnificent power, but they could only look. They might, however, have been employed when it was built: although the skilled work was done by navvies, there was casual employment for local farm labourers. Some may even have worked on the bridge that took the railway over the old road.

It still makes for an impressive sight: the two forms of transport that not only assisted in the Industrial Revolution but wrenched Chorlton out of centuries of isolation. The station at Stretford brought people with money, who began to buy houses along the route from the station to the village.[619] Thirty years later another railway line, with its station on the edge of the village, sparked a second building boom on land that had been agricultural. By then the old road was just a lane, used by farmers and for leisure.[620]

---

618 *Ibid.*

619 Stretford station was opened in 1849, Chorlton station in 1880.

620 A road from Chorlton to Barton was cut in 1811, and Edge Lane and High Lane were main roads to Stretford as early as 1841; passengers and farm traffic may have used these roads. By 1888 a picture shows what appear to be warehouses and a crane along the canal by the bridge at Stretford station.

Trees are what the traveller notices most on this route. There are elms growing straight and tall, having apparently triumphed over the Dutch elm disease of the 1960s and '70s. Trees are everywhere: what was once arable, meadow and pasture is now woodland. In some cases planted since the 1970s, they have destroyed many indigenous plants and have made it difficult for some animals to survive.

Just half an hour or so after having set out, we reach journey's end at the Cut Hole Aqueduct and the equally charming Cut Hole Bridge. Once under the twin tunnels the road rejoins the present day. Turn to the right and you reach Edge Lane, the station, Chester Road and Stretford's Arndale Centre. To the left another track follows the old overflow channel from the weir into Kicketty Brook. Take this path and you can walk past growing woodland and fields that are still farmed, before reaching the banks of the Mersey.

twenty-four

LANE END NORTH AND SOUTH

A choice of walks out of the township, with the opportunity to view Hough End Hall

Lane End to Hough End Hall and north to Dog House Farm

Lane End is another of those place names that has fallen from common usage, and yet it describes perfectly the point where High Lane and Moss Lane join Barlow Moor Lane. Even today this is an important junction, and whichever direction the traveller chooses he will be heading out of the township: west along High Lane to Stretford, south down Barlow Moor Lane to Didsbury, north through Martledge to Whalley Range and to the city, or east along Moss Lane and then due north into Hulme, Chorlton-upon-Medlock and Manchester.

Moss Lane is now Sandy Lane. There was a cluster of properties at its junction with Barlow Moor Lane, including the wheelwright William Brownhill's workshop, a pub and a beershop, a collection of cottages and, a little further away, two farms. By any criteria William Brownhill was an enterprising man. When he started his business in the 1830s he was not the only wheelwright in Chorlton, but a decade and a bit later he was – and doing well enough to engage an apprentice, who was still with him as a qualified wheelwright in the 1850s. Brownhill also ran a beershop (probably from his home) and rented property. His workshop and home have gone: they were on the southern side of the lane, not far from the junction with Barlow Moor Lane and probably on the site of the semi-detached houses that stand here today. The eleven brick cottages he built and rented out were a more lasting legacy. They were a little further down on the south side and were only demolished in the 1970s, having been condemned as unfit in 1972. They stood for over 140 years but their time had come. In some cases the external walls had perished, while the roofs were sagging and the floors damp and springy; added to this there were inadequate natural light and ventilation.[621] The site today is a small gated community that retains an element of the old name. Somewhere between Lane End and Brownhill's Buildings was the Black Horse, with a reputation for after-hours drinking on a Sunday and a 'rough and low company' no doubt attracted by the nasty spectacle of badger fighting.[622]

That was it on the south side of Moss Lane. Looking down this road today, a modern traveller is presented with rows of late 19th-century houses and the little roads like Whalley Road that run off from Sandy Lane to Chorlton Park.

On the northern side of the road in 1847 we would have had a view of Caleb Jordrill's wattle and daub cottage, roughly where the church stands on the corner. He was not the most popular man in the township, being one of the ringleaders who instigated the bouts of public humiliation directed against both wrongdoers and those unlucky enough to have unfaithful wives or husbands. His wife lived in the cottage after his death and, helped by a granddaughter and parish relief, lived into the 1850s.

Setting off along the road towards the modern St Werburghs Road, in 1847 we would have encountered fields on both sides. On the corner with Hartington Road was the home and garden of William Gresty, who made a living as a gardener and whose house sat in the orchard he rented. Unlike Caleb's house this was a brick-built six-roomed cottage with a slate roof, outhouses and water pump.[623]

Still further down the road, opposite Whalley Avenue, was the home of another gardener, George Lunt. His was a smallholding consisting of 2 acres of land, which was mostly orchard, stretching back from Moss Lane to Rough Leach Gutter (which today runs roughly under Corkland Road). This was a smallish amount of land, and like many of our market gardeners Lunt may also have had other jobs as well. He had six children, all of whom were old enough to help on the land as well as performing the usual chores, like collecting water from the pump beside the house and assisting on market days. Sadly no picture of his home has survived, and the building may have been demolished to make way for Chorlton High School in the 1920s.

The journey down Moss Lane arrived at Park Brow Farm, one of the bigger ones in the township. In 1847 it was in the hands of James Bankcroft, who farmed 47 acres of mixed arable and meadow. This was still a working farm in the 1960s and the farmhouse and outbuildings still exist today. The substantial brick farmhouse had eight rooms and a scullery; its south side looked out on the garden while the north fronted the farmyard and outbuildings. Despite the alterations that have been made it is still possible to see much

621 Compulsory Purchase Order, Manchester City Council, April 1972.

622 Ellwood, chapter 8, 1885.

623 One undated picture exists of the house which is titled Croton's Farm. Charles Croton was there in 1901 running a coach business, and appears in the census returns and directories up to 1929.

that is original and would have been familiar to both James Bankcroft and Leonard Bailey, the last farmer at Park Brow. From the south little has changed except that the door to the garden has been bricked up, and the scullery transformed into a living area. On the northern side some of the buildings have been developed into residential accommodation, and the yard has become a car-park.

Park Brow faces both south and north, and we can either head south along Nell Lane and past Hough End Hall and to Didsbury, or north by way of Dog House Farm and towards the city.

Hough End Hall is strictly not in the township and yet all historians of Chorlton from John Booker in 1853 have included it in their accounts. In 1847, walking from Park Brow down Nell Lane and standing on the low bridge over the Brook, the Hall would have been clearly visible. This would not have been the most impressive of views, however: the northern side was partly hidden by farm buildings at the back and side. At the front and rear were gardens, while the house was set back from the road and partially screened by hedges. Built in 1596, it is a traditional Elizabethan brick house designed to imitate the letter E. The design of these houses tended to follow the same pattern: on the ground floor there was the hall, which took up most of the building and had a long gallery directly above it. This latter was used for a variety of purposes, including entertaining, a family area, displaying the family portraits and walking when the weather was poor. There were windows on three sides and a fireplace on the fourth. The kitchen and living areas were contained in the two arms that jutted out from the main part of the building. The large communal areas were sometimes later partitioned off as smaller rooms, and the census of 1911 describes Hough End Hall as having eleven rooms.[624] Today some of its charm has been overshadowed by the office blocks that obscure its graceful appearance. Nor has the inside escaped: a fine oak staircase was taken out by the Egerton family, and the ground floor has been knocked through to accommodate a restaurant.

Had we stood outside the Hall in 1841 we might have caught a glimpse of Henry Jackson who rented it from the Egertons. Within the decade it would pass to Samuel Lomas, whose family would still be there in 1911. In 1851 Samuel was just thirty-four and farmed 220 acres; he employed five labourers and two house servants.

Directly opposite Hough End Hall was Brookfield House. Set in its own grounds, it faced south with views across what is now Chorlton Park. The grounds included two ponds fed from the brook and trees in all directions. In 1841 it was home to John and Elizabeth Stanway; he was an accountant and they had four young children. Ten years

---

624 A ground floor plan exists from 1938.

later it was the family home of the doctor James Partington.[625] It is possible that the house dates from the late 18th century, and both Greenwood's map of 1818 and Yates's of 1784 show a building with a similar footprint. It currently belongs to the Corporation and is still there in the park.

From here the road continued until it joined Burton Lane in Withington. Had we turned north at Park Brow we would still be on Moss Lane. This, as we know, went from Lane End, following the modern Sandy Lane as far as Park Brow Farm. It then headed north along what is now St Werburghs Road before turning at right angles towards Dog House Farm. It is still possible to follow this route by picking up St Werburghs Road at Park Brow and walking north to join Kings Road, then along Kingsbrook Road. Dog House Farm stood on the site of the present cricket and tennis pavilion. Today this walk takes us past rows of mid-20th-century housing, but in 1847 we would have walked along a country lane almost empty of houses. There was just one group: Moss Cottages, on the south side of what is now Kings Road between Daventry and Withington Roads. This was home to eight households consisting of forty-two people in total, ranging from sixty-five years of age to two months. They were mainly families who made their living from the land: while there was a joiner, the rest gave their occupations as farmer, gardener or agricultural labourer.[626] How big the cottages were is unknown, but it is unlikely they would have had more than four rooms. In the case of two households this meant cramming ten people into one house and six into another. This isolated little community was surrounded by fields and ponds. Some of its inhabitants must have worked for Dog House Farm. This was one of the largest farms in the area: in 1851 John Chorlton farmed 380 acres and employed eighteen labourers, eight of whom lived on the farm. Nothing of Dog House Farm or the surrounding fields are left: the farm was demolished in 1960.

We have reached the sports pavilion on Kingsbrook Road; we are out of Chorlton and in Whalley Range. This is now a densely packed residential area, so utterly different from the 19th-century scene – and thus a fitting close to the last of our walks along Chorlton's roads.

---

625 James Partington was fifty-one in 1847 and lived with his family south of Hough End Hall on Nell Lane: Enu. 2c, p.23. Ten years earlier he was living on Oxford Street: Enu. 29, p.7, Chorlton-upon-Medlock 1841 (third house from Boundary Street West heading south on the west side).
626 There were two farmers, one gardener, four agricultural labourers, a farm servant and a joiner. 1841 census, Enu. 6, p.8, Withington.

twenty-five

WALKING SOUTH THROUGH THE TOWNSHIP TO HARDY AND THE MERSEY

To the remotest parts of the township

This is another pleasant walk, to Hardy Lane and then west to Jackson's Boat and the Mersey. The starting point is the junction of the Row and Barlow Moor Lane. Today, standing on the corner with the bus station behind us and looking east and south, there is the usual mix of shops and houses, including an undistinguished alley with workshops and some blocks of modern flats. Hidden from view down the alley is the first building of interest. This is Lime Bank, one of the few remaining buildings from before the middle of the 19th century. In 1847 it was the home of Charles Morton and commanded fine views in all directions. To the south, partially obscured by a line of trees, was Chorlton Brook, to the east Hough End Hall and just a little to the north the walled estate of the Holt family. For anyone walking up the Row on a dark winter's morning the lights of Lime Bank would have been clearly visible. Certainly on those nights that Charles Morton attended the Vestry meetings in the schoolhouse on the Green his first sight of home would have been as he passed Sutton's Cottage, roughly on the corner of today's Wilton Road and Beech Road.

Leaving Lime Bank and walking south down Barlow Moor Lane there were fields on either side, and just before the bridge over the Brook was Brook Bank Farm. This stood on the eastern side of the road, on a site that today is occupied by a row of houses and shops and a car-park.[627] It gave its name to the bridge close by. Just beyond was Oak House Farm.[628] Long gone, it is still possible to follow the path that led off the lane to the farm.

---

627 This was the home of Elizabeth Whitelegg. She rented 4 acres from the Lloyd estate and her house and garden from Henry Jackson.

628 John Brundrett farmed Oak House, consisting of 19 acres rented from the Egerton estate, and owned small parcels of land around the Row.

This is the stretch of Cundiff Road that leads to Oak House Drive. Both farms were set back from the road and date from the 18th century or before.

The remaining section of the road up to Hardy Lane was pleasant if unremarkable.

The modern Hardy Lane has been realigned so that it is directly opposite Mauldeth Road West, but originally it curved round from Barlow Moor Lane; its earlier path is evident from the position of the drain grids on the northern corner. From the vantage point at this corner we can get a clear idea of how the land lay: to the east across what is now Chorlton Park there were two very large ponds, close to where the tennis courts are now, and beyond was Hough End Hall.

Barlow Moor Lane continued south, passing close to Barlow Hall and Red Bank Farm, where the Mersey performs one of its more dramatic twists.

Dominating this part of Hardy Lane was Hardy House. Charles Wood, who lived here, farmed on a large scale: his 60 acres were a mix of arable and meadow and his land stretched down to the Mersey. This was the floodplain, and much of his holding was meadow. He employed three farm servants who lived with the family. All were young men, two from Withington and the third from Baguley, and their pay reflected the fact that their board and food were provided.[629] Some farm servants slept in the family home but others stayed in the shippon, the space above the cow house. The Woods were to prosper over the next twenty years, and by 1861 they had increased their land from 60 to 92 acres. A traveller might have caught a glimpse of the Woods' house, but that would be all. It was set well back from Hardy Lane behind a large garden and orchard.

Back in the 19th century Hardy Lane was unlike its modern counterpart. Now a broad thoroughfare bordered on both sides by social and private housing, it was narrower, and separated from the fields by high hedges. Along its course beyond Hardy House there was just Hardy Farm, close to where the modern road ends. The Cook family, who lived here, farmed 29 acres of mixed arable, meadow and pasture. In 1841 there were eight of them in all, inhabiting six rooms.[630] This was a remote spot, and while it may have been pleasant enough in the summer months it was grim and foreboding in winter. The farmhouse was built on a rise; just beyond the buildings the land falls away. This gave the Cooks some protection from the Mersey, for flooding was a constant danger.

Beyond Hardy Farm, the lane ran into a track before reaching the river. This had been the centre of the hamlet of Hardy and the cottages were old. Like Hardy Farm they were built on a slight rise, to protect them from flood water. By the 1840s there were only two left. John Burgess, a labourer, and his family lived in one and John Marsland, an agricultural

---

629 Joseph Whitefield was twenty, while Thomas Goodier and John Lamb were just sixteen.

630 John and Elizabeth Cook would have had one bedroom, and this left the rest to be divided up between four daughters: Hannah aged twenty-seven, Mary aged sixteen, Sarah aged fifteen and Elizabeth aged nine. There was also a son, Thomas, aged twenty-two.

labourer, shared the other with his wife and three sons. The cottages were on land farmed by Samuel Dean: his was the largest farm in the township, consisting of 290 acres centred on Barlow Farm, close to the Hall. It is more than likely that these families who lived here worked on the farm. Certainly the youngest Marsland boy worked for Samuel Dean, as he was at Barlow Farm at the time of the 1851 census. The route to the Burgess and Marsland cottages is not easy to track, and the exact location of Hardy Farm is no easier to find. The farm was demolished to make way for a university sports complex and the cottages were demolished following floods in 1854, when the surrounding land was under 3ft of water.

As isolated as the small hamlet of Hardy was, it had a pub over the water: The Greyhound. There was a ferry here until 1832.[631]

The noise of the motorway and rows of houses in the far distance intrude into a semi-rural picture. One has to remember that this isn't strictly the land that Samuel Dean, the Cooksons and Charles Wood farmed, but an artificial landscape created by Corporation rubbish tipping on the site and by the efforts of the Mersey Valley wardens to improve it.

---

631 Samuel Wilton levied a toll of ½d to cross the bridge. In 1881 the present bridge was built and the toll continued. There are those like Marjorie Holmes and the late Tony Walker who remember having to pay to cross. The toll was abolished sometime after Manchester Corporation took the bridge over in the 1940s.

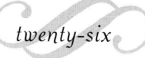
WATERCOURSES, PONDS AND LOST EXPANSES OF WATER, FORGOTTEN ROADS AND FOOTPATHS

Chorlton Brook, Longford Brook, Rough Leech Gutter, Acres Ditch, Blomley's Fishpond, the village fishpond, Sally's Hole and drainage ditches

C horlton was a township where people were never far from running water, which was all to the good as the first mains supply did not arrive until 1864.[632] Most people relied on wells, pumps and the many watercourses and ponds that abounded. Finding them today is not always easy: most have long since disappeared below ground, or filled in and built over – and in most cases long forgotten. Some watercourses have even suffered the indignity of becoming part of the sewer system.

Chorlton Brook

The most southerly of these watercourses is Chorlton Brook, which flows from the east into the township by Hough End. By the time it arrives at this point it is already the product of many smaller streams, of which the Gore and Red Lion Brooks are the last, joining by Hough End.[633] The best glimpse of any of these streams is at Hough End playing fields, where the Red Lion Brook comes out into the light and crosses the open before flowing underneath Hough End Crescent, where it becomes Chorlton Brook. Back in 1847 we would have been surrounded by open fields here, but at the point where the Red Lion and

---

632 This was supplied by Manchester Corporation. The 3in main came into the township from Stretford, along Edge Lane, then down St Clements to the Green.

633 From the north flowed Dog Kennel Brook, which originated in the Fallowfield area between Dickenson Road and Lloyd Street, the Platt Brook or Gore Brook from Levenshulme, the Ley Brook from Fallowfield and Lady Barn, and Shaw Brook slightly to the south, draining from a number of streams from the Heaton and Burnage area before flowing through Withington and becoming known as Red Lion Brook. Ashworth, *op. cit.*

Gore Brooks joined to become Chorlton Brook the landscape changed, the watercourse running through an area bordered by trees known as Hough End Clough. Sadly for the modern traveller the brook is lost again as it runs under Mauldeth Road West, before reappearing and flowing past the high school and under Nell Lane.[634]

Just a little to the west of this point is one of those mystery watercourses that might be flowing in an old brick tunnel or may just have dried up. Back in the 1840s it was clearly visible, coming in from the south across land farmed by Henry Jackson. It fed into Chorlton Brook just below where the brook now crosses Mauldeth Road West, through a wooded and wet area with the delightful name of Pitts and Bogs. In its journey from the south it fed a number of ponds, and as it flowed into the brook it broadened out, contributing to the swampy character of Pitts and Bogs. Tracking it today is difficult and the Environment Agency has no record, but it may have followed a route from the junction of Burton Road and Lapwing Lane, north towards the Brook and passing just east of Weller Avenue. If so it may well be that the railway line (now the Metro link to Didsbury) marks its course.[635] Yet another brook crossed Chorlton Park from two ponds just a little south and west of Brookfield House. From this point, with just a small break, we can walk alongside the brook as it wanders through Chorlton Park and under Barlow Moor Road. Back in 1847 the Nell Lane Bridge was a lower structure but it still gave good views. To the east there was Hough End Hall; directly south was Brookfield House. From here the brook remains open to the air until it meets the Mersey, but as its route flows through private property there is no access to it until it crosses Brookburn Road. A footpath used to run from Barlow Moor Road, skirting Oak House Farm by the modern Oak House Drive and running down behind the gardens on the north side of South Drive and Claude and Brookburn Roads, but this fell out of use and is now blocked off. This is a great pity, because it would allow our modern traveller to walk beside the brook along a steep wooded corridor known as the Cliffs, which ran roughly along the route of the footpath. Here the brook skirts the edge of the village. On the south side were Brook Cottage and Brook Farm. Here too was the village pond, which today is where the car-park of the Bowling Green Hotel stands. It stretched back from the lane to include all the modern bowling green to the edge of Finney Drive and from the brook to the hotel. It contained fish and was rented out to gentlemen.

Once across Brookburn Road the brook twists and turns before flowing into the Mersey. The land on either side would have been mainly meadows, and running from the watercourse would have been the ditches that allowed farmers to regularly water their

634 Environment Agency.

635 This was the Manchester South District line, running from Withington and Didsbury, north under Mauldeth Road West before running into Chorlton station.

land. Where young trees and bushes crowd in on the passer-by, in 1847 it would have been more open, with trees forming natural boundaries between fields. Not far from the bridge across the brook the land north was covered by an orchard, which ran up to and over the old road to the big pond on Turn Moss.

Longford Brook

To the north of the township flows Longford Brook, which rises in what is now Whalley Range. It winds across Chorlton before emptying into the Bridgewater Canal at Longford Bridge. If we had followed its route in 1847 our journey would have taken us from its source close by Dog House Farm across open land north of Longford to the canal. Today the brook rises on Withington Road opposite St Bede's playing fields. From here it flows under the northern end of Badminton Road, under the cricket ground and along Westfield Road to Brantingham Road and Manchester Road. It continues under Longford Road, across Longford Park and out towards Longford Bridge.[636] But as it passes through the township there is nothing to see. As recently as the 1940s the brook flowed above-ground by the swimming baths on Manchester Road, and again across part of Longford Park.[637]

Rough Leech Gutter

Rough Leech Gutter vanished a long time ago. It ran east to west across the township between the Chorlton and Longford Brooks. It is clearly shown on maps of the 1840s but there is no record of it today, and the Environment Agency does not include it in its list of watercourses. Its name may suggest that it wasn't a true brook, but there are other clues to its existence and so it is worthy of inclusion here.

The gutter flowed from just north of Park Brow Farm roughly parallel with Sandy Lane, and may be under the present Corkland Road. It crossed just south of the modern junction of Barlow Moor and Wilbraham Roads, and briefly followed Wilbraham Road before turning down towards High Lane. There is a possibility that it then ran along the modern Acres Road before flowing into Blomley's Fishpond on the Row, now Beech Road. If this is the route, it may explain the Edge Lane Lake that appears opposite St Clement's Church, and may have its origin in a weakening of the brick tunnel that carries the gutter under

---

636 Ashworth, *op. cit.*, p.50.

637 On quiet Sundays at the start of the 20th century the enclosed brook could be heard as it flowed under the road by Egerton Road North. Phillip Lloyd, June 2010.

High Lane. There was a ditch that ran from High Lane along the route of Acres Road, and exited where Blomley's Fishpond was.[638] The ditch became polluted and was covered with flagstones and earth, so it seems plausible that the Rough Leech Gutter fed the fishpond via the ditch along Acres Road. The only reference to it appeared in a newspaper article, which referred to it as a brook or rill.[639]

Evidence suggests that the fishpond was quite extensive, stretching from the modern Acres Road up to Chequers Road, and that it had a bridge allowing access from the Row to the fields on the other side. Jeremiah Brundrett used water from the pond during the building of the second Wesleyan chapel in 1825. All of this allows us to recreate what we could have seen in 1847. Rough Leech Gutter ran through open countryside, acting as a field boundary just north of Park Brow across to Oak Bank, a fine house in its own grounds just beyond the modern Needham Avenue. There is no way of telling how deep the watercourse was, if indeed it was anything more than a ditch, but it continued under Barlow Moor Lane and skirted Clough Farm. Given its close proximity to both Oak Bank and Clough Farm, it is reasonable to suppose that it provided some of their water, even if not drinking water. Beyond the farm the gutter continued to define field boundaries, and would have taken us to the bottom of George Grantham's orchard and garden, where Brundrett Road joins Wilbraham Road today, and so down to High Lane, where it may have run alongside the road before twisting down Acres Road and Blomley's Fishpond.[640]

Ponds and Ditches

Every village is supposed to have a village pond, and Chorlton had two. One was located behind the Bowling Green Hotel and the other was on the Row. There were plenty more spread across the township and to attempt to catalogue them all would be a Herculean undertaking. None now exist. Most seem to have been filled during the 19th century, including both the village pond and Blomley's on the Row. Others survived into the 20th century. Some ponds were just water-filled pits, the result of marl or clay extraction around Martledge. Some even date from the early 20th century when the brick works continued to extract clay from the Longford area and they could be particularly deep. One newspaper

---

638 Ellwood, chapter 6, 1885. There is one slight problem with this explanation: Ellwood refers to the polluted ditch as emptying into the sewer on High Lane.

639 *Manchester Guardian*, 15 January 1851. A rill is less a stream and more a narrow and shallow incision in topsoil layers resulting from erosion by overland flow or surface run-off. They are most common on slopes of agricultural land and if left may grow into gullies, streams or rivers.

640 This route seems to be confirmed by the memories of Ken Allan, who lived on Beale Grove and later at 29 High Lane, which is on the south-west corner of High Lane and Wilton Road. Both houses suffered from flooding. In the cellar of 29 High Lane the cellar could flood if the rubber seal around a grid was left open.

report of a drowning described a disused clay pit just 40yds from Longford Road, 'five feet deep within a yard of the side, and 100 yards long and 50 yards wide.'[641]

Drainage ditches are hardly the stuff of romance, but they were an important part of the agricultural scene and help us to understand how the land was worked. Maps from the 19th century show plenty of such ditches, many of which were part of a sophisticated system of water management. Most of these ditches have long since vanished but a few still exist on the land bordering the Mersey, a wonderful mix of small woodlands, rough grassland and ponds, developed after the closure of Withington sewage works in 1972. Another borders Barncroft Meadow, which is best reached down the lane from Brookburn Bridge and past the school. Alongside it is a ditch that heads off towards the Mersey. Properly worked meadow land was served by a series of ditches, which included a feeder ditch that brought water into the field and a corresponding ditch on the opposite side to take it away. Linking the two were a series of smaller channels running the length of the field.[642]

Now they have all gone but some evidence remains, including those who can still remember them. Ida Bradshaw remembers some of these ditches, including one that ran into Boat Meadow and others by Hardy Lane Farm. They were roughly knee deep and were crossed by planks.[643] There is also a late 19th-century photograph of a group of children standing beside a footbridge somewhere between Barncroft Field and the Mersey over what might have been an irrigation ditch. The historian John Lloyd placed this bridge at Boat Meadow, writing that it was part of the route that led from the village to Hardy Farm. Today it is possible to follow that route by walking out of Chorlton along Brookburn Road, south past the Bowling Green Hotel and over the road bridge. To the left was Lydia Brown's farmhouse, and on the right is the school. Brookburn Road twists at this point and ends at a stile. Beyond is the old track, past the football pitch and sewage works across open land to the Mersey. As we reach the river the land to the east of the track was Boat Meadow, farmed by Charles Wood of Hardy House. Continuing across it, it is possible to pick up the track towards Hardy Lane, past the lost cottages of Hardy to Hardy Farm and Hardy House. As we stand on this new track the bridge over the Mersey is at our back, and ahead in the distance is Hardy Lane. Not that this entirely solves the mystery of exactly where the footbridge was. There is a shallow watercourse that runs to the south of the old Hardy Farm and borders the golf course before cutting across open land and flowing into the Mersey, but this seems a little too far away for the footbridge. Perhaps its path has been diverted, or perhaps there was a smaller stream that crossed Boat Meadow.

641 *Manchester Guardian*, 13 August 1924. There were others during the interwar period.
642 Stephens, *op. cit.*, pp.672–3, Google edn pp.691–2.
643 'I remember playing beside them when I was young. You had to jump over them but if you went in they were deep enough to cover your knees and you had a devil of a time trying to get out.' Ida Bradshaw, July 2010.

Forgotten roads and footpaths

Chorlton had a lot fewer roads and a lot more footpaths in 1847. As the number of roads has increased so the number of footpaths has declined. Some of the roads have changed their names and some of the footpaths have been incorporated into the road network, while a few of both have disappeared completely. Some are easier to trace than others. Lloyd Street, included in the 1841 and 1851 census returns, became Whitelow Road. It is still possible to see an early stretch of the road: in the 1840s it ran north from the corner of the Row, ending just where the modern road curves left. Locations of others, like Half Street and Back More Lane, can only be guessed at.

Chapel Lane and Chorlton Lane later became Manchester Road. Chapel Lane ran from Pitts Brow where Edge Lane meets the modern Manchester Road past the Methodist church, before becoming Chorlton Lane from the Lloyds Hotel across Wilbraham Road to Oswald Road, finishing where Nicolas Road joins Barlow Moor Road. This was a pleasant route that took our 1847 traveller from William Chesshyre's home at Pitts Brow north to Ash Tree, through fields and orchards. Here the road became Chorlton Lane following the section of Wilbraham Road opposite the modern Lloyd Hotel before heading north into the present car-park of the precinct. Where the lane turned north was a fingerpost and the home of the Helsbys, who farmed 4 acres that stretched back to Oswald Road.[644] In time this would become known as Martledge Green. To complicate matters even further this part of the road was also known as Stretford Road. Lastly there was Back Lane, which was the official name for the old road that cuts from the east across Chorlton to Stretford.

---

644 A fingerpost, sometimes called a guidepost, was what today we would call a signpost, comprising one or more arms. Legislation enacted in 1697 enabled magistrates to place direction posts at crossroads.

twenty-seven

THE PEOPLE

Who they were, what they did and the sources

The lives of those who lived and worked in Chorlton can be tracked through a variety of records and sources, available online, from the city and county record offices, or from family members.

A starting point is the census returns, produced every ten years. The first census was in 1801, but the first that provides details of individuals was taken in 1841. In the following decades the returns became more detailed, so that by 1911 they show not only the number of children born to a family but those who died and those who survived. In Chorlton the earlier census returns do not always allow the historian to place individuals accurately: William Chesshyre, who compiled the 1841 and 1851 censuses, was a little cavalier in recording where people lived. There are also problems with the spelling of names, exact dates of birth and reluctance on the part of some to divulge personal details. In some cases there is the possibility that an illegitimate birth is covered up by passing off a child as the child of a grandparent. In other cases the place of birth is vague: this might be poor memory, lack of knowledge or the fault of the enumerator but sometimes it was deliberate. Many of those born in Ireland do not specify a county, which may have been reluctance on the part of those questioned to divulge too much or again a lack of interest. Census returns for Chorlton are available on microfilm in the Local History Library in Manchester or online from www.ancestry.co.uk and other sites.

Parish records detailing baptisms, marriages and burials are a rich source of detail. These are on microfilm in the Local History Library in Manchester, as are the records of the Wesleyan chapel on the Row. There are also the gravestones of those buried in the parish churchyard and in the grounds of the Methodist chapel. Sadly only a handful remain, and some are difficult to read.

There are no records for the administration of poor relief before 1838. This is all the more frustrating given that those for Stretford have survived; these provide names and details of payment. However, the minutes of the Vestry or ratepayers meetings still exist for the period 1839 to 1858. These handwritten documents record decisions about the setting of the local poor rate, the administration of poor relief and maintenance of the local highways, as well as showing who was nominated and elected as overseers, surveyors of the highways and constables. The minutes are available from the Manchester Archives and Local Studies Centre, reference number M10/8/8/30.

After 1837 it is possible to use the General Registry Office, which holds records of births, deaths and marriages. These certificates provide a wealth of information. Birth certificates give the maiden name of the mother, as well as the occupation of the father and the place of birth. A marriage certificate provides a date for the marriage, the names, ages and previous residences of the bride and groom and some details of their fathers. A death certificate gives the date of death and the age of the deceased, and also provides some indication of the cause of death. But there was a reluctance in the early years after 1837 to comply with registering, which may lead to gaps in a family history. Before applying to obtain a certificate some basic information is needed, usually the name, date and place of birth, marriage or death. The General Registry Office provides this search, but it charges – together with a fee for reproducing the certificate.

Street and trade directories also help to track individuals. They list the name and address of prominent people and those engaged in business and trade. The advantage of these lists is that they were published more regularly than the census returns, but the earlier ones do not include more humble individuals and tend to be centred on towns and cities. Those for Chorlton are often grouped together with Stretford, Urmston and Altrincham. These are also available from Manchester Local History Library on microfilm, and some online from Historical Directories and Ancestry.

Early electoral registers and the record of how people voted in the 1832 election are available from the Archive and Local History Library, Manchester, BR 352.042 M45, but are fragmentary and limited to a handful of men.

Then as now newspapers provide a rich source, including the stories of elections and sensational reports of murders and crimes, as well as adverts and announcements. Often stories were carried by newspapers outside Manchester: even if local coverage of an event has been lost it will still appear somewhere. There were a number of Manchester newspapers operating in the 19th century and these can be read on microfilm at Manchester Local Library, and the *Manchester Guardian* and *Observer* along with *The Times* are available online to members of Manchester Libraries. These and many other newspapers from the period can also be accessed from http://newspapers.bl.uk/blcs/, which has the added advantage that the researcher can employ a search engine to do some of the work. Some current newspapers also have a research facility for their papers.

In 1847 Archdeacon Rushton visited St Clement's and left a detailed report of the church. This is available from the Archives and Local History Library, Archdeacon Rushton's Visitation Returns Ref Nu MSf942.72 R121/Vol. 39.

For the township a useful source of information are the twenty-five articles written by Thomas Ellwood between the winter and spring of 1885 and 1886. These were published in weekly instalments in the *South Manchester Gazette* and reappeared as articles in the Wesleyan and parish magazines throughout the late 19th and early 20th centuries. Ellwood in turn drew on a work about the histories of the churches and chapels of south and east Manchester written thirty years earlier, as well as contemporary documents. The real strength of his account is that much of it is based on the oral testimonies of some of the oldest inhabitants of Chorlton, people who had been born at the very beginning of Elwood's century and who confidently recorded the customs and people of an even earlier time. The articles include not only the names of those who lived in the township but often some detail about their lives. All are available from the Manchester Local History Library on microfilm.

Finally there are the many sources that have been collected by the descendants of those who lived in Chorlton. These are not in the public domain but much can be found online. They include a cornucopia of biographies and events listed in chronological order by William Axon in 1885, in his *The Annals of Manchester*, available as a download from Google Books which constantly amazes me with the variety of obscure but important works that they publish.

What follows is an alphabetical list of individuals and families, including references to them in local and national sources.

Aldcroft family

A number of Aldcrofts crop up in the census records. James Aldcroft was born in 1786, was a labourer and in the 1840s rented a house and land on Oswald Field from Charles Bracegirdle for an annual rent of £6. He also appears in the rate book records. Another Aldcroft was a shoemaker. Charles and Margaret appear in the baptismal records for 1834.

Alderl[e]y family

There are two Alderley families, one which ran Barlow Hall Farm from about 1864 and the other which was in continuous occupation of Red Bank Farm from about 1851. Both farms were on the southern edge of the township. There are references to the families in the census records from the 1850s, the tithe schedule and the rate books. James Alderley of Red Bank can be found in the *Electors Guide* for 1854–55, where he qualifies for a parliamentary vote as occupier of 33 acres.

Allcock family

There are two Allcocks listed in the 1841 census. Richard and Elizabeth and their children lived in Martledge in Renshaw's Buildings, and Peter and Alice were on High Lane. Both Richard and Peter were labourers. At the 1851 census only Alice was left, living on an annuity in Brownhill's Buildings near Lane End. The gravestone of Peter, Alice and one of their daughters is in the parish churchyard. The two families may be connected as their children have similar forenames.

Ashcroft family

The Ashcrofts were a family of independent means living at Oak Bank, a substantial home near the end of Needham Avenue, and are mentioned in the 1841 census. Another Ashcroft family appear in the 1851 census. This was William and Sophie Ashcroft. He was a master slater employing two men, and their family gravestone is in the parish churchyard.

Axon family

The Axons appear in the parish burial records from the 1760s until 1863. John and James Axon were both in the first brass band, which dated from about 1826 (Ellwood). James was a Methodist who led the orchestra and made his own drum and 'bass violin' (Ellwood). James also appears in the baptismal records in the 1820s as a labourer. John was in the 1851 census aged fifty-four, living on the Row with his wife, Sarah, aged sixty-eight, and their two grown-up children. John was an agricultural labourer, Sarah and daughter Eliza were charwomen, their son was a shoemaker and their nephew was another agricultural labourer. John was born in Newton Heath, Sarah in Stretford and the children and nephew in Chorlton. John and his family are in both the 1841 and 1851 census. A Harriet Axon baptised an illegitimate son in 1832: parish records.

Baguley family

There were Baguleys in the township from the 18th century, and they appear in the burial records of the parish church. They include Thomas Baguley, tailor, Thomas Baguley, gardener, and James Baguley, agricultural labourer. The families appear in the 1841 and 1851 censuses and a James Baguley is listed in the tithe schedule as occupying land and living behind the National School. The 1851 census also highlights Hannah White *née* Baguley, who in 1841 is living with another family, and at the age of twenty gave birth to a son, James, out of wedlock, later marrying Samuel White and having another child in 1847. James, her first son, retained her maiden name. The gravestone of Thomas, Mary and their children can be found in the parish churchyard, and there are references to them in the parish baptismal record. They also appear in Ellwood.

Bailey family

The Bailey family were market gardeners on the Row. The tenancy passed to them from John Renshaw, who was related to Alice Bailey. The Renshaws had held it since 1767. The Bailey family appear in all the census records from 1841 to 1911, and are mentioned in the tithe schedule and rate books for the mid-century. They are also referred to in the private papers of the Bailey and Lewis families. They were related to the Taylors and Renshaws.

Bancroft family

The Bancroft family farmed about 60 acres at Park Brow Farm. They are recorded in census returns from 1841 to 1881 and can also be found in the tithe schedule, rate books and Vestry minutes. The gravestone of James and Elizabeth (Betty) is in the parish churchyard. James qualified for a parliamentary vote in 1840 and 1854–55 and can be found in the *Electors Guide*.

Bates family

James Bates appears in the rate books for 1845 and 1846, after which it appears that Samuel took tenancy of the house, which may have been on High Lane. Samuel was a shoemaker: he appears in the 1841 census and again in 1851, when he was married to Betty Bates. She was born in 1804, sang in the Methodist chapel, ran a sweet shop on the Green and died in 1884. She appears in the census from 1851 and is mentioned by Ellwood.

Beeston and Craven

The Beestons and Cravens lived on the Row and are in the 1861, 1871 and 1881 censuses.

Beswick family

The Beswicks were small-time market gardeners. They rented 2 acres, a mix of arable meadow and garden, from the Lloyd estate. They are in the 1841 and 1851 censuses, the tithe schedule, baptismal records of the Methodists between 1807 and 1828, the Vestry minutes and Ellwood. G. Beswick is referred to in Ellwood. A gravestone to the Beswicks can be seen in the churchyard.

Birley, Revd William

William Birley was in Chorlton from 1842 to 1859, during which time he was responsible for raising money for the building of the new school and rectory, and was also involved in the dispute over church rates. He appears in the 1851 census, in Ellwood, indirectly in the report made after Archdeacon Rushton's visit in 1847, in some newspaper reports (e.g. *Preston Guardian*, 51 August 1846, 24 December 1846; *Manchester Times*, 27 March 1852; *Hampshire Telegraph and Sussex Chronicle*, 18 September 1852; *Liverpool Mercury*, 16 September 1853; *Manchester Times*, 23 May 1855; *Preston Guardian*, 10 October 1863; *Liverpool Mercury*, 10 September 1863; *Derby Mercury*, 9 August 1865; *Newcastle Courant*, 4 August 1865; *Pall Mall Gazette*, 1 August 1865; *North Wales Chronicle*, 5 August 1865), in the minutes of the railway companies of which he was a shareholder (including the Birkenhead, Lancashire & Cheshire Junction Railway Company minutes, February 1857), in *The Annals of Manchester* by William Axon and in the National Probate Calendar of Wills and Administration, 1865. He can also be found in the *Electors Guide* for 1854–55 when he qualified to vote in parliamentary elections. There are also references to him in the 1861 census for Leaf Street (Enu 1, p.15, Pendleton).

Birkett, Thomas

Thomas Birkett's shop adjoined the Horse and Jockey (Ellwood).

Blomley family

Elizabeth and Samuel Blomley are shadowy people. She appears as living in Chorlton from 1821 to 1829, according to Pigot and Dean's New Directory of Manchester and Salford, 1821–22, where she is described as a gentlewoman, Baines Directory, 1824–25 and Pigot and Co.'s Commercial Directory, 1828–29. Samuel is listed in Pigot and Co.'s National Commercial Directory of 1834. There is a further reference to an Elizabeth and Samuel Blomley baptising a son in the parish church in 1807. Ellwood refers to Blomley's Pond.

Bracegirdle, Charles

Charles Bracegirdle owned 3 acres of land and also rented a small amount. He can be found in the tithe schedule, the rate books for 1846–51, Methodist burial records and Ellwood. He qualified for a parliamentary vote in 1840 and 1854–55, as he owned freehold buildings at Oswald Field.

Bradbury family

They are referred to in Ellwood as living in a wattle and daub cottage.

Brooks, Samuel

Samuel Brooks was a merchant and banker who bought Jackson's Moss north of the township in 1836. He drained it and built homes for the wealthy. His own house was called Whalley House and the area became known as Whalley Range. He can be found in the 1851 census, Enu. 2c, p.30, Withington, and the 1861 census (Enu. 5, p.22, Withington), the rate books for 1845–46 and Ellwood.

Brown family

Jonathan and Lydia Brown appear in the baptismal records for 1823, 1825, 1828 and 1831. Jonathan described himself as a publican, and according to Ellwood he was a tenant at the Horse and Jockey. Jonathan is in the electoral register for 1832, 1835 and 1840, with freehold buildings at Lane End and on the Row. Lydia Brown was a landowner. She appears in the rate books for 1845 and 1846 and the tithe schedule for 1847. She rented land to William Davies, the blacksmith. The Browns' gravestone is in the parish churchyard. There are references to Brown families in both the 1841 and 1851 census returns.

Brownhill, William

The Brownhill family lived at Lane End. William Brownhill was a wheelwright, landlord of Brownhill's Buildings and a beerseller. The family appear in all the census records from 1841 to 1911 and in the rate books. There are also references in Pigot and Co.'s Royal National and Commercial Directory of 1841 and in Slater's Directory for 1855 and 1869, as well as the *Manchester Times*, 11 September 1869, which reported that his beer licence had been refused. There is also a fine description of Brownhill's Buildings in the Compulsory Purchase Order, 1972, Report Number 7332 (Archives and Local History Library, Manchester, M646/1/Box 21). Brownhill was also involved in the inquest held at the Horse and Jockey into the murder of Francis Deakin, *Manchester Times and Gazette*, 7 May 1847.

Brundrett family

The numerous Brundrett family included prominent Methodists, shopkeepers and farmers. They can be found in the censuses, rate books, tithe schedule and in the baptismal and burial records of the Methodist chapel. They are also in Pigot and Co.'s National Commercial Directory of 1834 and 1841, Slater's Directory of 1855 and crop up in Ellwood on several occasions. They appear in the *Electors Guide* for 1832, 1835, 1840 and 1854–55. James was also part of the inquest held at the Horse and Jockey into the murder of Francis Deakin, *Manchester Times and Gazette*, 7 May 1847. Pictures of Jeremiah senior and Charles and Elisha were published in the souvenir of the grand bazaar produced by the Wesleyan church in 1908, and are included in this book.

Bythell [Bythel] family

The Bythell family appears in the 1841 census, where William is listed as a labourer, married to Ellen, and noted as a shopkeeper in Pigot's National Commercial Directory of 1834. Ellwood mentions Ellen as keeping a shop 'in an old wood and plaster house behind the National Schools. She sold groceries and provisions, but her chief business was in bread, for which she had a great name amongst the inhabitants of the village.' The picture is a little confusing as William also describes himself as a schoolteacher and later a joiner in the baptismal records. The family had moved to Hulme by 1851, where William described himself as a joiner: Enu. 2e, p.25, Hulme. Ellwood also makes reference to a William Bythell as the parish clerk, but no date is given. This may be the William Bythell listed in Pigot and Dean's New Directory of Manchester and Salford, 1821–22, as 'shopkeeper, overseer of taxes, Chorlton and Bridge Inn Salford'. The Bythells also appear generally in Ellwood.

Chesshyre family

William Chesshyre was a market gardener of 6 acres who lived at Pitts Brow. William was a Methodist but later the respected parish clerk, carrying out the 1841 and 1851 census collection. The family is mentioned in the census from 1841, the tithe schedule and rate books, the Methodist baptismal records as well as the parish baptismal and marriage records. He also appears in a report on a burglary at Pitts Brow in the *Manchester Times and Gazette* for 14 March 1837, indirectly in Archdeacon Rushton's visitation returns,

1847, the Bailey papers, and in Ellwood. The family gravestone can be found in the parish churchyard. He was also part of the inquest held at the Horse and Jockey into the murder of Francis Deakin, *Manchester Times and Gazette*, 7 May 1847.

Chorlton family

The Chorlton family farmed at Dog House Farm: this was strictly outside the township, but they feature here because Mary Moore, who was murdered in the summer of 1838, worked for them. They appear in the 1841 census (Enu. 6, p.7, Withington), the 1851 census and various newspaper reports concerning the murder.

Chorlton, Thomas

Thomas kept the Black Horse pub at Lane End, and there are references to him in Ellwood.

Clarke family

The Clarke family ran the blacksmith's on the Row from 1860 well into the 20th century. They are in the census returns from 1861 and appear in a photograph of the bottom of the Row showing the smithy in John Lloyd's book, *Looking Back at Chorlton-cum-Hardy*, Willow Publishing, Altrincham, 1985. The legal agreement between John Clarke to pay £55 for goodwill and fixtures of forge, pigsty and shed of Elizabeth Lowe widow on 23 October 1850 survives (MISC/675, Manchester Archives).

Cook family

The Cook family farmed 29 acres at Hardy Lane Farm on the southern edge of the township at Hardy. They appear in the census record from 1841, the tithe schedule and rate books, the baptismal and burial records of the Methodist chapel and the Vestry minutes. John Cook[e] is in Ellwood, as is Thomas Cook. He qualified for a parliamentary vote by occupying 16 acres of land and appears in the *Electors Guide* for 1854–55. The gravestone of Thomas and family is in the churchyard.

Cookson family

There were at least three Cookson families. William Cookson was an agricultural labourer with a large family, recorded in the 1841 census. John Cookson farmed 7 acres at Dark Lane and is mentioned in the 1841 and 1851 censuses, the tithe schedule, rate books, Vestry minutes and Methodist burial records, as well as Baines's Directory for 1824–25 and the *Electors Guide* for 1832, 1835, 1840 and 1854–55. In 1854 he qualified for two votes. There is a reference to him in Ellwood. He was present at the murder of Francis Deakin and gave evidence to the inquest, *Manchester Times and Gazette*, Friday 7 May 1847, *Daily News*, Thursday 19 August 1847. Thomas Cookson was also a farmer, and like his brother owned some land as well as renting. He farmed 29 acres, and is in the census returns for 1841 and 1851, the tithe schedule, rate books and the *Electors Guide* for 1832. They are referred to in Ellwood and he was part of the inquest held at the Horse and Jockey into the murder of Francis Deakin, *Manchester Times and Gazette*, 7 May 1847.

Cope family

The Cope family owned and lived at Oak Bank House. The tithe schedule for 1845 shows Frederick Cope renting the house and land to a John Hilton until 1850, when the Cope family took up residence. Frederick was a wine and spirit merchant in partnership with his brother Richard. They had various outlets, including the Exchange Tavern or Vault on St Mary's Gate and the Sawyers Arms on the corner of Deansgate and Bridge Street. There is a record of him in the electoral register, in the *Electors Guide* of 1832 (BR352042 M45) and the Manchester Poll Book 1839 (BR 352 042M45 A, Manchester Archives). He moved to Oak Bank in 1848 and appears in the rate books. He and his family can be found in the 1851 census and in a number of directories from the 1820s to the 1850s. The Copes left Chorlton in 1855 and rented Oak Bank House to Charles Clarke, finally selling it in 1860. A description of Oak Bank appears in the *Manchester Guardian*, 28 June 1845: 'a valuable Property for sale in Chorlton'. There is a reference to Frederick's will in 1874 in the England and Wales Probate Index of Wills and Administration 1861–1942 available online at Ancestry. There are also references to Frederick, his daughter Ann's marriage and the suicide of his son Frederick in the *Manchester Times* and the *Manchester Times and Gazette* for 1837 to 1854.

Crofton, Mrs

Mrs Crofton is a shadowy figure who appears only in the rate book for 1845, living in Oak Bank House – a substantial home near the end of Needham Avenue. This house had belonged to William Morton; Mrs Crofton paid her £90 rent to the Morton estate in 1845. In the 1841 census the Ashcroft family was there, and according to the rate books Mrs Crofton had gone by 1846.

Crowther family

The Crowther family was in Chorlton from 1732, when they were granted settlement (Lancashire County Records, QSP/1356/7). Mary was the subject of a removal order from Stretford to Chorlton in 1765 (Archives and Local History Library, Manchester L89/9/10/11) and is subsequently recorded in the parish records as giving birth to three illegitimate children. Her gravestone, along with that of one of her children, is in the parish churchyard, and there are references to her in Ellwood, who locates her wattle and daub house on the Row, on or close to the site of the Trevor Arms on Beech Road.

Cunliffe Brooks family

William, a banker, his wife Jane and their family lived at Barlow Hall from June 1848, and are in the 1851 census and the rate books. There is a monument in the parish church to their two infant children, who also appear in the parish records for burials. Photographs of the window that William donated can be seen in old pictures of the parish church and the lych-gate he paid for is still at the entrance to the graveyard. Ellwood mentions the family. William is also mentioned in the *Electors Guide* for 1854–55.

Davies, William

He was the village blacksmith and lived on the Row, renting land from Lydia Brown and John Brundrett. He can be found in Pigot and Co.'s National Commercial Directory of 1834, in the 1841 and 1851 censuses, baptismal records for the 1830s and the tithe schedule for 1845.

Deakin, Francis

Francis was a market gardener, murdered in 1847 when his wife had just given birth to their sixth child. He is mentioned in the census return for 1841, the rate books and tithe schedule, and his murder was covered by a number of newspapers, notably the *Manchester Times and Gazette*, 7 May 1847, the *Daily News*, 19 August 1847 and the *Manchester Guardian*, 18 August 1847. His funeral was reported in the *Manchester Guardian*, 12 May 1847. After his death his widow Martha continued the market garden and the family is recorded in later censuses. The family gravestone is in the parish churchyard. There are references to the family in the parish records.

Dean family

James and his son Samuel Dean farmed nearly 300 acres at Barlow Hall Farm. James appears in the electoral registers for 1832, 1835 and 1840. The family appear in the censuses for 1841 to 1861 and are also in the rate books and tithe schedule. James died in 1864 and there is a reference to his will in the National Probate Calendar Index of Wills and Administration for 23 August 1864. Samuel qualified for a parliamentary vote in 1854–55.

Downes, John

John Downes was a Methodist, who appears in the rate books and in Methodist baptismal records.

Fox family

The Foxes lived in Renshaw's Buildings and were paying 2s a week. John Fox was a tailor. They appear in the 1851 census, the rate books for the 1840s and the parish burial records. The family gravestone is in the churchyard.

Gilpin, William

William was the first police constable resident in the township (Ellwood). He and his family lodged with the Moores family on Chapel Lane (now St Clements Road) and are in the 1841 census.

Grantham family

George Grantham owned Grantham's Buildings on High Lane. The Granthams appear in the 1841 and 1851 censuses, the tithe schedule, rate books and the electoral registers for 1832, 1835 and 1840. They were Methodists and there are references to them in the chapel register as well as Ellwood.

Gratrix, Samuel

Samuel Gratrix farmed on the Row; his farmhouse was on what is now the corner of Beech Road and Beaumont Road. He is in the 1841 census, the rate books and tithe schedule, and his widow appears in the 1851 census. There is a photograph of their cottage reproduced in this book. A 'John Gratrix, wheelwright' appears in Pigot and Co.'s National Commercial Directory, 1834.

Green family

James Green was an agricultural labourer. The family rented a cottage for 1s 6d a week from Mrs Brown in 1845. They appear in the 1841 and 1851 censuses and rate books.

Gresty family

There were eighteen Grestys in 1851 divided between five families; they included a farmer, market gardener, hay cutter, labourer and charwoman. They are in the 1841 and 1851 censuses, the rate books and parish records. James Gresty was active in the brass band and is mentioned in the electoral register for 1840 and by Ellwood. His gravestone is in the parish church. John Gresty lived on the western side of the churchyard and is also mentioned in Ellwood. William Gresty was also in the brass band and appears in Ellwood. Thomas and Mary Gresty are in the parish records. William Gresty can be found in the electoral register for 1832 and 1835 and was part of the inquest held at the Horse and Jockey into the murder of Francis Deakin, *Manchester Times and Gazette*, 7 May 1847. The Gresty family is spread beyond the township, but some still live in Chorlton.

Griffiths family

The Griffiths family were active Methodists. They appear in the 1841 and 1851 censuses, tithe schedule, rate books and chapel registers. William was a market gardener and one of his sons a wheelwright. William is mentioned in Ellwood. William Griffiths is in the electoral registers for 1832, 1835 and 1840 by virtue of owning freehold houses in Lloyd Street.

Hardy family

They appear in the 1841 census and their gravestone is in the churchyard.

Hayson family

The Hayson family farmed Hobson Hall Farm. They appear to have prospered during the 1840s, increasing their tenancy from 37 to 45 acres between 1841 and 1851 and to 70 acres by 1861. They appear in the censuses for 1841, 1851 and 1861. They can also be found in the tithe schedule, rate books and the Vestry minutes: Thomas Hayson was at various times chairman, an assessor, surveyor of highways and constable. The family were indirectly connected with the murder of Francis Deakin: his death occurred in the beershop which, while it was run by Mrs Leach, was in the name of her relative Charlotte Hayson. Thomas Hayson had the vote in 1832, 1835, 1840 and 1854–55.

Healey, Ellen

Ellen Healey is another of those shadowy figures whose existence is limited to references in the rate book. She rented a cottage from the Renshaw executors, one of the New Buildings or Renshaw's Buildings; she paid 1*s* 6*d* a week.

Heath family

In 1851 George Heath was a coachman living in Holt Lodge, part of the Holt estate and at the top of the Row where it joined Barlow Moor Lane. In 1845 he paid a rent of 1s 6d. Three years later he was in Renshaw's Buildings, where he paid 1s 9d. His footprint is confined to the rate books and the 1851 census. His wife Harriet and their two children show up in the 1851 census.

Helsby family

There were two Helsby families and maybe more. They appear in the burial records of the parish church from 1823. Richard Helsby was a farmer and appears on the parish marriage records: his daughter Mary married John Gresty in 1838. His son married a Jane Haigh in 1853. There is a reference to a Richard Helsby living in a wattle and daub cottage near Lloyds Hotel (Ellwood). Richard and Martha Helsby baptised a number of children in the parish church between 1822 and 1832. Martha Helsby rented 4 acres from the Lloyd estate in 1847 and lived at the point where Wilbraham Road meets the small stretch of Manchester Road, probably in the cottage Ellwood refers to. She appears in the 1851 census as a widow and gardener and is also in the rate books. A second Helsby family lived at Brownhill's Buildings in 1851. John, the head of the household, was a labourer.

Hesketh family

The Hesketh family, like so many others, are difficult to track. There is a record of a Mary Hesketh in the 1841 and 1851 censuses and a reference to William and his son Samuel, who lived in a wattle and daub cottage on Manchester Road somewhere near the railway bridge (Ellwood).

Heywood family

It would appear that there were at least two Heywood families. A William Heywood was living in Renshaw's Buildings in 1846–47, paying 1s 6d a week in rent. Ellen Heywood was living in a wattle and daub cottage somewhere on the site of the modern Needham Avenue (Ellwood). She was buried in the churchyard in 1845 with her parents, John and

Martha. A more prosperous Heywood family lived at Brook Bank, which was on the north-west side of the Brook and is currently the site of a fast food outlet. William and his elder sisters, Helen, Sarah and Ann, were of independent means, living off annuities. They appear on the 1851 census, and William is in the Vestry minutes: he held the posts of chairman and assessor.

Higginbotham family

This was one of the core farming families of Chorlton. Their farm was on the west side of the Green directly opposite the school and the churchyard; the farmhouse still exists. The Higginbothams were there from 1841 into the late 20th century. They appear in all census returns from 1841, the tithe schedule, rate books and later street directories. James Higginbotham was active in local politics and there are references to him in the Vestry minutes in the role of chairman, overseer, assessor and constable; he was part of the inquest held at the Horse and Jockey into the murder of Francis Deakin, *Manchester Times and Gazette*, 7 May 1847. He is also in the electoral register for 1854–55. He buried his first wife and two children in the Methodist chapel graveyard, and there are references to him in the chapel records. Ellwood describes him as attending the chapel. There are photographs of the farmhouse and of one of his fields, and there is a record of his will in the National Probate Calendar for January 1877. There are also extracts from his farm accounts for the 1840s, but the authenticity of these records has yet to be verified.

Holland family

There are a number of Holland families. John Holland is mentioned by Ellwood as the first superintendent of the Sunday school. He appears in the electoral registers for both 1832 and 1835 by virtue of occupying 20 acres. He is in the 1841 and 1851 censuses as well as the rate books and the Vestry minutes, which document that he was an assessor. Joseph and Alice Holland were Methodists who appear in the chapel registers and were connected by marriage to the Granthams and Rhodes families. A Joseph Holland is listed as a labourer aged sixty in the 1841 census. His early occupation is given as shoemaker, and he may be the same Joseph Holland who in 1845 was running the Horse and Jockey pub. As well as the census returns for 1841 and 1851, there are references to him in the rate books, the tithe schedule and in Ellwood. Thomas Holland held 5 acres according to the tithe schedule and lived at the top end of Manchester Road, where it now joins

Wilbraham Road (Ellwood). By 1851 he was farming Brook Farm on 54 acres. He can be found in the rate books and in the Vestry minutes: he was an overseer, assessor and constable. William Holland was a warehouseman and is recorded in the 1851 census.

Holt family

There were three Holt families. One of them lived on the Row in Beech Cottage, later renamed Beech House. There are references to them in the census returns from 1841 to 1901. James and Hannah Holt were from Manchester and moved into the township in the 1830s. He had made his money from making calico engraving blocks. There are references to them in Pigot and Co.'s National Commercial Directory, 1834 and 1841, as well as Slater's Directory of Lancashire. They retained the family home in St John Street and there are references to them before their move to Chorlton in Pigot and Dean's Directory of Manchester and Salford of 1821. They also appear in the rate books for Chorlton and the tithe schedule. His son and later his grandson all moved into the township. The Holts retained a large portfolio of property in the city as well as in Chorlton. There are references to the extent of these holdings in their private papers. Beech House and James Holt are referred to in Ellwood. The property qualifications for their parliamentary votes along with their voting record for the 1835 general election can be seen in the *Electors Guide*.

By contrast William Holt was a labourer who lived on the Green with his wife Margaret and three children. They rented Holt Croft from the Egertons. Their cottage and land were at the end of Ivygreen Road, on the south side, where today there is a block of flats. They are in both the 1841 and 1851 censuses and the tithe schedule. A Mary Holt baptised two children out of wedlock in 1825 and 1829 according to the baptismal records. One of these may have been the same James Holt whose family gravestone is in the parish churchyard, although there is a discrepancy of seven years between his given birth on the gravestone and the baptismal record.

Hooley, John

John Hooley was a joiner who lived with his wife, Ann, a laundress, and their daughter, Mary Ellen, also a laundress, on the Row. They rented a cottage from James Holt that cost 3s 10d a week, which was one of the highest rents for a working man's cottage. They can be found in the 1841 and 1851 censuses, rate books and parish marriage records – when Mary Ellen married John Coppock in August 1851; he was a manufacturer from Didsbury.

Horden, Revd Peter

The Revd Peter Hordern was in Chorlton briefly from 1833 to 1836. He appears in the list of electors for both 1832 and 1835 and is mentioned by Ellwood.

Howarth, Edmund

Edmund Howarth is another shadowy figure who only appears as a Chorlton voter in the electoral registers for 1835 and 1840. He was an absent voter who lived at Sale Lodge in Cheshire but owned The Greyhound and some land at Jackson's Boat.

Jackson

There are a number of Jacksons referred to in Chorlton. Henry Jackson owned and rented land in the township according to the tithe schedule, but lived just outside at Hough End Hall. He appears in the rate books and is in the 1841 Withington census (Enu 6, p.9). The Hough End farm later included 220 acres. Henry appears in Ellwood. The contents of his farm are listed in an advertisement in the *Manchester Guardian*, 20 January 1849, on his death. Another Henry Jackson, aged thirty in 1841 according to the census, farmed Hardy House Farm. There is also a Henry Jackson listed in the tithe schedule as owning land in the township, as well as renting some from the Egertons. James Jackson lived in Hulme, and was listed in the 1821–22 edition of Pigot and Dean's New Directory of Manchester and Salford as a farmer and carrier. He owned 15 acres of land at Round Thorn, the area north of Chorlton Brook roughly covering the stretch from the allotments down to Nell Lane, but it was sold to James Holt in 1839 after he had gone bankrupt. There is a John Jackson described as a 'gentleman' in Baines's Directory of 1824 and Pigot and Co.'s National Commercial Directory of 1828–29. Sarah Jackson lived with her son Samuel and daughter Margaret on the Row, where she ran a shop. She rented from Thomas Taylor and paid 3s 10d in weekly rent. In Pigot's Directory for 1841 the twenty-year-old Samuel is listed as a beerseller, but in the same year in the census as an agricultural labourer. In 1849 he was running a beerhouse on the Green. One other Samuel Jackson appears in the 1851 census as lodging at the Travellers Rest on the Row. A William Jackson paid for the aisles in the parish church in 1837 (Ellwood). He was a churchwarden (also Ellwood). This may be the same William Jackson who qualified for a parliamentary vote because he occupied 33 acres at Hardy Lane.

Jordrill family

A number of Jordrill (or Jordrell) families appear in the parish church baptismal and burial records but only Caleb appears a number of times. In the 1841 census he is described as eighty years old and living at Lane End. Ellwood refers to his home as a wattle and daub cottage. He also appears in the tithe schedule for the same place, and is named by Ellwood as one of the leaders who took part in riding the stang. There are references to him in the 1841 and 1851 censuses, as well as the parish records. An Ann Jordrell, who may have been his wife, is in the 1851 census as a widow receiving parish relief and living with her granddaughter, Anne Kenyon. Anne's parents may well have been John and Ann Kenyon, who lived in a cottage on High Lane. He was an agricultural labourer and they had five children, of whom Ann was the youngest.

Johnson, John

He was one of the early Methodists in the township, and services were held at his cottage behind the National School before the first chapel was built. It was one of the old wattle and daub cottages (Ellwood). He is one of the three who set up the Loyal Lord Nelson Lodge on 9 January 1843 (also Elwood).

Kenyon families

There were a number of Kenyon families. Ellen Kenyon was living in Renshaw's Buildings from at least 1845 and appears in the rate books paying a rent of 1s 11d. She was a widow aged fifty-seven and worked as a charwoman. She also appears in the 1851 census. Charles and Francis only occur in the baptismal records. Samuel and Ann Kenyon baptised their daughter Charlotte in 1805. They were also the parents of John Kenyon of High Lane. Charlotte baptised her daughter Harriet in October 1823 when she was just eighteen, followed by her son George in May 1828, before marrying James Walley. He was twenty-two years older than Charlotte and it may be that George was his son. Either way he was no longer around by 1851, and Charlotte had married again. John and Ann Kenyon lived in a cottage on High Lane, for which they paid a weekly rent of 1s 6d. He was an agricultural labourer and they had five children. His wife was the daughter of Caleb and Ann Jordrell and appears in the baptismal record for 1802. They were Methodists and appear in the baptismal records for the chapel. William and Esther Kenyon are mentioned in both the 1841 and 1851 censuses, living on Dark Lane and later Oswald Lane. They had a number of children who appear in the baptismal records.

There was another John Kenyon, a market gardener who lived at Pitts Brow (Ellwood). One of his daughters married William Chessyhre, who took over the market garden. John Kenyon appears in the 1841 census and in the baptismal records for the chapel on the Row, as well as in Baines's 1824–25 Directory for Lancashire. Finally there is a reference to Kenyons living in wattle and daub cottages off Sandy Lane in Ellwood, but these had gone by the 1840s.

Knight family

The Knight family farmed in the township from at least 1832. William the elder qualified for a parliamentary vote and was on the electoral list for 1832, 1835 and 1840. During that time his occupancy of land rose from 24 acres to 46. He can be found in the 1841 census and the tithe schedule; he died in 1852. William the younger ran the Robin Hood pub in Stretford and appears in Pigot and Co.'s Royal National and Commercial Directory for 1841 and the census for the same year in Stretford (Enu 6, p.10, Stretford), before moving into Chorlton to farm on the Green in the 1850s. He is on the electoral register for 1854–55. He can also be found in the Vestry minutes and was part of the inquest held at the Horse and Jockey into the murder of Francis Deakin, *Manchester Times and Gazette*, 7 May 1847. The family gravestone is in the parish churchyard. Earlier in 1824 a Thomas Knight was listed in Pigot and Dean's Directory of Manchester and Salford as 'vict Old Greyhound, (boat house) Chorlton', and Martha Knight was listed in Baines's Directory for 1824–25 as running the 'Boat House' in Chorlton. This later became the Old Greyhound, then the Bridge Inn and today is Jackson's Bridge.

Lamb family

The Lamb family features in Chorlton during the 18th century and the family grave was inside the parish church where it can still be seen today, which suggests they were of some importance. Later in the early 19th century a Lamb family appears in the baptismal records of the chapel on the Row. By the 1850s there were two families who were engaged in agricultural work and laundry.

Langford family

The Langford family of market gardeners lived at Oswald Field in Martledge and later on the Row, at the farm formerly run by Samuel Gratrix; this became known as Bowling Green Farm. They appear in the 1841, 1851 and 1861 censuses and in the baptismal and marriage records of the chapel on the Row. They were related to the Lunt family. Peter Langford was part of the inquest held at the Horse and Jockey into the murder of Francis Deakin, *Manchester Times and Gazette*, 7 May 1847. John Langford, Peter's son, is mentioned in Ellwood.

Lewis, George,

There is a reference to George Lewis as a shopkeeper in Pigot and Co.'s National Commercial Directory, 1834.

Lloyd, George

George Lloyd was the second largest landowner. He was mentioned in the tithe schedule and in Ellwood. He qualified for the vote in 1832, 1835, 1840 and 1854–55. He lived at Stockton Hall near York.

Lomas, Samuel

Samuel Lomas farmed 220 acres, employing thirteen labourers at Hough End Hall – just outside the township. He took over the tenancy in 1849 and appears in the 1851 census for Withington (2c, p.23) as well as Ellwood.

Lunt, George

George Lunt was a market gardener of 2 acres farming Egerton land roughly half-way down what is now the north side of Sandy Lane. For this he paid an annual rent of £12 10s 5d a week. He appears in both the 1841 and 1851 censuses and the tithe schedule. The Lunts were Methodists and were related by marriage to the Cookson, Langford,

Moore and Renshaw families. Ellwood refers to them in his description of wattle and daub cottages and in his history of Methodism in the township. George was also active in the brass band (Ellwood). William Lunt was a gardener, but it is unclear how much land he rented. The family lived at Grantham's Buildings in the 1840s and 1850s and appears in the 1841 and 1851 censuses. They too appear in the baptismal records of the Methodist chapel. Mrs Lunt, who may be Ann Lunt, the wife of William, rented one of the cottages in Grantham's Buildings in 1845, paying 3s 5d a week. Earlier in the century the Lunts lived in a 'large antiquated, old thatched farmhouse on the site of Hardy House Farm' (Ellwood).

Lyth family

They appear in the graveyard and in the parish burial records.

Mason family

The Mason family was in Chorlton from at least the late 18th century and might have been here from the 1730s. The family gravestone is situated inside the parish church. Edward Mason, born in 1734, gained the first licence for the Bowling Green. He died in 1797. His son, also called Edward, took over the hotel and rented out the pond for fishing (Ellwood). Both Edward Mason senior and his son (1814–84) were land surveyors. Edward Mason senior appears in Pigot and Dean's New Directory of Manchester and Salford of 1821–22, Baines's Directory of 1824–25 and Pigot and Co.'s National Commercial Directory of 1834. By 1841 the Bowling Green was being run by William Whitelegg. Edward also appears to have had freehold buildings on the Row in 1832 and occupied 23 acres at Chapel End, which qualified him for a parliamentary vote: he is on the electoral register. Edward and Sarah appear in the baptismal records in 1822. There are other Masons buried in other plots in the churchyard, and also a James Mason who appears in Pigot and Dean's New Directory of Manchester and Salford of 1821–22 and Baines's Directory of 1824, and is listed as a gentleman.

Moore[s] family

There were at least four families of this name, and all appear in the 1841 and 1851 censuses. Some were Methodists and were linked by marriage with the Brundrett, Griffith, Kenyon and Lamb families, which underlines the close links that the Methodists fostered. Alice Moore was a widow by 1841. She may have been born in 1786 or 1791 and died in 1852. She appears in the census for 1841 and 1851 and is in the rate books as owning two cottages, one of which she lived in and one she rented for 1s 11d. Betty Moore was also a widow by 1841. She described herself as a charwoman and ten years later as a laundress. She had been married to Thomas Moore and appears in the baptismal records of the chapel as well as the census, and according to Ellwood was active in the chapel choir. Thomas collected subscriptions for the Methodist Sunday school (Ellwood). Catherine Moore baptised a daughter out of wedlock in 1830; she may have been the daughter of Thomas and Jane Moore. He was a labourer and his wife was the daughter of Samuel and Ann Kenyon. Catherine appears in the baptismal records for the chapel in February 1806. James Moore owned property on the Green, which he rented out. He qualified for a parliamentary vote in 1832, 1835 and 1840. John Moore supported his family as a labourer and lived on the Row in a wattle and daub cottage close to the modern Trevor Arms (Ellwood). William was a market gardener who rented 4 acres from the Egertons on the west side of Edge Lane, near what was then Cow Lane and today is Hampton Road. He was married to Margaret, and the family lived in a cottage on this land, paying an annual rent of £16 6s 1d a week. They appear in the census records, the tithe schedule, rate books and baptismal records of the chapel. There are two Moore gravestones in the churchyard.

Morton family

The Mortons lived at Oak Bank House. William was resident by 1824, appearing in Baines's Directory of Lancashire. He appears in the electoral registers for 1832 and 1835. He worked for an established Manchester bank where he was paid £2,000 a year, and there is a brief biography of him in Grindon, Leo H., *Manchester Banks and Bankers*, Palmer and Howe, Manchester, 1877, pp.178–9. William's will exists, and his gravestone can be found in the parish churchyard with other members of his family. Most notable of these is his son Charles, who worked for the same bank and lived at Lime Bank. This house still stands, and can be approached down the alley that runs from Barlow Moor Road opposite the bus terminus to Nell Lane. He appears in the 1851 and 1861 census returns, as well as the tithe schedule and the rate books. He played a prominent part in Chorlton's local government and is mentioned in the Vestry minutes. There are various newspaper references to some of the other children of William Morton, including, the death of one of his sons, William Henry, on the River Bony in Nigeria (*Preston Chronicle*, 1 September 1832), the marriage of his daughter, Jane (*Liverpool Mercury*, 19 August 1825), the death of his daughter Alice (*Manchester Times and Gazette*, 12 March 1847) as well as the marriage of Charles (*Manchester Times and Gazette*, 5 May 1838).

Morton, Revd John

See Ellwood. Morton presided over St Clement's from 1836 to 1842 and his gravestone is in the churchyard. He appears on the electoral roll for 1840.

Newton, Edwin

He was part of the inquest held at the Horse and Jockey into the murder of Francis Deakin, *Manchester Times and Gazette*, 7 May 1847.

Nixon family

Samuel senior was tenant of The Greyhound from perhaps 1832 or 1834 (Ellwood). He appears in Pigot and Co.'s National Commercial Directory for 1834 and Pigot and Co.'s Royal National and Commercial Directory for 1841 as well as the censuses for 1841 and 1851. He is also in the tithe schedule and the rate books, rented 5 acres of land and appears in the electoral register for 1835 and 1840. Samuel is listed in the burial records of the parish church. Samuel junior was tenant of the Travellers Rest (Ellwood). His gravestone along with that of his wife is in the parish churchyard. The third Samuel Nixon was the son and grandson of the two innkeepers and ran the post office. He is mentioned in various census returns. He also appears on an agreement with Mrs Jane Taylor over the lease of the post office dated 11 May 1882, at what is now 68 Beech Road. It refers to the Travellers Rest, now no. 70. Lionel Nixon was the great-grandson of Samuel senior. He appears in various census returns, ran the stationery shop and newsagent on the corner of Church Street (Chequers Road) and Beech Road, and married Hilda Brownhill.

Pearson families

Thomas Pearson appears on the electoral register for 1832 and 1835 as occupying 9 acres at Round Thorn on land owned by James Jackson of Hulme. Round Thorn was roughly the stretch of land east from Lane End on the south side of what is now Sandy Lane down towards Nell Lane. Thomas and his wife Elizabeth were Methodists and appear in the baptismal records during the early 19th century. They were related to William Lunt by marriage. Richard and Elizabeth Pearson lived on the Row, and appear in the censuses for 1841 and 1851, the baptismal records of the Methodist chapel and in the rate books. One of their daughters, Ann, was sent to trial in 1855 for the suspected murder of her infant child. The case was described in detail by the *Manchester Guardian*, 18 April 1855, and her acquittal was recorded in the England and Wales Criminal Register 1791–1892, available on Ancestry.

Phillips, Shakespeare

He lived at Barlow Hall and is mentioned by Ellwood. He appears in the rate books, the electoral register and in the poll books that show how he voted in the 1832 general election. Phillips's contribution to the election campaign of 1835 is recounted in the *Preston Chronicle*, 24 January 1835. He appears in various directories for the 1820s, including Pigot and Dean's Directory of Manchester and Salford for 1821–22.

Pickford, John Cornelius

John Cornelius Pickford appears in the 1835 electoral register with a vote by virtue of a freehold property called Grove House. There are two other references to him: the *Draper and Clothier*, Houlston and Wright, London, 1860 and the *London Gazette*, 14 June 1861: 'Pickford, Cornelius, John, formerly of Fallowfield, Brow, Manchester, in the county of Lancaster, afterwards of Carnforth in the said county, Commsission Agent, then Kent-lane, afterwards of Stainton, both in Kendal, in the county of Westmorland, Manager of an Artificial Manure Mill, and late of Carnforth, aforesaid, Commission Agent'. In 1841 he was at July Cottage, Fallowfield (Enu 5, p.9, Withington), and after that in Carnforth.

Pinnington family

The Pinnington family appear in the burial records from the 18th century. James and Mary Pinnington (or Pennington) baptised a number of their children at the parish church: Mary in 1805, Sarah in 1806, Martha in 1809, Hannah in 1811, Susanna in 1813, Elizabeth in 1816, George in 1819 and James in 1821. They appear in the parish records from the 18th century and their gravestone is in the parish churchyard. William and Mary are in the baptismal records in 1812 with their daughter Hannah. He ran a shop on the Green. This was one of the houses now incorporated into the House and Jockey. It is most likely that it now forms the last part of the pub on the east side. Miss Wilton took over the shop (Ellwood), and she lived in this section. Susannah Pennington (or Pinnington) had a child named Thomas out of wedlock, and the father is mentioned in a 'Notice of Intention to apply for an order against James White for maintenance of his bastard son by Susannah Pennington May 9th 1837' (Lancashire County Records Item QSP/3066/34, 9 May 1837). She appears in the 1841 census living with her sister Hannah and brother William. There are also other references in the census records for 1861 and 1871, after she had married Daniel Chester.

Pollit, Thomas

Thomas Pollit was one of those named as refusing to pay the church rate. He is on the 1851 census and appears in reports on the dispute: *Manchester Times*, 26 April 1851, *Preston Guardian*, 3 May 1851, and Ellwood.

Renshaw families

There are a number of Renshaw families interwoven into the history of Chorlton. They appear in the parish records, census returns, rate books and are on gravestones in the churchyard. They are connected in marriage to the Bailey, Chesshyre and Taylor families. James Renshaw began farming on the Row in 1767, and the family continued to work the land until 1844 when the tenancy passed to the Bailey family, who in turn stayed until the early 20th century when they moved to Park Brow. Alice Bailey was the niece of John Renshaw, who had occupied the farm until his death. John Renshaw also owned eleven cottages as well as Renshaw's Buildings. He is on the electoral register for 1832 and 1835. His will is in the Lewis and Bailey Collections. Other Renshaws appear in Ellwood. They include Charles, James the Methodist schoolteacher, Margaret, Thomas and William the haycutter and thatcher. One family is also to be found in the baptismal records of the Wesleyan chapel, including James and Elizabeth, whose daughter Elizabeth was married to Richard Pearson, John and Sarah, Joseph and Jane, Thomas and Sarah, and Thomas and Susannah.

Rhodes, Thomas

Organiser of musical evenings, he was a much-respected Methodist preacher. He appears in Ellwood. There is a photograph of him in the 1908 souvenir of the grand bazaar, included in this book. He is listed in the 1841 census.

Sadler family

There was a Sadler family recorded in the 1841 and 1851 censuses. George and Betty lived on the Row in 1841. He was a labourer. Ten years later he was a widower and described himself as infirm. He was living with his son William, who was a tailor, daughter-in-law Hannah and their son George.

Sharp, Daniel

He lived on the Row, can be found in the census returns, rate books and tithe schedule. He is listed in the electoral registers for 1840 and 1854–55. There is also a reference to a John Sharp in a legal document dated 1825.

Silgram family

Charles and Hannah lived on the Row. They appear in the 1841 census, rate books and baptismal records. He was an agricultural labourer and she was present at the discovery of Mary Ann Page's dead infant in 1849.

Sutton family

The Suttons lived on the Row and appear in census returns and rate books. Their cottage was demolished in July 1891 and stood on the corner of Beech and Wilton Road. A photograph of the houses appeared in the souvenir of the grand bazaar at the Wesleyan church, 1895.

Taylor families

There are a number of Taylor families and they appear on gravestones in the churchyard. There are references to them in the census records, rate books, parish records and the tithe schedule. Ellwood refers to them. Margaret Taylor is mentioned in the tithe schedule, farming 11 acres and living at the bottom of the Row (junction of Beech Road and Whitelow Road), and John Taylor rented a cottage on the south side of Ivygreen before Attercliffe Road. There is a reference to Thomas Taylor in the burial records for July 1841. He was seventy-one. Four Taylors appear on the electoral registers: John Taylor lived at 20 Dodge Hill, Heaton Norris, and qualified for a vote with 'freehold houses in Martledge in occupation of John Taylor & other' in 1854–55; Samuel Taylor lived on Chester Road but qualified in 1854–55 by owning freehold houses for rent in Martledge; Thomas Taylor senior qualified in 1832, 1835 and 1840 with freehold houses at Martledge; Thomas Taylor junior qualified in 1832, 1835, 1840 and 1854–55 as he had freehold houses for rent at the bottom of the Row. These included what are now 68–70 Beech Road and possibly whatever was on the site of the Beech Inn, and extended onto the modern Whitelow Road. His tenants were Sarah Jackson, James White and James Bates. Samuel Nixon junior rented the Travellers Rest, now 70 Beech Road, while Thomas Taylor occupied no. 68, a stationer's shop and the post office from 1857. He was also the tenant landlord of the Horse and Jockey in 1841, the pub owned by Thomas White. These Taylors were related to the Bailey, Chessyhre and Renshaw families. Thomas Taylor had married Elizabeth Renshaw, and their daughter Alice married Robert Bailey in 1816. There is also a reference to a Thomas Taylor of Chorlton in Pigot's Directory as 'acting overseer in Chorlton'.

Thomas, Daniel

He was a gardener from Wales and is credited with starting the brass band again in 1850, and canvassing the township for subscriptions (Ellwood). He also appears in the 1851 census.

Turner family

They lived on the Green and are recorded in the 1841 and 1851 censuses as a labouring family. A Margaret Turner was a servant for annual wages of £8 in 1844: Higginbotham's accounts.

Walker family

Thomas Walker was an 18th-century radical. He had a town house at South Parade, St Mary's, Manchester, where he lived in the winter. The road still exists, facing the gardens that were once the site of St Mary's Church. In the summer he stayed at Barlow Hall, and later moved to Longford Hall. He was active in the politics of Manchester, was put on trial for his beliefs and his house was attacked by a mob. His gravestone is in the parish church. The details of his trial are available in his book: Walker, Thomas, *A Review of some of the events of the last five years*, London, 1794, and he appears in Clarkson, Thomas, *History of the Rise, Progress, and Accomplishments of the Slave Trade*, John Parker, London, 1839, for the part he played in the campaign against the slave trade. Ellwood gives a brief description, and there are references made to him by Axon, William in *The Annals of Manchester*, John Heywood, Manchester, 1885. Other members of the family mentioned by Ellwood are his sons, Thomas and Charles. Thomas published a collection of his own thoughts on issues of the day in *The Original*, Henry Renshaw, London, 1850. Charles built a bridge across Chorlton Brook where it runs into the Mersey, and is listed in the tithe schedule.

Whitelock, Richard Hutchins

A curate between 1816 and 1833 (Ellwood).

Warburton, Ellen

Ellen lived in a wattle and daub cottage near the site of the Trevor Arms (Ellwood). She is recorded in the tithe schedule as renting a cottage and garden from the Lloyd estate.

White, James

James White was a beerseller according to Pigot's Commercial Directory for the Counties of 1841. There is also a reference to a labourer called James White in the 1841 census. He lived on Lloyd Street just off the Row, and was twenty-two when it was alleged he fathered Thomas Pinnington. By the age of twenty-five he was married with two children. His eldest was just a year younger than Thomas.

White, John and Mary

John appears in the 1832 and 1835 electoral registers as the occupier of 53 acres on the Green. He died in November 1835 and is in the parish burial records. Mary is listed in the 1841 census as a widow, and by 1845 had increased the land she rented from the Lloyd estate to 77 acres. She lived on the west side of the Green. Her house may be the brick house set back between Higginbotham's cottage to the south and a terrace of houses to the north. She is also in the 1851 census. Both John and Mary appear in the baptismal records for 1798 and 1816, and John is listed as constable in Pigot and Co.'s National Commercial Directory of 1834.

White, Thomas

He was the son of John and Mary White. He is mentioned in Ellwood as the first tenant of the Travellers Rest in 1832. He was still there in 1841, where he appears with his wife Harriet as a beerseller in the census. By 1845 he had bought the Horse and Jockey, which according to the electoral register was 'occupied by Joseph Holland and others'. The tithe schedule confirms he was renting land from the Lloyd estate. He appears in the rate books as owning the pub and another cottage, which may have been in the same row. In 1851 Thomas and Mary appear in the 1851 census as living with his mother Mary on the Green.

Whitehead family

John and Jane Whitehead lived on the Row with their five children and are in the 1841 census and the rate books. John was a labourer. Ten years later the census shows that he is a widow, his daughter is a washerwoman and they lived at Lane End.

Whitelegg families

Elizabeth Whitelegg is in the 1841 census, where she is recorded as of independent means and living with her son James, a cotton dealer, and four other children. The tithe schedule has her renting a house and garden from Henry Jackson at Brook Farm, just north of the Brook Bridge. The site is currently occupied by a fast food outlet, car-park and video shop. The tithe also shows that she rented 4 acres of meadow and arable land, along with her garden, from the Lloyd estate. George Whitelegg is one of those enterprising inhabitants who diversified into farming, running a pub and property. In the 1841 census he described himself as the publican of the Bowling Green and a farmer. He appears in the rate books as renting the pub and land from the Egertons, and the tithe schedule shows him renting 36 acres from the Egertons. This was a mix of arable, meadow and pasture, along with a pond and the pub. He had already moved into property, and rented a cottage and garden to Alice Daniels at Martledge, which may have been on the site of the old Royal Oak and is just north of the present Royal Oak. In the 1851 census, while still at the Bowling Green, he reduced the land he farmed to 22 acres and by the 1860s had built two prestigious houses called Stockton Range at the junctions of High Lane, Edge Lane, St Clements and Whitelow Road. He was active in local politics, and there are references to him in the Minutes of the Overseers for Chorlton-cum-Hardy, holding various positions, and he is on the electoral registers for 1840 and 1854–55, by virtue of his renting land around the Green. He is mentioned in Ellwood and in the deeds for Stockton Range. William Whitelegg farmed at Red Gates Farm at Martledge, roughly where Chorlton Library now stands. He is in the 1841 and 1851 censuses, rate books, tithe schedule and the electoral registers for 1835, 1840 and 1854–55 as occupier of 42 acres. There is an advertisement for the sale of the farm contents in the *Manchester Examiner and Times* of 3 November 1855. He also appears in the Minutes of the Overseers for Chorlton-cum-Hardy, holding various positions, and was summoned to appear at the New Bailey prison in 1848 for irregularities in the collection of the poor rate while he was overseer in 1848: *Manchester Guardian*, 29 July 1848 and 24 February 1849.

Whittaker family

James and Ann Whittaker were selling grocery provisions on the Row according to the 1851 census, and the business lasted until well into the 20th century.

Wilton family

Samuel and Mary can be found in the baptismal records from 1812, where he variously described himself as a builder, victualler and publican. In 1816 he built the first bridge across the river at what is now Jackson's Boat. It was a wooden construction and survived until 1880. He is mentioned in Ellwood, as is his daughter. During the 19th century he rented what is now the Green from the Egertons. The 1845 tithe schedule records refer to this plot as 'garden and pond', and the occupier was Mary Wilton. According to Ellwood there was a large pit on part of this land, and after it was filled in the area was given over to cultivation. Part was retained as the family garden and some was sublet. There was a grassed section by the church which children played on. The enclosed area was still visible in a photograph taken between 1887 and 1895. In the 1850s a number of tall Italian poplar trees grew on the north and west side. The Wiltons owned a cottage in the block, which included the Horse and Jockey. Mary Wilton is recorded there in the rate books and on the 1841 census. There is a reference in Ellwood to a Mary Wilton taking over a shop that became her home. This may have been Samuel's widow, who was there in 1841 living with one of her daughters. The property has now been incorporated into the pub and forms its eastern end. Various of the daughters lived there until the last; Fredereka, died there in 1895 aged eighty. On her death the Egertons returned it to public use.

Williamson, Ann

She was a pork butcher, and is listed in Pigot and Co.'s National Commercial Directory for 1828–29.

Williamson, James

James was a farmer and is mentioned in Ellwood. He lived on what is now Sandy Lane on the site of William Gresty's farm.

Williamson, John

John Williamson kept the badgers for Thomas Chorlton's pub at Lane End and appears in Ellwood. He lived on High Lane. William Williamson was a farmer of '27 acres at Sandy Brow' who can be found in the electoral register for 1832 and 1835.

twenty-eight

FINDS AND EVIDENCE

Clay pipes, archaeological digs, and voices from the past

Some of the most revealing clues about how people lived are contained in the rubbish they threw away. Across Chorlton one of the most common items to resurface is the humble clay pipe. Usually these are broken and often turn up on their own, although sometimes a whole batch has been unearthed over a period of time close together. They were the pipe of the working man, and some working women. Inexpensive, easy to make, and made in huge quantities, they are a true example of a throwaway product. They were smoked in the home, in the pub and at the workplace. The evidence from sites in some of the poorer parts of London show that the owners smoked heavily.[645] Clay pipes come in many different sizes, some with long stems and decorated bowls, and date from the 17th to the 20th century. The last clay pipe manufacturer in Manchester only ceased trading in 1990. The most interesting pipe to be found in the township was discovered in the archaeological dig at the church site in the 1980s. It can be dated to between 1830 and 1832, and may have been bought to commemorate the coronation of William IV. It bears the inscription 'William IV and Church' around the rim and is decorated with the royal coat of arms flanked by a lion on one side and a unicorn on the other. It is unusual because it was found in one of the graves inside the church. This was Thomas Watson aged fifty-four, who was buried in 1832. It is unusual for the bowl to survive; more commonly it is the stem that turns up, and even these are usually fragments. No other decorated pipes have been found in Chorlton: the rest seem to be the simplest and therefore the cheapest. Most would have come into the township via a carrier or itinerant trader, who bought them in bulk from one of the thirteen tobacco and pipe-makers in Manchester and Salford, or from one of 130 tobacco shops around the two cities.[646]

---

645 Pearce, Jacqui, *Living in Victorian London: The Clay Pipe Evidence*, Geography Department at Queen Mary, University of London, 2007.
646 Slater's Directory of Manchester and Salford, 1850, Historical Directories, p.496.

The series of archaeological digs during the 1970s and early 1980s at the church revealed a varied collection of everyday objects, from coins to commemorative medallions and even shirt buttons, and shed fresh light on the history of the two churches built on the site and some of the people buried there. The dig owes much to Angus Bateman, who lived close to the churchyard in a 1960s development that replaced the farm, small smithy and workshops that bordered the Green to the east of the church. While his main interest was the churchyard and its church, he saw the need to develop the surrounding area in a way that retained its original village character, and from 1965 pushed for the City Council to incorporate the Green and churchyard in an integrated plan of improvement. Angus began 'some exploratory and very amateurish digs, at weekends, intermittently between October 1970 and August 1972'[647] and concluded that he needed to gain more experience in running a dig. He enrolled in a course in archaeology at Manchester University, and the subsequent 1977 dig formed the project for that certificate. It led to further digs, culminating in the 1980–81 season, carried out with South Trafford Archaeological Group. The excavations and subsequent research have helped with an understanding of the two churches that stood on this site from about 1512 until 1949 and a possible dating sequence for the extension of the graveyard in the early 19th century. The fragments from the later church were carefully analysed and recorded, and in some cases Angus was able to track the manufacturers, some of whom were still trading in the 1970s. He also undertook a very detailed record of all the gravestones, including an analysis of the style and composition of the inscriptions and the light they threw on life expectancy among the young.

Everyday personal possessions were also revealed. Sadly these are now missing, but they were carefully recorded. Most of the finds date from the 19th century. The earliest coin was a silver half-groat dating from Charles I's reign, which was found alongside pennies dating from 1797 and 1863. These pennies are notable in their own way. The 18th-century cartwheel penny was the first serious attempt by the government to produce low denominational coinage, while the 1863 bun penny represents the switch from copper to bronze. But it is the 18th-century Liverpool half-penny that raises questions about the life of ordinary people. This coin was not issued by the government but by an individual, and highlights the problem that many people had in obtaining low denominational coinage. This was partly addressed in the 17th century when private individuals began issuing tokens, usually as a mixture of half-pennies and farthings and were redeemable at the place of business of the issuer. This tied the individual to trading with the businessman who had issued the tokens, and were less useful to people living in rural areas because

647 Bateman, Angus J., *Excavations and Other Investigations at Old St Clement's Church Yard, Chorlton, 1977*, Report of work done in part fulfilment of the Certificate Course in Methods of Archaeology, Extra-mural Department, University of Manchester, held by South Trafford Archaeological Group, p.1.

most were issued in towns and cities. During the 17th century there were fifteen issues in Manchester, twelve in Liverpool, seventeen in Warrington, nine in Preston and more in some of the smaller Lancashire towns.[648] A second large issue of tokens across the county began sometime between 1783 and 1785. The Chorlton coin was issued in 1791 as part of a very large series by Thomas Clarke: he produced 10 tons of these copper coins between 1791 and 1794. Clarke was a Liverpool merchant, and his coins were only redeemable at his warehouse in Liverpool.[649] The coin itself, although common, is a beautiful piece of work. The obverse side shows a ship under canvas with crossed laurel branches beneath and the inscription 'Liverpool Half penny'. The reverse bears the motto and arms of Liverpool. In the late 1790s all these tokens were made obsolete by an issue of copper coinage by the government from Mathew Boulton's Soho Mint in Birmingham. This included Chorlton's cartwheel penny. The discovery of one Liverpool half-penny does not throw much light on the working of the local economy: it may just have found its way into the township as a curiosity rather than a means of exchange. But if it was in use as a substitute coin then this raises questions. Given that it was redeemable in Liverpool and that similar tokens were circulating in Manchester, was there an interchange between these companies, so a Liverpool half-penny could be exchanged in Manchester? And if so, was there a trade in the tokens between small businesses, allowing someone to exchange their token in a local shop that would then redeem them at the issuing warehouse? All this is speculation – and, of course, this 1791 half-penny sits outside our story.

The Queen Victoria medallion, however, would have been the stuff of recent history. Victoria was crowned in 1838, and the medallion commemorated her coronation. It was a yellow metal medallion, with a diameter of 1in and less than 0.04in thick. A hole had been drilled so that it could be hung around the neck or perhaps even used as part of a wristband. On the obverse was a profile of the young queen in the centre and the inscription 'Her Gracious Majesty Victoria' around the edge. In the centre of the reverse side was a Crown, with the inscription 'Born May 24 1819' above and 'Crowned June 28 1838' below. There was also a 9 carat gold ring that had belonged to a child. This, like all the finds, had been lost when it fell through the floor of the church onto the sandy surface below. All of them were found in one of the side aisles, which date their loss to after 1837, which was the year the aisles were added to the church.

While finds like these are at the core of any dig, it was the unexpected skeletons that proved both disturbing to the team and the closest link with Chorlton's people. They were all found underneath the north aisle but had been buried before the extension of the church

---

648 'Ormskirk and West Lancashire Numismatic Society', www.numsoc.net.
649 Thomas Clarke was a grocer living at 12 Cable Street. He had a warehouse at 4 Marshall Street off Lord Street.

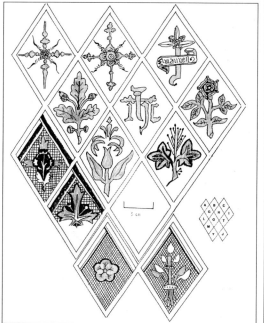 

Above left Fragments of window glass from the old parish church discovered during the excavation of its site in the 1980s. Similar designs can be seen in the new parish church on Edge Lane.

Above right The coin, token and button discovered during the excavation of the church and graveyard in the 1980s.

in 1837. In one case the excavation revealed a foot, leg and shroud pin, made of 'heavily tinned cooper wire'. With his usual attention to detail, Angus had taken the bones home, 'cleaned them and reassembled them, with the help of Gray's Anatomy,' a task which he admitted 'was very tricky for an amateur'.[650] But it was the complete and undisturbed skeleton of a new-born child that most affected members of the team. Even today, thirty years on, something of the drama and sadness of the discovery is revealed in the report: 'It was found right against the 1780 wall at a depth of 70 cm. Every tiny bone I could see was collected, washed and taken home for analysis. I was impressed by the perfect condition of these bones when compared with the adult leg bones ... Because of the immature ossification, each vertebra was in 3 pieces, and the skull disarticulated into many separate bones. The cranial bones were the only damaged ones, presumably crushed by the collapsing coffin. They were paper thin.'[651] The same evening the skull of an adult, taken to be the mother, was unearthed from beside the child. Its teeth were in perfect condition, which

650 Bateman, *op. cit.*, p9.
651 Bateman, *op. cit.*, p.10.

The brass coffin plate of Jonathan Lowe. The Lowe family lived in the township during the late 18th and early 19th centuries, and some were buried in the parish graveyard.

led Angus to assume it was a young woman. But the documentary evidence was less conclusive. The only mother and child recorded to fit the grave position were Mary Lamb and her daughter Betty. They were buried in 1778, and while Betty fitted the profile, having died aged seven days, Mary was forty-four, which seemed too old for the skull. Young Betty died on 6 April and her mother three days later on the 9th. In the years stretching back to 1760, Mary and her husband had buried five other children.

Less gruesome but no less important was the discovery of a large collection of window glass and painted plaster. This was compared with examples in the new church and elsewhere. No conclusive date was possible for the window glass but expert advice suggested a date in the 1860s, although it is possible some could have been early 19th-century. A later date may fit with the improvements funded by William Cunliffe Brooks, who remained a supporter of the old church long after the new one had been built on Edge Lane. It is possible that some of the glass might have been from the large east window that Cunliffe Brooks donated.

The dig was supported where possible by oral testimony of people who knew the old church before it was demolished. They confirmed that it was still lit by oil lamps before the First World War and that it had painted plastered walls. One of those interviewed was able to identify what may have been part of the lectern. Marjorie Holmes also remembered the church that she attended as a child and visited just before its demolition. One of the most striking features was the east window and domed apse, decorated by a silver star that burst out across the blue painted ceiling. Photographs from the 1880s and 1930s clearly show this star, and some of the plaster found during the dig had a blue wash.

But memories of the church are fast fading from living memory. Walking through the landscaped graveyard today presents an altogether different picture to before the area was landscaped in the 1980s. There were 380 gravestones crowded together, marking more than 1,000 burials. Here the good and the great as well as the rich and the poor lay side by side and one on top of another. Some had managed to reach their eighth decade, but many failed to see their first birthday. Here there was a density of death. Today the place looks empty. Bushes and trees now hide some of the remaining gravestones, while a few selected ones mark the route past open grassland from the lych-gate to the Bowling Green entrance. Superficially it may seem an improvement on the run-down, overgrown and neglected former burial place, but many of the inscriptions on the grave-stones are beginning to suffer from being walked on. Some are already wearing thin, while others pass great parts of the year under a blanket of leaves, moss and cigarette ends. Given this slow degradation, it was timely that part of the dig project involved recording these inscriptions and filling in the gaps left from a simi-

The excavation was carried out by volunteers under the direction of Angus Bateman in September 1981.

lar exercise that had been undertaken by the Corporation. This part of Angus's records has yet to come to light, but his description of the dig undertaken by the teams in the 1970s and '80s remains a very important link with Chorlton's past. The fact that some of the information from the digs has been lost serves to remind us that knowledge that is found can be lost again.

It is a powerful observation but one that can also work in reverse. Just as the book was finished I came across the report of a visit by Alexander Somerville to Chorlton in the summer of 1847. He had come looking for potato blight – that disease which had rav-aged the crops of Ireland and had been reported just a little further south in Derbyshire, and what he found was a group of farmers and labourers all too happy to show him they were blight-free. Here were many of the people I had come to know, including James Higginbotham, farmer on the Green, Lydia Brown, whose farm was just a little east of the Bowling Green Hotel, and old Samuel Nixon, market gardener and landlord of the Greyhound just over the river. It is a remarkable piece because Somerville reported and in places quoted what they said. Nothing quite prepares you for hearing their voices, talking of farming issues, joking about what the newspapers publish and complaining about their landlords. These are authentic voices of 165 years ago.

Nor is that quite it. For when Somerville and Higginbotham inspect the potato field I know where it was. It is the strip of land that ran from the Row along what is now the Rec beside Cross Road, and when they stood admiring the Rose of Sharon apple trees and the Newbridge pears, we are just behind the Trevor Arms on what is now Beech Road. It doesn't take much imagination to recreate that orchard scene with the smell of William Davis's smithy hard by and perhaps even the noise of the children in the nearby National School on the Green. Likewise I am pretty sure I can locate the large bank of earth with ash trees which Lydia Brown was so unhappy about and fully understand why she might contemptuously refer to George Lloyd the landlord as Squire Lloyd because of his refusal to allow her to cut the trees back.

Above all it is that calm and steady confidence of the farmer that shines through. Along with Higginbotham's pleasure that the weather has won out there is the certainty of a life-time of experience that allows George Whitelegg to assert that he didn't believe in blight. Whitelegg, who ran the Bowling Green Hotel, also farmed 36 acres and later would go into speculative building.

So I shall close by quoting Somerville's article and allow their voices to come through:

Mr Higginbotham was only afraid that the blight might come. When it does come it will be time enough to raise the alarm.

Mr Whitelegg, of Chorlton, told me that he was a potato grower, had heard of the blight, had looked for it, could not find it, and did not believe in it.

Crossing the green meadows I was told at Brook Farm to go down a path under some trees and examine a field, 'for,' said the workman who bad me to go, 'it is best for those who want to find the potato disease to look for it themselves and find their own disappointment.' I told him that I did not want to find it; that I should be well satisfied to find that the blight was not there, to which he replied briefly, 'Then, sir, you get satisfaction. The best grown potatoes in this part of the country are in that field, and never since the day that you and I were born did the plants look better.'

I found them after close examination to be all that he described them. A large bank of earth with ash trees growing upon it – trees which are not only objectionable as all other kinds are in and around cultivated fields but positively poisonous to other vegetation, ran through the ground causing much waste of land, waste of fertility, and doing no good what-ever. Squire Lloyd is the landlord. Mrs Brown, a widow, is tenant. She keeps the farm in excellent order so far as the landlord's restrictions will allow. But neither myself nor her workmen must 'crop or lop top' a single branch from the deleterious ash trees.

Again I was in the green meadows, where the rain that had newly fallen, and the fresh wind that was blowing, and the luxuriant herbage on every side, and the wild flowers prodigal of bloom, all proclimed that the insurgents now in rebellion against bountiful Providence must soon be defeated and humiliated.

At 'Jackson's Boat' where I crossed the Mersey into Cheshire by the bridge which has superseded the boat, the bridge keeper [Samuel Nixon] said, 'I have been a farmer all my days and never saw anything that can grow out of land look better. It is only int paper; they must have something to say in paper.' [652]

652 *Manchester Examiner*, 19 June 1847.

twenty-nine

AN ENDING AND A BEGINNING

The village as it had been, the promise of change and a hint of the suburb to come,
of canals, railways, water and bricks, post offices, telegrams and telephones

I n many ways the summer of 1847 was one of the last in the old township. Not that anyone would have thought so at the time. Most of the people who feature in our story were making their living in a way that had not changed much for 100 years. Even the coming of the railway to Stretford in 1849 did not seem to threaten the township's traditional way of life. However, with the railway came the beginning of new housing along the Edge Lane and High Lane corridor into Chorlton. These were grand houses, belonging to comfortably off people whose homes stood proud and tall, isolated from the township by wide gardens at front and back. It would be another thirty years before the real housing boom threatened to spread across the fields. This came with a new railway that opened in 1880 and ran along the northern edge of the township with a station on Wilbraham Road. It was now possible to travel on one of fifty trains into and out of the city, a journey that took just 15 minutes. The railway's success can be gauged by the huge increase in the number of season tickets that were issued during the first few years. In January 1880 this stood at 200, but by 1886 it had risen to 600. It was now possible to work in the city but live on the edge of the countryside.

By 1901 a brickworks had opened on Longford Road, providing the material for more elegant villas and not so elegant terraces of brick houses, which stretched out towards Martlege and back along new roads to the village. As if to underline this new turn in Chorlton's history there were new people coming to build these houses – men like Henry Scott, from London, who was a plasterer, his two sons, who became builders of Chorlton houses in their own right, and William Rochell from Yorkshire. In a few short years they and others were transforming the township, so much so that the *Manchester Evening News* commented that there were 'great enterprises a foot and new roads are being monthly added to the local directory'.[653] Much of this new development was aimed at the clerical and artisan end of the market. As the same *Evening News* article said, 'The clerk no less than the merchant must be catered for.'[654] Joe Scott, son of Henry, built many of these smaller terraced houses around Beech Road. There was also the Sandy Lane 'colony', three long new roads named Nicholas, Beresford and Newport, and the 'six shilling a week homes' on Hawthorne Road. All were modest four-roomed houses, with a small front garden and back yard. In that respect the township remained a very down-to-earth place. There may well have been the grand houses that sat well back on Edge and High Lane, but they were matched by those rows of small terraces. In the same way, while there remained private schools offering refined education, the provision of schooling for the majority was increased, first with a new church school and later with the building of a board school at Oswald Road. During this expansion of the township there was a clear shift of the centre of Chorlton to the area around the station, so much so that there seemed to be a clear divide between the new community and the older centre of population around the Green and the Row. This divide was still there to some as late as the 1970s, when people still spoke about old and new Chorlton.

Although the coming of the railway was important, it is only part of the explanation for the housing boom. A good supply of clean water was also a factor. Chorlton relied on wells, ponds and watercourses for all its water, and even in the 1840s and '50s these were only just adequate. By the 1880s wells were either polluted or drying up, and watercourses were disappearing into culverts. When in 1860 George Whitelegg's fashionable new houses on Edge Lane had been finished he had supplied them with an indoor well. Just a few years later Manchester Corporation, responding to a request from seventeen ratepayers, resolved 'to authorise the laying of a [water] service Main in Edge Lane ... for the supply of the houses included in the Schedule submitted and situate in Chorlton-cum-Hardy'.[655] The 3in main extended down Edge Lane, along St Clements Road to the Horse and Jockey. At the time there were only eleven houses along its course, but during the next thirteen years it was frequently extended, until in 1877 a new 12in main was laid from Brooks Bar, along Manchester Road, Wilbraham Road and Edge Lane to Stretford. This was just as well: within another ten years the remaining wells were all but empty and becoming contaminated. There were also plans to improve the sanitation of the township,

---

653 From a series of articles entitled 'History of the Suburbs of Manchester', *Manchester Evening News*, 20 September 1901, Archive and Local History Library, Q942 733 951 Ch (318).

654 *Ibid.*

655 Minutes of the Water Works Committee of Manchester Corporation, No. 10, 28 January 1864 (Archive and Local History Library, M231/1/2/1/10). The 3 inch main extended down Edge Lane, along St Clements Road to the Horse and Jockey and cost £180. Ellwood, chapter 22, 1886.

which led to the building of a sewage farm in 1879. The provision of clean water marked the moment that a rural community began to see itself as an urban one. This was even further advanced when in 1904 Chorlton elected to join the city of Manchester.

But despite all that the city had to offer, Chorlton remained a place that had much which James Higginbotham and James Renshaw would have recognised. South from Beech Road in 1907 there was open land as far as the Brook and beyond to the Mersey, while cows were still walked back onto the Green. As late as the 1930s children were being sent to buy jugs of milk from local farms, and getting to school late because they stopped to watch the local blacksmith.

There seems to have been a deliberate decision on the part of big landowners to sell land for housing rather than industrial purposes. The brickworks, which was the only departure from this rule, was to have a short existence. The Chorlton Land and Building Company gained permission to work the clay and make bricks for about ten years, and while it was later bought by the Jackson family it ceased activity by the middle of the 20th century. Nor was the housing boom as all-encompassing as it might seem. During the late 19th century speculative builders were denied the opportunity of building on much of the farmland. There were, according to the *Manchester Evening News*, 'countless eligible plots still tempting the speculators. It hurts the feelings of people to know that £30 an acre would be refused for a field which may be earning as little as 50s from the farmer.'[656] Even into the late 20th century there were still a few patches of open land that had yet to be developed. Nor had the link with the farming past been completely lost. Well into the 1950s the Bailey family, who had farmed on the Row for most of the 19th century and then moved to the bottom of Sandy Lane at the start of the 20th century, kept bulls on a thin strip of land on the north side of the railway line, drove their pigs through Chorlton and watered the elephants from a travelling circus which camped on open land by St Werburghs.[657]

But these are stories that properly belong to another history of Chorlton.

656 'History of the Suburbs of Manchester: Chorlton-cum-Hardy', *Manchester Evening News*, 20 September 1901.
657 These come from the memories of Oliver Bailey. There are pictures of the bulls in the Local History Image collection. The thin strip of land on the northern side of the railway line east of the bridge is now the site of Adastral House.

BIBLIOGRAPHY

Adams, Samuel and Sarah, *The Complete Servant*, Knight & Lacey (1826)

Agricultural Labourers' Earnings, Parliamentary Papers (1861)

Archdeacon Rushton's Visitation Returns, Reference Number MSF 942.72 R121/Vol. 39, Manchester Archives and Local Studies Centre

Ashworth, Geoffrey, *The Lost Rivers of Manchester*, Willow Publishing (1987)

Axon, William, *The Annals of Manchester*, John Heywood (1885)

Bailey Papers, Collection of family documents covering Bailey and Renshaw families from late 18th to 20th centuries. Privately held

Baines Directory of Manchester (1824–25)

Bateman, Angus J., *Excavations and Other Investigations at Old St Clement's Church Yard, Chorlton, 1977*, Report of work done in part-fulfilment of the Certificate Course in Methods of Archaeology, Extra-mural Department, University of Manchester, held by South Trafford Archaeological Group

Beech Road Baptismal Records 1807–47 from the Register of Baptisms in the Wesleyan Chapel Radnor Street Circuit 1830–7, microfilm MFPR2120, Beech Road Baptismal Records 1807–50, own MSS, vol. 42, Manchester Archive and Local Studies Centre

Beeton, Isabella, *The Book of Household Management*, S.O. Beeton (1863)

Bloy, Dr Marjorie, www.historyhome.co.uk.

Bonham-Carter, Victor, *The English Village*, Penguin (1952)

Booker, Revd John, *A History of the Chapels of Didsbury and Chorlton*, Chetham Society (1857)

Briggs, John Joseph and Melbou Brundrett, Charles, *Brundrett Family Chronicle*, The Book Guild (1984)

Bush, Michael, *The Casualties of Peterloo*, Carnegie Publishing Ltd (2005)

Buxton, Richard, *A Botanical Guide to the Flowering Plants Ferns Mosses & Algae found indigenous with 16 miles of Manchester*, Abel Heywood (1849)

Census of Education, Routledge (1851)

Census of Religious Worship, Routledge (1851)

Cheshire Tithe Maps and schedule

Cheshire County Records of Chorlton-cum-Hardy, Q942 733 951 Ch (318), Manchester Archives and Local History Centre

Chorlton cum Hardy, Maintenance, Removal, Settlement, Orders, L89 Manchester Archives and Local History Centre

'Chorlton-cum-Hardy and its Methodism, A Sunday School Centenary' (18 May 1905), in the collection of The Oxford Centre for Methodism and Church History, Oxford Brookes University (1905)

Chorlton-cum-Hardy Rate Books, 1844–76, Microfilm Rolls 297–9, Manchester Archives and Local History Centre

Chorlton-cum-Hardy Wesleyan Church Souvenir of the Grand Bazaar (1908)

Cliff, Karen and Masterton, Vicki, *Stretford: An Illustrated History*, Breedon (2002)

Cook, Chris, *Britain in the Nineteenth Century 1815–1914*, Routledge (2005)

Crofton, H.T., A *History of the Ancient Chapel of Stretford in Manchester Parish, vol. 3*, Chetham Society (1904)

Culpeper, Nicholas, *The English Physician* (1652)

DeLacy, Margaret, *Prison Reform in Lancashire 1700–1850*, Manchester University Press (1968)

Duffield, H.G., *The Strangers Guide to Manchester* (1850), reprinted by Neil Richardson (1984)

Dunkerley, Philip, 'The Early Dunkerleys and the Domestic System of Cotton Working', http://dunkerley-tuson.co.uk/jame_tuson_longton.aspx.

Ellwood, Thomas L., *South Manchester Gazette* articles (1885–86)

Evidence on Poor Law Medical Relief Taken before the Select Committee of the House of Commons, on Poor Relief, England, HMSO (1861)

Faucher, Leon, *Manchester 1844, Its Present Condition and Future Prospects*, Abel Heywood (1844)

Fife, N., Letter to Anthony Walker (February 1984), and 'A time to look back and think' (1981)

Frow, Edmund and Ruth, *Radical Salford*, Neil Richardson (1984)

Further Report of the Commissioners for Inquiring Concerning Charities, HMSO (1830)

Gaskell, Elizabeth, *Mary Barton* (1848), Penguin edition (1970)

Gaulter, Henry, *Origin and Progress of the Malignant Cholera in Manchester*, Longman (1833)

Grindon, Leo H., *Manchester, Banks and Bankers*, Simpkin Marshall & Co. (1877)

Gritt, A.J., 'The Survival of service in English Agricultural Labour Force: lessons from Lancashire *c*.1650–1851', *Agricultural History Review*, 50 (2002)

Groves, Jill, 'Such a Day as is Seldom Seen, The Memorandum Book of a Cheshire Yeoman, Jon Ryle of High Greaves, Etchells, 1649–1721', *Manchester Region Review*, vol. 4 (1990-1)

Gurney, Joseph, *The Whole Proceedings on the Trial of an Indictment against Thomas Walker*, T. Boden, Manchester (1794)

Harland, John, *Ballads and Songs of Lancashire*, Whittaker & Co. (1865)

Herbert, B.J., *A Norfolk Diary 1850–1888, c*.1949, quoted by Russell, G.E and K.F., *The English Countryside*, Bloomsbury (1953)

Higginbotham's farm accounts, 1845–48

'History of the Suburbs of Manchester: Chorlton-cum-Hardy', *Manchester Evening News* (20 September 1901)

Home Office: Convict Transportation Registers (the National Archives Microfilm Publication HO11); the National Archives of the UK (TNA), Kew, Ancestry.com, Australian Convict Transportation Registers – Other Fleets & Ships (1791–1868)

Horn, Pamela, *The Rise and Fall of the Victorian Servant*, Alan Sutton Publishing Ltd, Stroud (1995)

Hostettler, John, *A History of Criminal Justice in England & Wales*, Waterside Press (2009)

Jenkins, Mick, *The General Strike of 1842*, Lawrence & Wishart (1980).

Kay, James Phillip, *The Moral and Physical Condition of the Working Classes Employed in the Cotton Manufacturing in Manchester*, James Ridgway (1832)

Lancashire County Records Office for Bastardy, Removal, Settlement, and Lancashire Quarter Sessions Records

Leech, Sir Bosdin, *Old Stretford*, Manchester City News Co. Ltd (1910)

Leach, Sir Bosdin, *Old Stretford*, privately printed (1910)

Legal Agreements, Agreement of John Clarke of Partington, blacksmith, MISC/675 Manchester Archives and Local Studies Centre, Manchester (1860)

Leslie, Miss, *The Behaviour Book*, Willis P. Hazzard (1839)

Lewis, Samuel, *A Topographical Dictionary of England*, S. Lewis & Co., vols 1 and 3, (1840)

Lloyd, John, *Looking Back at Chorlton-cum-Hardy*, Willow Publishing (1985)

Lloyd, John, *The Township of Chorlton Cum Hardy*, E.J. Morten (1972)

Lumley, G.W., *The Poor Law Election Manual*, third edition, Shaw and Sons (1867)

Manchester Botanical Gardens Old Trafford: http://manchesterhistory.net/manchester/gone/botanicgardens.html

Manchester City Council, Housing Department Compulsory Purchase Order CPO Records, M646/1/Box 14 and Box 21, Archive and Local History Library

Marland Hilary, *The Medical Activities of Mid 19th century Chemists & Druggists with special reference to Wakefield & Huddersfield, vol. 3*, Medical History Wellcome Trust Centre for the History of Medicine at UCL (October 1987)

Million, Ivor, *A History of Didsbury*, J. Morten (1969)

Minutes of the Water Works Committee of Manchester Corporation No. 10, 28 January 1864, M231/1/2/1/10, Manchester Archives and Local History Studies

Morton, A.L., *A People's History of England*, Lawrence & Wishart (1974)

Ormskirk and West Lancashire Numismatic Society, www.numsoc.net

Overseers Meetings including minutes and accounts, Chorlton-cum-Hardy, M10/8/8/1Manchester Archives & Local Studies (1839-58)

Pereira, Jonathan, *A Treatise on Food and Diet*, J. & H.G. Langley (1843)

Philip, Robert Kemp, *Dictionary of Daily Wants*, Houlston & Wright (1863)

Pigot and Co.'s National Commercial Directory (1828–29, 1834)

Pigot and Co.'s Royal National and Commercial Directory (1841)

Pigot and Dean's New Directory of Manchester and Salford (1821–22)

Pigot and Slater's Directory of Manchester and Salford (1841)

Porter, Valerie, *Yesterday's Farm*, David & Charles (2008)

Rate Book for Chorlton-cum-Hardy, 1844–76, Microfilm 297. Manchester Archives and Local History Studies

Reay, Barry, *Rural England*, Palgrave Macmillan (2004)

Records of the City Manchester Petty Sessions Court Licensing Records M117/4/3, Manchester Archives and Local Studies

Relief of the Poor, Township of Stretford, St Matthew's, Microfilm MRPR 2042, Manchester Archives and Local Studies

Report of Special Assistant Poor Law Commissioners on the Employment of Women and Children in Agriculture, HMSO (1843)

Report of the Poor Law Commissioners, HMSO (1840)

Scola, Roger, Feeding the Victorian City, Manchester University (1992)

Slater's Directory, Manchester and Salford (1850, 1855, 1863)

Slugg, T.J., Reminiscences of Manchester, J.E. Cornish (1881)

Smith, L., Thornton, S.J., Reinarz, J., Williams, A.N., 'Please, sir, I want some more', British Medical Journal (17 December 2008), BMJ 2008;337:a2722

St Clement's parish magazine (1896), Manchester Archives and Local Studies Centre

Stephens, Henry, The Book of Farming, William Blackwood & Sons (1852)

Stratton, J.M., 'Agricultural Records AD 220–1977', John Baker, second edition (1978)

Stretford, St Matthew Overseers of the Poor, L89/9/14, Manchester Archives and Local Studies

The Eighth Annual Report of the Poor Law Commissioners, HMSO (1842)

The Electors Guide 1832. List of Manchester voters who voted at the elections in December 1832, with residences, qualifications, candidates and who they voted for. Compiled from poll books. Includes photograph of the original which was held in the Guildhall Library until it was destroyed in the Second World War. BR 352042 M45, Manchester Archives and Local Studies

The Family Save-All, W. Kent & Co., second edition (1861)

Report of the General Board of Health on the Epidemic Cholera of 1848 & 1849, HMSO (1850)

Thompson, E.P., Customs in Common, Penguin (1993)

Thompson, E.P., The Making of the English Working Class, Pelican Books (1968)

Thompson, Flora, Lark Rise to Candleford, Penguin Classics (2000)

Tithe Map and Schedule, Chorlton cum Hardy, 1845

Turner, William, Riot, The Story of East Lancashire Loom Breakers in 1826, Lancashire County Books (1992)

Voting Register Southern Division of the County of Lancaster Salford Hundred, f324.4272 L1 (1832) and f352.04272La1 (1835), Archive and Local History Library

Wadsworth, A.P. and De Lacy Mann, Julia, The Cotton Trade and Industrial Lancashire, 1680–1780', Manchester University Press (1931)

Walker, Thomas, A Review of some of the events of the last five years (1794)

Waugh, E., Lancashire Sketches, Alexander Ireland & Co. (1869)

Wheeler James, Manchester Its Political, Social & Commercial History, Ancient & Modern, Whitaker & Co. (1836)

Williams, Richard, Village Pumps, Shire (2009)

Williamson, W.C., Sketches of Fallowfield and Surrounding Manors Past and Present, John Heywood (1888)

Wombwell, Margaret, Milk, Muck and Memories, Derbyshire County Council (2007)

Wythen Baxter, G.R., The Book of the Bastilles, John Stephens (1841)

INDEX